MW01042457

UNDERSTANDING MINIMALISM

Understanding Minimalism is a state-of-the-art introduction to the Minimalist Program – the current model of syntactic theory within generative linguistics. Accessibly written, it presents the basic principles and techniques of the Minimalist Program, looking first at analyses within Government-and-Binding Theory (the predecessor to minimalism), and gradually introducing minimalist alternatives. Minimalist models of grammar are presented in a step-by-step fashion, and the ways in which they contrast with GB analyses are clearly explained. Spanning a decade of minimalist thinking, this textbook will enable students to develop a feel for the sorts of questions and problems that minimalism invites, and to master the techniques of minimalist analysis. Over one hundred exercises are provided, encouraging them to put these new skills into practice.

Understanding Minimalism will be an invaluable text for intermediate and advanced students of syntactic theory, and will set a solid foundation for further study and research within Chomsky's minimalist framework.

NORBERT HORNSTEIN is Professor of Linguistics at the University of Maryland. His most recent books are *More! A Minimalist Theory of Construal* (2001), *Working Minimalism* (co-edited with Sam Epstein, 1999), and *Chomsky and his Critics* (co-edited with Louise Antony, 2003). He is author of over seventy book chapters and articles in major linguistics journals, and is on the editorial board of the journals *Linguistic Inquiry* and *Syntax*.

JAIRO NUNES is Associate Professor of Linguistics at the Universidade de São Paulo, Brazil. He has lectured as a visiting professor at several universities worldwide and is author of *Linearization of Chains and Sideward Movement* (2004). He has published articles in several major journals in the field and is co-editor of the journal *Probus*.

KLEANTHES K. GROHMANN is Assistant Professor of Linguistics at the University of Cyprus. He is author of *Prolific Domains: On the Anti-Locality of Movement Dependencies* (2003) and co-editor of *Multiple Wh-Fronting* (with Cedric Boeckx, 2003). He has written for many international journals, serves on the expert panel of "Ask-a-Linguist," and is on the editorial board of the *Linguistic Variation Yearbook* and the advisory board of the Elsevier North-Holland Linguistic Series: Linguistic Variations.

Understanding Minimalism

In this series:

UNDERSTANDING MINIMALISM

NORBERT HORNSTEIN
University of Maryland

JAIRO NUNES
Universidade de São Paulo

KLEANTHES K. GROHMANN
University of Cyprus

CAMBRIDGE UNIVERSITY PRESS
Cambridge, New York, Melbourne, Madrid, Cape Town, Singapore, São Paulo

Cambridge University Press
The Edinburgh Building, Cambridge CB2 2RU, UK

Published in the United States of America by Cambridge University Press, New York

www.cambridge.org
Information on this title: www.cambridge.org/9780521824965

First published 2005
Third printing 2006

Printed in the United Kingdom at the University Press, Cambridge

A catalogue record for this book is available from the British Library

ISBN-13 978-0-521-82496-5 hardback
ISBN-10 0-521-82496-6 hardback
ISBN-13 978-0-521-53194-8 paperback
ISBN-10 0-521-53194-2 paperback

Contents

Preface

One problem students face in "getting into" minimalism is the difficulty in seeing how the specific proposals advanced reflect the larger programmatic concerns. This book is our attempt to show why minimalism is an exciting research program and to explain how the larger issues that motivate the program get translated into specific technical proposals. We believe that a good way of helping novices grasp both the details and the whole picture is to introduce facets of the Minimalist Program against a GB-background. In particular, we show how minimalist considerations motivate rethinking and replacing GB-assumptions and technical machinery. This allows us to construct the new minimalist future in the bowels of the older GB-world and gives the uninitiated some traction for the exhausting work of getting to a minimalist plane by leveraging their efforts with more familiar GB-bootstraps. In the end, we are confident that the reader will have a pretty good picture of what minimalism is and how (and why) it came about, and should be well equipped to pursue minimalist explorations him- or herself.

Given this pedagogical approach, this book has an intended audience. Although it does not presuppose any familiarity with minimalism, it is written for those who already have a background in linguistics and syntax. This ideal reader has taken a course in *GB* and this is an introduction to *minimalism* for such a person; it is not an intro to syntax nor an intro to linguistics. Before we embark on our various minimalist voyages, we summarize the main GB-assumptions and technical apparatus of concern. These summaries are intended to help the reader remember relevant GB-background material and to provide pointers for where to look for further readings. We stress that these GB-sections are summaries. They are not full elaborations of even standard GB-positions. If the reader hasn't taken a course in GB, it would be very useful to track down these pointers and become comfortable with the relevant background material.

Although the first two authors wrote the bulk of the book, each chapter was thoroughly checked by the third author, who made valuable refinements and improvements, took care of the notes and references, and ensured internal coherence within and among chapters.

The three of us are extremely grateful to all the people who read (parts of) the manuscript, gave us feedback, helped us with data, and tested some of the chapters in their classes. Special thanks to Marina Augusto, Christopher Becker, Cedric Boeckx, Željko Bošković, Noam Chomsky, Norbert Corver, Marcel den Dikken, Ricardo Etxepare, Koldo Garai, Kay Gonzalez, Eleni Gregoromichelaki, Joy Grohmann, Jiro Inaba, Mary Kato, Winnie Lechner, Jürgen Lenerz, Anikó Lipták, Horst Lohnstein, Ruth Lopes, Eric Mathieu, Jason Merchant, Rafael Nonato, Masayuki Oishi, Jamal Ouhalla, Phoevos Panagiotidis, Eduardo Raposo, Martin Reitbauer, Henk van Riemsdijk, Ian Roberts, Anna Roussou, Ed Rubin, Joachim Sabel, Raquel Santos, Usama Soltan, Volker Struckmeier, Juan Uriagereka, Amy Weinberg, an anonymous reviewer, Elena Shelkovaya-Vasiliou for valuable help with the index, Jacqueline French for wonderful copy-editing, Dora Alexopoulou for safe delivery, and our editors at CUP, Mary Leighton and Andrew Winnard.

We would also like to thank the students at the institutions where we taught the materials of the book for their invaluable feedback: Michigan State University in East Lansing (LSA Summer Institute), Universidad de Buenos Aires, Universidade Estadual de Campinas, Universidade Estadual de Feira de Santana, Universidade de São Paulo, Universität zu Köln, Universität Stuttgart, University of Cyprus in Nicosia, and University of Maryland at College Park.

The second author would also like to acknowledge the support he received from Conselho Nacional de Pesquisa (grant 300897/96–0) and the Cátedra de Estudos Brasileiros of the University of Leiden while he was writing the book.

Norbert Hornstein   College Park
Jairo Nunes   São Paulo
Kleanthes K. Grohmann   Nicosia
                           June 2005

Abbreviations

[±interpretable]	(un)interpretable [feature]
±an	(non-)anaphoric
±pro	(non-)pronominal
1/2/3	first/second/third [person]
$\forall$	universal quantifier/scope
$\exists$	existential quantifier/scope
α	placeholder
β	placeholder
γ	placeholder
Δ	empty position
λ	LF-object
π	PF-object
ϕ^-	uninterpretable ϕ-features
ϕ^+	interpretable ϕ-features
ϕ-features	phi-features [person, number, gender]
σ	[lexical] subarray
θ-role	theta- or thematic role
A	admissible convergent derivation
A (A^0)	adjective (head)
A-movement	argument movement
A′-movement	non-argument movement ["A-bar"]
AAEV	African-American English Vernacular
ABS	absolutive
ACC	accusative
Adj	adjunct
Agr (Agr^0)	agreement (head)
AgrIO ($AgrIO^0$)	indirect object agreement (head)
AgrIOP	indirect object agreement phrase
AgrO ($AgrO^0$)	[direct] object agreement (head)
AgrOP	[direct] object agreement phrase

AgrP	[general] agreement phrase
AgrS (AgrS⁰)	subject agreement (head)
AgrSP	subject agreement phrase
A-P	articulatory-perceptual [interface]
AP	adjective phrase
ASL	American Sign Language
Asp (Asp⁰)	aspect (head)
AspP	aspect phrase
AUX	auxiliary
BEV	Black English Vernacular
C	convergent derivation
C(omp) (C⁰)	complementizer (head)
CAUS	causative
c-command	constituent-command
CH	chain
C-I	conceptual-intentional [interface]
CL	clitic
Compl	complement
CP	complementizer phrase
D	set of all possible derivations
DET **D(et) (D⁰)**	determiner (head)
DAT	dative
DEF	definite
D-linking	discourse-linking
DP	determiner phrase
DS	D-Structure ["deep"]
E	[some] expression
e	empty node
ec	empty category
ECM	exceptional Case-marking
ECP	Empty Category Principle
EPP	Extended Projection Principle
ERG	ergative
EXPL	expletive
F_1-F_6	"big facts"
FEM	feminine
FF	formal features
FIN	finite
Foc (Foc⁰)	focus (head)

FocP	focus phrase
FT	future tense (particle)
G	gender
GB	Government-and-Binding [Theory]
GEN	genitive
GF	grammatical function
G_L	grammar of a particular language
H	[some] head
HAB	habitual
I(nfl) (I^0)	inflection (head)
i/j/k/l/m	index [sub- or superscripts]
INF	infinitival
IO	indirect object
IP	inflection phrase
LCA	Linear Correspondence Axiom
LF	Logical Form [semantic component]
LI	lexical item
LOC	locative
MASC	masculine
m-command	maximal projection c-command
MinD	minimal domain
Move F	Move Feature
Move-α	"Move anything anywhere anytime"
N	number
N	numeration
N (N^0)	noun (head)
NEUT	neuter
NOM	nominative
NP	noun phrase
OB	[direct] object
OBJ	objective
OBL	oblique
OP	null/zero/empty operator
P	person
P&P	Principles-and-Parameters [Theory]
P (P^0)	preposition (head)
PART	participle
PERF	perfective
PF	Phonetic Form [phonetic component]

PG	parasitic gap
PIC	Phase Impenetrability Condition
PISH	Predicate-Internal Subject Hypothesis
PL	plural
PLD	primary linguistic data
POSS	possessive
PP	preposition phrase
PRES	present tense
PS	phrase structure [rules]
PUNC	punctual perfect
Q	interrogative complementizer
QP	quantifier phrase
R-expression	referential expression
S	sentence
S'	Comp-projection above S ["S-bar"]
SC	small clause
SG	singular
Spec	specifier
SS	S-Structure ["surface"]
SU	subject
SUBJ	subjective
SUBJ-PRT	subjunctive particle
SUP	superessive
t	trace
T (T^0)	tense (head)
Top (Top^0)	topic (head)
TopP	topic phrase
TP	tense phrase
TP	tense particle
TR	transitive prefix
TRAP	Theta-Role Assignment Principle
UG	Universal Grammar
***v* (v^0)**	light verb
V (V^0)	verb
***v*P**	light verb phrase
VP	verb phrase
X/X'/XP	any head / intermediate projection/phrase

1 *The minimalist project*

1.1   The point of this book

This book is an introduction to the art of minimalist analysis. What we
mean by this is that it aspires to help those with an interest in minimalism
to be able to "do" it. Partly this involves becoming acquainted with the
technology that is part and parcel of any specialized approach. Partly it
involves absorbing the background assumptions that drive various aspects
of the enterprise. However, in contrast to many earlier approaches to
grammar, we believe that "doing minimalism" also involves developing
an evaluative/aesthetic sense of what constitutes an interesting problem or
analysis and this is not a skill that one typically expects a text to impart. So,
before we begin with the nuts and bolts of the Minimalist Program, we'll
spend some time outlining what we take the minimalist project to be and
why its ambitions have come to prominence at this time.

But before we do that, let us briefly address who this book is for. It aims
to introduce the reader to the minimalist approach to the theory of
grammar. It doesn't start at zero, however. Rather, it presupposes an
acquaintance with the large intellectual concerns that animate generative
linguistics in general and some detailed knowledge of generative syntax in
particular. Our optimal reader has a good background in the Principles-
and-Parameters (P&P) approach to grammar, in particular the model
generally referred to as Government-and-Binding (GB) theory.[1] However,

---

1 For early introductions to generative grammar, see, e.g., Jacobs and Rosenbaum (1968),
  Perlmutter and Soames (1979), and Radford (1981) in the framework generally known as
  (Extended) Standard Theory; for earliest introductions to the incarnation of the P&P
  model referred to as GB, see van Riemsdijk and Williams (1986) and Lasnik and
  Uriagereka (1988). Two good comprehensive and accessible textbooks on GB, which we
  recommend as useful companions to this book to brush up on some concepts that we do not
  deal with in detail here, are Radford (1988) and Haegeman (1994). Roberts (1996), and
  Carnie (2001) also offer solid introductions to GB and include a number of early minimalist
  ideas as well.

we've tried to make the discussion accessible even to the reader whose familiarity with GB is a little more wobbly. For this purpose, each chapter starts off with a quick review of the GB approach to the main topic. This review is not intended to be comprehensive, though. Its purpose is to reanimate in the reader knowledge that he or she already has but may have mislaid in memory. It'll also serve as a starting point for the ensuing discussion, which outlines an alternative minimalist way of looking at the previously GB-depicted state of affairs. The bulk of each chapter presents conceptual and empirical reasons for shifting from the GB to the minimalist perspective. Most importantly, the material contained in this book does not presuppose familiarity with or even exposure to the Minimalist Program. To help the reader move from passive participant to active collaborator, we offer exercises as the discussion gets technical. These should allow the reader to practice "doing" some minimalism in a safe and controlled setting. To aid memory, we list all minimalist definitions at the end of the book.

1.2   Some background

Since the beginning, the central task of generative grammar has been to explain how it is that children are able to acquire grammatical competence despite the impoverished nature of the data that is input to this process. How children manage this, dubbed *Plato's problem* (see Chomsky 1986b), can in retrospect be seen as the central research issue in modern generative linguistics since its beginnings in the mid-1950s.

Plato's problem can be characterized abstractly as follows. Mature native speakers of a natural language have internalized a set of rules, a *grammar*, that is able to generate an unbounded number of grammatical structures. This process of grammar or language acquisition is clearly influenced by the linguistic data that the native speaker was exposed to as a child. It's obvious to the most casual observer that there's a strong relation between growing up in Montreal, Conceição das Alagoas, or Herford, for instance, and speaking (a variety of) English, Brazilian Portuguese, or German. However, slightly less casual inspection also reveals that the grammatical information that can be gleaned from the restricted data to which the child has access, the *primary linguistic data* (*PLD*), is insufficient to explain the details of the linguistic competence that the mature native speaker attains. In other words, the complexity of the attained capacity, the speaker's grammatical competence, vastly exceeds that of the PLD, all the linguistic information available to and taken in by the child.

To bridge the gap between the attained capacity and the PLD, generative grammarians have postulated that children come biologically equipped with an innate dedicated capacity to acquire language – they are born with a language faculty.[2] The last five decades of research can be seen as providing a description of this faculty that responds to two salient facts about human natural language: its apparent surface diversity and the ease with which it's typically acquired despite the above noted poverty of the linguistic stimulus. In the last two decades, a consensus description of the language faculty has emerged which is believed to address these twin facts adequately. It goes as follows.

Kids come biologically equipped with a set of principles for constructing grammars – principles of *Universal Grammar* (*UG*). These general principles can be thought of as a recipe for "baking" the grammar of a particular language G_L by combining, sifting, sorting, and stirring the primary linguistic data in specifiable ways. Or, to make the same point less gastronomically, UG can be thought of as a function that takes PLD as input and delivers a particular grammar (of English, Brazilian Portuguese, German, etc.), a G_L, as output. This is illustrated in (1):

(1)   PLD $\rightarrow$ $\boxed{\text{UG}}$ $\rightarrow$ G_L

More concretely, the principles of UG can be viewed as general conditions on grammars with open parameters whose values are set on the basis of linguistic experience. These open parameters can be thought of as "on/off" switches, with each collection of settings constituting a particular G_L. On this view, acquiring a natural language amounts to assigning values to these open parameters, i.e. "setting" these parameters, something that children do on the basis of the PLD that they have access to in their linguistic environments.[3]

Observe two important features of this proposal. First, the acquisition process is sensitive to the details of the linguistic/environmental input as

2 This faculty of language is one of the domains in our brains specialized for cognitive processes, alongside other faculties each specialized for things like colors, numbers, vision, etc. For an approach to the "modularity of mind" from a general cognitive/philosophical point of view, see the influential work of Fodor (1983); for a more linguistic perspective, see, e.g., Curtiss (1977), Smith and Tsimpli (1995), and Jenkins (2000); for latest views within minimalism, see Chomsky (2000, 2001, 2004). See also Carston (1996) and Uriagereka (1999b) for a discussion of the Fodorian and Chomskyan notions of modularity.
3 For expository purposes, this brief presentation oversimplifies many issues regarding parameter setting (for relevant discussion, see Hornstein and Lightfoot 1981, Manzini and Wexler 1987, Lightfoot 1991, Meisel 1995, Baker 2001, Crain and Pietroski 2001,

it's the PLD that provides the information on the basis of which parameter values are fixed. Second, the shape of the knowledge attained is not restricted to whatever information can be garnered from the PLD, as the latter exercises its influence against a rich backdrop of fixed general principles that UG makes available.

Observe further that each characteristic of this model responds to one of the two basic features noted above. The fact that particular grammars are the result of setting parameter values in response to properties of the PLD allows for considerable diversity among natural languages. If UG has a tight deductive structure, then even a change in the value of a single parameter can have considerable ramifications for the structure of the particular G_I being acquired.[4] Thus, the fine details of a native speaker's linguistic competence will always go way beyond the information the PLD may provide.[5] In sum, a speaker's linguistic capacities are a joint function of the environmental input *and* the principles of UG, and though these principles can be quite complex, they need not be learned as they form part of the innately endowed language faculty.

Davis 2001, and Fodor 2001, among others). For instance, one has to properly identify which properties of languages are to be parameterized in this way and which structures should count as positive evidence to the learner for purposes of parameter setting. One must also determine whether the parameters are all available at birth or some parameters may "mature" and be activated before others. In either scenario, it's still possible that in order to activate a given parameter P_1, another parameter P_2 must be set on a specific value. Besides, parameters need not have only binary on/off options and it may be the case that (some) parameters establish one of its options as the default setting to be assumed in absence of disconfirming evidence. Further complexities are easily conceived. For problems of computational complexity arising in the parameter model, see Berwick (1985), Clark and Roberts (1993), Gibson and Wexler (1994), and Dresher (1998), among others. Some useful introductory texts on child language acquisition in a generative framework can be found in Cook and Newson (1996) and Crain and Lillo-Martin (1999). Other works that illustrate this approach more thoroughly include Crain and Thornton (1998), Lightfoot (1999), and Guasti (2002).

4 Take, for example, the null-subject or *pro*-drop parameter (see Rizzi 1980), arguably one of the better studied ones (see the papers collected in Jaeggli and Safir 1989 for pertinent discussion). It has been argued that languages that have an "on"-setting, thus allowing for null-subjects, also show lack of *that*-trace effects and overt expletives, and allow for free subject inversion, long *wh*-movement of subjects, and empty resumptive pronouns in embedded clauses (see Chomsky 1981: 240ff.).

5 That the complexity of a native speaker's competence vastly exceeds the complexity of the linguistic environment is transparently shown by the emergence of creoles, which have all the properties of natural languages but take a drastically impoverished linguistic environment, a pidgin, for input. For a discussion of the differences between the grammatical properties of creoles and pidgins, see among others Holm (1988, 2000), Bickerton (1990), Lightfoot (1991), deGraff (1999a), and the collection of papers in deGraff (1999b).

This picture of the structure of the language faculty has been dubbed the *Principles-and-Parameters Theory*.[6] To repeat, it now constitutes the consensus view of the overall structure of the language faculty. The Minimalist Program adopts this consensus view. In effect, minimalism assumes that a P&P-architecture is a boundary condition on any adequate theory of grammar. Adopting this assumption has one particularly noteworthy consequence. It changes both the sorts of questions it's worthwhile focusing on and the principles in terms of which competing proposals should be evaluated. Let us explain.

As in any other domain of scientific inquiry, proposals in linguistics are evaluated along several dimensions: naturalness, parsimony, simplicity, elegance, explanatoriness, etc. Though all these measures are always in play, in practice some dominate others during particular periods. In retrospect, it's fair to say that explanatory adequacy, i.e. the ability to cast some light on Plato's problem, has carried the greatest weight. The practical import of this has been that research in the last decades has focused on finding grammatical constraints of the right sort. By *right sort* we mean tight enough to permit grammars to be acquired on the basis of PLD, yet flexible enough to allow for the observed variation across natural languages. In short, finding a suitable answer to Plato's problem has been the primary research engine within generative linguistics and proposals have been largely evaluated in terms of its demands. This does not mean to say that other methodological standards have been irrelevant. Simplicity, parsimony, naturalness, etc. have also played a role in adjudicating among competing proposals. However, as a practical matter, these considerations have been rather weak as they have been swamped by the need to develop accounts able to address Plato's problem.

In this context, the consensus that P&P-style theories offer a solution to Plato's problem necessarily affects how one will rank competing proposals: if P&P-theories are (to put it boldly) assumed to solve Plato's problem, then the issue becomes which of the conceivable P&P-models is best. And this question is resolved using conventional criteria of theory evaluation. In other words, once explanatory adequacy is bracketed, as happens when only accounts that have P&P-architectures are considered, an opening is created for simplicity, elegance, and naturalness to emerge from the long shadow cast by Plato's problem and to become the critical

---

6 See Chomsky (1981, 1986b) for a general outline of the model, the succinct review in Chomsky and Lasnik (1993), and the introductory texts listed in note 1.

measures of theoretical adequacy. The Minimalist Program is the concrete application of such criteria to the analysis of UG. But this is no easy task. To advance in this direction, minimalism must address how to concretize these evaluative notions – simplicity, naturalness, elegance, parsimony, etc. – in the research setting that currently obtains. Put another way, the task is to find a way of taking the platitude that simpler, more elegant, more natural theories are best and giving them some empirical bite.

To recap, once P&P-theories are adopted as boundary conditions on theoretical adequacy, the benchmarks of evaluation shift to more conventional criteria such as elegance, parsimony, etc. The research problem then becomes figuring out how to interpret these general evaluative measures in the particular domain of linguistic research. As we concentrate on syntax in what follows, one important item on the minimalist agenda is to find ways of understanding what constitutes a more-or-less natural, more-or-less parsimonious, or more-or-less elegant syntactic account. Note that there's little reason to believe that there's only one way (or even just a small number of ways) of putting linguistic flesh on these methodological bones. There may be many alternative ways of empirically realizing these notions. If so, there will be no unique minimalist approach; rather, we'll have a family of minimalist programs, each animated by similar general concerns but developing accounts that respond to different specific criteria of evaluation or even to different weightings of the same criteria.

It would be very exciting if minimalism did in fact promote a research environment in which various alternative, equally "minimalist" yet substantially different, theories of grammar thrived, as it would then be possible to play these alternatives off against one another to the undoubted benefit of each. This possibility is worth emphasizing as it highlights an important feature of minimalism: minimalism is not a theory so much as a program for research. The program will be successful just in case trying to work out its main ideas leads to the development of interesting analyses and suitable theories. In this sense, there's no unique minimalist theory, though there may be a family of approaches that gain inspiration from similar sources. Theories are true or false. Programs are fecund or sterile. Minimalism aims to see whether it's possible to interpret the general methodological benchmarks of theory evaluation in the particular setting of current syntactic research in ways that lead in fruitful and interesting directions. The immediate problem is not to choose among competing implementations of these methodological yardsticks but to develop even a single, non-trivial variant.

One last point. There's no a priori reason to think that approaching grammatical issues in this way guarantees success. It's possible that the language faculty is just "ugly," "inelegant," "profligate," "unnatural," and massively redundant. If so, the minimalist project will fail. However, one can't know if this is so before one tries. And, of course, if the program proves successful, the next question is *why* the language faculty has properties such as elegance and parsimony.[7]

1.3   Big facts, economy, and some minimalist projects

The question before us now is how to implement notions like elegance, beauty, parsimony, naturalness, etc. in the current linguistic context. One way into this question is to recruit those facts about language that any theory worthy of consideration must address. We can then place these "big facts" as further boundary conditions on theoretical adequacy. We already have one such big fact, namely that the theory have a P&P-architecture. Other big facts regarding language and linguistic competence that afford additional boundary conditions to structure a minimalist inquiry of UG include the following:

F_1:   Sentences are basic linguistic units.
F_2:   Sentences are pairings of form (sound/signs) and meaning.
F_3:   Sentences are composed of smaller expressions (words and morphemes).
F_4:   These smaller units are composed into units with hierarchical structure, i.e. phrases, larger than words and smaller than sentences.
F_5:   Sentences show displacement properties in the sense that expressions that appear in one position can be interpreted in another.
F_6:   Language is recursive, that is, there's no upper bound on the length of sentences in any given natural language.

F_1–F_6 are uncontentious. They are properties that students of grammar have long observed characterize natural languages. Moreover, as we'll see, these facts suggest a variety of minimalist projects when coupled with the following two types of economy conditions. The first comprise the familiar methodological "Occam's razor" sort of considerations that relate to theoretical parsimony and simplicity: all things being equal, two primitive

---

7 See, e.g., Uriagereka (1998, 2002), Chomsky (2000, 2001, 2004), and Lasnik and Uriagereka with Boeckx (2005).

relations are worse than one, three theoretical entities are better than four, four modules are better than five. In short, more is worse, fewer is better. Let's call these types of considerations principles of *methodological economy*.

There's a second set of minimalist measures. Let's dub these principles of *substantive economy*. Here, a premium is placed on least effort notions as natural sources for grammatical principles. The idea is that locality conditions and wellformedness filters reflect the fact that grammars are organized frugally to maximize resources. Short steps preclude long strides (i.e. Shortest Move), derivations where fewer rules apply are preferred to those where more do, movement only applies when it must (i.e. operations are greedy), and no expressions occur idly in grammatical representations (i.e. Full Interpretation holds). These substantive economy notions generalize themes that have consistently arisen in grammatical research. Examples from the generative history (see the texts suggested in note 1 for more details on these) include, for example, the A-over-A Condition (Chomsky 1964), the Minimal Distance Principle (Rosenbaum 1970), the Subjacency Condition (Chomsky 1973), the Superiority Condition (Chomsky 1973), Relativized Minimality (Rizzi 1990), and the Minimal Binding Requirement (Aoun and Li 1993). It's natural to reconceptualize these in least effort terms. Minimalism proposes to conceptually unify all grammatical operations along these lines.

These two kinds of economy notions coupled with the six big facts listed above promote a specific research strategy: look for the simplest theory whose operations have a least effort flavor and that accommodates the big facts noted above. This proposal actually has considerable weight. Consider some illustrative examples of how they interact to suggest various minimalist projects.

The fact that the *length* of sentences in any given natural language is unbounded (cf. F_6) implies that there's an infinite *number* of sentences available in any given natural language: for instance, you can always create another sentence by embedding and re-embedding it. This, in turn, implies that grammars exist, i.e. rules that can apply again and again to yield an unbounded number of different structures. The fact that sentences have both form and meaning properties (cf. F_2) implies that the sentential outputs of grammars "interface" with systems that give them their articulatory and perceptual (A-P) properties and those that provide them with their conceptual and intentional (C-I) characteristics.[8] More specifically, if

---

8 The term *articulatory-perceptual* (or *sensorimotor*) is to be understood as independent of the modality of the output system, in order to capture both spoken and sign languages (see Chomsky 1995: 10, n. 3).

one is considering a theory with levels, e.g. a *Government-and-Binding* (*GB*)-style theory, this implies that there must exist grammatical levels of representation that interface with the cognitive systems responsible for A-P and C-I properties. In effect, the levels Logical Form (LF) and Phonetic Form (PF), sometimes also called Phonological Form, must exist if any levels exist at all.[9] In this sense, LF and PF are conceptually necessary. Further, as methodological economy awards a premium to grammatical theories that can make do with these two levels alone, one minimalist project would be to show that all levels other than LF and PF can be dispensed with, without empirical prejudice.

More concretely, in the context of a GB-style theory, for example, this would amount to showing that D-Structure (DS) and S-Structure (SS) are in principle eliminable without any significant empirical loss. This in turn would require reconsidering (and possibly reanalyzing) the evidence for these levels. For instance, in GB-style theories recursion is a defining characteristic of DS. Given F_6, a mechanism for recursion must be part of any grammar; thus, if DS is to be eliminated, this requires rethinking how recursion is to be incorporated into grammars. We do this in chapters 2 and 6.

Consider a second minimalist project. The above considerations lead to the conclusion that grammars must interface with the C-I and A-P systems. Given this, there's a premium on grammatical principles that originate in this fact. For example, if some sorts of grammatical objects are uninterpretable by the C-I or A-P interface, then the grammatical structures (e.g. phrase markers) that contain these might be illegible to (i.e. non-readable by) these interfaces. It would then be natural to assume that such structures would be ill-formed unless these wayward objects were dispatched before the structures that contained them gained interpretation at these interfaces. If so, we could regard the interfaces as imposing bare output conditions that all grammatical objects have to respect. On this view, accounts exploiting bare output conditions to limit grammatical structures would be very natural and desirable. See especially chapters 2, 7, and 9 for more elaboration.

Let's push this one step further. Substantive economy prompts us to consider how strings are generated ("What are the relevant derivational

---

9 For minimalist approaches that attempt to eliminate all levels of representation, see, e.g., Uriagereka (1997, 1999c), Epstein, Groat, Kawashima, and Kitahara (1998), and Epstein and Seely (2005).

resources and how are they economized?"), as well as how they are interpreted ("What are the bare output conditions of the interfaces and what restrictions do these place on the structure of grammatical outputs?"). In other words, we should examine how derivations might be "minimalized" and how exactly Full Interpretation is to be understood.[10] For example, we should consider theories that have a least effort flavor, e.g. requiring that derivations be short, or movements be local or operations be simple or that there be no vacuous projections or operations, etc. In sum, given the general setting outlined above, we would begin to look for two kinds of conditions on grammars: conditions that correspond to the filtering effects of the interfaces (bare output conditions) and conditions that correspond to the derivational features of the grammar (economy conditions). Filtering mechanisms that resist interpretation in one of these ways are less favored. See especially chapters 4 through 7 and chapter 10 on this.

Consider another set of questions minimalist considerations lead to. What are the basic primitives of the system, i.e. the basic objects, relations, and operations? If phrases exist and if they are organized in an X′-format, as standardly assumed, then a set of privileged relations is provided. In X′-Theory, phrases have (at least) three parts – heads, complements, and specifiers – and invoke (at least) two relations, head-complement and specifier-head. Given the obvious fact that natural languages contain phrases (cf. F₄), UG should make reference to phrases and the pair of relations phrase structure exploits. Therefore, parsimony counsels that at most these objects and relations should be part of UG. This implies, for example, that sentences be analyzed as types of phrases and not as idiosyncratic structures. This is essentially the conclusion GB has already drawn. Labeling sentences as IPs or CPs embodies this consensus.

---

10 Throughout the book we'll be assuming that the computational system of the language faculty is "weakly" derivational (weakly in the sense that it admits the levels of PF and LF, which are representations by definition). See Brody (1995) for a weakly representational version of the Minimalist Program and Epstein, Groat, Kawashima, and Kitahara (1998) and Uriagereka (1999c), for example, for strongly derivational alternatives. Beyond the occasional remark, we'll discuss some arguments in favor of derivational approaches in chapter 10. For critical comparison between strongly representational approaches, such as constraint-based frameworks like Pollard and Sag's (1994) Head-driven Phrase Structure Grammar (see Sag and Wasow 1999 for a comprehensive introduction) and derivational implementations of minimalism, see Johnson and Lappin (1997, 1999). From within the P&P camp/minimalism, Lasnik (2001a) offers a brief summary of some of the issues involved in the derivational/representational debate.

The recognition that phrases are a minimally necessary part of any theory of grammar further suggests that we reexamine whether we need government among the inventory of basic grammatical relations. Methodological simplicity urges doing without this extra notion, given that we already have two others (namely, the head-complement and head-specifier relations). All things being equal, we should then adopt government only if the X′-theoretic relations we already have prove empirically inadequate.

Now, rethinking the structure of UG without government constitutes a vast project all by itself. As the reader might already know (and will soon be reminded of again), every module of grammar within GB exploits the government relation in stating its operative procedures and principles; government is implicated in Case- and θ-role assignment, trace licensing, in establishing binding domains, and in determining the distribution of PRO. Within GB, it's the relation that unifies these otherwise diverse modules. As such, dispensing with government in line with our methodological reflections involves revisiting each grammatical module to see if (and how) the empirical virtues government affords can be attained without its use. In particular, we consider replacing government by accounts that use only "natural" relations made available by the conceptually necessary (cf. F$_4$) theory of phrases embodied in X′-Theory. This is done in chapter 3 with respect to Theta Theory, in chapter 4 with respect to Case Theory and the PRO Theorem, and in chapter 8 with respect to Binding Theory.

We can, of course, go further still. We can reconsider X′-Theory itself. How natural is it? The fact that phrases exist does not imply that they have an X′-structure. Thus, we should investigate what features of phrasal organization follow from the mere fact that they exist and which ones require more elaborate justification. For example, are bar-levels basic features of phrases or simply the reflections of something more basic? Is the fact that heads take maximal projections as complements and specifiers a primitive principle or the reflection of something more fundamental? How much of X′-Theory needs to be assumed axiomatically and how much results from the fact that phrases must be constructed and interpreted? We review these issues in chapter 6.

Consider one last illustrative example. As mentioned above, displacement is one of the big facts about natural languages (cf. F$_5$). Assume, for sake of argument, that displacement is due to the fact that grammars have movement rules like those assumed in typical GB-accounts, such as *wh*-movement in questions or NP-movement in passives. We can then ask how much of the GB-theory of movement is motivated on minimalist grounds. In standard GB, movement is defined as an operation that leaves traces. Are traces conceptually required? In part perhaps, insofar as they model displacement by providing a mechanism for coding the fact that expressions can be interpreted as if in positions distinct from the ones they overtly appear in. But does displacement *by itself* motivate the GB-view that traces are indexed categories without lexical content (i.e. [*e*]$_i$)? Or does the existence of displacement phenomena suffice to ground the claim that traces are subject to special licensing conditions (such as the Empty Category Principle) that don't apply to lexical items more generally? This is far less clear.

Traces in GB are grammar-internal constructs with very special requirements that regulate their distribution. Historically, the main motivation for traces was their role in constraining overgeneration in the context of a theory where movement was free, i.e. based on a rule like Move-α. Their peculiar properties (e.g. they were phonetically null categories left only by movement) and restrictions on them (e.g. they had to be properly governed) were postulated with this in mind. However, on purely conceptual grounds, traces are dubious theory-internal entities. In a minimalist context where movement isn't free (as opposed to GB) but only occurs if it must, i.e. only if needed to produce an object that the interpretive interfaces can read, the special nature and needs of traces seem methodologically odd. If so, we should resist postulating traces as grammatical formatives unless strong empirical reasons force this conclusion.

Say you agreed with this. What could then replace traces? Well, we independently need words and phrases (cf. F$_3$ and F$_4$). Why not assume that they are used by the grammar to accommodate displacement? In other words, assume that traces are not new kinds of expressions, but that they are copies of expressions that are already conceptually required. This seems simpler than postulating a novel construct if one's main goal is to accommodate displacement. In short, GB-traces must earn their keep empirically; all things being equal, a copy theory of traces is preferable. We elaborate this argument in chapters 6, 7, and 8.

What holds for traces holds for other grammar-internal formatives, as well: PRO, null operators and chains, to name three more. It also brings into question the value of modules like the Empty Category Principle (ECP), Control Theory and Predication, whose purpose is to monitor and regulate the distribution of these null (grammar-internal) expressions.

None of this means that the best theory of UG will not contain such entities or principles. However, minimalist reasoning suggests that they be adopted only if there's strong empirical motivation for doing so. On conceptual grounds, the burden of proof is on those who propose them. At the very least, minimalist scruples force us to reconsider the empirical basis of these constructs and to judge whether their empirical payoffs are worth the methodological price.

These sorts of considerations can be easily amplified, as we'll see when we get into details in the chapters that follow. This suggests that the big facts listed in F_1–F_6 above in tandem with the principles of methodological and substantive economy can in fact be used to generate interesting research projects. We'll present some of them later on in this book. These considerations prove more fruitful still when the proposals they prompt are contrasted with an appropriate foil. The GB-framework proves to be an admirable straight man to the minimalist jokester.

1.4   Using GB as a benchmark

GB is the most successful P&P-theory elaborated to date. It thus affords a useful starting point for the minimalist methodological concerns outlined above. In what follows, we'll constantly be assuming (one of) the standard GB-approaches to a particular problem and asking whether we can do better. In effect, the GB-story will set the mark that any competing minimalist reanalysis will have to meet or beat.

As a general rule, we'll start by discussing the empirical bases of various modules of GB. This means that we'll ask what data lie behind the Case Theory or the X'-Theory, for instance. Then, we'll examine whether the GB-approach to the grammatical phenomenon in question (the leading idea as well as its technical implementation) is really the best that we can come up with. In this respect, we'll ask whether there's anything minimalistically undesirable about it. For example, does it use undesirable primitives or rely on operations and levels that are not conceptually necessary? We'll then proceed to consider minimalist alternatives that might do better.

For example, consider again the fact that sentences pair form and meaning. Within GB this big fact (cf. F_2) is accommodated by having PF and LF levels. A reasonable minimalist question given GB as a starting point is whether the other two GB-levels, DS and SS, are dispensable and if not, why not. Observe that even in case we come to the conclusion that one or the other (or maybe even both of these levels) must be retained, we'll have a far better understanding about what justifies them if we go through this minimalistically inspired process. Of course, it's always possible that we might discover that DS and SS are convenient but not really necessary. This discovery would, in turn, prompt us to see whether certain technical alternatives might allow us to get the results for which we postulated these levels – but without having levels at all. Chomsky (1993) attempts this and suggests that perhaps our acceptance of a four-level theory (consisting of DS, SS, PF, and LF, as in GB) was somewhat hasty.

It's very important to keep in mind that the fact that an analysis is minimalistically suspect does *not* imply that it's incorrect. To repeat, minimalism is a project: to see just how well designed the faculty of language is, given what we know about it. It's quite conceivable that it has design flaws, a conclusion we might come to by realizing that the best accounts contain a certain unavoidable redundancy or inelegance. It's also conceivable that GB is roughly right and that when all the relevant facts are considered, it's the best theory of grammar we can devise. From a minimalist perspective, even this conclusion would be interesting. For it would indicate that even starting from different initial considerations, we end up with the conclusion that GB is roughly right. In what follows you'll see that this is not the conclusion that many have come to. However, it could have been and still could be. This does not remove the interest of analyzing GB-accounts in minimalist terms. For what minimalism does is afford us the opportunity of rethinking the empirical and theoretical bases of our claims and this is always worth doing.

This said, the reader will observe that grammars that arise from minimalist reflection have a very different "look" from the standard GB-varieties. One aim of what follows is to escort readers through the complexities of some current speculations that fly under the minimalist flag.

1.5   The basic story line

The Minimalist Program explores the hypothesis that the language faculty is the optimal realization of interface conditions. In other words, it's a non-redundant and optimal system in the sense that particular phenomena are not overdetermined by linguistic principles and that the linguistic system is subject to economy restrictions with a least effort flavor. The program also addresses the question of what conditions are imposed on the linguistic system in virtue of its interaction with performance systems (the bare output conditions).

Earlier versions of the P&P-theory worked with the hypothesis that the linguistic system has several levels of representation encoding systematic information about linguistic expressions. Some of these levels are conceptually necessary, since their output is the input to performance systems that interact with the linguistic system. The Minimalist Program restricts the class of possible linguistic levels of representation to only the ones that are required by conceptual necessity, namely, the ones that interface with performance systems.

As a working hypothesis, these performance systems are taken to be the A-P system and the C-I system. The linguistic levels that interface with A-P and C-I are PF and LF, respectively. Assuming that these are the only interface levels, PF and LF can be conceived of as the parts of the linguistic system that provide instructions to the performance systems. Under the minimalist perspective, all principles and parameters of the linguistic system should either be stated in terms of legibility at LF or PF (perhaps as modes of interpretation by the performance systems) or follow as byproducts of the operations of the computational system. Linguistic expressions are then taken to be optimal realizations of interface conditions, where optimality is determined by economy conditions specified by UG.

Another assumption is that the language faculty comprises a lexicon and a computational system (see note 10). The lexicon specifies the items that enter into the computational system and their idiosyncratic properties, excluding whatever is predictable by principles of UG or properties of the language in question. The computational system arranges these items in a way to form a pair (π, λ), where π is a PF object and λ is an LF object. The pair (π, λ) is subject to Full Interpretation, a principle of *representational economy* (itself part of substantive economy) that requires that all the features of the pair be legible at the relevant interfaces. If π and λ are legitimate objects (i.e. they satisfy Full Interpretation), the derivation is said to *converge* at PF and at LF, respectively. If either π or λ doesn't satisfy Full Interpretation, the derivation is said to *crash* at the relevant level.

A derivation is taken to converge if and only if it converges at both LF and PF. Thus, if D is the set of permissible derivations that yield a pair (π, λ), the set of convergent derivations C is the subset of D whose members satisfy Full Interpretation at LF and at PF. That is, the set of legible syntactic objects is a subset of the set of all combinations that the grammar can construct.[11] Considerations of *derivational economy* (which

11 As Chomsky (1995: 221) observes, if nonconvergent derivations could be taken into consideration for economy purposes, a derivation that employs no operation would

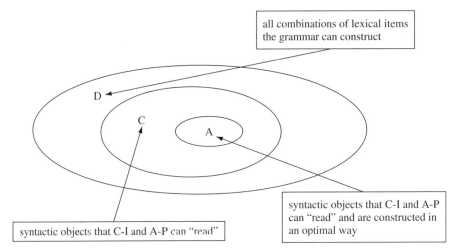

Figure 1 *Subset relationship among derivations*

is also part of substantive economy considerations) in turn select derivations where legible pairs (π, λ) are built in an optimal way. (We discuss derivational economy in chapter 10.) In other words, the set of admissible derivations A constitutes the subset of C that is selected by optimality considerations. Figure 1 offers a visual summary of these subset relations.

This chapter has presented an overall picture of the Minimalist Program. In the chapters that follow, we elaborate this general conception and discuss specific aspects of minimalism, as formulated in these general terms.

1.6   Organization of *Understanding Minimalism*

As we mentioned at the end of section 1.1, each chapter starts off with a quick review of the GB-approach to the main issues under consideration before we suggest one or more alternative ways of understanding them in minimalist terms. In addition, each chapter contains exercises at the relevant parts in the text, which are meant to allow the reader to practice (and go beyond!) the acquired knowledge. Let's see what else is in stock in terms of content.

Chapter 2 reviews the basics of GB, concentrating on two issues, the architecture of the grammar (levels of representation and modular structure) and its conditions, principles, and operations (government, movement, etc.). We'll then pose a methodological question as to whether the

always block any derivation that employs some operation. Thus, only convergent derivations can be compared in terms of economy.

complex architecture of the GB-grammar is really necessary, focusing on the levels of representation. Our answer will be a unanimous *No*. Since this negative answer has a lot of consequences for the theoretical framework, we'll examine in detail some of the relevant conditions, principles, and operations assumed in GB. We dismantle the empirical and theoretical arguments put forth in favor of DS and SS, which leads us to the conclusion that neither may be needed. The agenda is now on the table and the subsequent chapters deal with a more thorough implementation of the new tools introduced and the line of thinking presented in this chapter.

In chapter 3, we deal with theta domains, that is, argument structure at large and its relation to and dependence on syntactic structure. We focus on two aspects, the realization of external arguments (*qua* the Predicate-Internal Subject Hypothesis) and the structure of ditransitive constructions for internal arguments (in terms of VP-shells or by introducing *v*P, the light verb projection). This chapter lays the foundations for the structure of VP assumed throughout.

Once thematic relations are minimalized, it's time to tackle Case domains, which we do in chapter 4. This chapter presents a minimalist rethinking of traditional Case Theory and argues in favor of a unified structural relation for the licensing of Case properties, the specifier-head configuration. Just as the previous chapter discusses the structure of VP, this chapter also deals with the finer articulation of Infl, which may be split in terms of Agr-projections or remain unsplit and be associated with multiple specifiers of *v*P.

These possible structures for Infl will be revisited in chapter 5, which introduces a hotbed in minimalist research: the relevance of minimality for movement. We'll also discuss the role of features in the syntactic computation. Here we'll tie the so-called minimality effects not to heads or phrases, but to individual features.

Chapter 6 explores phrase structure. After reviewing the basic properties of X'-Theory, we'll outline a more dynamic approach to structure in terms of structure-building based on the single operation Merge. This theory of bare phrase structure, again connecting to much of what we've assumed earlier, allows at least two things. First, the GB-conception of a preformed clausal skeleton can be dropped, something alluded to in chapter 2, when we dispense with DS. Second, Trace Theory can be reduced to the copy theory of movement.

Linearization of syntactic constituents is the topic of chapter 7. We introduce a mapping procedure, the Linear Correspondence Axiom

(LCA), and discuss its relevance to variation in word order across languages. We also show that deletion of traces (copies) is determined by the linearization procedures that the grammar makes available.

Chapter 8 develops an alternative to Binding Theory within GB, which does without indices and without appealing to levels of representation other than LF (and PF). In particular, we show that standard DS and SS arguments for the application of certain binding conditions can be expressed in terms of LF only. We appeal to the copy theory of movement and explore an implementation for binding properties in language. While conceptually desirable for obvious reasons (the purpose of this book!), the approach developed in this chapter suggests strongly that a minimalized formulation of the classic binding conditions, Principles A, B, and C, is technically feasible as well.

In chapter 9, we focus on checking theory, which was used in previous chapters to handle the licensing of specific lexical features in a syntactic structure (Case, for instance). Framing the discussion in a broader perspective, we address the issue of what checking really consists of, by examining the relationship between feature interpretability and feature checking.

Chapter 10 introduces a number of related developments in more recent minimalist research, such as the preference for Merge over Move and the concepts of subnumerations and phases. At this point, the general outline of the Minimalist Program will have been spelled out so that it can be applied by the reader. In this sense, chapter 10, the big finale, acts as a looking glass on the current state of the minimalist endeavor.

Turn the page and enjoy!

2 *Some architectural issues in a minimalist setting*

2.1 Introduction

Minimalism (at least as presented here) takes GB as its starting point. The reason for this is twofold. First, GB is a very successful theory of grammar with a very interesting theoretical structure and ample empirical coverage. The former property provides grist for the methodological concerns that minimalism highlights. The latter property permits discussion to move beyond mere methodology by setting empirical bars for prospective theories to clear. Second, GB is the most fully worked out version of a P&P-approach to UG. As such, considering a GB-style theory from the vantage point of minimalist methodological concerns is a good way of getting into substantive issues quickly. So, let's start!

Section 2.2 will review the major architectural properties that are shared by most (if not all) incarnations of GB. Section 2.3 will then introduce some basic minimalist qualms with the GB-architecture of the grammar, focusing on its levels of representation and critically evaluating the evidence in favor of S-Structure (SS) and D-Structure (DS). The exercise of abolishing SS and DS will introduce some key minimalist themes and technical proposals, to be further explored in the subsequent chapters. The upshot of this chapter is a simplified architecture of the grammar consisting solely of the only true interface levels, Logical Form (LF) and Phonetic Form (PF). Section 2.4 will wrap up and sketch the picture of the grammar developed up to that point.

2.2 Main properties of a GB-style theory[1]

2.2.1 General architecture

First and foremost, GB has a P&P-architecture. This means that UG is taken to be composed of principles with open parameter values that are set

---

1 This overview section recaps the cornerstones of GB. For a more comprehensive and detailed presentation, see, for example, Radford (1988), Haegeman (1994), Roberts (1996), or Carnie (2001).

by experience, i.e. by PLD. The driving force behind P&P-theories is the need to answer Plato's problem in the domain of language. By having innate general principles with open parameter values, one can deal with two basic facts that characterize language acquisition: (i) it's considerably fast despite the very serious deficiency in the data that the child can use in fixing his or her competence, and (ii) languages display an intricate surface variation. This dual problem is adequately accommodated if P&P is roughly correct. The ease of acquisition is due to the rich innate principles that the child comes equipped with. In turn, the variation can be traced to the fact that different parameter values can result in significantly different outputs.

2.2.2   Levels of representation

GB-theories identify four significant levels of grammatical representation: D-Structure (DS), S-Structure (SS), Logical Form (LF), and Phonetic Form (PF). These levels are formal objects with specific functional and substantive characteristics. Let's consider these.

2.2.2.1   D-Structure

DS is substantively described as the phrase marker at which "pure GF-θ" is represented, i.e. the one-to-one correspondence between grammatical function and thematic or θ-role. This means that DS is where an expression's logical/thematic role θ perfectly coincides with its grammatical function *GF*: logical subjects are DS (grammatical) subjects, logical objects are DS (grammatical) objects, etc. Thus, at DS, positions that are thematically active must all be filled and positions with no thematic import must be left empty.

An example or two will help fix ideas. Consider the verbs in (1), for instance:

(1)   John persuaded Harry to kiss Mary.

Thematically, *persuade* requires a "persuader," a "persuadee," and a propositional complement, whereas *kiss* requires a "kisser" and a "kissee." Given that (1) is an acceptable sentence, each of these θ-roles must then correspond to filled positions in its DS representation, as illustrated in (2):

(2)   DS:
      [John$_{persuader}$ persuaded Harry$_{persuadee}$ [ec_{kisser} to kiss
      Mary$_{kissee}$]$_{proposition}$]

The details of constructions like (1) are not important here. What is key is that once we assume the notion of DS, (2) must have a filler in the position associated with the "kisser" θ-role, despite the fact that it's not phonetically realized. In other words, this position is filled by a (phonetically) empty category (*ec*). In GB, the empty category in (2) is an obligatorily controlled PRO, whose antecedent is *Harry*.

By contrast, let's now consider the verbs of the sentences in

(3)   a. John seems to like Mary.
       b. It seems that John likes Mary.

Like has two θ-roles to assign (the "liker" and the "likee"), whereas *seem* has only one θ-role to assign to its propositional complement. Crucially, it doesn't assign a θ-role to the position occupied by *John* in (3a), as can be seen by the fact that this position may be filled by an expletive in (3b). This means that *John* in (3a) wasn't base-generated in the position where it appears, but must have gotten there transformationally. Thus, the matrix subject position of the DS representation of (3a) is filled by nothing at all, not even a null expression, as shown in (4), where Δ represents an empty position.

(4)   DS:
       [Δ seems [John$_{liker}$ to like Mary$_{likee}$]$_{proposition}$]

As for its functional characterization, DS is defined as the "starting point" for a derivation; that is, it's the phrase marker that is the output of phrase-structure operations plus lexical insertion and the input to transformational operations. By being the locus of phrase-structure rules, DS is the locus of a grammar's recursivity. By being the input to the computations that will lead to an LF object and a PF object, DS also ensures that the pair form/meaning is compatible in the sense that the two objects are based on the same lexical resources; after all, any adequate theory of grammar must ensure that the PF output associated with the sentence in (5) should mean 'Mary likes John' and not 'I don't think that Mary likes John', for instance.

(5)   Mary likes John.

There's some interesting evidence for DS within GB. The best of it revolves around distinguishing raising from control, which we'll return to in section 2.3.2.2. There's also some interesting evidence against the existence of a DS level that we'll review when we consider minimalist objections to DS.

2.2.2.2 S-Structure
SS can be functionally characterized as the point in which the derivation splits, sending off one copy to PF for phonetic interpretation and one copy to LF for semantic interpretation. Substantively, SS is the phrase marker

where several grammatical modules ply their trade; thus, it's the place where Case is assigned, some aspects of Binding Theory are inspected, null operators are identified, some aspects of the ECP apply (γ-marking of argument traces) and Subjacency holds.[2] In addition, SS has been used to describe language variation. For instance, *wh*-movement is taken to occur before SS in English, but after SS in Chinese, and V-to-I movement is assumed to take place before SS in French, but after SS in English.[3]

It's fair to say that SS is the queen of GB-levels. It's the most theory-internal level of the grammar and a large number of modules apply there to filter out unwanted derivations. One of the most interesting sets of arguments spawned by the Minimalist Program argues that SS is both dispensable and undesirable. We return to these below.

2.2.2.3   PF and LF

PF and LF are interface levels within GB. This means that they provide the grammatical information required to assign a phonetic and semantic interpretation to a sentence. Various proposals have been put forward about what operations apply at these levels. The most important of these is the ECP-filter that functions to weed out derivations with unlicensed traces at LF.[4] Binding Theory and the control module are also thought to apply at LF. By contrast, it's very unlikely that any syntactic condition can apply at the PF level itself, given it is not a phrase marker; however, this doesn't rule out the possibility that syntactic conditions may apply during the mapping from SS to PF, while syntactic structures are still available.[5]

2.2.3   The "T-model"

Another core feature of GB is that the grammar has a T-type organization in the sense that SS is the only level that directly relates to the others, as illustrated in (6):

---

2 For more discussion on the properties of SS, and why certain conditions hold there and only there (and others don't), see especially Chomsky (1981: chap. 3, 1986b) and Lasnik and Saito (1984).

3 Huang (1982) proposed that *wh*-movement can apply before or after SS; thus, in *wh*-in situ languages (such as Chinese or Japanese), the *wh*-phrase moves covertly. In the same vein, Pollock (1989), building on work by Jackendoff (1972) and Emonds (1976, 1978), argues for application of verb movement before or after SS.

4 The ECP says that traces must be properly governed (see Chomsky 1981, 1986a, Kayne 1981, Lasnik and Saito 1984, 1992, among others).

5 See, for instance, Aoun, Hornstein, Lightfoot, and Weinberg's (1987) proposal that head-government applies on the PF-side of the grammar.

(6)   *The GB T-model of the grammar*

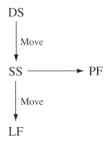

The Move operation that applies on the mapping from SS to LF is the same operation that applies before the split, the only difference being that one is *overt* (from DS to SS) and the other *covert* (from SS to LF). However, since LF and PF are not directly connected, the outputs of Move that are obtained after SS, i.e. covert movement, don't have a reflex at PF. Examples of covert movement operations include *wh*-movement, expletive replacement, and anaphor raising, which we'll address in due time.

2.2.4   The Projection Principle

The Projection Principle makes derivations monotonic by requiring that some kinds of information from earlier structures, such as thematic information, be preserved at later levels of derivation, in particular, DS, SS, and LF (PF is not so constrained). One consequence of this is that traces are required to preserve the thematic and structural information encoded at DS. If a verb takes an object at DS, for instance, the Projection Principle requires that it take one at SS and LF as well. Thus, if the object moves, some residue of its prior position must be maintained or the verb will "detransitivize," violating the Projection Principle. In effect, the Projection Principle forces each movement to leave a trace behind to mark the position from which it has taken place.

Within GB, the Projection Principle is generally augmented to include a stipulation that all clauses must have subjects. This is the "Extended" Projection Principle (EPP).[6]

2.2.5   The transformational component

GB embodies a very simple transformational component. It includes two rules: Bind and Move. Bind allows free indexing of DPs and Move allows anything to move anywhere anytime. Due to the Projection Principle, Move leaves behind

---

6 The EPP was first proposed in Chomsky (1982). We'll return to its status in the Minimalist Program in sections 2.3.1.3 and 9.3.3.

traces with the form [$_X$ *e*], i.e. a constituent X with null phonetic content. By definition, traces are silent and are coindexed with what has been moved.

2.2.6   *Modules*

The two very general rules of the transformational component massively overgenerate unacceptable structures. To compensate for these very general rules, GB-grammars deploy a group of information-specific modules that interact in such a way as to bar unwanted overgeneration and "prepare" a phrase marker for interpretation at LF and PF. These modules track Case-features (Case Theory), θ-roles (Theta Theory), binding configurations (Binding Theory), trace licensing (ECP and Subjacency), phrase-structure (X'-Theory), and control relations (Control Theory).[7] These different kinds of information may be inspected at different points in a derivation. For instance, phrase markers that fail to conform to the required specifications of X'-Theory are weeded out at D-Structure, the Case Theory determines at SS how a pronoun is to be phonetically realized, and Binding Theory excludes unwanted coindexation of DPs at LF.

2.2.7   *Government*

The fundamental grammatical relation within GB is government. The conceptual unity of GB-modules resides in their conditions exploiting the common relation of government. As noted, the kinds of information that GB-modules track are very different. Thus, θ-roles are different from Case-features, anaphors are different from bounding nodes, reciprocals are not empty categories, and so on. What lends conceptual unity to these diverse modules is the fact that their reach/applicability is limited to domains defined in terms of government. Case is assigned under government, as are θ-roles. Binding is checked within minimal domains that are defined using governors. The ECP and Subjacency are stated in terms of barriers, which are in turn defined via government. There is thus an abstract conceptual unity provided by this key relation to otherwise very diverse modules.

2.3   Minimalist qualms

Despite its successes, there are reasons for rethinking the standard GB-assumptions reviewed in section 2.2, at least from a minimalist point

---

7 For early minimalist perspectives on the status, history, and place of GB-modules, see, for example, the collection of papers in Webelhuth (1995b).

of view. Recall the question that animates the minimalist enterprise: to what extent are the minimal boundary conditions on any adequate P&P-theory also maximal? We fleshed these minimal conditions in terms of methodological and substantive economy conditions (see sections 1.3 and 1.5). The question that then arises is whether these are sufficient to construct empirically viable accounts of UG. In other words, how far can one get exploiting just these considerations?

In the remainder of this chapter, we begin the task of reconsidering the status of the broad systemic features of GB against the methodological backdrop of minimalism, by examining the four-level hypothesis. As reviewed in section 2.2.2, GB identifies four critical levels in the structural analysis of a sentence: its DS, SS, LF, and PF representations. Why four levels? From a minimalist perspective, if levels are at all required (see notes 9 and 10 of chapter 1), LF and PF are unobjectionable. Recall that one of the "big facts" about natural languages is that they pair form and meaning. LF and PF are the grammatical inputs to the Conceptual-Intentional and Articulatory-Perceptual systems, respectively. As any adequate grammar must provide every sentence with a form and a semantic interpretation, any adequate grammar must thus have a PF and an LF representation. In this sense, LF and PF are conceptually necessary parts of any adequate model of grammar.

What of SS and DS? Let's consider these in turn, starting with SS.

2.3.1   Rethinking S-Structure

SS is a theory-internal level. This means that it's not motivated by the general sorts of considerations outlined in chapter 1. Thus, the motivation for SS is empirical, not conceptual. This, it's important to emphasize, is *not* a criticism. It's merely an observation that points to another question, namely: how strong is the evidence for postulating SS? What empirical ground would we lose if we dropped the assumption that SS exists?

On the face of it, we would lose quite a bit. First, within GB both Case and Binding Theory apply at SS, as does γ-marking in various *Barriers*-versions of GB.[8] Second, SS serves an important descriptive function in that it marks the border between overt and covert syntax. As much language variation has been treated in terms of rules applying before or after SS, it would appear that dispensing with SS would leave us without

---

8 See Lasnik and Saito (1984) on the notion of γ-marking and its applicability to proper government, and Chomsky (1986a) and Lasnik and Saito (1992) for further discussion.

the descriptive resources to characterize this variation.[9] Lastly, there are various kinds of phenomena that seem tied to SS. Parasitic gap licensing, for example, is one classic example of this.[10] So, it would appear that SS has considerable empirical value, even if it's conceptually unmotivated.

The minimalist project is, however, clear: to show that appearances here are deceiving and that it's possible to cover the same (or more) empirical ground without the benefit of SS. This is what Chomsky (1993) tries to do with respect to Case Theory, Binding Theory, and cross-linguistic variation. Let's review his reasoning.

2.3.1.1 Case Theory considerations: assignment vs. checking

The standard GB-conception of Case Theory is that in order to be well-formed, DPs must be assigned Case by a governing verb, preposition, or finite Infl at SS.[11] Why at SS? Because Case has been argued to be relevant at both LF and PF and not to be relevant at DS.

That Case can't be assigned at DS is shown by passive and raising constructions like (7) and (8), respectively:

(7) a. He was seen.
    b. <u>DS</u>:
        [$_{IP}$ Δ was + Infl [$_{VP}$ seen he]]
    c. <u>SS</u>:
        [$_{IP}$ he$_i$ was + Infl [$_{VP}$ seen t$_i$]]

(8) a. He seems to be likely to win.
    b. <u>DS</u>:
        [$_{IP}$ Δ Infl [$_{VP}$ seems [$_{IP}$ Δ to [$_{VP}$ be likely [$_{IP}$ he to win]]]]]
    c. <u>SS</u>:
        [$_{IP}$ he$_i$ Infl [$_{VP}$ seems [$_{IP}$ t$_i$ to [$_{VP}$ be likely [$_{IP}$ t$_i$ to win]]]]]

In both the DS of (7a) and the DS of (8a), the pronoun *he* is not governed by a Case-assigning element: *seen* in (7b) is a passive verb and the most embedded Infl in (8b) is non-finite. What these data suggest, then, is that passivization voids a verb of its (accusative) Case-marking capacity and

---

9 This was explicitly expressed by Pollock (1989) and Chomsky (1991). See also, among many others, Huang (1982) on *wh*-movement, Rizzi (1986) on licensing *pro*, and the collection of papers in Freidin (1991).

10 For early descriptions of parasitic gaps, see Taraldsen (1981), Chomsky (1982, 1986a), Engdahl (1983), Kayne (1984). Culicover and Postal (2001) contains a more recent collection of articles; see also Nunes (1995, 2001, 2004), Nissenbaum (2000), and Hornstein (2001).

11 We won't take side on the issue of whether Case is assigned to DPs or NPs. For purposes of exposition, we'll assume that it's assigned to DPs.

non-finiteness doesn't give Infl the power to assign (nominative) Case; only after the pronoun moves to the specifier of a finite Infl (see (7c) and (8c)) can it then be assigned Case (nominative in both instances). Thus, Case Theory cannot apply at DS; otherwise, the sentences in (7a) and (8a) would be incorrectly ruled out.

Notice that to say that Case-assignment in (7) and (8) must take place after the movement of the pronoun does not necessarily mean that it takes place at SS. Thus, why not assume that it takes place at LF or PF? Consider LF. Recall that, given the T-model of grammar (see section 2.2.3), the output of covert operations is phonetically inert. Thus, if Case were assigned at LF, PF wouldn't take notice of it. However, the roots of Case Theory rest on the fact that what Case DP receives quite clearly has phonological implications. English pronouns surface as *he, she*, etc. if assigned nominative Case, but as *him, her*, etc. if assigned accusative Case; other languages, such as Latin or German, Case-mark all DPs with a phonological reflex. Therefore, Case can't be assigned at LF.

What about PF, then? Again, the argument relates to the T-model organization of the grammar. Most late versions of GB assume that Case Theory and Theta Theory are linked by the Visibility Condition in (9):[12]

(9)   *Visibility Condition*
       A DP's θ-role is visible at LF only if it is Case-marked.

Empirical evidence for the Visibility Condition is provided by contrasts such as the one in (10), which involve null operators (OP):[13]

(10)   a. I met the man [OP_i that Mary believed t_i to be a genius]
        b. *I met the man [OP_i that it was believed t_i to be a genius]

---

12 See Chomsky (1981: chap. 5) for early discussion of the Visibility Condition, building on an idea by Aoun (1979) and especially a 1977 letter from Jean-Roger Vergnaud to Noam Chomsky and Howard Lasnik which circulated in the linguistic community (see also Vergnaud 1982).

13 Null operators (also known as empty or zero operators) were introduced by Chomsky (1982), on a par with their overt cousins (Chomsky 1981), for elements that are not phonetically realized but display operator properties, such as the ability to license variables, for example. See, among others, the works of Jaeggli (1982), Stowell (1984), Aoun and Clark (1985), Haïk (1985), Browning (1987), Authier (1988), Lasnik and Stowell (1991), and Contreras (1993) for the properties of and evidence for null operators. In the case of a relative clause such as (10), OP is the covert counterpart of a *wh*-relative pronoun, such as *who* in (i) below. Under this analysis (see Chomsky 1986a and Chomsky and Lasnik 1993, for instance), *that* in (10a) is indeed analyzed as a regular complementizer, not as a non-interrogative relative pronoun.
    (i)   I met the man [who_i Mary believed t_i to be a genius].

Under the plausible assumption that the null operators in (10) are DPs (they stand for *the man*), the Visibility Condition requires that they (or their chains, i.e. $<OP_i, t_i>$) be assigned Case despite the fact that they don't have phonetic content. Hence, the contrast in (10) follows from the fact that (the trace of) the null operator can be assigned Case by the active *believed* in (10a), but not by the passive *believed* in (10b). In other words, the unacceptability of (10b) is analyzed as a Theta-Criterion violation: the "subject" θ-role of the lowest clause is not visible at LF as the trace is not Case-marked. In general terms, then, if Case were assigned at PF, the θ-roles borne by DPs wouldn't be visible at LF and any sentence containing argument DPs would violate the Theta-Criterion. The conclusion is therefore that Case must not be assigned at PF.

In short, the GB-theory of Case requires that Case-assignment take place after DS, feed PF, and feed LF. SS is the level that meets all three requirements and so seems to be the appropriate locus for Case-assignment. This looks like a very good argument for the existence of SS, given the strong empirical evidence in favor of Case Theory.

However, appearances are deceptive here. Chomsky (1993) shows that the conclusion above crucially rests on an unwarranted *technical* assumption about how Case is implemented within GB and that if we adopt slightly different (but no less adequate) technology, then the need for SS disappears. In particular, the above arguments rest on the assumption that Case is *assigned*. It now behooves us to consider what Case-assignment is.

Let's do this by taking a closer look at the specific details of the derivation of (7a–c), where the boldfaced NOM(inative) indicates the property assigned by finite Infl (*was*):

(11)   He was seen.

(12)   a. <u>DS:</u>

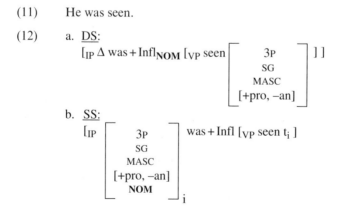

b. <u>SS:</u>

At the DS representation of (11), the pronoun is inserted as a bundle of features with no Case specification and the finite Infl is inherently specified as bearing nominative Case, as shown in (12a). The pronoun then moves to [Spec,IP] and the nominative Case-feature of Infl is "transmitted" to the feature matrix of the pronoun, yielding the SS representation in (12b). Finally, the modified feature matrix is realized at PF as *he*.

The standard mechanics of Case Theory in GB thus assumes (i) that on lexical insertion DPs have no Case and (ii) that Case is acquired through the course of the derivation. With this technology at hand, we've seen above that Case Theory must then hold of SS in order to be empirically adequate. However, why assume that this is the way that Case Theory works? What would go wrong if we assumed that (i) DPs have Case-features at DS and (ii) the appropriateness of these features is checked derivationally?

Consider such a checking account applied to the derivation of (11), as shown in (13), where crossing out annotates feature checking (relevant feature NOM in boldfaced type):

(13)   a. <u>DS</u>:
              [$_{IP}$ Δ was + Infl$_{NOM}$ [$_{VP}$ seen he$_{NOM}$]]
         b. <u>SS</u>:
              [$_{IP}$ he$_{\mathbf{NOM}}$ was + Infl$_{\mathbf{NOM}}$ [$_{VP}$ seen t]]

When the pronoun is inserted at DS, it's fully specified, as shown in (13a) by the form *he* rather than a feature-bundle, but its Case-feature can't be licensed in this structure because it isn't governed by a Case-bearing element. The pronoun then moves to [Spec,IP], where its Case-feature is paired with the Case-feature of the governing Infl. Once these features match, Case Theory is satisfied and the pronoun is licensed in the structure.

In general terms, instead of requiring that DPs be assigned Case by a governing head, we say that the Case-feature of a DP must be licensed by matching the Case-feature of a governing head. In place of assignment, we substitute checking. There seems to be no empirical reason for preferring Case-assignment to Case-checking. However, and this is the surprise, if we assume that Case is checked rather than assigned, then the above arguments in favor of SS evaporate. In later chapters we'll revisit Case Theory from a minimalist perspective and change some fundamental assumptions of the GB-approach. However, the present argument does not rely on any major revisions of Case Theory. It only relies on substituting checking for assignment. All else can be left in place. Chomsky's point is that this trivial technical emendation suffices to undercut the Case-based arguments in favor of SS.

Consider the details. Recall that the main argument in favor of the claim that we needed to check Case at SS and not at LF was that Case may have phonetic consequences: *he* differs from *him*, *she* differs from *her*, etc. Given our assumptions about the T-model organization of the grammar, we couldn't assume that Case is assigned at LF. However, with the proposed new machinery reviewed above, this problem disappears. If all DPs already have their Case-features specified at DS, the phonological/phonetic component already has the relevant piece of information for a pronoun to be realized as *he* and not as *him*, for instance. All we need to be sure of is that the right Case appears in the right place, e.g. that *he* appears in the specifier of finite Infl ([Spec,IP]), and not in the object position of transitive verbs. However, this sort of checking *can* be delayed until LF at no empirical cost. So, if we replace assignment with checking and assume that the Case Filter applies at LF (something like, "by LF all Cases must be appropriately checked"), then all goes swimmingly even without SS.

Consider a couple of concrete examples to see that this is indeed so:

(14)   a. *Mary to leave would be terrible.
         b. *It was seen them.
         c. *John loves they.

On the assignment story, (14a) is out because *Mary* is Caseless (recall that the governing infinitival Infl assigns no Case) in violation of the Case Filter. On the checking story, *Mary* has a Case-feature but there's nothing to check it as its governing head is the non-finite Infl, which is not a Case-active head; hence, *Mary* violates the Case Filter at LF by having an unchecked Case. The same story extends to (14b). The passive verb *seen* is not a Case-assigner, nor a Case-checker. So, *them* can't get Case under the assignment approach, nor have its accusative Case checked under the checking approach, and the Case Filter is violated. (14c) is a little different. Here *they* has the "wrong Case," nominative instead of accusative. On the assignment story, this follows because *loves* only assigns accusative Case and *they* is governed by *loves*. Similarly, we can assume that *loves* only checks accusative Case and that the Case mismatch between nominative-marked *they* and accusative-bearing *loves* results in ungrammaticality.

Finally, let's consider the existential construction like (15a) below. There are as many analyses of existential constructions as there are versions of GB and minimalism.[14] Leaving a more detailed discussion of these constructions to chapters 9 and 10, we would just like to point out that in addition to resorting to SS, the analysis in terms of Case-assignment may also require a considerable enrichment of the theoretical apparatus. Let's see why.

(15)   a. There is a cat on the mat.
        b. SS:
           $[_{IP}$ there^i is + Infl $[_{SC}$ [a cat $]^i$ [on the mat]]]

Under many analyses, the DP *a cat* in (15b) is not in a Case-marked position because it's not governed by the finite Infl (see section 4.2 for a review of the role of government in Case Theory).[15] If so, it should violate the Case Filter at SS and the sentence would be incorrectly ruled out. In order to prevent this undesirable result a new primitive, *CHAIN*, is introduced into the theory.[16] A CHAIN is taken to encompass both regular chains formed by movement and "expletive-associate" pairs such as (*there^i*, [a cat $]^i$) in (15b), whose members are related by a mechanism of co-superscripting. Under such an analysis, the finite Infl in (15b) would assign its Case to *there*, as in standard instances of nominative-assignment, and this feature would be transmitted to the co-superscripted associate of *there*, allowing the DP *a cat* to satisfy the Case Filter at SS.

Under a checking-based alternative, on the other hand, all that needs to be said is that *a cat* in (15a) must check its (nominative) Case against Infl *by* LF. If *a cat* moves covertly to a position where it can be governed by Infl, say, if it adjoins to IP, as shown in (16), it will have its Case checked and the Case Filter would be satisfied at LF.[17]

(16)   LF:
        $[_{IP}$ [a cat $]_i$ $[_{IP}$ there is + Infl $[_{SC}$ t$_i$ [on the mat]]]]

14 On the rich literature on expletive/existential constructions, see among others Chomsky (1981, 1986b, 1991), Belletti (1988), Authier (1991), Lasnik (1992a), Chomsky and Lasnik (1993), Rothstein (1995), and Vikner (1995) within GB, and Chomsky (1993, 1995, 2000), den Dikken (1995b), Groat (1995), Lasnik (1995c), Castillo, Drury, and Grohmann (1999), Boeckx (2000), Grohmann, Drury, and Castillo (2000), Hornstein (2000), Felser and Rupp (2001), Bošković (2002b), Nasu (2002), and Epstein and Seely (2005) under minimalist premises (see Sabel 2000 for a brief overview).

15 We assume in (15b) that the string *a cat on the mat* forms a small clause (SC), a type of predication structure with special properties (see, among others, the collection of papers in Cardinaletti and Guasti 1995 for relevant discussion). However, as the argument unfolds below, nothing hinges on this assumption; SC may very well be a regular VP whose external argument is *a cat* and whose head *is* raises to Infl.

16 See Burzio (1986) and Chomsky (1986b) for discussion.

17 See Chomsky (1986b) for this approach.

The theoretical apparatus is thus kept constant. The only special proviso that needs to be made concerns the feature specification of *there*: the checking approach must assume that it doesn't have a Case-feature. But this assumption seems to be comparable to a tacit assumption in the assignment approach: that *there* can't "withhold" (i.e. it must "transmit") the Case-feature it receives. All things being equal, methodological considerations would thus lead us to choose checking instead of assignment.

In sum, as far as standard instances of Case-related issues go, the checking approach covers virtually the same empirical ground as the assignment approach. However, with checking in place of assignment, we can assume that the Case Filter applies at LF and dispense with any mention of SS. What this shows is that our earlier Case-based arguments in favor of SS rested on a technical implementation that is easily avoided and that these sorts of arguments shouldn't stand in the way of the minimalist project of doing away with SS. Moreover, we've also seen that, depending on how existential constructions are to be analyzed, the combination of the assignment technology with the claim that the Case Filter applies at SS has the undesirable result of complicating the picture by requiring Case "transmission" in addition to standard Case-assignment.

Exercise 2.1

Explain in checking terms what is wrong with the following sentences, where (id) is supposed to mean 'she likes herself', with *she* A-moving from the object to the subject position:

(i)   a. *Her likes he.
      b. *John doesn't expect she to leave.
      c. *It was believed her to be tall.
      d. *She likes.

Exercise 2.2

Consider how subject-verb agreement works. There are two possible approaches: either a DP assigns agreement features to a finite V, or a DP checks the agreement features of a finite V. Discuss these two options in relation to the sentences below.

(i)   a. The men are/*is here.
      b. There *are/is a man here.

2.3.1.2 Binding Theory considerations: what moves in wh-movement?
There's another set of arguments for SS from Binding Theory that
Chomsky (1993) discusses. Let's outline these here after reviewing some
preliminary background.

First, let's examine the application of Principle C of the Binding Theory
to data such as (17) and (18).

(17)   a. *He$_i$ greeted Mary after John$_i$ walked in.
        b. DS/SS/LF:
           *[he$_i$ [greeted Mary [after John$_i$ walked in]]]

(18)   a. After John$_i$ walked in, he$_i$ greeted Mary.
        b. DS:
           *[he$_i$ [greeted Mary [after John$_i$ walked in]]]
        c. SS/LF:
           [[after John$_i$ walked in]$_k$ [he$_i$ [greeted Mary t$_k$]]]

Principle C says that referential or R-expressions must be free, i.e. not
coindexed with any other c-commanding (pro)nominal expression. Thus,
if we were to compute Principle C at DS, we would incorrectly predict that
both (17a) and (18a) should be unacceptable because they arguably have
identical DS representations, as shown in (17b) and (18b), and *he* c-commands
John in these representations. By contrast, if Principle C is computed at SS
or LF, we get the facts right: (17a) is predicted to be unacceptable and (18a),
acceptable; crucially, after the adjunct clause moves in (18c), the pronoun
doesn't c-command *John*. The question now is at which of these two levels
Principle C should apply. In order to address this question, we'll examine
slightly more complicated data involving covert *wh*-movement.

Consider the sentence in (19) below, for instance. (19) contains two
wh-elements and has a multiple interrogative structure. A characteristic
of such sentences is that they allow (in English, they require) a *pair-list*
reading, that is, they require answers that pair the interpretations of the
wh-elements. An appropriate answer for (19) would thus associate eaters
with things eaten, as in (20), for instance.

(19)   Who ate what?

(20)   John (ate) a bagel, Mary (ate) a croissant, and Sheila (ate) a muffin.

Under most GB-analyses, it is assumed that *in situ*, non-moved
wh-phrases (i.e. those left behind at the end of overt syntax) covertly
move to a position associated with an interrogative complementizer.[18]

---

18 See Huang (1982) and much subsequent work.

If so, the object *wh*-phrase of (19) appears *in situ* at SS, as represented in (21a) below, but moves covertly to the position containing the overtly moved *wh*-element, yielding the LF representation in (21b). Semantically, we can understand the structure in (21b) as underlying the pair-list answer in (20); the two *wh*-elements in CP form an "absorbed" operator that ranges over *pairs* of (potential) answers (pairs of eaters and things eaten in the case of (19)).[19]

(21)   a. <u>SS</u>:
         [$_{CP}$ who$_i$ [$_{IP}$ t$_i$ ate what]]
        b. <u>LF</u>:
         [$_{CP}$ what$_k$ + who$_i$ [$_{IP}$ t$_i$ ate t$_k$]]

Given this background, let's consider the standard GB-analysis of the binding data in (22)–(24):

(22)   a. Which picture that Harry$_i$ bought did he$_i$ like?
        b. <u>SS/LF</u>:
         [$_{CP}$ [which picture that Harry$_i$ bought]$_k$ did [$_{IP}$ he$_i$ like t$_k$]]

(23)   a. *He$_i$ liked this picture that Harry$_i$ bought.
        b. <u>SS/LF</u>:
         *[$_{CP}$ he$_i$ liked this picture that Harry$_i$ bought]

(24)   a. *Which man said he$_i$ liked which picture that Harry$_i$ bought?
        b. <u>SS</u>:
         *[$_{CP}$ [which man]$_k$ [$_{IP}$ t$_k$ said he$_i$ liked which picture that Harry$_i$ bought]]
        c. <u>LF</u>:
         [$_{CP}$ [which picture that Harry$_i$ bought]$_m$ + [which man]$_k$ [$_{IP}$ t$_k$ said he$_i$ liked t$_m$]]

As reviewed above, the LF and SS representations are basically identical in the case of the sentences in (22a) and (23a), as shown in (22b) and (23b), but considerably different in the case of (24a), as shown in (24b–c), due to the covert movement of the *wh*-object to the matrix [Spec,CP].

   Let's now examine the potential coreference between *he* and *Harry* in the sentences above. If Principle C held of LF, we would correctly predict that coreference is possible in (22a) (because at LF, *Harry* is not c-commanded by *he*) and impossible in (23a) (because at LF, *Harry* is c-commanded by *he*), but would incorrectly predict that coreference in (24a) should be possible, because after the object *wh*-phrase moves, *Harry* ends up in a position where it's not c-commanded by *he*. On the other hand, if Principle C applied at SS, we would get the right results: coreference would be allowed for (22a), while

---

19 See Higginbotham and May (1981) for relevant discussion.

it would be ruled out for (23a) and (24a). Therefore, it appears that we have an argument for SS in terms of Binding Theory here.

However, once again, appearances are somewhat deceiving. Note that the above argument for SS relies on the assumption that the LF representation of (24a) is (24c), i.e. that covert *wh*-raising moves the *whole wh*-phrase. By contrast, if we assumed that in order to establish a structure sufficient for question interpretation, covert *wh*-raising moves *only* the *wh*-element, then the LF structure for (24a) should be (25), rather than (24c):

(25)   LF:
        *[$_{CP}$ which$_m$ + [which man]$_k$ [$_{IP}$ t$_k$ said he$_i$ liked [t$_m$ picture that Harry$_i$ bought]]]

Given that *Harry* is c-commanded by the pronoun in (25), their coindexation leads to a Principle C violation. In other words, we now have an empirically adequate alternative LF-account of the coreference possibilities of the data in (22)–(24).

Thus, the evidence for SS reviewed above is as good as the supposition that covert *wh*-raising involves movement of *whole wh*-phrases. What then are the arguments for this? As it turns out, the arguments are quite weak.[20] Even if we assume that paired readings in multiple questions require covert *wh*-movement, it's not clear that it requires moving the whole *wh*-expression rather than just the relevant *wh*-part. Aside from the observation that in overt syntax one can move the whole *wh*-phrase, there's little reason to think that in covert syntax one must do so. In fact, even in overt syntax, it's not always necessary to move the whole *wh*-phrase.

Consider the French and German data in (26) and (27), for instance.[21]

(26)   *French*
        a. [Combien   de livres]$_i$ a-t-il   consultés t$_i$?
           how.many   of books   has-he consulted
        b. Combien$_i$ a-t-il   consultés [t$_i$ de livres]?
           how.many   has-he consulted   of books

---

20 See Hornstein and Weinberg (1990) for relevant discussion.
21 This paradigm was first noted by Obenauer (1976). See also Obenauer (1984, 1994), Dobrovie-Sorin (1990), Rizzi (1990, 2001), Adger (1994), Laenzlinger (1998), Starke (2001), and Mathieu (2002) for the phenomenon in French, including the role of agreement, adverb placement, and issues of interpretation. The relevance of the German phenomenon in (27) was observed by van Riemsdijk (1978). For a comprehensive discussion and further references, see Butler and Mathieu (2004), who discuss the syntax and semantics involved in such split constructions in a uniform way.

    c. *[De livres]ᵢ a-t-il   consultés [combien   tᵢ]?
       of   books   has-he consulted   how.many
       'How many books did he consult?'

(27)   *German*
    a. [Was für Bücher]ᵢ hast du tᵢ gelesen?
       what for   books   have you   read
    b. Wasᵢ hast du [tᵢ für Bücher] gelesen?
       what   have you   for books   read
    c. *[Für Bücher]ᵢ hast du   [was tᵢ] gelesen?
       for books   have you   what   read
    'What books did you read?'

Leaving details aside (such as why stranding of the preposition phrase is possible, i.e. why the PP *de livres* or *für Bücher* may stay behind), (26a–b) and (27a–b) show that a *wh*-word such as *combien* or *was* need not drag its complement structure along. In turn, the contrasts in (26b–c) and (27b–c) indicate that what is really necessary for a *wh*-question to converge is that the *wh*-word is appropriately licensed.

    Even more telling are the English constructions in (28), where the relative clause *that Harry likes* moves along with the *wh*-phrase *which portrait* in (28a) but not in (28b):

(28)   a. Which portrait that Harry likes did he buy?
       b. Which portrait did he buy that Harry likes?

(28b) structurally resembles the proposed LF representation in (25) and, interestingly, we find that it does not allow coreference between *he* and *Harry* either, as opposed to (28a), where the relative clause moves overtly along with the *wh*-phrase.[22] Notice that if the relative clause of (28b) does not move covertly to adjoin to *which portrait*,[23] its SS and LF representations will be the same, as shown in (29) below. Thus, we can also account for the different coreference possibilities in (28a) and (28b) in LF terms: Principle C is satisfied in (29a), but violated in (29b).

---

22 Some early discussion of related data can be found in van Riemsdijk and Williams (1981), Freidin (1986), and Lebeaux (1988).
23 Covert adjunction of the relative clause in (28b) can be prevented in various ways. For instance, we could assume that covert movement carries along as little material as possible, or that all things being equal, at LF it's preferable to modify variables rather than operators. At any rate, it seems possible to defuse the premise that is causing the problems without too much trouble. See Hornstein and Weinberg (1990), Chomsky (1993), and also sections 8.3.1 and 9.4 below.

(29)   a. <u>SS/LF</u>:
        [[which portrait that Harry$_k$ likes]$_i$ did he$_k$ buy t$_i$]
       b. <u>SS/LF</u>:
        *[[which portrait]$_i$ did he$_k$ buy [t$_i$ that Harry$_k$ likes]]

The data above suggest that what is at stake is actually not where Principle C applies, but what moves under *wh*-movement, that is, why pied-piping is optional in some cases and obligatory in others. If we don't let this independent question obscure the issue under discussion, it's safe to conclude that the binding-theoretic argument for SS based on data such as (22)–(24) is weak at best. Given that LF is a conceptually motivated level of representation, methodological considerations then lead us to prefer the LF-based analysis sketched above over the traditional SS-based competitor.

Exercise 2.3

In (i) below, *himself* is ambiguous in being able to take either the matrix or the embedded subject as its antecedent, whereas in (ii) it must have the embedded subject reading. Discuss if (and how) such an asymmetry can be captured under either approach to covert *wh*-movement discussed in the text (movement of the whole *wh*-phrase or only the *wh*-element).

    (i) [[which picture of himself$_{i/k}$]$_m$ did Bill$_k$ say John$_i$ liked t$_m$]

    (ii) [who$_k$ said John$_i$ liked [which picture of himself$_{i/*k}$]]

Exercise 2.4

Assuming that the ECP holds at LF, explain how the data below may provide an argument for one of the approaches to covert *wh*-movement discussed in the text. (For present purposes, assume that the description of the judgments is essentially correct; to brush up on the ECP, see any of the GB-texts suggested in note 1 of chapter 1.)

    (i) Which man said that which events were in the park?

    (ii) *Which event did you say that was in the park?

    (iii) *Who said that what was in the park?

2.3.1.3   Movement parameters, feature strength, and Procrastinate
Another kind of argument advanced in favor of SS has to do with cross-linguistic variation. It's well known that languages differ in many respects in their overt properties. For example, *wh*-questions in English are formed by moving *wh*-expressions to the specifier of CP, i.e. [Spec,CP], while in (Mandarin) Chinese *wh*-expressions don't – they remain *in situ*.[24]

---

24 See the pioneering work of Huang (1982) and much subsequent work.

(30)   What did Bill buy?

(31)   *Mandarin Chinese*
Bill mai-le   shenme?
Bill buy-ASP what
'What did Bill buy?'

Similarly, languages like French raise main verbs to finite Infl overtly, while in English these verbs stay in place; hence, main verbs follow VP adverbs in English, but precede them in French:[25]

(32)   John often drinks wine.

(33)   *French*
Jean bois   souvent du vin.
Jean drinks often   of wine
'Jean often drinks wine.'

The way these differences are managed in GB is to say that Chinese does covertly what English does overtly and that English does covertly what French does overtly. In other words, a standard assumption is that all languages are identical at LF and that the overtly moved cases tell us what all languages "look like" at LF. The reasoning behind this assumption is the familiar one from poverty of the linguistic stimulus: data bearing on possible LF-variation is taken to be only sparsely available in the PLD (if present at all). Once LF-parameters couldn't be reliably set, LF should have no variation and be the same across grammars.[26] Postponing further discussion to chapter 9, let's assume that this is indeed so. Thus, after SS, English main verbs adjoin to Infl and *wh*-phrases in Chinese move to [Spec,CP].

To say that movement operations must apply prior to SS in some languages, but after SS in others crucially adverts to SS in the descriptive statement and thereby appears to lend empirical support for the postulation of SS. Once again, it's questionable whether this line of argument actually establishes the need for a level that distinguishes overt from covert movement. Buried in the assumptions of GB-style theories that incorporated SS was the assumption that languages differed on where operations applied because some morphological difference forced an operation to apply either before or after SS. Pollock (1989) and Chomsky (1991), for

---

25 Classic references include Emonds (1978) for early discussion and the seminal paper by Pollock (1989).

26 For relevant discussion, see Higginbotham (1983, 1985), Hornstein and Weinberg (1990), Chomsky (1993), Hornstein (1995), and also section 9.4 below.

instance, distinguished French and English Infls in terms of strength, with only strong Infl being capable of supporting main verbs before SS. As Chomsky (1993) observes, however, once we rely on something like morphological strength, it's no longer necessary to advert to SS at all.

Consider the following alternative. Assume, as in the discussion about Case Theory (section 2.3.1.1 above), that movement is driven by the need to check features. Assume further that features come in two flavors: weak and strong. Strong features are phonologically indigestible and so must be checked before the grammar splits; weak features, on the other hand, are phonologically acceptable and need only be checked by LF. Assume, finally, that grammars are "lazy" in that one doesn't check features unless one must; let's call this condition *Procrastinate*. Thus, since weak features need not be checked overtly, Procrastinate will require that they be checked covertly. By contrast, if strong features aren't checked before the grammar splits, the derivation will phonologically gag. So strong features must be checked by overt movement. We can now say that the differences noted among languages is simply a question of feature strength. Consider how this works with the examples above.

Simply translating Pollock's approach, we may say that features of the inflectional system of English and French are the same, only differing in terms of strength: finite Infl in French has a strong V-feature, whereas finite Infl in English has a weak V-feature. Verb movement in French must then proceed overtly to check the strong V-feature of Infl and make it phonetically inert; on the other hand, since the V-feature of Infl in English need not be checked overtly, verb movement will take place covertly in compliance with Procrastinate. Hence, main verbs will surface as preceding VP-adverbs in French, but following them in English, as schematically shown in (34) and (35):

(34) *French*
   a. <u>DS</u>:
      $[_{IP} \ldots Infl_{\text{strong-V}} \quad [_{VP} \text{ adverb } [_{VP} V \ldots]]]$
   b. <u>SS/LF</u>:
      $[_{IP} \ldots V_i + Infl_{\text{strong-V}} [_{VP} \text{ adverb } [_{VP} t_i \ldots]]]$

(35) *English*
   a. <u>DS/SS</u>:
      $[_{IP} \ldots Infl_{\text{weak-V}} \quad [_{VP} \text{ adverb } [_{VP} V \ldots]]]$
   b. <u>LF</u>:
      $[_{IP} \ldots V_i + Infl_{\text{weak-V}} [_{VP} \text{ adverb } [_{VP} t_i \ldots]]]$

What about auxiliaries in English? It's also well known that as opposed to main verbs, English auxiliaries like *be* (as well as auxiliary *have*, dummy *do*, and the modals *may*, *shall*, *can*, etc.) do precede VP-boundary elements such as negation, as exemplified in (36):[27]

(36)   a. John is not here.
       b. *John plays not here.

Under the approach sketched above, the most natural approach is to encode this idiosyncrasy on the lexical entry of the auxiliary itself, that is, to say that the V-feature of *be* is strong, requiring overt checking against Infl.[28] One common implementation is direct insertion of the auxiliary into Infl. Notice that since auxiliaries are functional elements (as opposed to lexical elements like main verbs or nouns), this suggestion is consistent with the standard assumption within P&P that parametric variation should be tied to functional elements.[29]

As for *wh*-movement, we can account for the differences between English and Chinese by assuming that the *wh*-feature of interrogative complementizers is strong in English but weak in Chinese. Hence, in order for the derivation to converge at PF, a *wh*-phrase must overtly move and check the *wh*-feature of C^0 in English, whereas in Chinese, *wh*-expressions only move covertly in order to satisfy Procrastinate, as represented in (37) and (38).

(37)   *English*
       a. <u>DS</u>:
          $[_{CP} C_{\text{strong-}wh}$ $[_{IP} \ldots WH \ldots]]$
       b. <u>SS/LF</u>:
          $[_{CP} WH_i C_{\text{strong-}wh} [_{IP} \ldots t_i \ldots]]$

(38)   *Mandarin Chinese*
       a. <u>DS/SS</u>:
          $[_{CP} C_{\text{weak-}wh}$ $[_{IP} \ldots WH \ldots]]$
       b. <u>LF</u>:
          $[_{CP} WH_i C_{\text{weak-}wh} [_{IP} \ldots t_i \ldots]]$

Notice that if it is the *wh*-feature of C^0 that is strong, as in English, then overt movement of a single *wh*-phrase suffices to check the strong feature

27 See, e.g., Jackendoff (1972), Emonds (1976, 1978), Pollock (1989), and much subsequent work.
28 See Lasnik (1995a) and Roberts (1998) for relevant discussion, and Roberts (2001) for an overview of general issues relating to head movement and available diagnostics.
29 This was first argued by Borer (1984) and Fukui (1986, 1988).

and Procrastinate prevents other existing *wh*-phrases from moving overtly, as illustrated in (39).

(39)   a. Who gave what to whom?
         b. *Who what to whom gave?

However, if the *wh*-feature of *wh*-phrases itself were strong, all *wh*-phrases should overtly move to have their strong feature checked. This is presumably what happens in languages such as Bulgarian, for instance, where all *wh*-phrases move overtly in multiple questions, as illustrated in (40).[30] Again, since *wh*-elements pertain to functional categories (they are determiners), parametric variation with respect to the strength of their features shouldn't be surprising; what seems to vary is the locus of this strength (C^0 or the *wh*-determiner).

(40)   *Bulgarian*
         a. *Koj dade   kakvo na   kogo?
             who gave   what   to   whom
         b. Koj kakvo na kogo dade?
             who what   to   whom gave
             'Who gave what to whom?'

Once we adopt this notion of feature strength, the EPP, which requires that all clauses must have a subject at SS, may then be re-described by saying that Infl has a strong D- or N-feature; thus, some element bearing a D/N-feature must occupy [Spec,IP] before the computation splits, so that the strong feature is appropriately checked.

In sum, contrary to first impressions, the overt/covert distinction exploited in accounts of parametric variation does not require invocations of SS. A technology based on feature strength coupled with an economy principle (Procrastinate) may be all that we need to accommodate variation. A question worth asking then is whether this use of features is better or worse than the earlier GB-treatment in terms of rules that apply before and after SS. At first sight, there's not much of a difference because in neither case have we *explained* why movement occurs the way it does. Ask why it is that English *wh*-phrases are moved overtly while Chinese ones are moved covertly. Answer: there's no principled account. That's just the way things are! So, within standard GB we have no account for *why* some

---

30 The classic reference is Rudin (1988a). For relevant discussion and further references, see among others Sabel (1998), Richards (2001), Bošković (2002a), and Boeckx and Grohmann (2003).

operation occurs prior to SS in one language and after SS in another. Similarly, we have no account in terms of feature strength as to why, for example, some features are strong in English and weak in Chinese. What seems clear is that invoking features leaves us *no worse off* than assuming that some operations are pre-SS and some post-SS.

Does it leave us better off? Yes and no. There's nothing particularly principled (or particularly deep) about an account based on strong/weak features. They are too easy to postulate and thus carry rather little explanatory power. However, *in the present context* the feature-based approach tells us something interesting: that variation provides no evidence for a level like SS. The reason is that we can deploy technology that is no less adequate and no less principled, but that does not need SS at all. This is an interesting conclusion, for it suggests that SS may be an artifact of our technical implementation, rather than a level supported on either strong conceptual or empirical grounds.

2.3.1.4   An excursion to *wh*-movement in Brazilian Portuguese

But even at a very descriptive level, it seems that we may get much simpler systems if we analyze parameters of movement in terms of feature strength, rather than the timing of the operation with respect to SS. Consider, for instance, the following descriptive facts about *wh*-movement in Brazilian Portuguese.[31]

(where the *wh*-phrase is marked in boldface)

>   A. *Wh*-movement in matrix clauses is optional with a phonetically null interrogative C⁰, but obligatory with an overt interrogative complementizer:

(41)   *Brazilian Portuguese*
   a. **Como** você consertou o   carro?
      how   you   fixed   the car
   b. Você consertou o   carro **como**?
      you   fixed   the car   how
      'How did you fix the car?'

(42)   *Brazilian Portuguese*
   a. **Como** que você consertou o   carro?
      how   that you fixed   the car

---

31 For discussion of *wh*-movement in Brazilian Portuguese, see Mioto (1994) and Kato (2004), among others. For purposes of presentation, we put aside possible interpretive differences between moved and *in situ* *wh*-phrases.

b. *Que você consertou o   carro **como**?
   that you fixed   the car   how
   'How did you fix the car?'

B. *Wh*-movement within embedded interrogative clauses is obligatory regardless of whether the complementizer is null or overt:

(43) *Brazilian Portuguese*
   a. Eu perguntei **como** (que) você consertou o   carro.
      I asked   how   that you fixed   the car
   b. *Eu perguntei (que) você consertou o   carro **como**.
      I asked   that you fixed   the car   how
      'I asked how you fixed the car.'

C. *Wh*-movement (of arguments) from within embedded clauses is optional if no island is crossed, but prohibited if islands intervene (island bracketed):

(44) *Brazilian Portuguese*
   a. **Que livro** você disse que ela comprou?
      which book you said that she bought
   b. Você disse que ela comprou **que   livro**?
      you said that she bought   which book
      'Which book did you say that she bought?'

(45) *Brazilian Portuguese*
   a. ***Que livro** você conversou com o   autor [que escreveu]?
      which book you talked   with the author   that wrote
   b. Você conversou com o   autor [que escreveu **que   livro**]?
      you talked   with the author   that wrote   which book
      'Which is the book such that you talked with the author that wrote it?'

D. *Wh*-movement of inherently non-D-linked elements is obligatory:[32]

(46) *Brazilian Portuguese*
   a. **Que diabo** você bebeu?
      what devil you drank
   b. *Você bebeu **que   diabo**?
      you drank what devil
      'What the hell did you drink?'

32 Pesetsky (1987) introduced the term D(iscourse)-linking for *wh*-phrases of the form *which N*; inherently or "aggressively" non-D-linked *wh*-phrases are those that can never have a discourse-linked interpretation (see den Dikken and Giannakidou 2002). For further discussion on the effects D-linking has on the syntax and interpretation of questions, see Grohmann (1998, 2003a), Pesetsky (2000), and Hirose (2003), among others.

The paradigm in (41)–(46) shows that we can't simply say that *wh*-movement in Brazilian Portuguese may optionally take place before or after SS, for overt movement is obligatory in some cases and impossible in others. Analytically, this runs us into trouble if we want to parameterize structures strictly in terms of applicability before or after SS.

Under a feature-based story, what we need to say to account for the data above is that in Brazilian Portuguese, (i) the null (i.e. phonetically empty) embedded interrogative complementizer, the overt interrogative complementizer *que*, and inherently non-D-linked elements all have a strong *wh*-feature, triggering overt movement (see (42), (43), and (46)), and (ii) there are two matrix null interrogatives C^0, one with a strong *wh*-feature and the other with a weak *wh*-feature.[33] Under this view, the "optionality" in (41) and (44) is illusory, for each "option" is associated with a different C^0, and the obligatoriness of the *in situ* version when islands intervene (see (45)) just shows that there's no convergent derivation based on the C^0 with a strong *wh*-feature.

To repeat, we're not claiming that the paradigm in (41)-(46) is *explained* if we adopt the feature specification suggested above. The claim is much weaker. We're just saying that the technology based on feature strength can adequately *describe* the facts in a trivial way, whereas standard approaches based on the timing of movement with respect to SS seem to require a much more baroque description. Given this, we're free to consider discarding SS.

Exercise 2.5

The standard analysis of sentences such as (ia) below is that *wh*-movement proceeds in a successive-cyclic way from [Spec,CP] to [Spec,CP], as represented in (ib). Assuming that overt *wh*-movement is triggered by the need to check a strong wh-feature, what other assumptions must be made to derive (ia)? Do these assumptions prevent overgeneration, correctly excluding unacceptable sentences like (ii)? If not, try to formulate an alternative account of (i) and (ii).

  (i)   a. What do you think John bought?
        b. [CP what$_i$ do you think [CP t$_i$ John bought t$_i$]]

  (ii) *You think what John bought.

Exercise 2.6

In French, *wh*-movement is optional if launched from the matrix clause, but not if launched from the embedded clause (see, e.g., Chang 1997, Bošković 1998, Cheng and Rooryck 2000), as illustrated in (i) and (ii) below. Can an analysis along the

---

33 Kato (2004) shows that each of these null complementizers is associated with a different intonational contour.

lines of the one suggested for Brazilian Portuguese in the text be extended to the French data in (i) and (ii)? If not, try to formulate an alternative account.

(i) *French*
  a. Qui   as   tu   vu?
     whom   have   you   seen
  b. Tu   as   vu   qui?
     you   have   seen   who
     'Who did you see?'

(ii) *French*
  a. Qui a   dit   Pierre que Marie a   vu?
     who has   said   Pieere   that   Marie   has   seen
  b. *Pierre a   dit   que Marie a   vu   qui?
     Pierre   had   said   that   Marie   has   seen   who
     'Who did Pierre say that Marie saw?'

Exercise 2.7

The data in (i) and (ii) below illustrate the fact that some languages don't allow long-distance *wh*-movement, but instead resort to an expletive-like *wh*-element (*was* 'what' in this case) and short movement of the real question phrase (see among others McDaniel 1986, 1989 and the collection of papers in Lutz, Müller, and von Stechow 2000). Can your answer to exercise 2.6 also account for these data? If not, how can your previous answer be modified in order to incorporate the new data?

(i) *German (some dialects)*
  *Wen   glaubt   Hans   dass   Jakob   gesehen   hat?
  who   thinks   Hans   that   Jakob   seen   has
  'Who does Hans think that Jakob saw?'

(ii) *German (all dialects)*
  Was   glaubt   Hans   wen   Jakob   gesehen   hat?
  what   thinks   Hans   who   Jakob   seen   has
  'Who does Hans think Jakob saw?'

2.3.1.5 A note on Procrastinate

One last point. Note that Procrastinate is stated as a preference principle. Thus, Procrastinate illustrates the second type of condition mentioned in chapter 1 that minimalist approaches have employed. It's not a bare output condition reflecting the interpretive demands of the interface (like, for example, the PF requirement that strong features be checked); rather, it characterizes the derivational process itself by ranking derivations: derivations that meet Procrastinate are preferable to those that do not, even though the derivations that violate it may generate grammatical objects that the interfaces can read. The intuition here is that derivations that comply with Procrastinate are more economical and that a premium is placed on the most economical ones.

Invoking a principle like Procrastinate raises further questions to the minimalist. The prime one is why it should be the case that covert operations are preferable to those that apply in overt syntax. Is this simply a brute fact? Or does it follow from more general considerations relating to the kinds of operations that the grammar employs? Put another way, is this cost index extrinsic to the grammar or does it follow in some natural way from the intrinsic features of the computational procedures? Clearly, the second alternative is the preferable one. We'll return to these issues in chapter 9, suggesting some ways in which Procrastinate might be rationalized along these lines.

2.3.1.6   Computational split and Spell-Out

There's one more pointed question that we need to address before moving on. Doesn't the very distinction between overt and covert operations presuppose a level like SS? That is, given that the computation must split in order to form a PF object and an LF object, isn't SS then conceptually justified as a level of representation in virtue of being *the point* where such splitting takes place?

The short answer is *No*. What a theory that incorporates the T-model assumes is that the phrase markers that feed the C-I and A-P interfaces are structurally different, though they share a common derivational history; thus, the computation must split. Let's then assume (with Chomsky 1993) that at some point in the derivation, the computational system employs the rule of *Spell-Out*, which separates the structure relevant for phonetic interpretation from the structure that pertains to semantic interpretation and ships each off to the appropriate interface. Now, postulating SS amounts to saying that there's a point in every derivation where Spell-Out applies, namely SS, and that there are filtering conditions that apply *at this point* (see the characterization of SS in section 2.2.2.2). However, the T-model is consistent with a weaker claim: that in every derivation Spell-Out applies at some point, not necessarily at the *same* point in every derivation (and not even necessary that it applies only once); thus, the application of Spell-Out can be governed by general conditions of the system and need not be subject to filtering conditions that would render it a linguistic level of representation.

Let's consider the logical possibilities. If Spell-Out doesn't apply in a given computation, we simply don't have a derivation, for no pair (π, λ) is formed; hence, Spell-Out must apply at least once. If a single application of Spell-Out is sufficient for the derivation to converge, economy considerations should block further applications.[34] If Spell-Out applies before strong features are checked, these unchecked features will cause the derivation to crash at PF; thus, "overt movement" must take place before Spell-Out. On the other hand, if a movement operation that takes place before Spell-Out only checks weak features, the derivation (if convergent) will be ruled out by Procrastinate; hence, if no strong feature is involved, the checking of weak features must proceed through "covert movement," that is, after Spell-Out. Thus, if applications of Spell-Out during the course of the derivation are independently regulated by convergence and economy conditions in this fashion, we account for the overt/covert distinction without committing hostages to an SS level.

Therefore, the computational split required by the T-model is not by itself a compelling argument for SS to be added into the theory.

2.3.1.7 Summary

We've seen that there are methodological reasons to hope that SS doesn't exist: it's not conceptually required, because it's not an interface level. Moreover, we've reviewed GB-arguments in favor of the idea that SS is required, and concluded that the empirical evidence for the postulation of SS is weak, at best. These arguments, we've seen, only go through on the basis of certain technical assumptions that are of dubious standing. If we replace these with other implementations, we're left with accounts no less empirically adequate than the standard GB-accounts, but without an SS level. This suggests that the standing of SS in GB is less empirically solid than generally believed. There are still other considerations that favor postulating an SS level, to which we return after we get some grasp on more technical apparatus. What we have hopefully shown so far, however, is that it's not *obviously* empirically hopeless to try to eliminate SS.

One last point. The reasoning till this point has been very conservative. We've taken the conceptual architecture behind the GB-apparatus largely at face value and seen that small technical changes allowed us to remove what appeared to be a deeply entrenched architectural property, namely,

34 However, convergence conditions may in principle require multiple applications of Spell-Out, if a single application leads to a derivational crash (see Uriagereka 1999c, 2002, Chomsky 2000, and Nunes and Uriagereka 2000, for instance). We discuss this possibility in sections 7.5 and 10.4.2 below.

the postulation of an SS level. Later on we'll suggest more radical revisions of GB. However, it's surprising how salutary thinking the details afresh has been just for our appreciation of GB itself.

2.3.2   Rethinking D-Structure

Let's now examine in more detail how DS is characterized within GB and see how solid it remains after some minimalist scrutiny.

Substantively, DS can be described as the level where lexical properties meet the grammar, so to speak. Thus, logical objects are syntactic objects at this level, logical subjects are syntactic subjects, etc. The satisfaction of these lexical properties within phrasal structures at DS is governed by two grammatical modules, Theta Theory and X′-Theory. Theta Theory ensures that only thematic positions are filled and X′-Theory ensures that the phrasal organization of all syntactic objects has the same general format, encoding head-complement, Spec-head, and adjunct-head structural relations.

DS is also the place where grammatical recursion obtains. Recall that one of the "big facts" discussed in section 1.3 is that sentences can be of arbitrary length. We capture this fact at DS by allowing a category A to be embedded within another category of type A, as exemplified in (47) below, and by imposing no upper limit on the number of adjuncts or coordinates in a given structure, as illustrated in (48) and (49). In fact, given that movements and construal processes don't (generally) enlarge sentences, sentence length is mainly a function of DS.

(47)   a. [$_{DP}$ [$_{DP}$ the boy] 's toy]
        b. [$_{PP}$ from out [$_{PP}$ of town]]
        c. [$_{IP}$ John said that [$_{IP}$ Mary left]]

(48)   a. [a tall man]
        b. [a tall bearded man]
        c. [a tall bearded man with a red shirt]

(49)   a. [John and Mary]
        b. [Peter, John, and Mary]
        c. [Susan, Peter, John, and Mary]

Finally, DS can be functionally defined as the level that is the output of phrase-structure operations and lexical insertion, and the input to overt movement operations. It's thus the "starting point" of a syntactic derivation ensuring compatibility between the members of the pair (π, λ).

When we ask if DS exists, or if it's required, we're asking whether there's a need for a level of grammatical representation meeting all of the requirements above. Below we discuss the conceptual and empirical arguments that underlie these requirements to see if they prove tenable from a minimalist perspective.[35]

2.3.2.1   Recursion and the operation Merge

We've seen above that DS is the generative engine of the grammar in the sense that it's the level where recursion is encoded. Of course, we do want to preserve recursion in the system, since it's responsible for one of the "big facts" about human grammars, namely that there's no upper bound on sentence size. The question that we should then ask is whether grammatical recursion is inherently associated with DS. In other words, would we necessarily lose recursion if we dumped DS? A quick look at the history of the field prompts us to give a negative answer to this question. Earlier approaches to UG adequately captured recursion but didn't postulate DS;[36] in its place were rules that combined lexical atoms to get bigger and bigger structures. We should thus be able to revert to this sort of theory and thereby account for grammatical recursion without DS. Let's see how.

Say that we have a lexicon where lexical atoms are housed and a grammatical operation that puts the lexical items together, organizing them into phrasal structures that comply with X'-Theory. Call this operation *Merge*. Leaving details for section 6.3.2, let's just assume that Merge takes two syntactic objects and forms a new syntactic constituent out of them. In order to derive the sentence in (50) below, for instance, Merge takes the two lexical items *saw* and *Mary* and forms the VP in (51a); this VP is then merged with Infl, yielding the I' in (51b). Further applications of Merge along the lines of (51c–g) finally yield the IP in (51g).

(50)   John said that Bill saw Mary.

(51)   a. *saw* + _{Merge} *Mary* →
             [_{VP} saw Mary]
         b. VP + _{Merge} Infl →
             [_{I'} Infl [_{VP} saw Mary]]

---

35 Within GB, DS is also the locus of directionality parameters; thus, whether a verb precedes or follows its complement in a given language, for instance, was taken to be determined at DS (see Koopman 1984 and Travis 1984, for instance). We postpone the discussion of word order until chapter 7, where we revisit directionality parameters from the perspective of Kayne's (1994) Linear Correspondence Axiom (LCA).

36 Recursion came to be encoded at DS in Chomsky (1965). For recent relevant discussion, see Frank (2002).

   c. I′ + $_{\text{Merge}}$ *Bill* →
      [$_{IP}$ Bill [$_{I'}$ Infl [$_{VP}$ saw Mary]]]
   d. IP + $_{\text{Merge}}$ *that* →
      [$_{CP}$ that [$_{IP}$ Bill [$_{I'}$ Infl [$_{VP}$ saw Mary]]]]
   e. CP + $_{\text{Merge}}$ *said* →
      [$_{VP}$ said [$_{CP}$ that [$_{IP}$ Bill [$_{I'}$ Infl [$_{VP}$ saw Mary]]]]]
   f. VP + $_{\text{Merge}}$ *Infl* →
      [$_{I'}$ Infl [$_{VP}$ said [$_{CP}$ that [$_{IP}$ Bill [$_{I'}$ Infl [$_{VP}$ saw Mary]]]]]]
   g. I′ + $_{\text{Merge}}$ *John* →
      [$_{IP}$ John [$_{I'}$ Infl [$_{VP}$ said [$_{CP}$ that [$_{IP}$ Bill [$_{I'}$ Infl [$_{VP}$ saw Mary]]]]]]]

The sentence in (50) is a standard example of grammatical recursion, for its structure involves a VP embedded within another VP, an I′ embedded within an I′, and an IP embedded within another IP, as shown in (51g). The important thing for us to have in mind is that such recursion was appropriately captured without any mention of DS. Thus, recursion alone is not a sufficient justification for the postulation of DS.

This is admittedly the weakest kind of argument against DS that we can formulate. It just says that we can provide an alternative account of the recursion property of human languages without DS. However, it's sufficient for minimalist eyebrows to be raised, for a conceptually unmotivated level of representation is being postulated when another seemingly plausible technology would perfectly do the job DS is supposed to do. Below we'll see that when some empirical facts are considered, we can make a much stronger case against DS.

2.3.2.2 Control and raising constructions

The main empirical motivation for adopting DS is that it enables us to account for the differences between raising and control structures. So, let's review some of the main properties of these two types of constructions and see how a DS-based approach handles them.

Raising and control constructions contrast in the following ways:[37]

  A. The subject of a control structure is understood as playing a semantic role with respect to both the control and the embedded predicate, whereas the subject of a raising structure is interpreted as playing only a role associated with the embedded predicate. Thus, in

37 See Rosenbaum (1967), Bowers (1973), and Postal (1974) for early, and, e.g., Bošković (1997, 2002b), Hornstein (1998, 1999, 2001, 2003), and Grohmann (2003b, 2003c) for more recent discussion.

a control construction like (52a), *Mary* is understood as a "hoper" and a "kisser," but in a raising construction like (52b), *Mary* is a "kisser," though not a "seemer" in any sense.

(52)   a. Mary hoped to kiss John.
           b. Mary seemed to kiss John.

    B. Expletives may occupy the subject position of raising, but not control structures:

(53)   a. It$_{EXPL}$ seems that John leaves early.
           b. *It$_{EXPL}$ hopes that John leaves early.

(54)   a. There$_{EXPL}$ seemed to be a man at the party.
           b. *There$_{EXPL}$ hoped to be a man at the party.

    C. Idiom chunks may occur in the subject position of raising, but not control predicates:

(55)   a. The shit seemed to hit the fan.
           b. *The shit hoped to hit the fan.

(56)   a. All hell seemed to break loose.
           b. *All hell hoped to break loose.

    D. Raising structures are "voice transparent," but control structures aren't. Thus, although the sentences in (57) are tolerably good paraphrases of one another (both are true in the same contexts), the sentences in (58) clearly have different meanings.

(57)   a. The doctor seemed to examine John.
           b. John seemed to be examined by the doctor.

(58)   a. The doctor hoped to examine John.
           b. John hoped to be examined by the doctor.

Let's now see how these differences are explained in GB-style theories. Recall that within GB, DS is the pure representation of thematic properties in phrasal garb; hence, all lexical/thematic properties must be satisfied there. Take the control structure such as (52a), for instance. Given that the verb *hope* requires a proposition for a complement (the state hoped for) and a "hoper" for its external argument, the DS of a well-formed sentence involving *hope* must have its subject and object positions "saturated," as illustrated in (59) below. By the same token, the embedded verb *kiss* must discharge its "kisser" and "kissee" θ-roles. This means that the subject position associated with *kiss* in (59) must be filled at DS, despite the fact that there's no phonetically realized element to occupy this position. In GB, this position should then be filled by the (phonetically) empty category PRO, which is later coindexed with the matrix subject, yielding the interpretation where *Mary* appears to be playing two different semantic roles.

(59)   DS:
        [Mary$_{hoper}$ hoped [PRO$_{kisser}$ to kiss John$_{kissee}$]$_{proposition}$]

Observe that the empty category in the embedded subject position of (59) can't be a trace. Why not? Because traces are by definition produced by movement and DS is taken to precede all movement operations. In effect, the GB-view of DS and the necessity of an expression like controlled PRO are very intimately connected. Given the plain fact that verbs can take non-finite complements, as illustrated by (52a), the requirements of DS force the postulation of empty categories such as PRO, which are not formed by movement.

Consider now what DS imposes on raising verbs when they take non-finite complements. The verb *seem* in (52b), for instance, takes a proposition for a complement, but its subject position is non-thematic. Thus, *Mary* can't occupy this position at DS. On the other hand, the embedded verb *kiss* in (52b) assigns two θ-roles, but only one argument surfaces in the embedded clause. The DS representation of (52b) must then generate *Mary* in the embedded clause and leave the matrix subject position empty, as illustrated in (60):

(60)   DS:
        [Δ seemed [Mary$_{kisser}$ to kiss John$_{kissee}$]$_{proposition}$]

Given the DS in (60), *Mary* moves to the matrix subject position to satisfy the EPP and check its Case, yielding the SS in (61). Since *Mary* was only associated with the "kisser" θ-role during the course of the derivation, that's how it's going to be interpreted. Thus, the semantic difference between raising and control structures (the property listed in (A) above) is accounted for.

(61)   SS:
        [Mary$_i$ seemed [t$_i$ to kiss John]]

If control and raising constructions are assigned different structures at the level of DS as described above, the remaining differences in (B)–(D) follow straightforwardly. The fact that control predicates don't tolerate expletives in their subject position (see (53b) and (54b)) follows from a Theta-Criterion violation at DS: the control predicate must assign its external θ-role and expletives are not θ-bearing expressions. By contrast, since the subject position of raising verbs is non-thematic, it may be filled by an expletive (see (53a) and (54a)).

Similarly, on the reasonable assumption that idioms chunks can't bear regular θ-roles, they are barred from θ-positions.[38] A sentence such as (55b), for instance, should be derived by raising *the shit* from the embedded subject position of the structure represented in (62a) below; however, (62a) is excluded as a DS representation because *hope* doesn't have its "hoper" θ-role discharged. Therefore, there's no grammatical derivation for (55b). By contrast, no problem arises in the case of raising constructions because the matrix subject position is non-thematic; hence (62b), for instance, is a well-formed DS for (55a).

(62)   a. <u>DS</u>:
            *[Δ hoped [the shit to hit the fan]]
        b. <u>DS</u>:
            [Δ seemed [the shit to hit the fan]]

Finally, the difference between raising and control constructions with respect to "voice transparency" trivially follows from their DS representations. In the raising sentences in (57), for instance, *John* is assigned the same θ-role at DS in both the active and the passive construction, as illustrated in (63) below. By contrast, in the DS representations of the control sentences in (58), *John* has different θ-roles, as shown in (64).

(63)   a. <u>DS</u>:
            [Δ seemed [the doctor to examine John$_{examinee}$]]
        b. <u>DS</u>:
            [Δ seemed [to be examined John$_{examinee}$ by the doctor]]

(64)   a. <u>DS</u>:
            [the doctor hoped [PRO to examine John$_{examinee}$]]
        b. <u>DS</u>:
            [John$_{hoper}$ hoped [to be examined PRO by the doctor]]

In sum, by assuming DS, we're able to derive the intricate differences between raising and control structures. And this *is* a big deal. The issue we turn to now is whether we need DS to do this or if there is another way.

Let's start by taking a closer look at where and how thematic relations are established. Within GB, the Theta-Criterion holds of DS and, due to the Projection Principle (see section 2.2.4), at SS and LF, as well. Assuming that LF is the input to rules mapping to the semantic interface, it seems

---

38 For relevant discussion, see, e.g., Marantz (1984).

reasonable that notions such as agent, patient, etc. are encoded at this level
and, therefore, it makes sense that we have something like the Theta-
Criterion at LF. Now, should it also apply at DS? Notice that the
Projection Principle ensures that some kinds of information are preserved
in the course of the derivation by inspecting them at subsequent levels of
representation. Thus, the Projection Principle ends up rendering the system
intrinsically redundant. In particular, the thematic relations encoded at DS
are a subset of the ones encoded at LF. Suppose then that we eliminate such
redundancy and simply assume the null hypothesis under minimalist guidelines, namely that the Theta-Criterion holds at the conceptually required
level of LF. How can we now account for the differences between raising
and control structures just by inspecting their thematic properties at LF?

Let's reexamine the reasoning underlying the claim that the fact that
Mary is understood as both "hoper" and "kisser" in (65) can be captured
by the structure in (66), but not by the one in (67).

(65)   Mary hoped to kiss John.

(66)   [Mary$_i$ hoped [PRO$_i$ to kiss John]]

(67)   *[Mary$_i$ hoped [t$_i$ to kiss John]]

If we buy the existence of DS and further assume that the Theta-Criterion
must also hold of this level, we're forced to choose the representation in (66),
because in (67) *Mary* was not in the matrix subject position at DS and the
Theta-Criterion is violated at this level. However, if we don't take the
existence of DS for granted, we may still be able to single out (66) as the
adequate representation of (65) by exploring the different empty categories
that each structure employs. We may take the postulated difference between
PRO and the trace to be indicating that θ-relations must be established upon
lexical insertion and can't be established by movement. This reinterpretation
of the facts appears to make the right distinction but does not presuppose DS.

To make it more precise, let's assume that recursion/generativity is
captured by the operation Merge, as proposed in section 2.3.2.1, and
adopt the principle in (68), which we may call the *Theta-Role Assignment
Principle (TRAP)*:

(68)   *Theta-Role Assignment Principle (TRAP)*
        θ-roles can only be assigned under a Merge operation.

Note that the TRAP is not stated on any level of representation. Rather,
it's a condition on grammatical operations and in this sense it's not

different from the requirement that θ-roles be assigned under government, for instance. According to the TRAP, the structure in (66) is well formed because the "kisser" θ-role was assigned to PRO when it was merged with the embedded I′ and the "hoper" θ-role was assigned to *Mary* when it merged with the matrix I′. Thus, when the Theta-Criterion applies at LF, the derivation will be judged as convergent. By contrast, although *Mary* can receive the "kisser" θ-role in (67) when it merges with the embedded I′, it can't receive the "hoper" θ-role because it's connected to the matrix clause by Move and not by Merge. Once the "hoper" θ-role hasn't been discharged, (67) violates the Theta-Criterion at LF and the derivation crashes.

The same reasoning ascribes the LF representation in (69a) to the raising construction in (52b), and not the one in (69b). (69a) is well formed because *Mary* receives its θ-role when it merges with the embedded I′ and moves to a non-thematic position. In (69b), on the other hand, *Mary* receives no θ-role when it merges with the matrix I′, violating the Theta-Criterion and causing the derivation to crash at LF.

(69)   a. <u>LF</u>:
           [Mary$_i$ seemed [t$_i$ to kiss John]]
       b. <u>LF</u>:
           *[Mary$_i$ seemed [PRO$_i$ to kiss John]]

Consider now how the TRAP fares with respect to the other differences between raising and control discussed above. Expletives may occupy the subject position of raising verbs because this position is non-thematic, as shown in (70a). In (70b), on the other hand, the expletive *it*, as a non-θ-bearing element, can't be assigned the "hoper" θ-role when it merges with matrix I′. Since this θ-role is not discharged, the Theta-Criterion is violated and the derivation crashes at LF.

(70)   a. <u>LF</u>:
           [it$_{EXPL}$ seems [that John leaves early]]
       b. <u>LF</u>:
           *[it$_{EXPL}$ hopes [that John leaves early]]

As for the relevant LF representations involving idiom chunks, (71a) below is similar to (67) in that it violates the Theta-Criterion because the "hoper" θ-role was not discharged; crucially, it couldn't be discharged under movement of *the shit*. Under the reasonable assumption that PRO can't form idiomatic expressions due to its lack of lexical content, it can't receive the "idiomatic" θ-role when it merges with the embedded I′ in (71b) and (72a), yielding a violation of the Theta-Criterion. (72a) should also be ruled out by the Theta-Criterion because *the shit* is assigned no θ-role when it merges with the matrix I'. Thus, the only convergent derivation involving the idiomatic expression is the one in (72b), where *the shit* receives its idiomatic θ-role upon merger and moves to a non-thematic position.

(71)   a. <u>LF</u>:
    *[[the shit]$_i$ hoped [t$_i$ to hit the fan]]
    b. <u>LF</u>:
    *[[the shit]$_i$ hoped [PRO$_i$ to hit the fan]]

(72)   a. <u>LF</u>:
    *[[the shit]$_i$ seemed [PRO$_i$ to hit the fan]]
    b. <u>LF</u>:
    [[the shit]$_i$ seemed [t$_i$ to hit the fan]]

Finally, the explanation for the "voice transparency" in raising but not control structures is the same as before, with the only difference being that it is stated in LF terms. That is, at LF *John* exhibits the same θ-role in active/passive pairs involving the raising structures of (73) below, but a different θ-role in the control structures of (74). That we should capture this difference just by replacing DS with LF should come as no surprise. Recall that in GB the Projection Principle requires that thematic information not change from one syntactic level to the other.

(73)   a. <u>LF</u>:
    [[the doctor]$_i$ seemed [t$_i$ to examine John$_{examinee}$]]
    b. <u>LF</u>:
    [[John$_{examinee}$]$_i$ seemed [t$_i$ to be examined t$_i$ by the doctor]]

(74)   a. <u>LF</u>:
    [[the doctor] hoped [PRO to examine John$_{examinee}$]]
    b. <u>LF</u>:
    [John$_{hoper}$ hoped [PRO$_j$ to be examined t$_j$ by the doctor]]

To sum up, the TRAP in (68) allows us to make the desired distinction between raising and control structures, without assuming that we need a level like DS. The reason isn't hard to spot. The TRAP functions in a derivational system exactly like DS functions in GB, in that both approaches rule out movement to θ-positions. Thus, it turns out that the DS level is not actually required to handle the contrast between raising and control structures. It is sufficient, but not necessary. To the extent that this distinction was perhaps the major empirical argument in favor of DS, it is fair to say that the grounds for postulating DS have been considerably shaken. In the next two sections, we'll see that the damage is even worse.

Exercise 2.8

What is the DS representation of the sentences in (i) below? Provide independent evidence for your analysis (see the differences between control and raising reviewed in the text) and discuss whether the TRAP approach suggested above can also account for these structures.

(i) a. John was persuaded to kiss Mary.
    b. John was expected to kiss Mary.

Exercise 2.9

In this section, we discussed the TRAP within a derivational approach, that is, assuming that syntactic objects are built in a step-by-step fashion, regulated by conditions on rule application; hence, the TRAP was defined in (68) as a condition on θ-role assignment.

But the TRAP can also be reinterpreted in a representational approach, according to which the computational system builds syntactic objects with a single application of the operation *Generate* and then applies licensing conditions to the objects so constructed. Under this view, the TRAP could be redefined as an LF wellformedness condition on A-chains (see Brody 1995), along the lines of (i).

(i) Given an A-chain CH, only its tail (i.e. the lowest link) can be θ-marked.

Consider the raising and control structures discussed in this section and examine whether they can all be correctly analyzed in terms of (i). What can we conclude regarding the need of DS in a representational approach to syntactic computations?

2.3.2.3 Headless relative clauses

Recall that DS is functionally defined as the output of phrase-structure rules and lexical insertion and the input to movement operations. We've already considered the first half of such a characterization. Let's now take a closer look at DS as the input to movement.

Within GB, the derivation of (75), for instance, proceeds along the lines of (76).

(75)   I wonder who you said asked what Bill ate.

(76)   a. <u>DS</u>:
        [I wonder [$_{CP}$ Δ C^0 [$_{IP}$ you said [$_{CP}$ Δ C^0 [$_{IP}$ who asked [$_{CP}$ Δ C^0 [$_{IP}$ Bill ate what]]]]]]]
    b. <u>SS</u>:
        [I wonder [$_{CP}$ who$_k$ C^0 [$_{IP}$ you said [$_{CP}$ t$_k$ C^0 [$_{IP}$ t$_k$ asked [$_{CP}$ what$_i$ C^0 [$_{IP}$ Bill ate t$_i$]]]]]]]

The DS of (75) is generated with empty positions in each [Spec,CP], as shown in (76a), and later these positions are filled by movement of *who* and *what*.

Not only must DS precede every movement operation in GB, but the movement operations themselves must apply in a bottom-up, successive-cyclic fashion.[39] Roughly speaking, movement must first take place in a more embedded CP before applying to a less embedded CP. In other words, the SS in (76b) is derived by first moving *what* and then moving *who*. The reasons for such a cyclic approach to syntactic derivations are empirical.

Consider the sentence in (77) below, for instance. If movement must proceed in a cyclic fashion, we can explain its unacceptability as a Subjacency violation. Given the DS in (78), movement of *how* to the lowest [Spec,CP] in (79a) complies with Subjacency, but the subsequent movement of *what* to the higher [Spec,CP] in (79b) doesn't.

(77)   *I wonder what you asked how John fixed?

(78)   DS:
        [I wonder [$_{CP}$ Δ C^0 [$_{IP}$ you asked [$_{CP}$ Δ C^0 [$_{IP}$ John [$_{VP}$ [$_{VP}$ fixed what] how]]]]]]

(79)   a. [I wonder [$_{CP}$ Δ C^0 [$_{IP}$ you asked [$_{CP}$ how$_i$ C^0 [$_{IP}$ John [$_{VP}$ [$_{VP}$ fixed what] t$_i$]]]]]]
        b. SS:
           *[I wonder [$_{CP}$ what$_k$ C^0 [$_{IP}$ you asked [$_{CP}$ how$_i$ C^0 [$_{IP}$ John [$_{VP}$ [$_{VP}$ fixed t$_k$] t$_i$]]]]]]

However, if movement could proceed in a non-cyclic manner, there's a potential derivation for (77) where no Subjacency violation obtains. Given the DS in (78), *what* could first move to the lower and then to the higher [Spec,CP], as illustrated in (80a–b) below. Assuming that the operation of deletion can apply freely up to recoverability (that is, it can apply if it doesn't cause loss of overtly expressed information),[40] it could then eliminate the intermediate trace of *what*, yielding (80c). Finally, *how* could move to the vacated [Spec,CP] position, yielding the same SS representation of the derivation in (79), but with no movement violating Subjacency.

---

39 See Chomsky (1965, 1973) and Freidin (1978) on early and Freidin (1999), Svenonius (2001, 2004), and Grohmann (2003b, 2003c) on more recent discussion of the cycle.
40 On free deletion up to recoverability, see among others Chomsky (1965, 1977), Kayne (1975, 1976), Chomsky and Lasnik (1977), and Lasnik and Saito (1984).

(80)   a. [I wonder [$_{CP}$ Δ C^0 [$_{IP}$ you asked [$_{CP}$ what$_k$ C^0
        [$_{IP}$ John [$_{VP}$ [$_{VP}$ fixed t$_k$] how]]]]]]
       b. [I wonder [$_{CP}$ what$_k$ C^0 [$_{IP}$ you asked [$_{CP}$ t$_k$ C^0
        [$_{IP}$ John [$_{VP}$ [$_{VP}$ fixed t$_k$] how]]]]]]
       c. [I wonder [$_{CP}$ what$_k$ C^0 [$_{IP}$ you asked [$_{CP}$ Δ C^0
        [$_{IP}$ John [$_{VP}$ [$_{VP}$ fixed t$_k$] how]]]]]]
       d. <u>SS</u>:
        [I wonder [$_{CP}$ what$_k$ C^0 [$_{IP}$ you asked [$_{CP}$ how$_i$ C^0
        [$_{IP}$ John [$_{VP}$ [$_{VP}$ fixed t$_k$] t$_i$]]]]]]

Given these remarks regarding cyclicity and the view of DS as the input to movement operations, we should ask how these ideas are to be interpreted in a system where there's no DS and syntactic generativity is captured by the structure-building operation Merge. We've seen in section 2.3.2.1 that successive applications of Merge may yield structures that mimic DS representations. What then happens when movement operations are involved? Must all applications of Merge precede all applications of Move? Does anything go wrong if applications of Merge and Move are interspersed?

   Take the simple sentence in (81) below, for example. Is there anything wrong with the derivation sketched in (82), where the *wh*-phrase is moved to [Spec,CP] in (82e) *before* the rest of the structure is assembled by Merge?

(81)   I wonder what Bill ate.

(82)   a. *ate* +$_{Merge}$ *what* →
        [$_{VP}$ ate what]
       b. VP +$_{Merge}$ Infl →
        [$_{I'}$ Infl [$_{VP}$ ate what]]
       c. I' +$_{Merge}$ *Bill* →
        [$_{IP}$ Bill [$_{I'}$ Infl [$_{VP}$ ate what]]]
       d. IP +$_{Merge}$ C^0 →
        [$_{C'}$ C^0 [$_{IP}$ Bill [$_{I'}$ Infl [$_{VP}$ ate what]]]]
       e. Move *what* →
        [$_{CP}$ what$_i$ C^0 [$_{IP}$ Bill [$_{I'}$ Infl [$_{VP}$ ate t$_i$]]]]
       f. CP +$_{Merge}$ *wonder* →
        [$_{VP}$ wonder [$_{CP}$ what$_i$ C^0 [$_{IP}$ Bill [$_{I'}$ Infl [$_{VP}$ ate t$_i$]]]]]
       g. VP +$_{Merge}$ Infl →
        [$_{I'}$ Infl [$_{VP}$ wonder [$_{CP}$ what$_i$ C^0 [$_{IP}$ Bill [$_{I'}$ Infl [$_{VP}$ ate t$_i$]]]]]]
       h. I' +$_{Merge}$ *I* →
        [$_{IP}$ I [$_{I'}$ Infl [$_{VP}$ wonder [$_{CP}$ what$_i$ C^0 [$_{IP}$ Bill [$_{I'}$ Infl [$_{VP}$ ate t$_i$]]]]]]]

We may think of the assumption that DS precedes all movements as another way to rule out instances where an element moves to an unfilled thematic position. We've seen in section 2.3.2.2, however, that such undesirable cases can be adequately accounted for if we assume that θ-roles must be assigned under Merge, but not under Move (i.e. the TRAP in (68)). If so, there seems to be no reason for movement operations necessarily to follow all applications of Merge. In fact, there's interesting evidence to the contrary.[41]

Consider the Portuguese sentence in (83) below, which contains a "headless relative clause."[42] Intuitively, *com quem* 'with who' is understood as a complement of both *conversa* 'talks' and *concorda* 'agrees'. But if so, what is the DS representation that underlies this sentence? If *com quem* is generated as the embedded object, as shown in (84), the matrix verb can't have its selectional/thematic properties satisfied, for it doesn't select for a propositional complement, as illustrated in (85).

(83) *Portuguese*
  Ele só   conversa com quem ele concorda.
  he   only talks   with who   he   agrees
  'He only talks with who he agrees with.'

(84) <u>DS</u>:
  *[$_{IP}$ ele só   conversa [$_{CP}$ ele concorda com quem]]
    he   only talks   he   agrees   with who

(85) *Portuguese*
  *Ele conversou que   ela   saiu.
   he   talked   that she   left
  '*He talked that she left.'

Suppose then that at DS, *com quem* in (83) is generated as the object of the matrix verb and a null operator OP is generated in the embedded object position, as shown in (86a); this OP would later move to [Spec,CP] and get coindexed with the matrix complement, yielding the relevant interpretation.

(86) a. <u>DS</u>:
      [$_{IP}$ ele só   conversa [com quem] [$_{CP}$ ele concorda OP]]
        he   only talks   with who   he   agrees
    b. <u>SS</u>:
      [$_{IP}$ ele só   conversa [com quem]$_i$ [$_{CP}$ OP$_i$ ele concorda t$_i$]]
        he   only talks   with who   he   agrees

---

41 This argument is based on Kato and Nunes (1998).

42 A *headless relative clauses* is, as the term suggests, a relative clause without a head noun, sometimes also called "nominal relative clauses." The following bracketed expressions illustrate this construction in English. See, e.g., Grosu (2003) for recent overview and references.

  (i) a. Call me [what you want].
      b. Tell us [when you are ready].
      c. [Where to eat] is every night's question.

The problem with the derivation outlined in (86) is that it has been standardly assumed that null operators can only be DPs and not PPs. Consider the contrast in (87) below, for instance.[43] The null operator can be properly licensed by the DP *the person* in (87a), but not by the PP *at the person* in (87b).

(87) a. [Mary laughed at [$_{DP}$ the person]$_i$ [$_{CP}$ OP$_i$ John was looking at t$_i$]]
  b. *[Mary laughed [$_{PP}$ at the person]$_i$ [$_{CP}$ OP$_i$ John was looking t$_i$]]

Thus, the unfortunate conclusion for a DS-based theory seems to be that there is no appropriate DS representation that captures the "double complement" role of *com quem* in (83).

Assume now that we dump DS, and that Merge and Move operations may intersperse. The derivation of (83) may then proceed along the following lines. Applications of Merge assemble the embedded clause, as illustrated in (88a) below. Since we have overt movement of the complement PP, let's assume, following the discussion in section 2.3.1.3, that C^0 has a strong *wh*-feature, which is checked after *com quem* moves and adjoins to CP, as shown in (88b). The structure in (88b) then merges with *conversa* and after further applications of Merge, we obtain the final structure in (88d).

(88) a. *Applications of Merge:*
      [$_{CP}$ C$_{strong-wh}$ ele concorda com quem]
              he agrees   with who
    b. *Move com quem:*
      [$_{CP}$ [com quem]$_i$ [$_{CP}$ C ele concorda t$_i$]]
        with who   he agrees
    c. *Merge conversa:*
      [$_{VP}$ conversa [$_{CP}$ [com quem]$_i$ [$_{CP}$ C ele   concorda t$_i$]]]
        talks   with who   he   agrees
    d. *Further applications of Merge:*
      [ele só   conversa [$_{CP}$ [com quem]$_i$ [$_{CP}$ C ele concorda t$_i$]]]
        he only talks   with who   he agrees

The crucial steps for our discussion are the ones in (88b–c). Assuming with Chomsky (1993) that an element adjoined to an XP may check the relevant features of its head X (see chapter 5 for further discussion), the adjoined PP in (88b) checks the strong feature of C, allowing the derivation to converge

---

43 For relevant discussion, see among others Jaeggli (1982), Aoun and Clark (1985), Stowell (1984), Haïk (1985), Browning (1987), Authier (1988), Lasnik and Stowell (1991), and Contreras (1993).

at PF. Furthermore, the structure resulting from the merger between *conversa* 'talks' and CP places this verb and the moved PP in a mutual c-command configuration (crucially, PP is not dominated by CP). Under standard assumptions, this is a configuration that allows thematic/selectional requirements to be established. Hence, the derivation can converge at LF because the thematic/selectional requirements of both the embedded and the matrix verb were satisfied in the course of the derivation. Notice that the θ-role assignment to the PP in (88c) is in full compliance with the TRAP. Although the PP has moved in a previous derivational step, it isn't assigned a θ-role through movement; θ-role assignment only takes place when the verb *conversa* merges with CP.

The above considerations show not only that there's no problem if applications Move and Merge intersperse, but also that empirical problems may arise if they don't. In particular, if it is assumed (i) that DS must precede movement operations and (ii) that all the thematic/selectional properties must be inspected at DS, there seems to be no trivial DS representation for constructions involving headless relative clauses. In other words, it seems that a successful analysis of these constructions can be achieved only if we give up on DS. Needless to say, if this line of reasoning is correct, then it is a powerful argument against DS.

Exercise 2.10

In exercise 2.9, you saw that the representational version of the TRAP as an LF wellformedness condition along the lines of (i) below can adequately distinguish raising from control structures. Now, consider the headless relative clause in (ii) and discuss if (and how) it's also properly handled by (i).

(i)   Given an A-chain CH, only its tail (i.e. the lowest link) can be θ-marked.

(ii) Mary would laugh at whomever she would look at.

2.3.2.4   Intermezzo: A quick note on cyclicity

If the operations Merge and Move can freely intersperse, one might ask the obvious question: what about cyclicity? Leaving further discussion for chapters 8 through 10, let's assume that empirical arguments like the one discussed in relation to (77) require that cyclicity should also hold of a system that doesn't assume DS. In fact, let's generalize this requirement, taking it to hold of Merge as well and assume the Extension Condition in (89), where a *root syntactic object* is a syntactic tree that is not dominated by any syntactic object.

(89)   *Extension Condition* (preliminary version)
        Overt applications of Merge and Move can only target root syntactic objects.

Let's now consider the derivation of the sentence in (90) below. Two applications of Merge targeting root syntactic objects yield the structure in (91b).

(90)   The woman saw George.

(91)   a. *saw* + $_{\text{Merge}}$ *George* →
           [$_{\text{VP}}$ saw George]
        b. VP + $_{\text{Merge}}$ Infl →
           [$_{\text{I}'}$ Infl [$_{\text{VP}}$ saw George]]

If the computational system proceeds to Merge *woman* with I′, as illustrated in (92a) below, there will be no convergent continuation for the derivation. Crucially, the Extension Condition in (89) prevents *the* from merging with *woman* in (92a), because *woman* isn't a root syntactic object anymore, and merger of *the* with the root IP doesn't yield a structure where *the woman* forms a constituent, as shown in (92b):

(92)   a. I′ + $_{\text{Merge}}$ *woman* →
           [$_{\text{IP}}$ woman [$_{\text{I}'}$ Infl [$_{\text{VP}}$ saw George]]]
        b. IP + $_{\text{Merge}}$ *the* →
           [$_{\text{DP}}$ the [$_{\text{IP}}$ woman [$_{\text{I}'}$ Infl [$_{\text{VP}}$ saw George]]]]

The Extension Condition thus forces merger of *the* and *woman* before they end up being part of IP, as illustrated in (93):

(93)   a. *saw* + $_{\text{Merge}}$ *George* →
           [$_{\text{VP}}$ saw George]
        b. VP + $_{\text{Merge}}$ Infl →
           [$_{\text{I}'}$ Infl [$_{\text{VP}}$ saw George]]
        c. *the* + $_{\text{Merge}}$ *woman* →
           [$_{\text{DP}}$ the woman]
        d. I′ + $_{\text{Merge}}$ DP →
           [$_{\text{IP}}$ [$_{\text{DP}}$ the woman] [$_{\text{I}'}$ Infl [$_{\text{VP}}$ saw George]]]

Notice that before Merge applies in (93c), there are three root syntactic objects available to the computational system: *the*, *woman*, and I′. That shouldn't come as a surprise once we give up the GB-assumption that the computational system arranges all the structures within a single phrase marker before movement may take place. In fact, it won't be uncommon that in building a sentence we may have several "treelets" around prior to their combining into a single big tree. In the next section, we'll see that even standard GB may need to resort to more than one phrase marker in order to account for some tough constructions.

Exercise 2.11

Assuming the Extension Condition in (89), derive the sentences in (i) and explain why one of them must involve two complex treelets at some derivational step, while the other doesn't need to.

(i) a. I greeted John and Mary.
    b. John and Mary greeted me.

2.3.2.5 *Tough*-movement constructions

A serious empirical problem for DS as conceived by GB is posed by the so-called *tough*-constructions like (94):[44]

(94) *Moby Dick* is hard for Bill to read.

There seems to be no way of accounting for this kind of construction if we assume DS. Let's see why by inspecting some of its properties.

The fact that replacing *Moby Dick* in (94) with *these books* in (95) changes the agreement features of the copula indicates that these elements occupy the matrix subject position of their sentences.

(95) These books are hard for Bill to read.

On the other hand, *Moby Dick* in (94) seems to be thematically related to the embedded object position; that is, it is understood as the thing read. This is further confirmed by the fact that (94) can be paraphrased as in (96), where *Moby Dick* actually occupies the embedded object position and the matrix subject position is filled by an expletive.

(96) It is hard for Bill to read *Moby Dick*.

At first sight, we're dealing with a trivial instance of movement from a θ-position to a non-θ-position. Indeed, *tough*-constructions such as (94) do exhibit the traditional diagnostics of movement. Thus, if an island intervenes between the matrix subject and the object of *read*, we get an unacceptable sentence, as exemplified in (97) with a *wh*-island:

(97) *These books are hard for Bill to decide when to read.

---

44 There's a rich literature on the *tough*-construction. For earlier analyses, see Postal and Ross (1971), Lasnik and Fiengo (1974), Chomsky (1977, 1981), Williams (1983), Culicover and Wilkins (1984), Levine (1984), and Jones (1985), among many others. For a minimalist analysis of these constructions, see Hornstein (2001). See also Hicks (2003) for an overview of *tough*-constructions in both GB and minimalist frameworks.

The problem, however, is that it's quite unclear what sort of movement this could be. Suppose, for instance, that *Moby Dick* in (94) moves directly from the embedded object position to the matrix subject position, as illustrated in (98):

(98)   [*Moby Dick*$_i$ is hard [for Bill to read t$_i$]]

As a trace of A-movement, *t$_i$* in (98) is an anaphor and should thus be bound within the embedded clause in order to comply with Principle A of Binding Theory. Since *t$_i$* is unbound in this domain, the structure should be filtered out. The structure in (98) should also be excluded for minimality reasons (see chapter 5): on its way to the matrix subject position, *Moby Dick* crosses the embedded subject. Finally, the motivation for the movement of *Moby Dick* is somewhat up in the air (especially if one goes in a minimalist direction). A-movement is generally driven by Case requirements, but the embedded object position in (98) is already a Case-marked position. The conclusion seems to be that whatever sort of movement we have here, it can't be A-movement.

Chomsky (1981) suggested that it's actually an instance of A'-movement with a null operator OP moving close to the *tough*-predicate and forming a complex predicate with it. The structure of (94), for instance, should be as shown in (99):

(99)   [*Moby Dick* is [hard [OP$_i$ [for Bill to read t$_i$]]]]

In (99), movement of the null operator allows the formation of the complex predicate *[hard [OP$_i$ [for Bill to read t$_i$]]]*, which is predicated of the subject *Moby Dick*. In effect, then, the matrix subject position in (99) *is* a θ-position, for *Moby Dick* receives a θ-role under predication.

Now, complex predicates are not quite as exotic as they may appear to be.[45] We find them in constructions involving relative clauses, for example, where a sentence can function as a kind of giant adjective. Consider (100), for instance:

(100)   a. John read a book that Bill enjoyed.
         b. [John read [[a book] [OP$_i$ [that Bill enjoyed t$_i$]]]]

---

45 In fact, the formation of complex predicates has been implemented in syntactic theory since Chomsky (1955); see, among others, DiSciullo and Williams (1987) on small-clause structures. For recent extensive discussion for a number of constructions, see Neeleman (1994) and the collection of papers in Alsina, Bresnan, and Sells (1997). See also Ackerman and Webelhuth (1998) for an HPSG-account of complex predication.

In (100b), *a book that Bill enjoyed* forms a constituent and carries the "readee" θ-role. Moreover, *a book* is intuitively understood as also playing the "enjoyee" θ-role. We know that relative clauses are formed via A′-movement. So it's possible that what looks like exceptional "long distance θ-assignment" of the "enjoyee" θ-role to *a book* in (100b) is actually local θ-assignment to a null operator, which then moves, yielding an open predicate. Under predication, this predicate is saturated by *a book*, which is then interpreted as the thing enjoyed by Bill.

The proposal that Chomsky makes is that the same thing happens in *tough*-constructions, with the difference that the adjective and its complement form a complex predicate. Let's assume that this account is on the right track and ask what this implies for DS.

The first problem that this analysis poses for DS regards the thematic status of the matrix subject in (99). (96) has shown us that the matrix subject of a *tough*-predicate is not inherently a θ-position, for it can be occupied by an expletive. This means that the matrix subject position in (99) is only a θ-position *after* A′-movement of the null operator has taken place and the complex predicate has been formed. Recall that we've already seen a similar case with headless relative clauses (see section 2.3.2.3); there, the matrix verb could have its thematic/selectional requirements satisfied only after the *wh*-phrase had moved. If the matrix subject position in (99) becomes thematic only after movement of the null operator, when then is *Moby Dick* inserted? If at DS, then it's not inserted *at the point when the matrix subject is a θ-position*. If after the null operator has moved, the conclusion then is that we can indeed have insertion into a θ-position *after* DS. Either way, there's a tension between the two leading claims of DS: that it precedes all movements and that all θ-positions are filled at DS (see section 2.2.2.1).

Chomsky attempts to solve this problem by weakening the θ-requirements on DS and allowing a lexical item to be inserted in the course of the derivation and get its θ-role assigned at LF.[46] In effect, lexical insertion and θ-assignment are pulled apart. Hence, the DS of (93) would be as (101a); *Moby Dick* would be inserted prior to SS and then receive a θ-role at LF under predication (indicated here by "i = j-indexation"):

(101)   a. <u>DS</u>:
             [is [hard [for Bill to read OP]]]

---

46 See Williams (1983) on this amendment of (strict) θ-requirements at DS, picked up in Williams (1994).

b. <u>SS</u>:
   [*Moby Dick*$_j$ is [hard [OP$_i$ [for Bill to read t$_i$]]]]
c. <u>LF</u> (i = j):
   [*Moby Dick*$_j$ is [hard [OP$_j$ [for Bill to read t$_j$]]]]

The problem with this amendment is that not only atomic lexical items, but also complex phrases can appear as the subject of a *tough*-construction. Consider the sentence in (102a), for instance, which, under the suggestion above, should have the DS in (102b):

(102)   a. These books are hard for Bill to read.
        b. <u>DS</u>:
           [are [hard [for Bill to read OP$_i$]]]

Now, we can't simply say that *these books* will be inserted prior to SS, because it's not an atomic lexical item, but a phrase. That is, in addition to allowing lexical insertion to take place after DS, we would also need a device to assemble phrases *after DS*.

Once phrases can in principle be of unbound complexity, the problem of structure building after DS may become even harder within standard GB. We may find as the subject of a *tough*-construction phrases that contain predicates, as illustrated in (103a), or even phrases that have a *tough*-structure themselves, as illustrated in (103b). If the predicates inside the matrix subject in (103) can assign their θ-roles after DS, why then shouldn't the predicates of "canonical" sentences do the same?

(103)   a. The books that Mary enjoyed are hard for Bill to read.
        b. *Moby Dick* being hard to read is tough for Bill to understand.

Interestingly, *tough*-constructions are not problematic if we dispense with DS. Recall that if DS is dispensed with, Move and Merge operations can be interspersed. Thus, the derivation of (94) can proceed along the lines of (104):

(104)   a. Applications of Merge →
           [$_{C'}$ for Bill to read OP]
        b. Move OP →
           [$_{CP}$ OP$_i$ [for Bill to read t$_i$]]
        c. CP + $_{Merge}$ *hard* →
           [$_{AP}$ hard [$_{CP}$ OP$_i$ [for Bill to read t$_i$]]]
        d. AP + $_{Merge}$ *is* →
           [$_{I'}$ is [$_{AP}$ hard [$_{CP}$ OP$_i$ [for Bill to read t$_i$]]]]
        e. I' + $_{Merge}$ *Moby Dick* →
           [$_{IP}$ *Moby Dick* is [$_{AP}$ hard [$_{CP}$ OP$_i$ [for Bill to read t$_i$]]]]

After *read* merges with the null operator and further applications of Merge, we obtain C′ in (104a). The null operator then moves, yielding the CP in (104b). After this CP merges with *hard*, as shown in (104c), they form a complex predicate that can assign a θ-role to the external argument. Thus, when *Moby Dick* merges with I′ in (104e), becoming the matrix subject, it will be θ-marked. Notice that such θ-marking conforms with the TRAP from (68), repeated in (105); in fact, it's no different to usual θ-role assignment to [Spec,IP].

(105)   *Theta-Role Assignment Principle (TRAP)*
         θ-roles can only be assigned under a Merge operation.

To sum up, what makes *tough*-constructions different is not where they discharge their thematic responsibilities, but that they involve complex rather than simple predicates. More important, it appears that we can only provide an adequate account of them if we don't assume DS and, of course, this is the strongest kind of argument against DS one can come up with.

Exercise 2.12

In this section, we have seen that the formation of complex predicates through the movement of a null operator provides evidence against the conception of DS within GB in that θ-roles may be assigned after movement operations. But upon close inspection, it seems that the appeal to null operators by itself already undermines the pillars of DS. Consider why, by examining the DS of the sentences in (i) and discussing how and where the verbs *ate* and *drink* can have their selectional requirements satisfied.

(i)   a. The bagel I ate was delicious.
      b. The caipirinha I drank was excellent.

2.3.2.6 The starting point and the numeration

Let's finally consider an important role that DS plays within GB, as the starting point for a derivation. Since DS is the point where lexical insertion takes place, it ensures that LF and PF are compatible in the sense that they are based on the same lexical resources and this is something that any adequate linguistic model must ensure. At the end of the day we want our theory to predict that the PF output associated with (106) means 'John left' and not 'I don't think John left'.

(106)   John left.

From a minimalist perspective, a starting point also seems to be necessary for economy reasons. If the computational system had direct access to
the lexicon at any time, it's not obvious how it could be determined when a
given derivation has finished and this in turn may lead to unwanted
economy computations. Let's see why.

It's natural to assume that economy considerations favor shorter derivations over longer ones. With this in mind, consider the following problem. We've seen that the recursion property of DS is captured within
minimalism by the operation Merge, which combines lexical items to
build phrases out of them. If the computational system could access the
lexicon directly at any point, the derivation of (106) should in principle
block the derivation of (107), for the former obviously requires fewer
applications of Merge, thereby being more economical than (107).

(107)   Mary said John left.

This undesirable result can be avoided if we assume instead that the
computational system doesn't have free direct access to the lexicon, but
only to a collection of lexical items that should function as the starting point
for a derivation. Now, if economy only compares derivations with the same
starting point, that is, the same collection of lexical items, the derivations of
(106) and (107) won't be compared for economy purposes, since they involve
different starting points; hence, they can be both admissible, for one won't
interfere with the other. Within GB, these different starting points correspond to different DS representations. The question for minimalists is then
how to resort to a starting point for a derivation, without invoking DS.

To say that we need a starting point for derivations in order to ensure
compatibility between PF and LF and prevent unwanted economy computations does not entail that we need DS. Recall that DS is much more
than a starting point. It's a formal object that is subject to several *linguistic*
wellformedness conditions; that is, DS must comply with X′-Theory, the
Theta-Criterion, etc. This is why DS is a level of *linguistic* representation
within GB. Thus, if we want a starting point for the reasons indicated
above, but we don't want to postulate levels that are not conceptually
required, what we need is just a formal object that is not subject to any
linguistic conditions other than the requirement that it contains the relevant lexical atoms that will feed the computational system.

Chomsky (1995) suggests that such a starting point is a *numeration*,
understood to be a set of pairs (LI, i), where *LI* is a lexical item and *i*

indicates the number of instances of that lexical item that are available for the computation. The numeration underlying the derivation of the sentence in (108a), for example, must contain two instances of *that* and one instance of *buy*, as shown in (108b):

(108)   a. That woman might buy that car.
        b. N = {might$_1$, that$_2$, buy$_1$, woman$_1$, car$_1$}

Given a numeration N, the computational system accesses its lexical items through the operation *Select*. Select pulls out an element from the numeration, reducing its index by 1. Applied to the N in (108b), for example, the computational system may select *car* and then *that*, yielding the reduced numerations N' and N'' in (109) and (110) below, respectively. The two lexical items can then merge, forming a DP, as shown in (111). Further applications of Select then exhaust the numeration and successive applications of Merge yield the structure corresponding to (108a), as illustrated in (112). A computation is taken to be a derivation only if the numeration has been exhausted, that is, a derivation must use up all the lexical items of its numeration.

(109)   a. N' = {might$_1$, that$_2$, buy$_1$, woman$_1$, car$_0$}
        b. *car*

(110)   a. N'' = {might$_1$, that$_1$, buy$_1$, woman$_1$, car$_0$}
        b. *car*
        c. *that*

(111)   a. N'' = {might$_1$, that$_1$, buy$_1$, woman$_1$, car$_0$}
        b. *car* +$_{\text{Merge}}$ *that* → [$_{\text{DP}}$ that car]

(112)   a. N''' = {might$_0$, that$_0$, buy$_0$, woman$_0$, car$_0$}
        b. [$_{\text{IP}}$ [$_{\text{DP}}$ that woman] [$_{\text{I'}}$ might [$_{\text{VP}}$ buy [$_{\text{DP}}$ that car]]]]

If the relevant starting point is a numeration, we may now prevent the unwanted comparison of the derivations of (106) and (107) by assuming that two derivations may be compared for economy purposes if (i) they are both convergent (otherwise, the most economical derivation will always be the one where nothing happens) and (ii) they are based on the same initial numeration. The compatibility between PF and LF is also ensured if the computational system accesses one numeration at a time; that is, PF and LF will be constructed with the same lexical resources.

Two things are worth mentioning about numerations. First, there's nothing wrong with "crazy" numerations like the ones in (113) below *as numerations*. Of course, there are no convergent derivations that can be built from any of these numerations. However, this can presumably be determined *at the interface levels*. If we start adding *linguistic* requirements about what is or isn't a well-formed numeration, we end up resuscitating DS. Since PF and LF already are responsible for filtering out crashing derivations, there's no need to filter out the numerations in (113), since derivations resulting from them will crash at LF and/or PF.

(113)   a. N_1 = {tree$_{43}$, of$_2$, buy$_1$}
        b. N_2 = {with$_{11}$, about$_{33}$, Mary$_2$, John$_7$}
        c. N_3 = {see$_7$, man$_1$, Infl$_{53}$}

The second important point to keep in mind is that this is a model of *competence*, rather than performance. Thus, it makes no specific claim as to how a speaker chooses to use certain lexical items and not others in a particular utterance. Note incidentally that in this regard, this is not different from a system that assumes DS (i.e. why does a speaker "choose" one rather than another DS?). All the proposal is saying is that the computational system that builds syntactic structures doesn't work with the whole lexicon at a time, but with collections of lexical items.

We'll have further discussion on the format of numerations in chapter 10, but for our current purposes we'll assume that the starting point of a syntactic derivation is a numeration as described above.

Exercise 2.13

In order to prevent (106) from blocking (107), we assumed that only derivations with the same starting point can be compared for economy purposes. That being so, provide the numerations that give rise to (106) and (107), and explain why we still need to assume that derivations must exhaust their numerations.

Exercise 2.14

Assuming the checking theory sketched in section 2.3.1.1, show why the pair of sentences in (i) can be derived from a common numeration, but the one in (ii) can't.

(i)   a. John said that Peter loves Mary.
      b. Peter said that John loves Mary.

(ii) a. John loves Mary.
      b. Mary loves John.

Exercise 2.15

One property of DS is that it's a single root syntactic object. In turn, a numeration, as a collection of lexical items, is not even a syntactic object. Discuss if it's useful to require singlerootedness in the computation and if so, where such requirement should be stated from a minimalist perspective.

2.3.2.7 Summary

In the previous subsections we've examined the major motivations for postulating DS as a level of representation within GB. We've seen that we need not postulate a level of representation to capture syntactic generativity or to have a starting point for derivations. Other plausible technologies (the operation Merge and the notion of numeration) may do equally well. DS should then be assumed mainly for empirical reasons. However, we've found that the complete separation of structure building and movement, which is inherent to a DS-based system, actually leads to serious empirical problems, as shown in the discussion of headless relative clauses and *tough*-movement constructions. More importantly, by simply assuming a condition on θ-role assignment (that it can take place under Merge, but not under Move), we were able to capture the beneficial features of DS, such as the differences between raising and control structures, without getting into the empirical troubles mentioned above. In effect, we have a much better theory, meeting empirical adequacy without the methodological burden of postulating a level that is not conceptually motivated. This provides hope that the methodologically best theory is also not too far removed from empirical adequacy.

2.4 The picture so far

DS and SS are central features of a GB-model of UG. From a minimalist point of view where we try to make do with the conceptually required levels only, DS and SS contrast with PF and LF in being methodologically dispensable. This chapter has reviewed the kinds of evidence put forward to support SS and DS. We've seen that with some technical changes, we're able to defuse these arguments and "save" the relevant data without assuming that DS or SS actually exist. Even more important, in some cases we came to the conclusion that a set of empirical phenomena could only be accounted for if we abandoned one of these levels. We haven't exhaustively reviewed all the empirical data that has been used to motivate SS or DS. However, we've taken a look at a fair sampling. It seems fair to conclude that it's reasonable to hope that eliminating DS and SS won't come at too great an empirical cost (if any). Thus, at least with respect to these issues, the minimalist goal of making do with the "obvious" (as outlined in chapter 1) is a viable project. In what follows we'll assume that further problems can be overcome and investigate what other changes to GB a serious commitment to minimalist goals would entail.

The picture of the grammar that we have thus far can be illustrated in the updated T-model given in (115) below. Given a numeration N (composed of lexical items A, B, C, etc., each with an index for the number of its occurrences), the computational system accesses the lexical items of N through the operation Select and builds syntactic structures through the operations Merge and Move. At some point in the derivation, the system employs the operation Spell-Out, which splits the computation in two parts, leading to PF and LF. The mapping that leads to LF is referred to as the *covert component* and the one that leads to PF as the *phonetic/phonological component*; the computation that precedes Spell-Out is referred to as *overt syntax*.

(114)   *A minimalist T-model of the grammar*

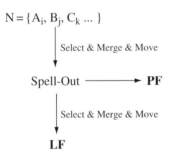

For any syntactic computation, if the computational system doesn't employ enough applications of Select, the numeration won't be exhausted and we won't have a syntactic derivation. If any strong feature is left unchecked before Spell-Out, the derivation crashes at PF. In addition, if an instance of overt movement only checks weak features, the derivation will be filtered out by the economy principle Procrastinate. Finally, two derivations will be compared for purposes of derivational economy only if both of them converge and start with the same numeration.

In order to ensure that we stick to the minimalist project as close as possible, we'll further assume that the mapping from a given numeration N to an LF object λ is subject to two conditions:[47]

---

47 See Chomsky (1995: 228–29).

(115)   *Inclusiveness Condition*
      The LF object λ must be built only from the features of the lexical items of N.

(116)   *Uniformity Condition*
      The operations available in the covert component must be the same ones available in overt syntax.

The Inclusiveness Condition is meant to save us from the temptation of introducing theoretical primes that can't be defined in terms of lexical features. The Uniformity Condition, on the other hand, aims at preventing SS from resurrecting through statements like "such and such operation must apply before/after Spell-Out." Notice that in principle, the Uniformity Condition does not ban the possibility that overt and covert syntax actually employ different operations, *if* the differences are independently motivated (in terms of the interface levels). If they are not, then a violation of the Uniformity Condition entails that Spell-Out is in fact being treated as a level of representation, being responsible for ruling out unwanted overt applications of "covert operations." The computations of the phonetic component aren't subject to these conditions, since they employ different operations and may add information that is not present in the numeration (intonation, for instance).

The forcefully parsimonious apparatus imposed by these conditions clearly call into question many of the traditional GB-entities and some of the minimalist assumptions discussed so far. For instance, the Inclusiveness Condition leads us to ask how traces and null operators are to be described in terms of the lexical features of a given numeration. In turn, the Uniformity Condition calls for an independent explanation for why movement before and after Spell-Out is different in terms of derivational cost, which is postulated by Procrastinate (see section 2.3.1.3), or for why movement before Spell-Out must be cyclic, but movement after Spell-Out need not be, as dictated by the Extension Condition (see (89)). We'll return to these issues in the chapters that follow and present approaches that are more congenial to the minimalist project.

Exercise 2.16

As mentioned in section 2.2.5, GB allowed free indexing of DPs. Is this feature of GB consistent with Inclusiveness and Uniformity? If not, outline a proposal of how indexing should be reinterpreted in a way compatible with these conditions.

Exercise 2.17

In section 2.3.1.2, the unacceptability of (i) below was accounted for in LF terms, under the assumption that its LF structure is (iia), rather than (iib). Is this analysis compatible with Inclusiveness and Uniformity? If not, discuss under which scenario the LF analysis of (i) can satisfy these conditions.

(i) *Which man said he$_i$ liked which picture that Harry$_i$ bought?

(ii) a. LF:
     *[$_{CP}$ which$_m$ [which man]$_k$ [$_{IP}$ t$_k$ said he$_i$ liked t$_m$ picture that Harry$_i$ bought]]
   b. LF:
     [$_{CP}$ [which picture that Harry$_i$ bought]$_m$ [which man]$_k$ [$_{IP}$ t$_k$ said he$_i$ liked t$_m$]]

3   *Theta domains*

3.1   Introduction

Let's get back to basics once again. One of the "big facts" listed in section 1.3 is that sentences are composed of phrases organized in a hierarchical fashion. Given our GB starting point, this big fact is captured by X′-Theory, according to which (i) phrases are projections of heads; (ii) elements that form parts of phrases do so in virtue of being within such projections; and (iii) elements within a phrase are hierarchically ordered. More specifically, phrases are endocentric objects with complements being in the immediate projection of the head and specifiers being outside the immediate projection of the head. Given this background, chapter 1 sketched as a minimalist project the elimination of government as a primitive relation within the theory of grammar. The conceptual motivation for dropping government is that once we need phrases anyhow, we should in principle stick to the structural relations that phrases bring with them. Thus, it is methodologically cost-less to avail oneself of the head-complement and specifier-head (henceforth, Spec-head for short) relations – and on the same token, it becomes costly to assume that we need more than these two relations. In particular, government comes out of this discussion as a methodological encumbrance worth dumping.

In this chapter, we examine whether government can be dispensed with within the domain of Theta Theory, the grammatical module responsible for licensing thematic or θ-roles.[1] In particular, we will discuss θ-assignment in structures involving external arguments in sections 3.2 and 3.4 and ditransitive predicates in section 3.3. Along the way we introduce some revisions of (X′) phrase structure, namely on the VP-level, for which we present two versions of so-called VP-shells. Section 3.5 concludes this chapter.

---

1 See Williams (1995) for a post-GB overview of GB's Theta Theory.

3.2   External arguments

3.2.1   *θ-marking of external arguments and government*

GB makes a distinction between internal and external arguments.[2] Internal arguments are typically objects and their θ-role is determined by the verb they are associated with. By contrast, external arguments are typically subjects and their θ-role appears to be determined in part by the internal argument. For illustration, consider the following paradigm:[3]

(1)   a. She took the book.
       b. She took a rest.
       c. She took a bus.
       d. She took a nap.
       e. She took offence.
       f. She took office.
       g. She took her medicine.
       h. She took her time.

Naïvely, it seems that *she* plays a different role in each of these constructions and this role is related to the role that the object has in each. Thus, one takes a book rather differently than one takes a bus or takes a rest. (We are here putting aside exotic and exciting cases, such as Godzilla taking a bus the same way you or we might take a book.) In fact, it seems that in each case the "taking" is somewhat different. An inelegant solution would be to suggest that *take* has several homophonous entries in the lexicon, one expressing each use; just consider how many verbs can have such alternate interpretations depending on which object they take (*throw a fist* vs. *throw a fit*, *kill a knight* vs. *kill a night*, etc.). Thus, trying to pin down the different thematic roles assigned to the subject to different entries of a verb is very messy.

One can track this difference more easily and elegantly by assuming that there is an external/internal argument distinction and that the external θ-role, the one that the subject receives, is actually assigned not by the verb alone, but by the whole VP (the verb plus the internal argument). If this is so, the role that *she* has in each example of (1) is different because, strictly speaking, the VPs are different as the internal arguments differ; in other words, *she* receives its θ-role from *take the book* in (1a) and from *take a nap*

2 See Williams (1981) and Marantz (1984), among others, and Williams (1995) for a brief overview.
3 These data were first discussed in Marantz (1984) and picked up more recently by, e.g., Kratzer (1996).

in (1b), for example. This assumption maintains a single entry for a verb like *take*, whose interpretation depends on the object it combines with. This combination, minimally the V′ containing verb and object, is the predication structure relevant for determining the external θ-role.

Let's assume that this is correct and examine how θ-marking of external arguments fits in the configurations for θ-assignment allowed by GB. One point that is uncontroversial is that the configurations for θ-assignment must be local in some sense. After all, we don't want any verb or VP of a given structure to assign its θ-role to any DP, but only to the ones close by. The issue is what *close by* means.

Within GB, the relevant notion of locality is stated in terms of government, which for current purposes is defined along the lines of (2) and (3):[4]

(2)   *Government*
       α governs β iff
       (i) α c-commands β and
       (ii) β c-commands α.

(3)   *C-Command*
       α c-commands β iff
       (i) α does not dominate β;
       (ii) β does not dominate α;
       (iii) the first branching node dominating α also dominates β; and
       (iv) α does not equal β.

Thus, under the assumption that α may assign a θ-role to β only if α governs β,[5] it must be the case that in, say, (4) the verb *saw* governs *Mary* and the VP *saw Mary* governs *John*.

(4)   John saw Mary.

The required government relations were not a problem in early GB-analyses that assigned a representation like (5) below to the sentence in (4).[6] In fact, θ-marking of the internal and the external arguments in (5) both take place under sisterhood (mutual c-command), the "core" case of government: *saw* is the sister of *Mary* and the VP is a sister of *John*.

---

4 See, e.g., Reinhart (1976), Chomsky (1981, 1986a), or Aoun and Sportiche (1983) on various definitions of c-command and government.
5 See Chomsky (1981: 36–37).
6 Recall that [s NP Infl VP] was in fact the original structure assumed in GB (Chomsky 1981), where *S* for sentence was carried over from earlier generative models (cf. Chomsky 1957, 1965, 1970, and all work in Standard Theory and Extended Standard Theory).

(5)   [$_S$ John INFL [$_{VP}$ saw Mary]]

However, with a more articulated clausal structure like (6), which adopts binary branching and endocentricity (see chapter 6),[7] the VP and the subject no longer c-command each other and something must be said with respect to how the external argument is θ-marked.

(6)   [$_{IP}$ John [$_{I'}$ I^0 [$_{VP}$ saw Mary]]]

One possibility is to resort to Spec-head relations in addition to government. More specifically, VP in (6) could assign its θ-role to I^0 under government and this θ-role would then be "reassigned" to *John* under Spec-head relation.[8] Another possibility is to relax the notion of government and state it in terms of m-command, as in (7) and (8) below, rather than c-command.[9] Since the VP and *John* in (6) share all maximal projections (i.e. IP), VP would m-command and govern *John* and could thus θ-mark it.

(7)   *Government*
         α governs β iff
         (i) α m-commands β and
         (ii) β m-commands α.

(8)   *M-Command*
         α m-commands β iff
         (i) α does not dominate β;
         (ii) β does not dominate α;
         (iii) every maximal projection dominating α also dominates β; and
         (iv) α does not equal β.

Note that if any maximal projection intervenes between VP and the position where the external argument is generated, both proposals may face problems. Suppose, for instance, that there is an intervening agreement projection for the object in (6), call it AgrOP, as illustrated in (9).

(9)   [$_{IP}$ John [$_{I'}$ I^0 [$_{AgrOP}$ AgrO [$_{VP}$ saw Mary]]]]

---

7 The structure in (6) crystallized in Chomsky (1986a). See Jackendoff (1977) for early discussion on phrase structure in X'-terms and Bresnan (1972), Fassi Fehri (1980), and Stowell (1981) on clause structure, in particular; see also Kayne (1984) for early arguments in favor of binary branching.

8 Chomsky (1986a) explicitly assumes this VP-assignment of the subject θ-role mediated by Infl, extending previous work in Chomsky (1981) and Marantz (1984).

9 M-command was introduced by Aoun and Sportiche (1983) and implemented in the way portrayed here by Chomsky (1986a).

Given that AgrO is involved in checking object agreement and accusative Case (see chapters 4 and 5 for discussion), the external argument should not be generated in its specifier. Thus, even if AgrO could reassign the θ-role it receives from VP to its specifier, *John* in (9) would not be in the appropriate Spec-head configuration to receive this θ-role. Moreover, the VP in (9) doesn't m-command *John*, for AgrOP dominates VP but not *John*; hence, VP can't assign the external θ-role to *John* under the definition of government in (7) either.

We won't attempt to change the notion of government so that the potential problems posed by structures such as (9) can be circumvented. The little discussion above shows that having government as our starting point may lead to the introduction of additional provisos, and minimalist parsimony tells us to avoid enriching theoretical apparatus whenever possible. Let's see if this is indeed possible by exploring a different starting point.

Exercise 3.1

It has been observed that there are many, many idioms of the V + OB variety across languages (see Marantz 1984), such as

- *hit the roof, kick the bucket,* and *screw the pooch* in English;
- *esticar as canelas* 'to die' (lit.: 'to stretch the shinbones'), *quebrar um galho* 'to solve a problem' (lit.: 'to break a branch'), and *pintar o sete* 'to act up' (lit.: 'to paint the seven') in Brazilian Portuguese;
- *die Luft anhalten* 'to hold one's tongue' (lit.: 'to stop the air'), *(nicht) die Kurve kriegen* 'to (not) get round to something' (lit.: 'to get the bend'), and *sich den Kopf zerbrechen* 'to rack one's brains' (lit.: 'to break one's head') in German.

In these cases, V + OB functions as a semantic unit that may take any appropriate DP for its subject. In contrast to V + OB cases, there are very few (if any) idioms of SU + V form, that is, idioms where SU + V constitutes a semantic unit that may take any appropriate DP for its object. Using the distinction between internal and external arguments reviewed in the text, explain in some detail why this contrast might hold and discuss how idioms might arise and how they should be stored in the lexicon.

3.2.2   *The Predicate-Internal Subject Hypothesis (PISH)*

Assume for a moment that all we have are the minimalistically acceptable relations, the ones derived from phrase-structure notions. What should we then do with external arguments? Clearly, their θ-roles can't be assigned under the head-complement relation, as this is the configuration under which internal arguments are θ-marked. This leaves the Spec-head configuration. If we assume that all θ-roles associated with a head H are assigned within projections of H, then it is reasonable to think that external arguments are generated in the specifier of the lexical head with which they enter into a θ-relation. Let's refer to this hypothesis as the *Predicate-Internal Subject Hypothesis* (*PISH*).[10]

According to the PISH, in the derivation of (4) *John* must start out in a configuration like (10).

(10)   [$_{VP}$ John [$_{V'}$ saw Mary]]

In (10), *John* is in the specifier of *saw*; it is also "external" to the projection immediately dominating the verb and the internal argument. This last point is important for it allows us to distinguish internal from external arguments, which, as we saw in section 3.2.1, is a difference worth tracking. Given that I^0 in English has a strong D/N-feature (i.e. the EPP holds), *John* in (10) must then move to [Spec,IP] before Spell-Out, yielding the structure in (11) (see section 2.3.1.3).

(11)   [$_{IP}$ John$_i$ [$_{I'}$ I^0 [$_{VP}$ t$_i$ [$_{V'}$ saw Mary]]]]

So, it is actually possible to find a representation that is minimalistically respectable in that government is not used (X$'$-theoretic notions are substituted) and which captures the internal/external argument distinction. Note also that the configuration in (10) is in accordance with the proposal that θ-roles are only assigned under a Merge operation (see section 2.3.2.2): in (10) *John* is θ-marked as it merges with *[saw Mary]*.

In the next section we will see that besides being conceptually sound from a minimalist perspective, the PISH is also strongly supported by empirical evidence.

3.2.3   Some empirical arguments for the PISH

3.2.3.1 Idioms and raising
A very interesting property that idioms appear to have is that they correspond to syntactic constituents. Thus, we may find numerous instances

---

10 The idea that subjects begin within VP was proposed within a GB-setting by various authors, including Zagona (1982), Kitagawa (1986), Speas (1986), Contreras (1987), Kuroda (1988), Sportiche (1988), and (the creators of the term VP-Internal Subject Hypothesis) Koopman and Sportiche (1991). For a nice review of the PISH, see McCloskey (1997). The next section steals liberally from the last two.

where a verb and its object form an idiomatic expression excluding the subject as in *hit the roof*, for example, but we don't seem to find idioms involving the subject and the verb, excluding the complement.[11] This systematic gap is accounted for if we assume the VP-structure in (12).

(12)   [$_{VP}$ SU [$_{V'}$ V OB]]

In (12), the verb and its complement form a syntactic constituent that is independent of the subject, namely V′, but the subject and the verb alone don't form a constituent; hence, we find idiomatic expressions with the form *[X [V OB]]* (e.g. *John/Mary/the students **hit the roof***), but not with the form *[SU[VX]]* (e.g. **The roof hit** *John/Mary/the students*), with elements in bold forming an idiom and X being the non-idiomatic material.

Idiomaticity can thus be used as a test for detecting syntactic constituenthood. In fact, we have already used idioms to argue that the element that appears in the subject of raising structures gets to this position by movement (see section 2.3.2.2). Let's review the argument by considering the sentences in (13).

(13)   a. The shit hit the fan.
        b. The shit seemed to hit the fan.

(13a) has an idiomatic reading which means, more or less, that things got very bad. What is crucial here is that in this sentence, *the shit* is not referential, but part of a larger sentential idiom. (13b) in turn shows that the idiomatic reading is also kept when *the shit* appears in the subject position of *seem*, a raising verb. Given the fact that idioms must form a syntactic constituent (at some point in the derivation) and the fact that raising predicates do not impose selectional restrictions on their subjects, we were led to the conclusion that in (13b), *the shit* raises from the embedded clause to the matrix IP.

What holds for raising in (13b) holds for modals, aspectual verbs, tenses, as well as negation. So, the following sentences are all fine *with the idiomatic reading*.

(14)   a. The shit may/should/might/can hit the fan.
        b. The shit hit/will hit/is hitting/has hit the fan.
        c. The shit did not hit the fan.

---

11 See Marantz (1984) for the original observation and, e.g., Bresnan (1982) and Speas (1990) for discussion.

What (14) indicates is that the idiomatic reading is unaffected by the presence of modals, different tenses, different aspects, or negation. The preservation of the idiomatic reading in (13b) and (14) follows if indeed the PISH is correct and the structure of the idiom is roughly as in (15).

(15)   [$_{VP}$ the shit [$_{V'}$ hit the fan]]

Given (15), the reason why this sentential idiom is insensitive to the modality, polarity, tense, or aspect of the sentence it is embedded in is simply that it does not contain any such information. The idiom is just the VP part indicated in (15); the rest is non-idiomatic and is added as the derivation proceeds. The sentences of (14a), for instance, are derived after a modal merges with the VP in (15) and *the shit* raises to check the EPP, as illustrated in (16) below. Put another way, tense, modals, negation, and aspect act like raising predicates.

(16)   [$_{IP}$ [the shit]$_i$ [$_{I'}$ may/should/might/can [$_{VP}$ t$_i$ [$_{V'}$ hit the fan]]]]

The derivation of the sentences in (13) and (14) is therefore analogous to the derivation of (17a), which contains the idiom *hit the roof*:

(17)   a. John hit the roof.
         b. [$_{IP}$ John$_i$ [$_{I'}$ I^0 [$_{VP}$ t$_i$ [$_{V'}$ hit the roof]]]]

The only relevant difference between (16) and (17b) is that the idiom in (16) is the whole VP, whereas the idiom in (17b) involves just the verb and the object. Thus, the idiomatic reading in (17) is also preserved if the subject varies, as illustrated in (18).

(18)   John/Mary/the students will/has/didn't hit the roof.

Note that the argument is not that idioms must exclude Infl information such as tense, for example. Like any other constituent, IPs and CPs may in principle be associated with an idiomatic reading and we do indeed find frozen expressions with such structures, as illustrated in (19).

(19)   a. A rolling stone gathers no moss.
         b. Is the Pope catholic?

As we should expect, if the material within these structures varies, the idiomatic reading is lost, as (20) and (21) illustrate (indicated by the hash mark '#').

(20)   a. #A rolling stone gathered/might gather/is gathering no moss.
         b. #A rolling stone seemed to gather no moss.

(21)   a. #Was the Pope catholic?
        b. #Mary wonders whether the Pope is catholic.

To recap. If we assume that subjects are merged in [Spec,IP], we fail to account for the fact that some sentential idioms are insensitive to information associated with inflectional projections. The reason is the following. If (13a), for instance, were associated with the structure in (22) below, we'd be tacitly admitting that idiomatic expressions could be syntactically discontinuous, for the tense information in Infl is not frozen, as can be seen in (14). But if we took this position, we'd then be unable to account for the lack of discontinuous idioms of the sort *[SU [VX]]*, where the subject and the verb form an idiomatic expression excluding the object.

(22) $[_{IP} [$ the shit $] [_{I'} I^0 [_{VP}$ hit the fan $]]]$

On the other hand, if we take the PISH to be correct, we can account for both facts. That is, the PISH allows us to maintain the plausible assumption that idioms must correspond to syntactic constituents (at some point in the derivation). Thus, the insensitivity of the sentential idiom in (13a) to information relating to Infl is due to the fact that the idiom corresponds to the VP, as shown in (15), and *the shit* gets to [Spec,IP] by movement, as shown in (23) below. In turn, the non-existence of subject-verb idioms, i.e. those with the format *[SU [VX]]*, is due to the fact that the subject and the verb don't form a constituent in this structure.

(23) $[_{IP} [$ the shit $]_i [_{I'} I^0 [_{VP} t_i [_{V'}$ hit the fan $]]]]$

3.2.3.2   The Coordinate Structure Constraint
A well-known fact about coordinate structures is that (in general) one cannot extract out of a single conjunct, though extraction from all conjuncts in an across-the-board (ATB) fashion is permissible.[12] The effects of this Coordinate Structure Constraint can be seen in (24), where extraction from the first conjunct yields a strongly unacceptable result unless it co-occurs with extraction in the second conjunct.

---

12 This important observation is due to Ross (1967), which inspired a lot of subsequent research on ATB-issues. Further classic references on ATB and coordination include Jackendoff (1977), Williams (1978), Gazdar, Pullum, Sag, and Wasow (1982), Sag, Gazdar, Wasow, and Weisler (1985), and Goodall (1987), among others. See also Munn (1993) for a succinct summary.

(24)   a. *[$_{CP}$ what$_i$ did [$_{IP}$ John eat t$_i$] and [$_{IP}$ Bill cook hamburgers]]
         b. [$_{CP}$ what$_i$ did [$_{IP}$ John eat t$_i$] and [$_{IP}$ Bill cook t$_i$]]

Leaving a detailed discussion of ATB-extraction aside, let's consider the coordinated structure in (25).

(25)   The girls will write a book and be awarded a prize for it.

If subjects of transitive clauses were generated in [Spec,IP], (25) should have the structure in (26) below. Given that (26) has a trace in only one of the conjuncts, it should violate the Coordinate Structure Constraint and we incorrectly predict that the sentence in (25) should be unacceptable.

(26)   [$_{IP}$ [the girls]$_i$ will [$_{VP}$ write a book] and [$_{VP}$ be awarded t$_i$ a prize for it]]

This problem does not arise if the PISH is adopted and the subject of the first conjunct is generated in [Spec,VP], as illustrated in (27).[13]

(27)   [$_{IP}$ [the girls]$_i$ will [$_{VP}$ t$_i$ write a book] and [$_{VP}$ be awarded t$_i$ a prize for it]]

Note that (27) has a trace in each of the conjuncts. Thus, under the PISH, the structure in (27) is actually a case of ATB-extraction analogous to (24b). The PISH therefore provides us with a straightforward account of the apparent lack of Coordinate Structure Constraint effects in sentences such as (25).

3.2.3.3   Binding effects
The PISH is also supported by binding phenomena.[14] Consider the pair of sentences in (28), for instance.

(28)   a. Which stories about each other did they say the kids liked?
         b. ... but listen to each other, they say the kids won't.

In (28a), the anaphor *each other* is ambiguous in that it can have either the matrix or the embedded subject as its antecedent. In (28b), on the other hand, *each other* cannot be licensed by the matrix subject and must be interpreted as *the kids*. The question is what prevents *each other* in (28b)

---

13 This argument was brought up in Burton and Grimshaw (1992), building on an old observation expressed in Schachter (1976, 1977), Williams (1977), Gazdar (1981), Goodall (1987), and van Valin (1986).
14 This argument has been brought up by Huang (1993), building on work by Cinque (1984) and Barss (1986).

from being bound by *they*, given that this sentence seems structurally analogous to (28a).

The PISH provides an answer. If the PISH is correct, the embedded subject of the sentences in (28) must have been merged in [Spec,VP] before raising to [Spec,IP], as shown in (29).

(29)   a. [$_{VP}$ [the kids] [$_{V'}$ liked [which stories about each other]]]
        b. [$_{VP}$ [the kids] [$_{V'}$ listen to each other]]

After subject raising and further computations, we obtain the simplified representations in (30):

(30)   a. [$_{CP}$ [which stories about each other]$_i$ did [$_{IP}$ they say [$_{CP}$ t$_i$ [$_{IP}$ [the kids]$_k$ [$_{VP}$ t$_k$ liked t$_i$]]]]]
        b. [$_{CP}$ [$_{VP}$ t$_k$ listen to each other]$_i$ [$_{IP}$ they say [$_{CP}$ t$_i$ [$_{IP}$ [the kids]$_k$ won't t$_i$]]]]

Leaving for now the precise details on how to compute Principle A of Binding Theory (see section 8.2.2 for discussion), the reason why the anaphor of (28b) is not ambiguous like the one of (28a) now becomes clear. The trace t_k in (30b) is the local binder for the anaphor, thus preventing binding by the matrix subject. The PISH therefore plays an important role in the resolution of some binding puzzles.

3.2.3.4   Floating quantifiers

Consider the following near-paraphrases.

(31)   a. All the men have left the party.
        b. The men have all left the party.

(32)   a. The women each seemed to eat a tomato.
        b. The women seemed to each eat a tomato.

(33)   a. Both the girls may sing arias in the production.
        b. The girls may both sing arias in the production.

The second of each pair involves a "floating quantifier" (*all*, *each*, and *both*). In all the cases, the floating quantifier is semantically related to the DP it forms a constituent with in the first of each pair of sentences. Thus, *all* in (31b), for instance, is related to *the men* just as it is in (31a). This suggests that floating quantifier constructions are formed via movement, as follows. The quantifier and the DP form a constituent at some point in the derivation, call it Quantifier Phrase (QP), and in a later step, the DP may move out of this constituent, leaving the quantifier stranded. (31b), for instance, should be derived along the lines of (34).[15]

(34)   [$_{IP}$ [the men]$_i$ [$_{I'}$ have [$_{VP}$ [$_{QP}$ all t$_i$] left the party]]]

This analysis of floating quantifiers is not uncontroversial.[16] However, it has one very nice piece of data in its favor. In many languages, the floating quantifier agrees with the element that it is related to. In Portuguese, for example, the floating quantifier agrees in gender and number with the DP it is associated with, as shown in (35).

(35)   *Portuguese*
    a. As meninas tinham todas/*todos   almoçado.
       the girls   had   all.FEM.PL/all.MASC.PL   had.lunch
       'The girls had all had lunch.'
    b. Os meninos tinham todos/*todas   almoçado.
       the boys   had   all.MASC.PL/all.FEM.PL   had.lunch
       'The boys had all had lunch.'

Similarly, analogous constructions in German exhibit Case agreement between the floating quantifier and the DP it relates to, as illustrated by the minimal pair in (36), where the subject of the psych-verb[17] *gefallen* 'to please' receives dative Case and the subject of the regular transitive verb *mögen* 'to like' is marked nominative.[18]

(36)   *German*
    a. Diesen Mädchen gefällt der Peter *alle/allen.
       these.DAT girls   pleases the.NOM Peter all.NOM/all.DAT
       'These girls all like Peter.'

---

15 See Sportiche (1988) for a development of this argument.

16 See Bobaljik (2003) and Bošković (2004) for extensive reviews of, and a host of references to, movement and non-movement issues involved with floating quantifiers (interchangeably referred to also as floated or stranded quantifiers in the literature).

17 *Psych-verbs* (psychological verbs) form a special class of predicates whose arguments are "reversed" in the sense that the subject is the theme, while the object is the experiencer (see Belletti and Rizzi 1988). For relevant discussion, see among others den Besten (1985), Bouchard (1995), and Pesetsky (1995), and specifically for German, Fanselow (1992) and Abraham (1995).

18 Case-marking in German can best be seen on the determiner (article or demonstrative); the word *Mädchen* 'girl' in (36), for instance, is the same in all Cases (nominative, accusative, genitive, dative) in both numbers (singular and plural), with the possible exception of the formation of the genitive singular (*Mädchens*), which, however, is being used less and less for most nouns. For more on floating quantifiers in German, see Bayer (1987), Giusti (1989), and Merchant (1996).

b. Diese   Mädchen   mögen   den   Peter   alle/*allen.
   these.NOM   girls   like   the.ACC   Peter   all.NOM/all.DAT
   'These girls all like Peter.'

The agreement we find in (35) and (36) mimics the agreement pattern of the corresponding sentences where the quantifier is not stranded, as shown in (37) and (38) below. And this is exactly what we should expect, if floating quantifier constructions are indeed derived by movement along the lines of (34).

(37)   *Portuguese*
        a. Todas/*todos   as   meninas   tinham   almoçado.
           all.FEM.PL/all.MASC.PL   the.FEM.PL   girls   had   had.lunch
           'All the girls had had lunch.'
        b. Todos/*todas   os   meninos   tinham   almoçado.
           all.MASC.PL/all.FEM.PL   the.MASC.PL   boys   had   had.lunch
           'All the boys had had lunch.'

(38)   *German*
        a. Der   Peter   gefällt   *alle/allen   diesen   Mädchen.
           the.NOM   Peter   pleases   all.NOM/all.DAT   these.DAT   girls
           'All these girls like Peter.'
        b. Alle/*Allen   diese   Mädchen   mögen   den   Peter.
           all.NOM/all.DAT   these.NOM   girls   like   the.ACC   Peter
           'All these girls like Peter.'

Thus, if this analysis of floating quantifiers is on the right track, it provides further support for the PISH, as the stranded (= floating) quantifier can mark the VP-internal position where the subject is generated.

3.2.3.5 VSO order

A variety of languages display the word order indicated in (39) below. An example of this is Irish (Gaelic), a typical verb-initial language.[19]

(39)   finite verb > subject > complement(s)

(40)   *Irish*
        Thóg   sí   teach   dófa   ar   an   Mhullach Dubh.
        raised   she   house   for.them   on   the   Mullaghduff
        'She built a house for them in Mullaghduff.'

---

19 See especially McCloskey (1997) on subjects and subject positions in Irish. (40) is taken from McCloskey (2001: 161).

The PISH provides an easy way of understanding cases like (40). They may be analyzed as in (41), with the finite verb moving to Infl and the subject remaining in situ.

(41) $[_{IP} V_i + Infl [_{VP} SU [t_i OB]]]$

In addition to simple word order, different kinds of data indicate that the structure in (41) is indeed explored by many languages. Let's consider two such cases, starting with negative inversion in some dialects of Black English Vernacular (BEV), as illustrated in (42).[20]

(42)   *Black English Vernacular*
         a. Ain't nothin' happenin'.
         b. Didn't nobody see it.

At first sight, sentences such as the ones in (42) appear to involve movement of the negative auxiliary to C^0, as in auxiliary inversion in the standard dialects. If that were the case, such movement should be blocked if C^0 is phonetically realized. However, there are dialects that appear to allow this inversion even if there is a filled C^0. Labov, Cohen, Robins, and Lewis (1968), for instance, report that examples like (43), which involves a relative clause headed by an overt C^0, are acceptable in these dialects.[21]

(43)   *Black English Vernacular*
         I know a way that can't nobody start a fight.

As illustrated in (44), negative inversion also occurs in relative clauses lacking *that* and in embedded questions, and these are also environments that do not permit movement of auxiliaries in the standard dialects.

(44)   *Black English Vernacular*
         a. It's a reason didn't nobody help him.
         b. I know ain't nobody leaving.

If indeed the negative auxiliary in (42)–(44) has not moved to C^0, the subject must occupy a position higher than the main verb, but lower than the auxiliary in Infl. The PISH provides such a space: the subject in (42)–(44) has remained in [Spec,VP], where it was generated.

---

20 The classic study on BEV, also known as African-American English Vernacular (AAEV), is Labov, Cohen, Robins, and Lewis (1968). The syntactic properties of BEV/AAEV have more recently been investigated by Sells, Rickford, and Wasow (1996) and Green (2002).

21 There is some dispute about the relative acceptability of these sorts of cases with an overt C^0 (see Sells, Rickford, and Wasow 1996).

Consider now imperatives in West Ulster and Derry City English, which we simply call Irish English here.[22] A distinguishing feature of these dialects is that they have an imperative marker *gon* (from *go on*), as illustrated in (45).

(45)   *Irish English*
        Gon make us a cup of tea.

There is a kind of VP ellipsis in these dialects that suggests that *gon* appears in C^0. The ellipsis in (46), for instance, is parallel to the one in (47), which is standardly analyzed as having the auxiliary in C^0.

(46)   *Irish English*
        A: Gon make us a cup of tea.
        B: Gon you.

(47)   A: He made a cup of tea.
        B: Did he?

Assume that this is correct and let's examine (48a) below. If *gon* is in C^0, the verb must be lower than C^0 and the subject must be lower than the verb. This is all consistent with the idea that the subject in these constructions has remained *in situ* and the verb has moved to I^0. Under this view, (48a) is to be represented along the lines of (48b). The fact that weak pronouns can appear to the left of the subject, as illustrated in (49), is a further indication that the subject does not sit in a high position, for weak pronouns are assumed to obligatorily move from their original positions.[23]

(48)   *Irish English*
        a. Gon open you that door.
        b. [$_{CP}$ gon [$_{IP}$ open$_i$ + I^0 [$_{VP}$ you [$_{V'}$ t$_i$ that door]]]]

(49)   *Irish English*
        Gon make us you that cup of tea.

To sum up, the PISH provides the means for us to account for VSO word orders in constructions where the verb has not moved as far as C^0.

---

22 These data are taken from McCloskey (1997); see also Henry (1995) on related properties of the Belfast English dialect.
23 For discussion on the properties of weak (as opposed to strong and/or clitic) pronouns, see among others Cardinaletti and Starke (1999) and Grohmann (2000a), and the material in van Riemsdijk (1999).

3.2.4 Summary

As mentioned in section 2.2.7, GB takes the notion of government as one of its pillars as it is in terms of this notion that the otherwise diverse modules gain a measure of conceptual unity. GB states many different kinds of relations in terms of government and θ-assignment is not exceptional: both internal and external arguments are θ-marked under sisterhood, the core instance of government. However, with the refinement of clausal structure in the late 1980s, θ-marking of the external argument came to require a series of emendations that called into question the idea that government should be the structural configuration underlying θ-marking.

The GB-response to these concerns was the Predicate-Internal Subject Hypothesis. The PISH allowed external arguments to be θ-marked in a local fashion and did so in a way compatible with the finer articulation of Infl as several functional categories (see section 4.3 for discussion). From a minimalist perspective, the PISH was a welcome development within GB in the sense that it only resorted to the relations made available by X'-Theory, namely, Spec-head and head-complement relations, not making use of the notion of government.

The fact that this nice result from a conceptual point of view receives substantial empirical support, as reviewed in section 3.2.3, suggests that we may indeed be better off if we dispense with government, at least as regards Theta Theory (see sections 4.3 and 8.3 for further discussion). Thus, we will henceforth assume the basic idea underlying the PISH, reformulating it as we go along, on the basis of further refinements in the structure of VP that we'll discuss in the next sections.

Exercise 3.2

We have discussed the PISH only with respect to verbal predicates, but the PISH need not be so restricted. The same considerations applied to verbal predicates should be extended to other predicates as well. Bearing this in mind, discuss the structures of the sentences in (i).

    (i)   a. This book seems nice.
          b. The cat is on the mat.
          c. Peter is a linguist.
          d. The students were considered to be smart.
          e. Everything appeared to be in order.
          f. Mary's criticism of John was unfair.

Exercise 3.3

The sentence in (ia) below is ambiguous in that the anaphor *each other* may take either the matrix or the embedded subject for its antecedent; by contrast, (ib) only admits the embedded subject reading for the anaphor (see Huang 1993). Assuming the PISH, explain why the matrix subject reading is not available in (ib).

> (i)   a. They weren't sure which stories about each other the kids read.
>   b. The teachers weren't sure how proud of each other the students were.

Exercise 3.4

Show that the subject of the sentence in (i) is not thematically related to *were* and discuss how this sentence complies with the Coordinate Structure Constraint.

> (i)   The kids were relentless and out of control.

3.3   Ditransitive verbs

3.3.1   The puzzles

Under the assumption that the PISH is correct, let's now consider the structure of constructions involving two internal arguments. At first sight, the VP part of the sentence in (50) could be represented as in (51).[24]

(50)   Mary gave a book to John.

(51)

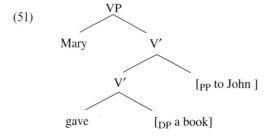

In (51), the distinction between external and internal arguments is maintained: the external argument is generated in [Spec,VP] and the internal arguments are generated in lower projections of V. As for the order

---

24 See Chomsky (1981), for instance.

of merger between the two internal arguments, it could be the case that the theme has a closer relation to the verb than the goal; hence, the verb merges with the theme and the resulting projection merges with the goal.

However, the representation in (51) faces some serious problems upon close inspection. Consider the sentences in (52)–(55), for instance.[25]

(52)   a. I presented/showed Mary to herself.
        b. *I presented/showed herself to Mary.

(53)   a. I gave/sent [every check]$_i$ to its$_i$ owner.
        b. ?? I gave/sent his$_i$ paycheck to [every worker]$_i$.

(54)   a. I sent no presents to any of the children.
        b. *I sent any of the packages to none of the children.

(55)   a. Which check did you send to whom?
        b. *Whom did you send which check to?

Each of the pairs in (52)–(55) illustrates a configuration where c-command is standardly taken to be relevant: in (52), the reflexive must be c-commanded by *Mary* in order to comply with Principle A of Binding Theory; in (53), the pronoun must be c-commanded by the quantifier in order to be interpreted as a bound variable; in (54), the negative polarity item *any* must be c-commanded by the expression headed by the negative quantifier *no/none* in order to be licensed; and in (55), a *wh*-expression cannot move to [Spec,CP] crossing another *wh*-expression that c-commands it, since this would constitute a violation of Superiority or the Minimality Condition (see chapter 5 for discussion).

If the structure of ditransitive constructions is as in (51), the paradigm in (52)–(55) cannot be explained. Leaving aside the external argument for the moment, the first sentence of each pair is abstractly represented in (56) and the second sentence in (57).

(56)

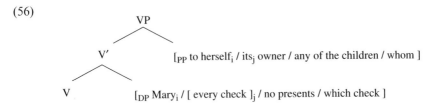

---

25 These data and much of the following discussion are taken from Larson (1988: 338). For relevant discussion, see, e.g., Barss and Lasnik (1986), Larson (1988, 1990), and Jackendoff (1990), as well as Anagnostopoulou (2003) and Beck and Johnson (2004) for more recent perspectives, and Emonds and Ostler (2005) for a succinct overview.

(57)

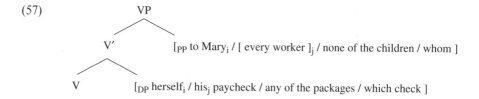

VP

V′   [PP to Mary_i / [every worker]_j / none of the children / whom]

V   [DP herself_i / his_j paycheck / any of the packages / which check]

The reflexive *herself*, the bound pronoun *its/his*, and the negative polarity item *any* are c-commanded by the relevant licenser neither in (56), due to the intervention of V′, nor in (57), due to the intervention of the PP headed by *to*. Hence, the structure in (51) leads to the incorrect prediction that both sentences of the pairs in (52)–(54) should be unacceptable. By the same token, given that neither *wh*-expression c-commands the other in (56) or (57), movement of either *wh*-phrase to [Spec,CP] should satisfy the Superiority/Minimality Condition and both sentences are predicted to be acceptable; again, an undesirable result, as shown in (55).

The contrasts in (52)–(55) can, however, be accounted for, if it is actually the theme DP that c-commands the goal PP within VP, as represented in (58) and (59).

(58)

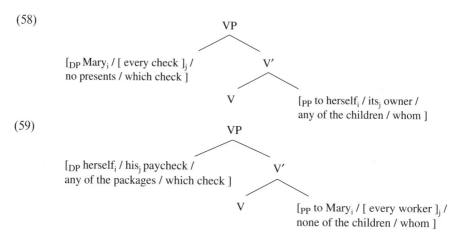

VP

[DP Mary_i / [every check]_j / no presents / which check]   V′

V   [PP to herself_i / its_j owner / any of the children / whom]

(59)

VP

[DP herself_i / his_j paycheck / any of the packages / which check]   V′

V   [PP to Mary_i / [every worker]_j / none of the children / whom]

Herself, its/his, and *any* are c-commanded by their relevant licenser in (58), but not in (59), explaining why the first sentence of (52)–(54) is acceptable, whereas the second one isn't. Furthermore, the movement of *which check* in (58) would cross no c-commanding *wh*-phrase, whereas the movement of *whom* in (59) would cross the c-commanding *wh*-expression *which check*, violating Superiority/Minimality; hence, the contrast between (55a) and (55b).

One could conjecture that the structures in (56) and (57) are indeed correct and that the required c-command relations observed in (52)–(55)

are established through movement of the theme DP to some higher position later on in the derivation. However, there is considerable evidence indicating that this is not the case. Take the idiomatic expressions italicized in (60), for example.[26]

(60)   a. Lasorda *sent* his starting pitcher *to the showers.*
        b. Mary *took* Felix *to the cleaners | to task | into consideration.*
        c. Felix *threw* Oscar *to the wolves.*
        d. Max *carries* such behavior *to extremes.*

In each of the sentences in (60), the verb and the complement PP form an apparent discontinuous idiom, skipping the direct object. As discussed in section 3.2.3.1, there are nevertheless strong reasons to believe that idioms must form a constituent (at some point of the derivation). Thus, it must be the case that (at some point in the derivation) the verb and the complement PP in (60) form a constituent that does include the direct object. If this is to be generalized to non-idiomatic ditransitive constructions, the relevant structures involving the two internal arguments of (52)–(55) should indeed be as in (58) and (59), and the one associated with our initial sentence in (50) as in (61).

(61)

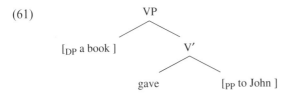

The structure in (61) captures the fact that the theme DP c-commands into the goal, yielding the contrasts in (52)–(55), and makes it possible to analyze the [V PP] idioms in (60) in consonance with our assumption that idioms must form a constituent.

Additional evidence that (61) is on the right track is provided by the interpretation dependency between the DP and the PP. Recall that the interpretation of external arguments in simple transitive constructions is determined by the verb together with the internal argument (see section 3.2.1). Since the DP in (61) is more "external" than the PP, we should in principle expect that the interpretation of the DP may vary, depending on the PP.[27] That this is indeed the case is illustrated by the sentences in

26 These data are taken from Larson (1988: 340).
27 See the discussion in Larson (1988: 340–41).

(62), where *Felix* is affected in a different manner, depending on the contents of the complement PP.

(62)   a. John took Felix to the end of the road.
        b. John took Felix to the end of the argument.
        c. John took Felix to the brink of disaster.
        d. John took Felix to the cleaners.

If the relative hierarchy between the direct and the indirect object is indeed as represented in (61), we now have a problem in conciliating it with the PISH, as shown in (63), where the external argument of (50) is added to the structure in (61).

(63)

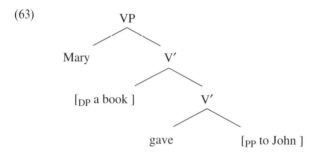

Under the standard assumption that main verbs do not move to I^0 in English (see section 2.3.1.3), after *Mary* raises to [Spec,IP] to check the EPP, we should obtain the structure in (64a), which yields the unacceptable sentence in (64b).

(64)   a. [$_{IP}$ Mary$_i$ [$_{I'}$ I^0 [$_{VP}$ t$_i$ [$_{V'}$ [$_{DP}$ a book] [$_{V'}$ gave [$_{PP}$ to John]]]]]]
        b. *Mary a book gave to John.

The task is thus to come up with a structure that retains all the advantages of the PISH and the partial structure in (61), while at the same time making the correct predictions with respect to the linear order of the constituents. Below we review two approaches to this issue, starting with one proposal developed within GB and then moving to its reinterpretation within minimalism.

3.3.2   *Verbal shells I*
Larson's (1988) solution for the puzzles reviewed above is to assign the VP-structure in (65) below to ditransitive constructions. To illustrate, (50) would receive the structure in (66):

(65)   [$_{VP}$ [external argument] [$_{V'}$ e [$_{VP}$ [direct object] [$_{V'}$ verb [indirect object]]]]]

(66)

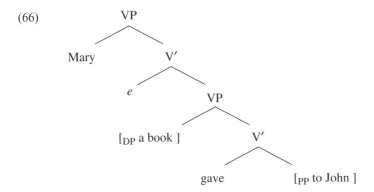

(66) involves two verbal "shells": a shell headed by *gave* and a shell whose head is empty. The empty head is just a place holder in an X'-skeleton and has no independent thematic requirement. By contrast, the verb *gave* in (66) still has to discharge its external θ-role. In order to do so, it then moves to the position of the empty head and assigns the external θ-role to the specifier of the upper VP-shell, as illustrated in (67).

(67)

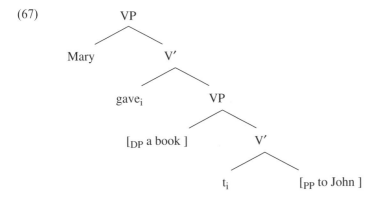

Given the structure in (67), the correct word order is derived after the external argument raises to [Spec,IP], as shown in (68).

(68) $[_{IP}$ Mary$_k$ $[_{I'}$ I^0 $[_{VP}$ t$_k$ $[_{V'}$ gave$_i$ $[_{VP}$ $[_{DP}$ a book $]$ $[_{V'}$ t$_i$ $[_{PP}$ to John $]]]]]]]$

In the next section, we present an alternative account of the higher shell, one that does not invoke an empty V.

3.3.3   Verbal shells II
The analysis presented in section 3.3.2 offers a potential argument against DS as conceived in GB. Notice that not all θ-roles can be assigned at DS;

the external θ-role of a ditransitive construction can only be assigned *after* verb movement proceeds.[28] Although this fits nicely with our discussion of θ-assignment in headless relative clauses and *tough*-constructions (see sections 2.3.2.3 and 2.3.2.5), other aspects of this analysis are undesirable from a minimalist point of view in that they crucially assume some other features of DS. More specifically, it allows empty heads that have no purposes other than holding a position in a single-rooted tree.

If we take the minimalist position that syntactic structures must be ultimately built from lexical items (one of the "big facts" from section 1.3), there is no room for analyses that invoke structures projected from empty heads (heads with no features whatsoever). We are thus back to the problem of conciliating the welcome aspects of the PISH and the partial structure in (61) with surface order.

Building on work by Hale and Keyser (1993), among others, Chomsky (1995) offers an answer to this puzzle by assuming that the upper verbal shell is not projected from an empty head, but from a phonetically null "light" verb v, as represented abstractly in (69) (see (65) for comparison).

(69)   [$_{vP}$ [external argument] [$_{v'}$ v [$_{VP}$ [direct object] [$_{V'}$ verb [indirect object]]]]]

Roughly speaking, a light verb is a verb whose meaning is heavily dependent on the meaning of its complement. As discussed in section 3.2.1, the "taking" in each of the sentences in (70) below, for instance, is rather different. This is due to the fact that *take* in these sentences is a light verb and its meaning hinges on the meaning of *shower* and *nap*. The light verb and its complement may thus be understood as forming a kind of complex predicate.[29]

(70)   a. John took a shower.
        b. John took a nap.

Given the proposal sketched in (69), the VP-structure of the sentence in (50), repeated below in (71a), should then be as in (71b), where the upper verbal shell is headed by a phonologically null light verb.

---

28 See Jackendoff (1990) for relevant discussion.
29 For relevant discussion on light verbs in several languages, see Grimshaw and Mester (1988), Hale and Keyser (1993, 2002), Trask (1993), Baker (1997), Miyamoto (2000), Lin (2001), Baker (2003), and Adger (2004), among many others.

(71)   a. Mary gave a book to John.
        b.

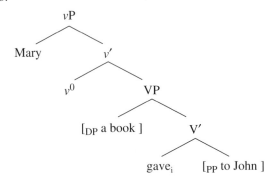

The surface order of (71a) is now obtained if the light verb has a strong V-feature, triggering overt movement of the contentful verb, as shown in (72), followed by movement of the subject to [Spec,IP], as shown in (73).

(72)

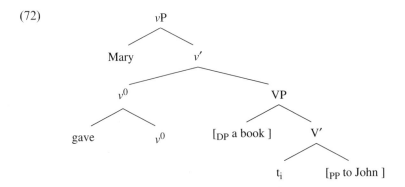

(73)   [$_{IP}$ Mary$_k$ [$_{I'}$ I^0 [$_{vP}$ t$_k$ [$_{v'}$ gave$_i$ + v^0 [$_{VP}$ [$_{DP}$ a book] [$_{V'}$ t$_i$ [$_{PP}$ to John]]]]]]]

Suggestive evidence for this approach is provided by some types of *serial verb* constructions that may be analyzed as involving an overtly realized light verb. Given the double-shell structure in (71b), the order of the constituents of the serial verbs in (74) and (75), for instance, is exactly what we should expect, if the verbs glossed as *take* are light verbs corresponding to *v* in (71b).[30]

---

30 This specific analysis of (74) (from Lefebvre 1991: 55) and (75) was proposed by den Dikken and Sybesma (1998).

(74)   *Fongbè*
        Kòkú **só**   flãsé   hélé   Àsíbá.
        Koku   take   French   teach   Asiba
        'Koku teaches French to Asiba.'

(75)   *Mandarin Chinese*
        Zhangsan **ba**   shu   gei   wo.
        Zhangsan   take   book   give   me
        'Zhangsan gave the book to me.'

To sum up, the verbal shell structure in (69) provides a representation that (i) is compatible with the PISH; (ii) captures the internal/external argument distinction (the external argument is in [Spec, vP], whereas internal arguments are within VP); (iii) accounts for the required c-command relation between the internal arguments; (iv) yields the correct surface order in languages like English, with a phonetically null light verb, and in languages like Fongbè and Mandarin Chinese, with an overtly realized light verb; and (v) is compatible with the idea that phrase structure is built from lexical items, one of the big facts listed in section 1.3 (see section 6.3 on bare phrase structure for further discussion).

Exercise 3.5

The sentence in (ia) below doesn't allow coreference between *him* and *John*, which suggests that the pronoun c-commands *John*, yielding a Principle C effect. However, if the structure of (ia) is along the lines of (ib), no such c-command relation obtains. This is so even if we analyze *to* as a morphological marking of dative Case, rather than a true preposition. Can the appropriate c-command relation be captured under a double verbal shell structure?

(i)   a. It seems to him$_{k/*i}$ that John$_i$ is a fool.
      b. [$_{IP}$ it [$_{VP}$ [$_{V'}$ seems [to him]] [$_{CP}$ that John is a fool]]]

Exercise 3.6

In this section, we have seen evidence for analyzing ditransitive structures in terms of one shell headed by a light verb and another one headed by the contentful verb. Are there reasons to extend this analysis to ditransitive structures involving nominalization? In other words, should the nominal structures in (i) be analyzed in terms of a light noun?

(i)   a. John's gift of a book to Mary
      b. John's donation of money to the church

Exercise 3.7

In addition to regular ditransitive constructions such as (i) below, many languages also allow *double object* constructions such as (ii), where the addressee is realized as a DP – instead of PP – which precedes the theme. Based on the tests discussed in section 3.3.1, determine what the c-command relation is between the two DPs of (ii) and provide a general structure for double object constructions, assuming a double VP-shell in terms of a light verb projection.

(i) a. [Mary gave [$_{DP}$ three books] [$_{PP}$ to her friend]]
     b. [I wrote [$_{DP}$ a letter] [$_{PP}$ to my wife]]

(ii) a. [Mary gave [$_{DP1}$ her friend] [$_{DP2}$ three books]]
     b. [I wrote [$_{DP1}$ my wife] [$_{DP2}$ a letter]]

3.4   PISH revisited

In section 3.3 we saw different kinds of motivation for postulating two verbal shells in ditransitive verb constructions. Furthermore, as discussed in section 3.3.3, the internal/external argument distinction can be nicely captured by placing the external argument in [Spec,*v*P] and the internal arguments within the VP projection. Assuming this to be on the right track, some questions arise with respect to simple transitive constructions, as well as to different types of intransitive structures. This section will address some of these.

3.4.1   *Simple transitive verbs*

Take a sentence like (76) below, for instance. With the above discussion in mind, here are two obvious questions. First, do we have one or two verbal shells? Second, where does the external argument sit?

(76)   TV violence harms children.

There are good reasons to believe that even simple transitive structures such as (76) involve two verbal shells, with the external argument occupying [Spec,*v*P] (at some point in the derivation), as illustrated in (77).[31]

(77)   [$_{vP}$ [TV violence] [$_{v'}$ *v* [$_{VP}$ harms children]]]]

---

31 Hale and Keyser (2002) offer recent discussion of the role of simple transitives for the PISH.

Consider, for instance, the paraphrase of (76) with the light verb *do* in (78) below. The subject in (78) arguably receives the causative θ-role in the specifier of the light verb *do*, as represented in (79). If (76) is to be associated with the structure along the lines of (77), the assignment of the external θ-role in (76) and (78) would then proceed in a uniform fashion. Given the similarity of their meanings, this is a welcome result.

(78)   TV violence does harm to children.

(79)   [$_{vP}$ [TV violence] [$_{v'}$ does [$_{NP}$ harm [$_{PP}$ to children]]]]

Similar considerations apply to the pair of sentences in (80) below. The fact that (80a) entails (80b) suggests that *John* has the same θ-role in both sentences. This is accounted for if *John* in (80) occupies [Spec,*v*P] (at some point of the derivation), regardless of whether the contentful verb is associated with one or two internal arguments.

(80)   a. John threw the ball to Mary.
        b. John threw the ball.

Another conceptual advantage of the double-shell structure for simple transitive constructions is that it provides a plausible explanation for the unexpected relation between accusative Case and external θ-role, which is captured under Burzio's Generalization.[32] According to this generalization, a verb assigns (structural) accusative Case to its object only if it θ-marks its subject. Consider the causative/inchoative pair in (81), for example.

(81)   a. The army sank the ship.
        b. The ship sank.

In (81a), the causative *sink* assigns its external θ-role to *the army* and accusative to *the ship*. In (81b), in contrast, the inchoative *sink* does not assign an external θ-role, and neither does it Case-mark its object; *the ship* must then move to [Spec,IP] in order to be Case-marked. If simple transitive constructions also involve two verbal shells and if the external argument is generated in the specifier of the outer shell, Burzio's Generalization may be interpreted as a statement about the role of the light verb: it is the element responsible for both external θ-role assignment and accusative Case-checking. Thus, the different properties of the causative/inchoative pair in (81) can be appropriately handled if their verbal structures are

32 See Burzio (1986) for the observation and relevant discussion.

analyzed along the lines of (82), with two shells for causatives and one shell for inchoatives.

(82)   a. [$_{\nu P}$ [$_{DP}$ the army] [$_{\nu'}$ ν [$_{VP}$ sank [$_{DP}$ the ship]]]]
        b. [$_{VP}$ sank [$_{DP}$ the ship]]

Independent evidence for distinguishing causative/inchoative pairs in terms of verbal shells is provided by languages where the causative instance must involve a verbal causative marker. In Kannada, for example, the causative version of (83a) requires the causative marker *-is-*, as shown by the contrast between (83b) and (83c).[33]

(83)   *Kannada*

        a. Neer   kud-i-tu.
           water.ACC   boil-PAST-1.S.NEUT
           'The water boiled.'
        b. *Naan-u   neer-annu   kud-id-e.
           I-NOM   water-ACC   boil-PAST-1.S
           'I boiled the water.'
        c. Naan-u   neer-annu   kud-**is**-id-e.
           I-NOM   water-ACC   boil-CAUS-PAST-1.S
           'I boiled the water.'

Given the analysis of (81) in terms of the structures in (82), English and Kannada may receive a uniform account if *-is-* in (83c) is actually an overtly realized light verb, analogous to the phonetically empty ν in (82a).

A related point involves active/passive pairs such as the one illustrated in (84).

(84)   a. John built that house last year.
        b. That house was built (by John) last year.

As is well known, passive constructions are taken to involve a process suppressing accusative assignment and changing the status of the external θ-role by realizing it as an adjunct (the *by*-phrase).[34] If the postulated light verb of simple transitive constructions is the element that assigns both the external θ-role and accusative Case, then it doesn't seem all that strange that a morphological process affecting the light verb can alter both its Case- and θ-properties.

---

33 See Lidz (2003).
34 See Jaeggli (1986) and Baker, Johnson, and Roberts (1989) for relevant discussion within GB.

Finally, there are languages where the phonetic realization of the light verb is not as restricted as in English but is a common way of expressing simple transitive structures, as illustrated by Basque in (85) and by Tibetan in (86).[35]

(85)   *Basque*
        Jonek   Aitorri   min   egin   dio.
        Jon.ERG   Aitor.DAT   hurt   do   AUX
        'Jon hurt Aitor.'

(86)   *Tibetan*
        Thubten-gyis   Lobsang-la   kha   byskal-song.
        Thubten-ERG   Lobsang-LOC   mouth   delivered-PERF
        'Thubten kissed Lobsang.'

Summing up, conceptual and empirical considerations indicate that the double-shell structure proposed to account for ditransitive constructions should be extended to transitive constructions involving a single internal argument, as represented in (87), where X is a cover symbol for lexical categories that can form a complex predicate with the light verb.[36]

(87)

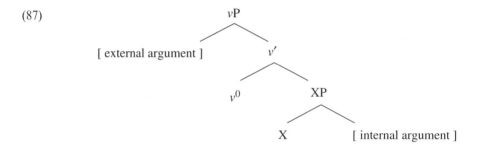

Exercise 3.8

The fact that (ia) may be paraphrased as (ib) suggests that *-en* and *make* are light verbs in these constructions (see Hale and Keyser 1993, 2002 for discussion). Assuming this to be so, provide the relevant structures for these sentences.

(i)   a. John thickened the gravy.
       b. John made the gravy thicker.

---

35 See Uribe-Etxebarria (1989) and Laka (1993) on Basque, and DeLancey (1997) on Tibetan.
36 For relevant discussion, see, e.g., Hale and Keyser (1993, 2002), Baker (1997, 2003), and Marantz (1997).

Exercise 3.9

Using double shells with a light verb, discuss why (ia) can be paraphrased as (ib), but not as (ic) (see Hale and Keyser 1993, 2002 for relevant discussion).

(i)   a. John put the boxes on the shelves.
      b. John shelved the boxes.
      c. John boxed the shelves.

Exercise 3.10

In the text, the fact that (ia) below entails (ib) was interpreted as indicating that the external argument is generated in the same position in both sentences, namely, [Spec,*v*P]. If this reasoning is correct, what does it imply for the position of the direct object in (i) and indirect object in (ii) and (iii)? Provide the relevant structure for all the sentences below and discuss whether or not they are problematic.

(i)   a. John threw the ball to Mary.
      b. John threw the ball.

(ii)   a. This reasoning leads us to a puzzling conclusion.
       b. This reasoning leads to a puzzling conclusion.

(iii)   a. They served wine to the guests.
        b. They served the guests.

Exercise 3.11

In English, the verb *give* may also be used as a light verb, as in *give a kick* for 'kick'. Interestingly, such light verb constructions employ the double object structure (see exercise 3.7), rather than the prepositional ditransitive structure, as illustrated in (i) and (ii) below. Can you think of reasons why this should be so?

(i)   a. John kissed Mary.
      b. John gave Mary a kiss.
      c. #John gave a kiss to Mary.

(ii)   a. I'll try the oysters.
       b. I'll give the oysters a try.
       c. #I'll give a try to the oysters.

3.4.2   *Unaccusative and unergative verbs*

A standard assumption within GB is that monoargumental verbs can be divided into two general types: unergative verbs, whose only argument behaves like the external argument of transitive verbs, and unaccusative verbs, whose only argument behaves like internal arguments.[37]

Consider the paradigms in (88)–(90), for example.[38]

(88)   *Italian*
   a. Giovanni   ha / *è   comprato   un   libro.
      Giovanni   has is   bought   a   book
      'Giovanni bought a book.'
   b. Giovanni   ha / *è   telefonato.
      Giovanni   has is   called
      'Giovanni called.'
   c. Giovanni   è / *ha   arrivato.
      Giovanni   is has   arrived
      'Giovanni arrived.'

(89)   *Portuguese*
   a. A   Maria   comprou   os   livros.
      the   Maria   bought   the   books
      'Maria bought the books.'
   b. Comprados   os   livros, ...
      buy.PART.MASC.PL   the   books
      'After the books were bought, ...'
   c. *Comprada   a   Maria, ...
      buy.PART.FEM.SG   the   Maria
      'After Maria bought (something), ...'
   d. Chegada   a   Maria, ...
      arrive.PART.FEM.SG   the   Maria
      'After Maria arrived, ...'
   e. *Espirrada   a   Maria, ...
      sneeze.PART.FEM.SG   the   Maria
      'After Maria sneezed, ...'

(90)   a. John smiled (a beautiful smile).
      b. John arrived (*an unexpected arrival).

In (88), we see that unergative verbs like *telefonare* 'to call' in Italian pattern like transitive verbs in selecting the auxiliary *avere* 'have', differing from unaccusative verbs like *arrivare* 'to arrive', which select the auxiliary *essere* 'be'. The structures in (89), in turn, show that the argument of unaccusative verbs such as *chegar* 'arrive' in Portuguese behave like the

---

37 See Perlmutter's (1978) influential Unaccusativity Hypothesis. For relevant discussion, see among others Burzio (1986) and Levin and Rappaport-Hovav (1995).
38 See Burzio (1986) on Italian and Eliseu (1984) on Portuguese.

internal argument of transitive verbs in that both can appear in participial temporal clauses, whereas the argument of unergative verbs like *espirrar* 'sneeze' and the external argument of transitive verbs can't. Finally, (90) shows that unergative verbs like *smile* may take a cognate object for a complement, but unaccusative verbs like *arrive* can't.

This distinction between the two classes of verbs has been traditionally accounted for in terms of the structural position where the only argument is generated: it is generated as the specifier of unergative verbs and as the complement of unaccusative verbs, as represented in (91).

(91)   a. Unergative verbs: [$_{VP}$ DP [$_{V'}$ V]]
        b. Unaccusative verbs: [$_{VP}$ V DP]

Hence, only verbs that require a specifier in Italian select for the auxiliary *avere* 'have' (see (88a, b)), only real complements may license participial temporal clauses in Portuguese (see (89b, d)), and unaccusative verbs cannot take cognate objects (see (90b)) because their complement position is already occupied (see 91b)).

Given the discussion about the structural position of external arguments in simple transitive constructions, we can now submit the structures in (91) to closer scrutiny. The first thing to note is that this structural distinction between the two kinds of verbs technically requires the adoption of vacuous projections in the theory. As will be discussed in detail in chapter 6, vacuous projections such as V' in (91a) are suspect from a minimalist perspective, because they alter labeling, but not constituency. It is very plausible to say that after V and DP in (91b) merge, a new constituent is formed, namely, VP. But what constituent does V merge with in (91a) in order to form V'? In other words, the distinction between V and V' in (91a) departs from minimalist guidelines in that it cannot be stated solely in terms of the lexical atoms that feed the computation.

Let's then suppose that the external argument of unergative verbs is generated in the same position as external arguments of transitive verbs, namely [Spec,*v*P], as represented in (92), where *X* is again a cover symbol for lexical heads that can form a complex predicate with *v*.[39]

---

[39] As will be discussed in section 6.3.1, the double status of X in (92) as a minimal and a maximal projection need not resort to vacuous projections.

(92)

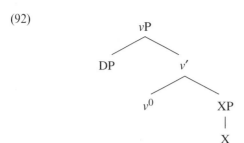

If unergative verbs are associated with a structure along the lines of (92), we can not only represent the unergative/unaccusative distinction and internal/external argument distinction within minimalist conceptual boundaries, but we can also assign a uniform configuration for the external arguments of pairs like the one in (93).

(93)   a. John sighed.
        b. John gave a sigh.

(93a) contains an unergative verb and (93b) a paraphrase with an overt light verb. Under the approach embodied by the representation in (92), *John* is assigned the external θ-role in the specifier of the covert, phonetically empty light verb *v* in (93a) and in the specifier of the overtly expressed light verb *give* in (93b), i.e. [Spec,*v*P] in both cases.

Interesting evidence for this proposal is found in languages like Basque, whose transitive and unergative constructions display an overt light verb, the boldfaced *egin* 'do' in (94)–(95) below, in contrast with unaccusative constructions, as illustrated in (96).[40]

(94)   *Basque* (transitive constructions)
        a. Jonek   Mireni   min   **egin**   dio.
           Jon.ERG   Miren.DAT   hurt   do   AUX
           'Jon hurt Miren.'
        b. Jonek   kandelari   putz   **egin**   dio.
           Jon.ERG   candle.DAT   blow   do   AUX
           'John blew out the candle.'

(95)   *Basque* (unergative constructions)
        a. Emakumeak   barre   **egin**   du.
           woman.DEF.ERG   laugh   do   AUX
           'The woman has laughed.'

---

40 For relevant discussion, see among others Uribe-Etxebarria (1989) and Laka (1993).

    b. Nik   eztul   **egin**   dut.
      I.ERG   cough   do   AUX
      'I have coughed.'

(96)   *Basque* (unaccusative constructions)

    a. Emakumea   erori   da.
      woman.DEF.ABS fallen   AUX
      'The woman has fallen.'

    b. Kamioiak   etorri   dira.
      truck.DET.PL   arrived   AUX
      'The trucks have arrived.'

Summarizing, we have seen conceptual as well as empirical motivation for a reinterpretation of the PISH in the domain of unergative verbs, according to which unergative structures involve a shell headed by a light verb and the external argument is generated in [Spec,vP].

Exercise 3.12

We have seen that with the help of the light verb v, we may account for the distinction between unaccusative and unergative verbs without resorting to vacuous projections. Discuss if we can obtain similar results under the original Larsonian VP-shell approach discussed in section 3.3.2.

Exercise 3.13

We have seen that the verbal structures underlying the sentences in (i) below are different in that *smile* is associated with an extra layer of structure headed by a phonetic empty light verb and such difference would be at the heart of the unergative/unaccusative distinction. Assuming this to be so, what do you have to say about their nominal counterparts in (ii)? Does the unergative/unaccusative distinction hold in (ii), as well? If so, how can it be structurally captured?

(i)   a. John smiled.
      b. John arrived.

(ii)   a. John's smile
      b. John's arrival

3.5   Conclusion

We have surveyed a range of data that support the view that external arguments are generated in a position lower than [Spec,IP] and that this fits well with the assumption favored by minimalist considerations that the

θ-position of arguments should be within the projections of the heads to which they are thematically related (the PISH). After taking a closer look at ditransitive constructions, we have been led to the conclusion that in the verbal domain, the PISH should be interpreted in terms of verbal shells. More specifically, the external argument of ditransitive, simple transitive and unergative constructions is generated in the specifier of a projection headed by a light verb, whereas internal arguments are generated within the shell structure headed by the contentful verb.

Recall that one of our motivations for exploring the PISH was the desire to remove government from the basic inventory of grammatical relations. We have shown how to do without government by adopting the PISH. The fact that there is considerable evidence supporting the PISH on empirical grounds shows that the methodological advantages of "going minimalist" are, in this instance, also empirically advantageous. It is always pleasant when methodological and empirical considerations dovetail in this way.

4 *Case domains*

4.1 Introduction

As we saw in section 2.3.1.1, one of the substantive principles that defines
S-Structure as a syntactic level of representation within GB is the Case
Filter. The idea that Case Theory should apply at SS is based on (i) the
empirical fact that DPs may have different phonetic shape depending on the
type of Case they bear, as illustrated in (1) below; (ii) empirical contrasts
such as the one in (2), which indicates that the chain $CH = (OP_i, t_i)$ must
have Case at LF (presumably to satisfy the Visibility Condition) despite its
lack of phonetic content; and (iii) the technical assumption that DPs are
not inherently specified with respect to Case at DS.

(1) $[_{IP}$ he$_{NOM}$ $[_{I'}$ I^0 $[_{vP}$ t admires him$_{ACC}$]]]

(2)   a. I met the man [OP$_i$ that Mary believed t$_i$ to be a genius]
       b. *I met the man [OP$_i$ that it was believed t$_i$ to be a genius]

If DPs acquire Case-specification after DS but before they are shipped
to the PF and LF components, it makes sense to take SS as the appropriate
level to filter out Caseless DPs. Under this view, the subject pronoun in
(1), for example, satisfies the Case Filter at SS after moving from its base
position to [Spec,IP] and receiving nominative Case from I^0; thus, it
complies with the Visibility Condition at LF and is phonetically realized
as *he*, and not as *him* or *his*.

This technical implementation of Case Theory in terms of Case-
assignment therefore requires the postulation of a non-interface level.
Section 2.3.1.1 presented a proposal outlined in Chomsky and Lasnik
(1993) and Chomsky (1993), which offers an alternative implementation
that accounts for the facts that standard Case Theory is designed to
explain, but does not rely on SS. The proposal is that lexical items
(including functional heads) enter the derivation with their features
already specified, and the system determines whether a given expression

X is licit in a given derivation by checking the features of X against the features of an appropriate head. From this perspective, *he* in (1) enters the derivation specified as bearing nominative Case and moves to [Spec,IP] to be checked against the finite I^0, which by assumption can only check nominative Case. If the subject in (1) were the genitive pronoun *his*, for instance, it would not have its Case-feature checked by I^0 and an ungrammatical result would obtain.

Given that both technical implementations of Case Theory reviewed above account for the core set of facts and that neither implementation is obviously conceptually better than the other, minimalist considerations led us in section 2.3.1.1 to choose the version of Case Theory stated in terms of checking, for it requires no non-interface level of representation. We will see in section 4.4 below that, when some complex paradigms are considered, the implementation of Case Theory in terms of checking is to be preferred on empirical grounds as well.

Assuming the checking approach, we now turn to a reevaluation of the structural configurations under which Case-checking can take place. Within GB, Case is assigned under government. This is not surprising, given that government is a unifying relation among the several modules of the GB-model (see section 2.2.7). However, as mentioned in sections 1.3 and 3.2.1, under minimalist considerations government is far from ideal. Recall that one of the "big facts" about language is that it is made up of phrases, elements larger than words and smaller than sentences (cf. F_4 in section 1.3). The center of any phrase is its head and a given syntactic constituent can be integrated into a phrase in basically two manners: it can be the complement or the specifier of the head of the phrase. Thus, one of our big facts already brings in its train two proprietary relations. From a minimalist perspective, this raises the question of why also postulate a third one (government), given that we already have two relations "for free," as it were.

In chapter 3, we examined the configurations for the establishment of θ-relations and reached the conclusion that in this domain, the head-complement and Spec-head relations are sufficient and there is no need to resort to government. At first sight, this welcome conclusion cannot be extended to Case-considerations, for Case-licensing appears to involve non-local relations in some instances, as in ECM-configurations, for example. We will see below that appearances here may also be misleading and that we can concoct an alternative that not only does not rely on government, but is also empirically more adequate.

We start by reviewing in section 4.2 the core configurations for Case-assignment within GB.[1] We then present an alternative approach based on Spec-head configurations in section 4.3, discuss some empirical consequences in section 4.4, and conclude in section 4.5.

On to the details!

4.2   Configurations for Case-assignment within GB

Within GB, the canonical configuration of government involves sisterhood (i.e. mutual c-command), as stated in (3).

(3)   *Government*
       α governs β iff
       (i) α c-commands β and
       (ii) β c-commands α.

Thus, verbs and prepositions typically assign Case to the DPs they are sisters of, as illustrated in (4):

(4)   a. [$_{VP}$ V DP]
           └──┘$_{ACC}$

       b. [$_{PP}$ P DP]
           └──┘$_{OBL}$

In addition to the head-complement configuration, Case-assignment may also take place under the Spec-head configuration, as illustrated in (5), where a finite Infl assigns nominative to the pronoun and the possessive determiner *'s* assigns genitive to *John*.

(5)   a. [$_{IP}$ he [$_{I'}$ I$_{FIN}$ VP]]
           └────┘ NOM

       b. [$_{DP}$ John [$_{D'}$'s NP]]
           └─────┘ GEN

The fact that a single relation (Case-licensing) should require two distinct structural configurations already intrigued researchers within the GB-model. It was actually proposed that the two configurations illustrated

---

1 See Webelhuth (1995a) for an overview of Case Theory which puts it into perspective regarding both pre-GB conceptions of Case-assignment (Chomsky 1970) and an early minimalist approach (Chomsky 1993).

in (4) and (5) should be unified under the refined notion of government as defined in (6) below.[2] Under such a definition, both the complement and the specifier of a head H m-command and are m-commanded by H (they are all dominated by the same maximal projections); hence, H governs both its complement and its specifier. Put in different terms, the Spec-head relation is treated as a sub-case of government.

(6)   *Government*
       α governs β iff
       (i) α m-commands β and
       (ii) β m-commands α.

(7)   *M-Command*
       α m-commands β iff
       (i) α does not dominate β;
       (ii) β does not dominate α;
       (iii) every maximal projection dominating α also dominates β; and
       (iv) α does not equal β.

Notice that the configurations in (4) and (5) already exploit the kinds of phrasal relations that come for free from the applications of the structure-building operation Merge (see section 2.3.2.1). Thus, from a minimalist perspective, the unification in (6), which incorporates a new relation (namely, m-command in (7)) into the theory, should be postulated only if demanded by empirical considerations.

Leaving this point in the back of our minds, let's now consider some instances of "exceptional" Case-marking (ECM), as illustrated in the (simplified) representations of (8).

(8)   a. [John [$_{VP}$ expects [$_{IP}$ her to win]]]
       b. [[$_{CP}$ for [$_{IP}$ him to leave]] would be terrible]

In (8a), *her* is Case-marked by the ECM-verb *expect* and in (8b), *him* is Case-marked by the complementizer *for*. Thus, if *expect* is passivized and therefore loses its Case-assigning powers, or if *for* is deleted, we get unacceptable sentences, as shown in (9) below. The problem that the constructions in (8) pose is that they cannot be handled by the basic head-complement and Spec-head relations: each pronoun in (8) occupies the specifier of an infinitival IP and therefore is neither the complement nor the specifier of its Case-assigner. An approach in terms of the notion of

---

2 Aoun and Sportiche (1983) first approached government in terms of m-command.

government given in (6) fares equally badly; since the pronouns and their Case-markers are not dominated by the same maximal projections (IP dominates the pronouns but not their Case-makers), *expects* does not govern *her* in (8a), neither does *for* govern *him* in (8b).

(9)   a. *[it was [$_{VP}$ expected [$_{IP}$ her to win]]]
       b. *[[$_{CP}$ him to leave] would be terrible]

GB attempts to get around this problem by reformulating the definition of government in terms of barriers, essentially along the lines of (10) and (11).[3]

(10)   *Government*
        α governs β iff
        (i) α m-commands β and
        (ii) there is no barrier γ that dominates β but does not dominate α.

(11)   *Barrier*
        α is a barrier iff
        (i) α is a maximal projection and
        (ii) α is not a complement.

According to (11), neither the IP in (8a) nor the IP in (8b) is a barrier for the pronoun in its specifier because it is a complement (of the verb in (8a) and of the preposition in (8b)). Hence, *expects* and *for* govern and may assign Case to the pronoun in [Spec,IP].

However, this move, even if successful, makes the unification somewhat suspect in minimalist terms. First, it extends beyond the purely local phrasal relations that come cost-free from a conceptual point of view; second, the notion of government in (10) is not particularly natural in the sense that it covers a motley of configurations, rather than a natural grouping; and, finally, yet another theoretical primitive (the notion of barrier) is being incorporated into the grammar.

To sum up. In the best of all possible worlds, we should make do with what is independently required. Given that the existence of phrases is one of the big facts about human languages, the relations that phrases exploit are conceptually required. The minimal theory of grammar should then make do with these phrasal relations and no more. However, it seems that exceptional Case-marking can't fit in this simpler picture and this is why GB resorted to the additional notion of government in its account of Case relations. These

---

3 The definition of government in (10) was first stated in Chomsky (1986a: 9), with a much more complex definition of a barrier.

considerations invite us to reanalyze Case Theory to see whether a minimalist alternative account might be workable that is conceptually superior to the GB analysis. Let's see what sort of story we might piece together.

4.3   A unified Spec-head approach to Case Theory

As seen in section 4.2, the GB-approach to Case takes head-complement as the paradigmatic configuration for Case-marking. In fact, government may be conceived of as a generalization of the basic verb-object relation so as to cover all the relevant empirical cases. We've suggested that this way of proceeding has several conceptual drawbacks and that we should look for another Case-configuration. Recall that two relations come for free, minimalistically speaking. Once the generalization of the head-complement relation faces conceptual problems, we are left with the Spec-head relation as the only "best" alternative. The question then is what we need to assume in order to implement a theory in which every type of structural Case is checked in a Spec-head configuration. Or putting this another way: let's assume that every type of structural Case is checked in the same manner nominative Case is; what sorts of assumptions must we then make to implement such an approach?

We will explore this approach in the sections below focusing the discussion on the Case-configurations that do not seem amenable to a Spec-head analysis.

4.3.1   *Checking accusative Case under the Split-Infl Hypothesis*
A standard assumption within GB is that clauses are ultimately projections of inflectional material. This is transparently encoded in the representation of clauses given in (12).

(12) $[_{IP} \text{ DP } [_{I'} \text{ I}^0 \text{ VP }]]$

A lot of intense research within GB has been devoted to investigating the nature of Infl and functional categories in general. Infl was first taken to be the head responsible for encoding inflectional information at DS; hence, it was assumed to bear tense/aspect affixes (or abstract features) as well as subject agreement affixes (or abstract features).[4] This could not be the whole story, however. As shown in (13)–(15), there are languages that

---

4 See Chomsky (1981). Some chief protagonists of Infl-related research within GB include Rizzi (1982), Emonds (1985), Kayne (1985, 1989, 1991, 2000), Roberts (1985, 1993),

exhibit object agreement in addition to subject agreement (object agreement is boldfaced).[5]

(13) *Basque*
Gizon-ek eskutitza-k Amaia-ri darama-**zki-o**-te.
man-ERG.PL letter-ABS.PL Amaia-DAT bring-3.PL.ABS-3.SG.DAT-
3.PL.ERG
'The men bring the letters to Amaia.'

(14) *Burushaski*
i:sɛ pfʊt jɛ ma:-r d-**i:**-uʃ-ʌm.
that spirit 1.SG 2.PL-for D-3.SG.MASC-turn.out-1.SG
'I'll turn out that spirit for you.'

(15) *Mohawk*
Sak **shako**-nuhwe'-s ne Uwari.
Sak MASC.SG.SUBJ+FEM.SG.OBJ-like-HAB NE Mary
'Sak likes Mary.'

The existence of agreement patterns such as the ones in (13)–(15) could in fact be easily accommodated in the theory. Once Infl was already associated with verbal inflectional morphology, it should in principle be able to bear object agreement affixes (or abstract features) as well.

Regardless of the exact content of Infl, it became clear in the late 1980s that the IP structure in (12) lacked enough landing positions for movement operations, in particular for different types of verb movement in different languages. Seminal work by Pollock (1989), for example, showed that in French, finite main verbs must precede adverbial expressions such as *à peine* 'hardly' and the negative element *pas* 'not', whereas their corresponding infinitival forms may optionally precede *à peine*, but cannot precede *pas*, as illustrated in (16)–(19).

(16) *French*
a. [V_{FIN} à peine]
b. *[à peine V_{FIN}]
c. [V_{FIN} pas]
d. *[pas V_{FIN}]

Uriagereka (1988), Pollock (1989), Belletti (1990), Chomsky (1991), and Rouveret (1991). For very useful recent reflections, see for example, the paper collection in the three-volume "syntactic cartography" (Cinque 2002, Belletti 2004, and Rizzi 2004) and the material in Baltin and Collins (2001), Bošković and Lasnik (2005), and Lasnik and Uriagereka (2005).

5 *D* in (14) is a gloss for "a verbal prefix which is lexically determined and which regularly precedes prefix agreement" (Holmer 2002: 18, citing the example from Lorimer 1935). *Shako* in (15) is a combined agreement morpheme, that is, it expresses *both* subject and object agreement. Notice that, in addition to subject and direct object agreement, (13) also exhibits agreement with the *indirect* object (see section 5.4.1.3 for more discussion).

(17)   *French*
       a. Pierre   parle   à peine   l'italien.
          Pierre   speaks   hardly   Italian
       b. *Pierre   à peine   parle   l'italien.
          Pierre   hardly   speaks   Italian
          'Pierre hardly speaks Italian.'
       c. Pierre   ne   parle   pas   l'italien.
          Pierre   CL   speaks   not   Italian
       d. *Pierre   ne   pas   parle   l'italien.
          Pierre   CL   not   speaks   Italian
          'Pierre doesn't speak Italian.'

(18)   *French*
       a. [V_{INF} à peine]
       b. [à peine V_{INF}]
       c. *[V_{INF}. pas]
       d. [pas V_{INF}]

(19)   *French*
       a. Parler   à peine   l'italien …
          speak-INF hardly   Italian
       b. À peine   parler   l'italien …
          hardly   speak-INF Italian
          'To hardly speak Italian …'
       c. *Ne   parler   pas   l'italien …
          CL   speak-INF   not   Italian
       d. Ne pas   parler   l'italien …
          CL not   speak-INF   Italian
          'Not to speak Italian …'

Based on facts such as (17) and (19), Pollock argued that in French, finite verbs must move to a position structurally higher than both *pas* and adverbials such as *à peine*, whereas infinitival verbs may optionally move to a position higher than *à peine* but lower than *pas*. He proposed that Infl should actually be split in two heads: a *T* head encoding tense and an *Agr* head responsible for (subject) agreement, with T being structurally higher than Agr, as represented in (20).

(20)   [$_{TP}$ … T … (pas) … [$_{AgrP}$ … Agr (à peine) [$_{VP}$ … V …]]]

Given (20), the facts in (17) and (19) are accounted for if finite verbs in French obligatorily move to T, whereas non-finite verbs optionally move as far as Agr.

Taking into consideration direct object agreement as well as subject agreement, Chomsky (1991) proposed a refinement of the clausal structure in (20), assuming two projections of Agr: *AgrS*, relevant for subject agreement, and *AgrO*, relevant for object agreement, as illustrated in (21).

(21)

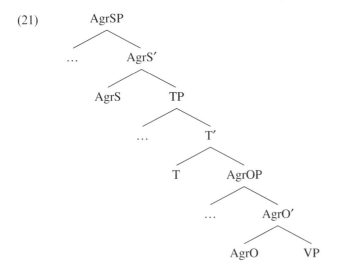

The interesting point for our current discussion is that the structure in (21), which was proposed based on different grounds, has the basic ingredients for a Case Theory that does not resort to government. Consider first how checking of nominative Case proceeds. Let's assume that the general correlation between nominative Case and subject agreement is captured by adjunction of T to AgrS at some point in the derivation (see section 5.4.1 for more detailed discussion). As before, checking of nominative Case and subject agreement may take place under the local Spec-head relation after the subject moves from its VP-internal position to [Spec,AgrSP], as illustrated in (22).

(22) $[_{AgrSP}\; SU_k\; [_{AgrS'}\; T_i + AgrS\; [_{TP}\; t_i \ldots [_{VP}\; t_k \ldots]\,]\,]\,]$

If accusative Case-checking is to parallel nominative Case-checking, the object should not check accusative Case in its base position, but should move to some Spec-position. Assume, then, that at some point in the derivation the verb raises to AgrO just as T raises to AgrS in (22). Now checking of accusative Case and object agreement can also proceed under the Spec-head configuration, as shown in (23).

(23) $[_{AgrOP}$ OB$_k$ $[_{AgrO'}$ V$_i$+AgrO $[_{VP}$ … t$_i$ t$_k$]]]

Recall that we are assuming that lexical items are already inflected upon entering the derivation and that feature-checking must take place *by* LF (see section 2.3.1.1). Thus, whether the configurations in (22) and (23) obtain overtly or covertly is simply a matter of strong or weak features (see section 2.3.1.3). In English, for instance, we may take the configuration in (22) to be established overtly, but the one in (23) to be established covertly (see section 4.4.2 below for further discussion); that is, in English AgrS has a strong D-feature (the EPP), which triggers subject movement before Spell-Out, whereas AgrO has a weak D-feature, which is checked after Spell-Out in compliance with Procrastinate (see section 2.3.1.5).

Putting irrelevant details aside, the LF structure of the sentence in (24a), for instance, should then be as in (24b).

(24)

   a.   He saw her.

   b. $[_{AgrSP}$ he$_s$ $[_{AgrS'}$ T$_i$+AgrS $[_{TP}$ t$_i$ $[_{AgrOP}$ her$_o$ $[_{AgrO'}$ saw$_v$+AgrO $[_{VP}$ t$_s$ $[_{V'}$ t$_v$ t$_o$]]]]]]]]

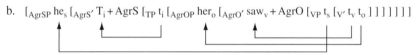

This reasoning extends straightforwardly to ECM-constructions. An example such as (8a), repeated below in (25a), should be associated with the (simplified) LF-structure in (25b).

(25)   a.   John expects her to win.

         b.   LF: [John $[_{AgrOP}$ her$_i$ $[_{AgrO'}$ expects$_v$+AgrO $[_{VP}$ t$_v$ $[_{IP}$ t$_i$ to win]]]]]

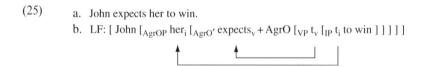

In (25b), the pronoun has moved covertly from the specifier of the infinitival clause to the specifier of the AgrO-projection that dominates the ECM-verb *expects*. After *expects* (covertly) adjoins to AgrO, checking of accusative Case and object agreement may then take place under the local Spec-head relation.

To sum up. Given GB-assumptions about Case-marking, significant complications must be introduced to get government to apply in ECM-constructions. With the revised minimalist assumptions discussed above, no analogous complications arise and so a conceptually satisfying unification of Case domains is achieved. The only apparent cost is the assumption that accusative Case-checking in English possibly involves covert object movement to the Case-checking position (see section 4.4 below for some evidence and further discussion). Notice, however, that covert movement is an option allowed in the system.

This line of reasoning has one interesting consequence. We saw in section 2.3.1.1 that replacing assigning with checking allowed us to dispense with SS. Here we see that to implement an empirically adequate approach to Case-configurations based on the Spec-head relation, we need checking once again. Consider why. Assume for a moment that Case is assigned rather than checked. Then, if *her* in (24a) or (25a) is not in a Case-configuration, it cannot be assigned Case in this position. This means that it must move to the specifier of an appropriate head to get Case. Notice, however, that it is phonetically realized as accusative. The problem is how to assign this Case to the pronoun *prior* to its moving to the appropriate Case-marking position.

The answer is now obvious: the pronoun surfaces with accusative Case because it has this Case-specification as it enters the derivation. In other words, *her* does not get its Case-specification via assignment; rather, the Case with which it enters the derivation is checked against an appropriate head (under a Spec-head relation). Note that such checking can be done at LF with no problems. If the Case the pronoun has does not match the features of V + AgrO, then the derivation crashes; if it does match, all is hunky-dory (see section 2.3.1.1). What checking does here, then, is allow us to get the right overt Case-morphology on the pronoun while still getting it checked in covert syntax. In short, if we assume that in languages such as English the object remains within VP in overt syntax, the unification of Case domains in terms of the cost-free Spec-head relation requires a checking approach to Case Theory (see section 4.4 below for further discussion).

Exercise 4.1

In this section, we have shown how we can account for nominative and accusative Case relations without invoking government, by resorting to the Spec-head relation. Given that c-command is also a relation that seems to be required independently, consider the following alternative approach to Case: a DP enters into a Case relation with the closest Case-bearing head that c-commands it. Describe how this proposal would account for the sentence in (i) below. Is it compatible with a checking or an assignment view of Case? Discuss its potential advantages and disadvantages when compared to the approach based on Spec-head relations.

(i)   She saw him.

4.3.2   *Checking accusative Case under the VP-Shell Hypothesis*

In chapter 3 we discussed several reasons for analyzing transitive construc-tions in terms of two verbal shells, as abstractly represented in (26).

(26)   [$_{vP}$ SU [$_{v'}$ *v* [$_{VP}$ V OB]]]

In (26), the light verb *v* is responsible for external θ-role assignment as well as accusative Case-checking (capturing Burzio's Generalization; see sec-tion 3.4.1), whereas the main verb V is responsible for θ-marking the internal argument.

As we will see in detail in section 5.4.2, this analysis may render the postulation of an AgrO projection unnecessary. Crucially, once we give up on DS and assume that structures are assembled by applications of the operations Merge and Move (see section 2.3.2.1), there should in princi-ple be no limit to the number of Specs a given category can have (see section 6.3 for further discussion). In the case at hand, the light verb in (26) may in principle license another specifier and allow the object to check its Case and object agreement under a Spec-head relation, as shown in (27).

(27)   [$_{vP}$ OB$_o$ [$_{v'}$ SU [$_{v'}$ V$_v$+*v* [$_{VP}$ t$_v$ t$_o$]]]]

In the relevant respects, the configuration in (27) is no different from the configuration in (23), with an AgrO-projection. We postpone the discussion of choosing between (23) and (27) until chapter 5. The important point here is that, under some very plausible assumptions, accusative Case may be checked under a Spec-head configuration even if we have reasons not to postulate AgrO. As before, once we assume that Case-checking must take place by LF (see sections 2.3.2.1 and 4.3.1), whether the configuration in (27) obtains overtly or covertly is a matter of strong features and Procrastinate. The troublemaker ECM-construction in (28a), for instance, can be analyzed without resorting to government if the pronoun in the specifier of the infinitival clause covertly moves to the specifier of the light verb associated with *expects*, as the (simplified) structure in (28b) illustrates.

(28)   a. John expects her to win.

    b. LF: [John$_k$ [$_v$P her$_i$ [v' t$_k$ [v' expects$_v$ + v [$_{VP}$ t$_v$ [t$_i$ to win]]]]]]

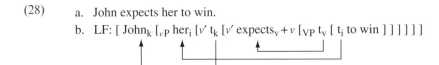

The reader may have observed that in both the AgrO and the light verb approaches to accusative Case-checking, the object moves across (the trace of) the subject in [Spec,VP/vP] and the subject may cross the object in [Spec,AgrOP/vP] in an apparent violation of Rizzi's (1990) Relativized Minimality. In addition, both approaches are tacitly assuming the Extension Condition as stated in (29) below (see section 2.3.2.4), which allows covert object movement to proceed non-cyclically. As noted in section 2.4, this is, however, inconsistent with the Uniformity Condition, for an unmotivated asymmetry between overt and covert syntax is being introduced into the system; this in turn has the unwanted consequence that Spell-Out ends up being treated as a syntactic level of representation.

(29)   *Extension Condition* (preliminary version)
        Overt applications of the operations Merge and Move can only target root syntactic objects.

These problems will be discussed in detail in chapters 5 and 9. For now, the relevant point to bear in mind is that two different hypotheses that were independently advanced within GB, the Split-Infl Hypothesis and the VP-Shell Hypothesis, already contained the essential ingredients for a minimalist analysis of accusative Case-licensing that exploits the cost-free Spec-head relation and dispenses with the non-local notion of government.

Exercise 4.2

Given the analysis of ECM in the text, how should the *for-to* construction in (8b), repeated below in (i), be analyzed?

    (i) [$_{IP}$ [$_{CP}$ for [$_{IP}$ him to leave]] would be terrible]

4.3.3   *Checking oblique Case*

Let us now reconsider the configuration for the assignment of structural oblique Case assumed in GB:

(30)   [$_{PP}$ P DP]

If structural Case-checking always exploits Spec-head configurations, oblique Case should also be checked under a Spec-head configuration, rather than the head-complement configuration in (30).

Suppose, for instance, that we extend the Agr-based approach to oblique Case-checking and assume that there is an Agr-projection dominating PP in (30). If so, oblique Case could then be checked under a Spec-head configuration after the preposition adjoins to Agr^0 and the oblique DP moves to [Spec,AgrP], as illustrated in (31).

(31) $[_{AgrP} DP_k [_{Agr'} P_i + Agr [_{PP} t_i t_k]]]$

Similarly to accusative Case-checking, whether the configuration (31) obtains before or after Spell-Out depends on the feature strength of the Agr-head. In English, for instance, Agr should have weak features and the movements displayed in (31) should take place in the covert component, in compliance with Procrastinate.

Two facts suggest that an approach along these lines may indeed be on the right track. The first one is that there are languages in which postpositions exhibit overt agreement, as exemplified in (32) for Hungarian.[6]

(32)   *Hungarian*
        a. én-mögött-**em**
           I-behind-POSS.1.SG
        b. te-mögött-**ed**
           you-behind-POSS.2.SG
        c. mi-mögött-**ünk**
           we-behind-POSS.1.PL
        d. ti-mögött-**etek**
           you-behind-POSS.2.PL
           'behind me / you (SG) / us / you (PL)'

The existence of agreement between the postpositions and the DP they select in (32) is no surprise if we assume that oblique Case-checking takes place in a configuration along the lines of (31).

More importantly, there seems to be a correlation between triggering agreement and being a preposition or postposition. As observed by Kayne (1994: 49, citing Ken Hale, p.c.), agreement in adpositional phrases is generally found in languages that employ postpositions, but not in

6 These data were provided by Anikó Lipták (personal communication).

languages that employ prepositions. This correlation mimics what we may encounter with respect to subject agreement. In Standard Arabic, for instance, subject-verb orders trigger "full" agreement, that is, the verb agrees with the subject in all ϕ-features (gender, number, person); by contrast, in verb-subject orders agreement for number is not triggered, as illustrated in (33).[7]

(33) *Standard Arabic*
    a. ?al-?awlaad-u   naamuu.
       the-children-NOM   slept.3.PL.MASC
    b. Naama   l-?awlaad-u.
       slept-3.SG.MASC the-children-NOM
       'The children slept.'

Assuming that the different word orders in (33) depend on whether or not the subject moves overtly to [Spec,IP/AgrSP], as represented in (34) (see section 3.2.3.), what the contrasting patterns of both standard subject agreement and agreement within adpositional phrases appear to indicate is that richness of morphological agreement depends on whether or not the Spec-head configuration is established overtly or covertly: full agreement if (34a) is established overtly and partial agreement if it is established covertly.

(34)   a. $[_{IP}\ SU_k\ V_i + I^0\ [_{VP}\ t_k\ [_{V'}\ t_i \ldots]]]$
        b. $[_{IP}\ V_i + I^0\ [_{VP}\ SU\ [_{V'}\ t_i \ldots]]]$

In the case of agreement in adpositional phrases, overt agreement may take place if the structural configuration in (31) is obtained overtly, that is, if we are dealing with postpositions rather than prepositions. This correlation is clearly seen in languages such as Hungarian, where the P-DP order is allowed only with adpositions that never admit agreement,[8] as illustrated in (35) and (36).

(35) *Hungarian*
    a. én-mögött-em
       I-behind-POSS.1.SG

---

7 Actually, the standard description is that in VS order only gender agreement obtains. See among others Mohammad (1990), Aoun, Benmamoun, and Sportiche (1994), and Ouhalla (1994).

8 The observation is due to Marácz (1989: 362). See Kayne (1994: 140, n. 43) for its interpretation under the LCA and section 7.4 for further discussion. For a recent discussion of Hungarian PPs, see É. Kiss (2002).

126 *Understanding Minimalism*

b. *mögött-em   én
   behind-POSS.1.SG   *I*
   'behind me'

(36)   *Hungarian*
a. *a   hídon   át
   the   bridge.SUP   *over*
b. át   a   hídon
   over   the   bridge.SUP
   'over the bridge'

A similar pattern is also found with the preposition *mesmo* 'even' in Portuguese. When it precedes its argument, it necessarily surfaces without agreement, as illustrated in (37a). When it follows its argument, then it may agree in gender and number, as shown in (37b).

(37)   *Portuguese*
a. Mesmo   as   meninas   criticaram   o   professor.
   even   the   girls   criticized   the   teacher
b. As   meninas   mesmas   criticaram   o   professor.
   the   girls   even.FEM.PL   criticized   the   teacher
   'Even the girls criticized the teacher.'

To summarize, if we assume that oblique Case-checking must also take place in a Spec-head configuration, we not only regularize the set of configurations for structural Case-checking but may also capture an interesting correlation between agreement within adpositional phrases and the order between the head of the adpositional phrase and the element it selects.

Exercise 4.3

Given the analysis of adpositions in the text, discuss how English expressions such as *thereafter, therein, thereabout, hereon, herewith, hereof*, etc. should be analyzed and how they might have arisen.

Exercise 4.4

In many languages, "active" and "passive" participles differ in that only the latter carry (obligatory) agreement features, as illustrated by the Portuguese pair in (i) below. Given the correlation between overt agreement morphology and structural configuration discussed in the text, how can the distinctive agreement morphology in (i) be accounted for? Can your answer also account for the agreement pattern in (ii)?

(i)   a. Maria   tinha   regado   as   plantas.
            Maria   *had*   *water.PART*   *the.FEM.PL*   *plant.FEM.PL*
            'Maria had watered the plants.'
      b. As   plantas   foram   regadas.
            the.FEM.PL   *plant.FEM.PL*   *were*   *water.PART.FEM.PL*
            'The plants were watered.'

(ii) As   plantas   tinham   sido   regadas.
       the.FEM.PL   *plant.FEM.PL*   *had*   *be.PART*   *water.PART.FEM.PL*
       'The plants had been watered.'

4.3.4   *PRO and Case Theory*

Once we are exploring an approach to Case Theory that does not rely on the notion of government, some discussion of the so-called *PRO Theorem*, stated in (38), is in place.

(38)   *PRO Theorem*
        PRO must not be governed.

The PRO Theorem follows from (i) the definition of binding domains for Principles A and B of Binding Theory in terms of a governing category (see (39)), which in turn is defined in terms of government (see (40)), and (ii) the specification of PRO as a hybrid category with both anaphoric and pronominal properties (see (41)).[9]

(39)   a. *Principle A*
         An anaphor must be A-bound in its governing category.
      b. *Principle B*
         A pronoun must not be A-bound in its governing category.

(40)   *Governing Category*
        α is a governing category for β iff
        (i) α is the minimal XP that dominates β and
        (ii) α is a governor for β.

(41)   *PROperties*
        PRO: [+ an, + pro]

Given (39) and (41), the only way for PRO to satisfy the contradictory requirements of Principles A and B is to do it vacuously; that is, PRO may

---

9 See, e.g., Haegeman (1994: chap. 5) for detailed presentation of the properties of PRO in GB.

comply with both principles if it does not meet the necessary requirements
for them to apply. If PRO does not have a governing category, for
instance, Principles A and B will be inapplicable; thus, PRO will certainly
comply with them in virtue of not violating them. Given (40), one
way for PRO to lack a governing category is to lack a governor; hence
the PRO Theorem in (38). Finally, once (38) is established, we are led
to the conclusion that PRO cannot be Case-marked either, given
that Case-assignment within GB must take place under government
(section 4.2).

   One of the conceptual problems with this picture is that it tacitly requires
nontrivial complications in the definition of government. For the sake of
discussion, take the definition in (6), repeated below in (42), which, as we
saw in section 4.2, allowed the finite Infl of a structure such as (43) to
govern and assign nominative Case to its Spec.

(42)   *Government*
       α governs β iff
          (i) α m-commands β and
          (ii) β m-commands α.

(43)
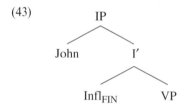

Now, compare (43) with (44), which is the typical configuration where we
find PRO.

(44)
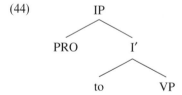

   The *structural configurations* in (43) and (44) are the same; thus, according to (42), the head of each IP should govern its Spec. This would be an
unwelcome result for (44), for PRO would have a governing category (IP)
and would not be able to satisfy both Principles A and B. The GB-solution

is to resort to the feature specification of Infl and say that finite Infl can be a governor, but non-finite Infl cannot.[10] This, however, does not seem to be a natural maneuver. It would be equivalent, for example, to postulating that a constituent X may c-command a constituent Y only if X has a given lexical feature.

Another problem with this picture is that if PRO is not Case-marked, it should violate the Visibility Condition, which requires argument chains to be Case-marked regardless of their phonetic content (see section 2.3.1.1). All things being equal, chains headed by PRO should be assigned Case for the same reasons an argument chain headed by a null operator must be.

This analysis of the distribution of PRO also makes wrong empirical predictions within GB. It predicts, for instance, that PRO should in general be allowed to move from a governed to an ungoverned position. Although this is certainly consistent with (45a), where PRO moves from the position governed by the passive verb to the specifier of the infinitival Infl, that is not the case of (45b), where movement of PRO from the position governed by the preposition should yield a licit result.[11]

(45)   a. [it is rare [PRO$_i$ to be elected t$_i$ in these circumstances]]
         b. *[it is rare [PRO$_i$ to seem to t$_i$ that the problems are insoluble]]

Chomsky and Lasnik (1993) outline an alternative approach to the distribution of PRO that circumvents these problems.[12] The basic idea is that PRO must indeed be Case-marked, but it is lexically specified as requiring *null Case* (a new sub-specification for Cases, on a par with nominative, accusative, etc.). Assuming that non-finite Infl is lexically specified as being able to assign null Case, the distribution of PRO then follows from Case-matching. In other words, Case-mismatch rules out PRO in the specifier of a finite Infl, for instance, in the same way it rules out a genitive pronoun in an accusative position.

---

10 As stated in Chomsky (1981: 50), for example: "INFL governs the sentence subject when it is tensed."
11 For further discussion, see among others Chomsky and Lasnik (1993), the source of (45b) and (46) below, Bouchard (1984), Lasnik (1992a), Chomsky (1993), vanden Wyngaerd (1994), Martin (1996), and Landau (1999); for a different perspective, see Hornstein (1998, 1999, 2001) and Boeckx and Hornstein (2003, 2004).
12 This approach develops ideas first proposed in Bouchard (1984), where the distribution of PRO was tied to Case Theory. Martin (1996, 2001) elaborates on Chomsky and Lasnik's (1993) null Case approach.

Under this approach, PRO is not exceptional with respect to the Visibility Condition and the configuration where PRO is licensed need not invoke lexical features. The contrast in (45), in turn, falls under the generalization that a given element cannot move from a Case-marked position to another Case-marked position (see section 9.3 below), as illustrated in (46) below. In (45a), PRO moves from a Caseless configuration within the passive predicate to [Spec,IP], where it can be licensed with respect to Case Theory. In (45b), on the other hand, PRO occurs in a configuration where oblique Case should be assigned/checked (see section 4.3.3) and cannot move out of it (cf. (46a)); however, if it does not move, the feature incompatibility between its null Case and the oblique Case associated with the preposition causes the derivation to crash.

(46)   a. *[it is rare [for John$_i$ to seem to t$_i$ that the problems are insoluble]]
        b. [it is rare [for it to seem to John that the problems are insoluble]]

Notice that what the account of the distribution of PRO in terms of null Case must abandon is the assumption that PRO is a pronominal anaphor (see (41)). If PRO is governed by *to* in (44), it does have a governing category according to (40), namely, the minimal IP that dominates it. Given that PRO is not bound within IP in (44), PRO must be a pronoun, rather than an anaphor. The anaphoric interpretation of PRO in environments of obligatory control should then be captured not in terms of Principle A, but by some other means, perhaps the control module.

In this work, we cannot enter into a detailed discussion of the distribution and interpretation of PRO from a minimalist perspective.[13] What is crucial from the above discussion is that if PRO is Case-marked, we can maintain the government-free approach to Case Theory sketched in this chapter. More precisely, null Case should be checked like all the Cases we have discussed: under the basic Spec-head relation. This also allows us to take another step in the direction of removing government from UG as it enables us to replace the standard account of the distribution of PRO within GB, which was intrinsically associated with the notion of government (via the PRO theorem), with a Case-based one that exploits Spec-head relations. We have suggested that by relating PRO to null Case, we reach a system that is

13 See, e.g., Hornstein (1998, 1999, 2001, 2003) and Boeckx and Hornstein (2003, 2004).

not only conceptually more elegant, but also empirically more adequate in the sense that it rules out sentences such as (45b).

> **Exercise 4.5**
>
> Contrast the properties of null Case and nominative Case, for instance. What do they have in common and how do they differ?

> **Exercise 4.6**
>
> In GB, the contrast in (i) follows from the assumption that PRO is governed by *seems* in (ia), but is ungoverned in (ib). Given the reanalysis of the distribution of PRO in terms of null Case, how can the contrast in (i) be accounted for?
>
> (i) a. *[it seems [PRO to visit Mary]]
>   b. [John wanted [PRO to visit Mary]]

> **Exercise 4.7**
>
> The unacceptability of (i) below could in principle be simply ascribed to a morphological incompatibility between the null Case of PRO and the oblique Case of the preposition *to*. However, the unacceptability of the sentences in (ii), where *John* is compatible with the Case properties of both the original and the derived position, indicates that a DP can't undergo A-movement from a Case-related position, regardless of feature compatibility. Assuming this to be so, discuss if this prohibition can be better captured under a checking or an assignment approach to Case relations.
>
> (i) *[it is rare [PRO$_i$ to seem to t$_i$ that the problems are insoluble]]
>
> (ii) a. *[it is rare [for John$_i$ to seem to t$_i$ that the problems are insoluble]]
>   b. *[John$_i$ seems [t$_i$ left]]

4.4   Some empirical consequences

In section 4.3 we have done some of the technical legwork necessary to develop an approach to Case Theory that dispenses with government and sticks to the cost-free Spec-head configuration. One consequence of this approach is that DPs check their (structural) Case in a position higher than the position where they are θ-marked. Although this may be no different from nominative and genitive Case-assignment in GB, it does contrast with the standard GB-analysis of accusative and oblique Case-assignment, which takes the Case- and the θ-position to be generally the same.

Consider, for example, the sentence in (47).

(47)   Mary entertained John during his vacation.

Within GB, (47) would be assigned the (simplified) LF structure in (48) below, with the object remaining in its base position. By contrast, under the unified approach to Case Theory in terms of the Spec-head relation outlined in section 4.3, (47) would be assigned one of the (simplified) LF structures in (49), depending whether one resorts to AgrOP or *v*P (see sections 4.3.1 and 4.3.2).

(48)

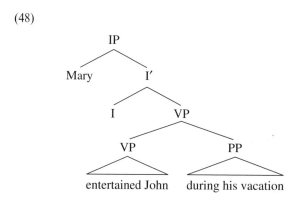

(49)   a.

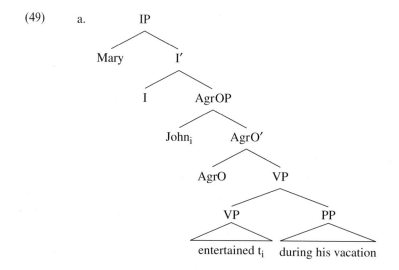

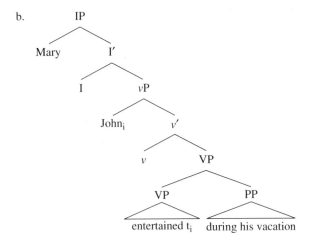

The fact that the object is taken to occupy a different position in each approach has interesting empirical consequences. We discuss two of such consequences in the next sections. For presentation purposes, we will take the AgrO-analysis to be representative of the Spec-head approach and compare it with the standard GB-approach.

4.4.1   *Accusative Case-checking and c-command domains*

The c-command domain of the object with respect to the adjunct PP in (48) and in (49a) is not the same. The object c-commands the material dominated by the PP in (49a), but not in (48); hence, the object may in principle bind into the PP-adjunct in (49a), but not in (48). So, the question is whether objects act as if their binding domains are as wide as expected given a minimalist account or as narrow as expected given a GB-story. Let's examine some concrete cases.

Consider the pair of sentences in (50).

(50)   a. The men entertained Mary during each other's vacations.
       b. *The men's mother entertained Mary during each other's vacations.

The contrast in (50) is a classic illustration of the effects of Principle A of Binding Theory (see (39a)). Given that reciprocals like *each other* require plural antecedents, only *the men* in (50) qualifies as a suitable antecedent. In (50a), *the men* is in the subject position and c-commands into the adjunct; hence, it can bind and license the anaphor *each other*; in (50b), by contrast, *the men* does not c-command – therefore does not bind – the anaphor and the sentence is ruled out by Principle A.

Let's now consider the interesting case in (51).[14]

(51)   Mary entertained the men during each other's vacations.

Here we have a perfectly well-formed sentence, which is understood as establishing an anaphoric link between *the men* and *each other*. Thus, it must be that the reciprocal is indeed bound by *the men* and Principle A is satisfied. What is interesting is that the minimalist approach to Case Theory outlined in section 4.3 has this desirable consequence, while the GB-approach does not. As discussed above, under the GB-approach the object remains in its base position at LF, as represented in (52) below, whereas under the Spec-head approach it moves to a position higher than the adjunct, as illustrated in (53). Hence, *the men* can bind the anaphor in (53), but not in (52). The acceptability of (51) is therefore predicted under the minimalist Spec-head approach, but left unexplained under the standard government-based approach.

(52)

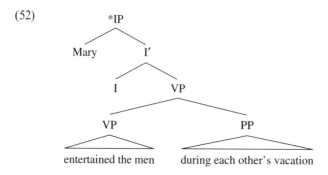

(53)

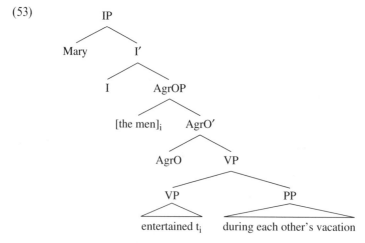

14 See Lasnik and Saito (1991) for original discussion.

The logic indicated above can be extended to the ECM-constructions in (54) in a straightforward manner.[15]

(54)   a. The DA proved the defendants$_i$ to be guilty during each other$_i$'s trials.
        b. *Joan believes him$_i$ to be a genius even more fervently than Bob$_i$'s mother does.
        c. The DA proved none of the defendants to be guilty during any of the trials.

On the GB-story, the embedded subject is Case-marked in the specifier of the infinitival clause, as represented in (55) below. Given (55), the acceptability pattern of the sentences in (54) is unexpected. The reciprocal *each other* in (55a), for instance, is not c-commanded by *the defendants*; hence, the corresponding sentence should be unacceptable, contrary to fact. Similarly, given that *him* and *Bob* in (55b) do not enter into a c-command relation, coindexation between them should be allowed by both Principles B and C, and the sentence in (54b) should be acceptable with the intended meaning, again contrary to fact. Finally, the structure in (55c) also predicts an incorrect result: as a negative polarity item, *any* should be c-commanded by a negative expression and that is not the case in (55c); hence, the sentence in (54c) is incorrectly predicted to be unacceptable.

(55)   a. [the DA [$_{VP}$ [$_{VP}$ proved [$_{IP}$ [the defendants]$_i$ to be guilty]] [$_{PP}$ during [each other]$_i$'s trials]]]
        b. *[Joan [$_{VP}$ [$_{VP}$ believes [$_{IP}$ him$_i$ to be a genius]] [$_{PP}$ even more fervently than Bob$_i$'s mother does]]]
        c. [the DA [$_{VP}$ [$_{VP}$ proved [$_{IP}$ none of the defendants to be guilty]] [$_{PP}$ during any of the trials]]]

By contrast, under the minimalist account sketched in section 4.3, the embedded subject moves (by LF) to a specifier position higher than the matrix VP, as illustrated in (56) below. Thus, the embedded subject actually c-commands the adjunct that modifies the matrix verb and this is what is needed to account for the data in (54). In (56a), *the defendants* binds *each other* in compliance with Principle A; in (56b), *Bob* is c-commanded by and coindexed with *him*, in violation of Principle C; and in (56c) the negative polarity item *any* is appropriately licensed by the c-commanding negative

15 See Postal (1974) for early and Lasnik and Saito (1991), Bošković (1997), and Runner (2005) for more recent discussion. Lasnik (1999) provides a minimalist analysis of ECM in line with the current presentation.

expression *none of the defendants*. Hence, the pattern of acceptability of the sentences in (54).

(56)   a. [... [$_{AgrOP}$ [the defendants]$_i$ [$_{VP}$ [$_{VP}$ proved [$_{IP}$ t$_i$ to be guilty]] [$_{PP}$ during [each other]$_i$'s trials]]]]

b. [... [$_{AgrOP}$ him$_i$ [$_{VP}$ [$_{VP}$ believes [$_{IP}$ t$_i$ to be a genius]] [$_{PP}$ even more fervently than Bob$_i$'s mother does]]]]

c. [... [$_{AgrOP}$ [none of the defendants]$_i$ [$_{VP}$ [$_{VP}$ proved [$_{IP}$ t$_i$ to be guilty]] [$_{PP}$ during any of the trials]]]]

Notice that if the movement of the embedded subject to the matrix [Spec,AgrOP] in (56) takes place in the covert component, as we have been assuming thus far (see section 4.4.2 below for further discussion), we may also take the pattern of acceptability of (54a) and (54b) as confirming independent evidence for the minimalist assumption that Binding Theory cannot apply prior to LF (see section 2.3.1.2). That is, if Principles A and C were checked prior to LF – say, at SS – (54a) would be ruled out by Principle A and (54b) would comply with Principle C. The fact that these are not the wanted results indicates that Binding Theory cannot be computed at a non-interface level such as SS.

The reader might have noted that the minimalist approach further predicts that the sentences in (54) should contrast with those in (57).

(57)   a. The DA proved the defendants$_i$ were guilty during each other$_i$'s trials.

b. Joan believes he$_i$ is a genius even more fervently than Bob$_i$'s mother does.

c. The DA proved none of the defendants were guilty during any of the trials.

If the embedded subjects in (54) move out of the embedded clause for Case-reasons, the ones in (57) should remain in the embedded [Spec,IP], given that they check nominative Case in this position. Thus, it is predicted that (57a) and (57c) should be unacceptable and the coindexation in (57b) should be allowed. Unfortunately, the contrast between the sentences in (54) and (57) is not nearly as sharp as we would like it to be. Of the lot, the contrast between (54b) and (57b) is the sharpest. The other examples contrast subtly. Recall that the relevant contrast in (57a,c) versus (54a,c) is one in which the *during*-phrase modifies the matrix verb *proved*. The reading in which the adjunct modifies the embedded clause is irrelevant as we expect it to be c-commanded by the relevant antecedent. With this proviso firmly in mind, the contrasts in (54) and (57) seem to support the claim that ECM objects are higher than embedded finite clause subjects.

To sum up, it appears that there is some empirical evidence in favor of the minimalist approach to Case Theory in terms of the cost-free Spec-head relation. There are some problems as well. However, the weight of the evidence supports the general thrust of the analysis outlined in section 4.3.

Exercise 4.8

Discuss if the data in (51) and (54) could be accounted for under the proposal suggested in exercise 4.1, according to which a DP establishes a Case relation with the closest c-commanding Case-bearing head.

4.4.2   *Accusative Case-checking and overt object movement*
The argument in section 4.3 assumed that a DP marked with accusative Case moves to its Case-checking position *by LF*. This is consistent with its moving earlier, in overt syntax. There is some interesting evidence that this possibility may indeed be realized. We review some of this here.

Some dialects of English allow the kind of elliptical construction illustrated in (58), which is referred to as *pseudogapping*.[16]

(58)   John ate a bagel and Susan did a knish.

The second conjunct of (58) is understood as 'Susan ate a knish', with *eat* being elided. Similarly, the second conjunct of (59a) and (59b) below reads 'Susan gave a knish to Mary' and 'Susan expected Sam to eat a bagel', respectively. The problem with the sentences in (59) is that if they were derived via deletion of the understood portions along the lines of (60), then deletion would be targeting non-constituents.

(59)   a. John gave a bagel to Mary and Susan did a knish.
         b. John expected Mary to eat a bagel and Susan did Sam.

(60)   a. John gave a bagel to Mary and Susan did give a knish to Mary.
         b. John expected Mary to eat a bagel and Susan did expect Sam to eat a
            bagel.

One could think that the derivations in (60) each involve two applications of deletion, rather than one application of deletion targeting a discontinuous element. If that were so, however, we should in principle expect deletion to apply independently to each of the constituents. In other

---

16 See Lasnik (1995b, 1999), who credits Levin (1978, 1979) for coining the term *pseudo-gapping*, for a brief history of the status of this construction in generative approaches.

words, we would in principle expect a well-formed result if deletion targeted only *give* in (60a) or *expect* in (60b), as shown in (61) below. That this is not the case is indicated by the unacceptability of the sentences in (62).

(61)   a. John gave a bagel to Mary and Susan did give a knish to Sam.
        b. John expected Mary to eat a bagel and Susan did expect Sam to eat a knish.

(62)   a. ??John gave a bagel to Mary and Susan did a knish to Sam.
        b. *John expected Mary to eat a bagel and Susan did Sam to eat a knish.

So the problem stands: how is the deletion in (60) effected if only constituents are manipulated by the grammar? The minimalist approach to Case Theory comes to rescue us from this problem. Let's assume that object movement for purposes of accusative Case-checking may proceed overtly. If so, the simplified structures of the second conjunct in (60) will be along the lines of (63).

(63)   a. [Susan did [$_{AgrOP}$ [a knish]$_i$ [$_{VP}$ give t$_i$ to Sam]]]
        b. [Peter did [$_{AgrOP}$ Sam$_k$ [$_{VP}$ expect t$_i$ to eat a bagel]]]

Given the structures in (63), deletion may then target VP, as shown in (64), and yield the sentences in (60). In other words, raising the object and ECM-subject to their Case position overtly allows us to analyze pseudo-gapping constructions in terms of the standard assumption that deletion can only target syntactic constituents.

(64)   a. [Susan did [$_{AgrOP}$ [a knish]$_i$]]
        b. [Peter did [$_{AgrOP}$ Sam$_k$]]

This analysis of pseudogapping raises the question of why the structures in (63) must trigger deletion and cannot surface as is:

(65)   a. *John gave a bagel to Mary and Susan did a knish give to Sam.
        b. *John expected Mary to eat a bagel and Susan did Sam expect to eat a bagel.

Suppose that verbs in English have some strong feature. By assumption, strong features are indigestible at PF and must be somehow rendered inert in the overt component. In section 2.3.1.3, we have explored the possibility that this is done by overt feature checking. What pseudogapping seems to show is that constituent deletion may also circumvent the indigestibility of strong features. In other words, if the strong feature of the verb in (63) has not been checked, deletion must take place in order for the derivation to converge at PF; hence, the contrast between (60) and (65).[17]

Pushing this idea further, let's assume for a moment that accusative Case in English is always checked overtly and examine what this implies for a simple transitive sentence like (66).

(66)   John ate a bagel.

As (66) plainly shows, the object is not pronounced preverbally. Thus, if *a bagel* has moved out of VP overtly, it must be the case that the verb has also moved overtly (recall that we are assuming that the verb has a strong feature), to a position higher than the position occupied by *a bagel*. Call the relevant projection XP for convenience. The overt structure of (66) must then be something like (67).

(67) $[_{IP}$ John $[_{XP}$ ate$_i$ + X^0 $[_{AgrOP}$ [a bagel $]_k$ $[_{VP}$ t$_i$ t$_k$ $]]]]$

This seems like a lot of movement with no apparent effect. Is there any payoff to doing all of this? Perhaps. Consider the distribution of adverbs. Just where adverbs hang is not entirely clear. However, it is very reasonable to assume that they can hang as low as VP and perhaps as high as I' (at least some of them). The sentences in (68) below also indicate that adverbs should be restricted to being in the same clause as the verbs they modify. Thus, *very sincerely* can be interpreted as modifying *believes* in (68a), but not in (68b).[18]

(68)   a. John very sincerely believes Mary to be the best candidate.
        b. #John believes that Mary very sincerely is the best candidate.

What is interesting for our purposes here is that (69) below seems quite acceptable with the intended modification. The problem is that if *Mary* is in the embedded [Spec,IP], as illustrated in (70), *very sincerely* is not a clause-mate of the verb *believe*; thus, (70) should pattern with (68b) rather than (68a).

(69)   John believes Mary very sincerely to be the best candidate.

(70)   [John believes $[_{IP}$ Mary $[_{I'}$ very sincerely [to be the best candidate $]]]]$

Notice that the problem posed by (69) arises in the GB-account of Case-assignment in ECM-constructions as well as in the Spec-head approach

17 See Lasnik (1999) for this proposal and further discussion.
18 The argument of adverbial modification originally goes back to Postal (1974). See also Koizumi (1993) and Runner (1995), and the overview in Runner (2005) for more recent discussion.

presented in sections 4.3.1 and 4.3.2, where the ECM-subject moves to the relevant accusative Case-checking position only in the covert component. Suppose, however, that accusative Case-checking takes place overtly, as suggested above. The overt structure of (69) should then be parallel to (67), as shown in (71), with both *Mary* and *believes* moving overtly.

(71)   [$_{IP}$ John [$_{XP}$ believes$_i$ + X^0 [$_{AgrOP}$ Mary$_k$ [$_{VP}$ very sincerely [$_{VP}$ t$_i$ [$_{IP}$ t$_k$ to be the best candidate]]]]]]

In (71) *very sincerely* is adjoined to the matrix VP and so can modify *believe*. Thus, on the assumption that accusative Case in English may be checked in overt syntax, the apparently anomalous modificational powers of *very sincerely* in (69) receives a simple account.

Exercise 4.9

Assuming that accusative Case relations are established in the way suggested in this section, discuss whether there are still reasons for preferring Case-checking to Case-assignment.

4.5   Conclusion

This chapter reviewed the configurational assumptions concerning Case-assignment/checking in GB. In addition to the local head-complement and Spec-head relations, GB uses the non-local notion of government in order to unify these two basic relations and to account for some instances of "exceptional" Case-marking. Starting with the assumption that expressions enter the derivation with their Case already specified (see section 2.3.1.1), we presented a minimalist alternative to Case Theory that dispenses with government. More specifically, we have explored the possibility that every structural Case is checked under the cost-free Spec-head configuration. The interesting result is that by doing so, we were able to account not only for the core set of empirical facts concerning structural Case, but also for facts that cannot be easily handled within standard GB-analyses without special provisos. The result is interesting from a minimalist point of view as we were able to expand the empirical coverage, while rejecting government and unifying all Case relations in terms of the methodologically more congenial Spec-head configuration.

5 *Movement and minimality effects*

5.1 Introduction

In chapter 3 we examined the reasoning that points to the conclusion that arguments are θ-marked within a lexical projection. In particular, we discussed several pieces of evidence for the Predicate-Internal Subject Hypothesis (PISH), according to which external arguments are θ-marked within a verbal projection. Under the PISH, *he* in (1), for instance, receives its θ-role when it merges with V′ or v′, depending on whether one assumes a single VP-shell or a double VP-shell involving a light verb v (see section 3.3), as respectively shown in (2).

(1)   He greeted her.

(2)   a. *he* + $_{\text{Merge}}$ [$_{V'}$ greeted her] →
            [$_{VP}$ he [$_{V'}$ greeted her]]
        b. *he* + $_{\text{Merge}}$ [$_{v'}$ v [$_{VP}$ greeted her]] →
            [$_{vP}$ he [$_{v'}$ v [$_{VP}$ greeted her]]]

In chapter 4, in turn, we discussed conceptual and empirical arguments for the proposal that by LF, DPs must uniformly check their structural Case requirements outside the domains where they are θ-marked.[1] More specifically, we discussed two possible scenarios depending on the choice between the theoretical possibilities in (2), as respectively illustrated in the simplified representations in (3).

(3)

a. [$_{\text{AgrSP}}$ he$_i$ [$_{\text{AgrS'}}$ AgrS [$_{\text{TP}}$ T [$_{\text{AgrOP}}$ her$_k$ [$_{\text{AgrO'}}$ AgrO [$_{\text{VP}}$ t$_i$ [$_{V'}$ greeted t$_k$]]]]]]]

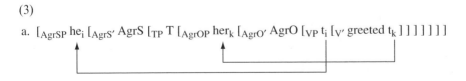

---

1 For a recent formulation of this dichotomy in terms of thematic and agreement or Case *domains*, see Grohmann (2000b, 2003b).

141

b. [$_{TP}$ he$_i$ [$_{T'}$ T [$_{vP}$ her$_k$ [$_{v'}$ t$_i$ [$_{v'}$ *v* [$_{VP}$ greeted t$_k$]]]]]]

Under the single-VP-shell approach sketched in (3a), the subject argument moves to [Spec,AgrSP] at some point in the derivation to check its nominative Case, and the object moves to [Spec,AgrOP] to check its accusative Case. Under the double-VP-shell approach in (3b), on the other hand, the object moves to an outer [Spec,*v*P] to check its accusative Case, whereas the subject moves to [Spec,TP] to have its nominative Case checked.

We'll leave the discussion of the choice between the two approaches sketched above for section 5.4 below. What is relevant for our current purposes is that in both approaches, the subject and the object chains interleave; as (3) shows, the moved object intervenes between the subject and its trace, and the trace of the subject intervenes between the moved object and its trace. However, such interventions go against the standard GB-wisdom that movement is restricted by minimality considerations, which, roughly speaking, prevent a given element from moving across another element of "the same type." Put in different words, the combination of the PISH with the proposal that arguments should uniformly check their structural Case outside the position where they are θ-marked leads to the incorrect prediction that a simple transitive sentence such as (1) should exhibit minimality effects and be unacceptable.

Given the substantial empirical weight that underlies the standard GB-conception of minimality, the task for a minimalist is, therefore, to look for an alternative notion of minimality that will allow movements such as the ones in (3), while still retaining the benefits of standard minimality. This chapter discusses attempts in this direction. We start by briefly reviewing in section 5.2 the core cases minimality was responsible for within GB. In section 5.3, we show in detail how the derivations sketched in (3) are at odds with the standard notion of minimality. Section 5.4 discusses two alternatives: one in terms of a single VP-shell and Agr-projections (cf. (3a)) and the other in terms of a double VP-shell with no Agr-projections (cf. (3b)). Finally, section 5.5 brings some evidence in favor of relativizing minimality in terms of features, rather than projections, and section 5.6 presents a summary of the chapter.

5.2   Relativized minimality within GB

It's a staple of the GB-framework theory that movement is restricted by minimality, along the lines of (4).[2]

(4)   *Relativized Minimality*
         X α-governs Y only if there is no Z such that:
         (i) Z is a typical potential α-governor for Y and
         (ii) Z c-commands Y and does not c-command X.

The intuition behind this version of minimality – where the notion "α-government" covers both head- and antecedent-government – is that movements must be *as short as possible* in the sense that one can't move over a position P that one could have occupied if the element filling P weren't there. Another way of putting this (equally fine for present purposes) is that the move required to meet some demand of a higher projection, e.g. to check Case, a *wh*-feature, or a V-feature, must be met by the closest expression that could in principle meet that requirement. (4ii) specifies that the relevant notion of closeness is defined in terms of c-command: Y is closer to X than Z is iff X c-commands Y and Y c-commands Z, as illustrated in the structure represented in (5) below. Notice that in (5), W and Z don't enter into a c-command relation; hence, neither W nor Z is closer to X than the other is.

(5)

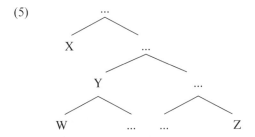

Note that this sort of restriction has the right kind of minimalist "feel." It places a shortness requirement on movement operations and this makes sense in least effort terms in that it reduces (operative) computational complexity by placing a natural bound on feature-checking operations; for example, a DP that needs to check its Case will be unable to do so once a second DP merges above it. In this sense, minimality is a natural sort of condition to place on

2 This definition is taken from Rizzi (1990: 7). See Rizzi (2001), who updates it in terms more congenial to minimalism in that it doesn't resort to government.

grammatical operations like movement (especially when these are seen as motivated by feature-checking requirements).

Moreover, there is interesting empirical support for minimality. Consider the paradigm in (6)–(8), for instance.

(6)   a. [it$_i$ seems [t$_i$ to be likely [that John will win]]]
      b. [John$_i$ seems [t$_i$ to be likely [t$_i$ to win]]]
      c. *[John$_i$ seems [that it is likely [t$_i$ to win]]]

(7)   a. [who$_k$ [t$_k$ wondered [how$_i$ you fixed the car t$_i$]]]
      b. [how$_i$ did you say [t$_i$ John fixed the car t$_i$]]
      c. *[how$_i$ do you wonder [who$_k$ [t$_k$ [fixed the car t$_i$]]]]

(8)   a. [could$_i$ [they t$_i$ [have left]]]
      b. [have$_i$ [they t$_i$ left]]
      c. *[have$_i$ [they could [t$_i$ left]]]

In (6a), the matrix and the most embedded Infl need to check their Case-features and this is done by the expletive *it* and *John*, respectively; the contrast between (6b) and (6c) in turn shows that the most embedded subject may move to check the Case-feature of the matrix clause (A-movement), as long as the expletive doesn't intervene. Similarly, (7) shows that *how* may move to check the strong *wh*-feature of the interrogative complementizer (A'-movement) only if it doesn't cross another *wh*-element on its way. Finally, (8) illustrates the same restriction with respect to head movement: the auxiliary *have* can check the strong V-feature of C^0 only if there is no other auxiliary that is closer to C^0.

In short, minimality seems like a conceptually congenial condition on grammatical operations from a minimalist perspective as it encodes the kind of least effort sentiments that minimalism is exploring. Moreover, there seems to be empirical support for this condition as well, in that it can be used to block unwanted derivations of unacceptable sentences. Let's then assume that minimality should hold in some fashion and reconsider the problem we pointed out in section 5.1.

Exercise 5.1

Icelandic shows a reordering phenomenon in the absence of an overt subject known as Stylistic Fronting, which is illustrated in (ia) and (iia) below (see, e.g., Jónsson 1991 and Holmberg 2000). Given the contrasts in (i) and (ii), can Stylistic Fronting be analyzed in a way compatible with Relativized Minimality?

(i) *Icelandic*

    a. Tekin   hefur   verið   erfið   ákvörðun.
       taken   has   been   difficult decision

    b. *Verið   hefur   tekin   erfið   ákvörðun.
       been   has   taken   difficult decision
       'A difficult decision has been taken.'

(ii) *Icelandic*

    a. Þeir sem skirfað munu hafa verkefnið   á morgun
       those that written will   have assignment.DEF tomorrow

    b. *Þeir sem hafa$_i$ munu skirfað verkefnið   á morgun
       those that have will   written assignment.DEF tomorrow
       'those who will have written the assignment by tomorrow'

Exercise 5.2

The sentences in (i) below show that in Italian, raising across experiencers is possible only if the experiencer is a clitic pronoun (see Rizzi 1986). Can this paradigm be accounted for in terms of Relativized Minimality?

(i) *Italian*

    a. [Gianni$_i$ sembra [t$_i$ essere stanco]]
       Gianni seems   be   tired
       'Gianni seems to be tired.'

    b. *[Gianni$_i$ sembra a Maria [t$_i$ essere stanco]]
       Gianni seems to Maria be   tired
       'Gianni seems to Maria to be tired.'

    c. [Gianni$_i$ gli   sembra [t$_i$ essere stanco]]
       Gianni him(DAT.CL) seems   be   tired
       'Gianni seems to him to be tired.'

Exercise 5.3

In contrast to Italian, English allows raising across full experiencers, as illustrated in (i) below. (ii) in turn suggests that the preposition *to* preceding the experiencer is just a morphological marking of dative Case, for it doesn't prevent the pronoun from c-commanding *John* and inducing a Principle C effect (see section 8.3.1 for further discussion). What kind of assumptions must be made if the Italian data in exercise 5.2 and the English data in (i)–(ii) below are to receive a uniform analysis? Can these assumptions also provide an account of (iii)? Is there any connection between the apparent exceptional violations of Relativized Minimality discussed here and Burzio's Generalization (see section 3.4.1)?

(i) a. [John$_i$ seems [t$_i$ to be ill]]
    b. [John$_i$ seems to Mary [t$_i$ to be ill]]

(ii) [it seems to him$_{k/*i}$ [that John$_i$ is ill]]

(iii) a. [it strikes me [that John is a genius]]
    b. [John$_i$ strikes me [t$_i$ as a genius]]

5.3   The problem

Recall that we came to the conclusion that arguments are uniformly θ-marked within their lexical predicates (see chapter 3) and uniformly check structural Case by moving (overtly or covertly) to positions outside their theta domains (see chapter 4). Let's consider what this entails with respect to minimality by examining in some detail the derivation of the sentence in (1), repeated here in (9), starting with the single-VP-shell approach.

(9)   He greeted her.

For our current purposes, let's ignore head movement and assume that movement of both subject and object takes place overtly so that the Extension Condition (see section 2.3.2.4) is satisfied. Proceeding in a bottom-up fashion in compliance with the Extension Condition, the system builds AgrO′ in (10a) below and the object moves to [Spec,AgrOP] to check accusative Case and object agreement, as show in (10b); the system then builds T′ and the subject moves to [Spec,TP] to check its nominative Case, as seen in (10d), and later to [Spec,AgrSP] to check subject agreement, as shown in (10e).

(10)   a. $[_{\text{AgrO}'}$ AgrO $[_{\text{VP}}$ he $[_{\text{V}'}$ greeted her $]]]$

        b. $[_{\text{AgrOP}}$ her$_i$ $[_{\text{AgrO}'}$ AgrO $[_{\text{VP}}$ he $[_{\text{V}'}$ greeted t$_i$ $]]]]$

        c. $[_{\text{T}'}$ T $[_{\text{AgrOP}}$ her$_i$ $[_{\text{AgrO}'}$ AgrO $[_{\text{VP}}$ he $[_{\text{V}'}$ greeted t$_i$ $]]]]]$

        d. $[_{\text{TP}}$ he$_k$ T $[_{\text{AgrOP}}$ her$_i$ $[_{\text{AgrO}'}$ AgrO $[_{\text{VP}}$ t$_k$ $[_{\text{V}'}$ greeted t$_i$ $]]]]]$

        e. $[_{\text{AgrSP}}$ he$_k$ AgrS $[_{\text{TP}}$ t$_k$ T $[_{\text{AgrOP}}$ her$_i$ $[_{\text{AgrO}'}$ AgrO $[_{\text{VP}}$ t$_k$ $[_{\text{V}'}$ greeted t$_i$ $]]]]]]$

The relevant steps for our discussion are the ones that form (10b) and (10d). In (10b), the object moves to [Spec,AgrOP], crossing the subject in [Spec,VP]. Similarly, in (10d) the subject, on its way to [Spec,TP], crosses the object in [Spec,AgrOP]. Given that [Spec,TP], [Spec,AgrOP], and [Spec,VP] arguably are all A-positions, the movements depicted in (10b) and (10d) violate Relativized Minimality, as defined in (4).

The double VP-shell approach faces a similar problem. After the light vP-shell is assembled in (11a) below, the object moves to an outer [Spec,vP] to check accusative Case and object agreement, skipping the subject in the inner [Spec,vP]. In turn, the subject crosses the object in the outer Spec on its way to [Spec,TP] to check the relevant features. Again, we incorrectly predict that a minimality effect should be observed.

(11)   a. [$_{vP}$ he [$_{v'}$ v [$_{VP}$ greeted her]]]
         b. [$_{vP}$ her$_i$ [$_{v'}$ he [$_{v'}$ v [$_{VP}$ greeted t$_i$]]]]
         c. [$_{T'}$ T [$_{vP}$ her$_i$ [$_{v'}$ he [$_{v'}$ v [$_{VP}$ greeted t$_i$]]]]]
         d. [$_{TP}$ he$_k$ T [$_{vP}$ her$_i$ [$_{v'}$ t$_k$ [$_{v'}$ v [$_{VP}$ greeted t$_i$]]]]]

One could think that in the case of A-movement, Relativized Minimality should hold only for positions in different clauses. With this amendment, movement of *John* over the expletive in a different clause in (6c), repeated below in (12), for instance, would still violate minimality, but the problematic movements in (10b) and (10d) or (11b) and (11d) would not, for only a single clause would be involved.

(12)   *[John$_i$ seems [that it is likely [t$_i$ to win]]]

Things can't be this simple, however. Recall that we are assuming that lexical items are already fully specified in the numeration and have their features checked in the course of the derivation (see the presentation throughout section 2.3.1). Thus, nothing prevents the assembling of the VP in (13) or the vP in (14) (depending on whether one assumes the single- or the double-VP-shell approach), where the internal argument bears nominative Case and the external argument bears accusative Case.

(13)   [$_{VP}$ her [$_{V'}$ greeted he]]

(14)   [$_{vP}$ her [$_{v'}$ v [$_{VP}$ greeted he]]]

If Relativized Minimality did not apply to arguments of the same clause, the computational system should then build the structure in (15) from (13) or the one in (16) from (14), by moving the arguments to their relevant Case-checking position (overtly or covertly).

(15)   [$_{AgrSP}$ he$_k$ AgrS [$_{TP}$ t$_k$ T [$_{AgrOP}$ her$_i$ [$_{AgrO'}$ AgrO [$_{VP}$ t$_i$ [$_{V'}$ greeted t$_k$]]]]]]

(16)   [$_{TP}$ he$_k$ T [$_{vP}$ her$_i$ [$_{v'}$ t$_i$ [$_{v'}$ v [$_{VP}$ greeted t$_k$]]]]]

If the verb in (15) or (16) moves higher than the object (in English or any other language), a sentence like (9) is then derived. In other words, we would incorrectly predict that a sentence like (9) (in English or some other language) should be ambiguous: it should yield the reading 'he greeted her' under the derivation in (10) or (11), and the reading 'she greeted him' under the derivation in (13)/(15) or (14)/(16). Note, incidentally, that the wild derivation in (13)/(15) or (14)/(16) is in a sense even more congenial to the standard notion of minimality. Since the external argument in these derivations never crosses the internal argument, they involve only one violation of minimality, whereas the derivations in (10) or (11) involve two violations each.

So, this is the puzzle we have to solve: figure out a way of allowing the derivation in (10) or (11), while at the same time excluding the derivations in (12), (13)/(15), and (14)/(16). Here's the general game plan. We'll explore attempts to relativize minimality with respect to domains in much the same way Principle B of Binding Theory is treated as holding of certain domains. More specifically, minimality will be relevant for relations between domains, but not for relations within a single domain. Of course, the question is what the relevant notion of *domain* is. This is the topic of the next section. We'll first discuss the issue under the single-VP-shell approach and then under the double-VP-shell hypothesis.

5.4   Minimality and equidistance

Below we explore the hypothesis that categories closely associated with a given head form a "closed" domain (the *minimal domain*), exempt from minimality considerations. But before we jump into the discussion proper, we need a couple of definitions. Two of them are the familiar definitions of containment and domination given in (17) and (18).[3]

(17)   *Containment*
        A category α contains β iff some segment of α dominates β.

(18)   *Domination*
        A category α dominates β iff every segment of α dominates β.

The distinction between containment and domination was introduced to account for relations involving adjunction. In a structure such as (19) below, for instance, where GP is adjoined to XP forming the two-segment category [XP, XP], we say that the category [XP, XP] only contains GP but doesn't dominate it, because not every segment of [XP, XP] dominates GP. On the other hand, [XP, XP] both contains and dominates MP, since every segment of [XP, XP] dominates MP. Furthermore, we may also say that Y is immediately contained by $[X^0, X^0]$, but immediately dominated by X': the immediate (the first) category containing Y is $[X^0, X^0]$ and the immediate (the first) category dominating Y is X'.

---

3 See May (1985) and Chomsky (1986a).

(19)

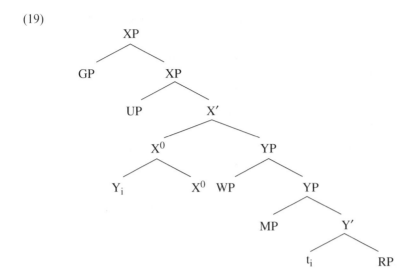

We may now move to the definition of minimal domain in (20) (adapted from Chomsky 1993), which will be crucial for our revision of minimality:[4]

(20)   *Minimal Domain*
         The Minimal Domain of α, or MinD(α), is the set of categories immediately contained or immediately dominated by projections of the head α, excluding projections of α.

The notion of minimal domain given in (20) captures the configurations that may allow the establishment of thematic, checking, or modification relations with projections of a given head. According to (20), MinD([X^0, X^0]) in (19), for instance, is the set comprising [YP, YP] (the complement of X^0), Y (the head adjoined to X^0), UP (the specifier of X^0), GP (the adjunct of XP), and, interestingly, WP (the adjunct of the complement of X^0). Notice that although WP is only immediately contained by [YP, YP], it's immediately dominated by X'; hence, WP also falls within MinD([X^0, X^0]), according to the definition in (20).

Let's finally inspect the relevant domain of the moved head Y in (19) more closely. Before it adjoins to X^0, its MinD is clear: WP, MP, and RP. The question is what happens after Y moves. Recall that within GB, a moved head in a sense preserves the relations it establishes before moving

---

4 The definition of MinD in (20) should remind you of the definition of government in terms of m-command. The idea to be incorporated here is essentially that expressions that m-govern one another are equidistant.

(the Government Transparency Corollary of Baker 1988); thus, a verb that has moved to Infl, for instance, is still able to govern and θ-mark its object at SS and LF, in compliance with the Projection Principle. As a starting point, let's then assume that movement of a head Y extends its MinD, along the lines of (21).

(21)   *Extended Minimal Domain*
The MinD of a chain formed by adjoining the head Y^0 to the head X^0 is the union of $MinD(Y^0)$ and $MinD(X^0)$, excluding projections of Y^0.

According to (21), a moved head may participate in more relations than the ones permitted in its original position. In the case of (19), for instance, $MinD(Y_i, t_i)$ is the set of categories present in $MinD(Y)$, namely, WP, MP, and RP, plus the set of categories of $MinD([X^0, X^0])$ excluding projections of Y (Y', YP), namely, UP and GP. Hence, after Y moves, it may in principle establish syntactic relations with UP and GP as well.

These are all the ingredients we need. Let's then get back to our minimality puzzle.

Exercise 5.4

Given the heads A, D, G, and J in the syntactic object in (i), determine their MinD and extended MinD.

(i)

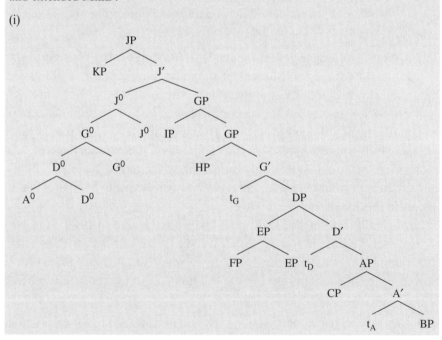

Exercise 5.5

In section 2.3.2.3, we suggested, following Kato and Nunes (1998), that headless relative clauses such as (i) should involve adjunction of the moved *wh*-phrase, as illustrated in (iia), rather than movement to a specifier, as represented in (iib). Given the definition of MinD in (20), explain why this should be so.

(i)   Mary laughs at whoever she looks at.

(ii)   a.   [$_{IP}$ Mary [$_{VP}$ laughs at [$_{CP}$ whoever$_i$ [$_{CP}$ C [$_{IP}$ she looks at t$_i$]]]]]
       b.   [$_{IP}$ Mary [$_{VP}$ laughs at [$_{CP}$ whoever$_i$ [$_{C'}$ C [$_{IP}$ she looks at t$_i$]]]]]

5.4.1   *Minimality and equidistance in an Agr-based system*

Given the definitions of MinD and extended MinD in (20) and (21), the proposal to be entertained here to account for the crossing between external and internal arguments in a simple transitive sentence is that minimality is inert for elements in a given MinD, as stated in (22).[5]

(22)   *Equidistance* (first version)
       Say that α is the target of movement for γ. Then for any β that is in the same MinD as α, α and β are equidistant from γ.

Consider what (22) says by examining the diagram in (23).

(23)

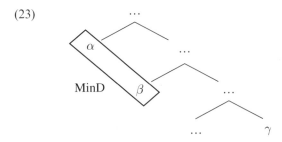

Given that α and β in (23) are in the same MinD, according to (22) none is closer to γ than the other is. In other words, the movement from γ to α doesn't count as longer than the movement from γ to β; hence, β in (23) doesn't induce a minimality effect for the movement from γ to α. In effect, it's as if minimal domains "flatten out" structures, allowing apparent violations of minimality to occur. Crucially, however, minimality comes into play again if the targets of movement are in different MinDs; hence the ungrammaticality of (12), repeated here in (24), where *John* moves to

5 This section is based on Chomsky's (1993) model.

the MinD of the matrix Infl skipping the expletive in the MinD of the intermediate Infl.

(24) $*[_{IP}$ John$_i$ $[_{I'}$ I^0 seems [that $[_{IP}$ it $[_{I'}$ is $+$ I^0 likely [t$_i$ to win]]]]]]

We now turn to the thorny issue of the crossings between subjects and objects.

5.4.1.1   Deriving simple transitive clauses

Let's now consider the details of the derivation of a simple transitive structure such as (25) below under the single VP-shell approach. For purposes of discussion, assume that both subjects and objects move overtly in English.

(25)   He greeted her.

After AgrO′ in (26) below is assembled by successive applications of Merge, the object should move to [Spec,AgrOP] to check accusative Case and object agreement. Suppose it does, as illustrated in (27).

(26) $[_{AgrO'}$ AgrO $[_{VP}$ he $[_{V'}$ greeted her]]]

(27) $[_{AgrOP}$ her $[_{AgrO'}$ AgrO $[_{VP}$ he $[_{V'}$ greeted t$_{her}$]]]]

In (27), *her* crosses *he* and according to the notion of minimality being entertained here, such movement should be licit only if [Spec,AgrOP] and *he* were in the same MinD. However, this is not the case: MinD(*greeted*) is {*he*, t$_{her}$} and MinD(AgrO) is {*her*, VP}. Once [Spec,AgrOP] and *he* are in different MinDs, a minimality effect should then arise as in (24), contrary to fact.

Notice, however, that there is an alternative derivational route starting from (26). Suppose that after AgrO′ is formed, the verb first adjoins to AgrO, as shown in (28a), *before* the object moves to [Spec,AgrOP], as shown in (28b).

(28)   a. $[_{AgrO'}$ greeted$_v$ $+$ AgrO $[_{VP}$ he $[_{V'}$ t$_v$ her]]]
        b. $[_{AgrOP}$ her greeted$_v$ $+$ AgrO $[_{VP}$ he $[_{V'}$ t$_v$ t$_{her}$]]]

According to (21), the extended MinD created by adjunction of *greeted* to AgrO in (28) includes the positions of MinD(*greeted*) before the movement and MinD(AgrO) minus VP, which is a projection of *greeted*. That is, the extended MinD(*greeted*$_v$, t$_v$) in (28b) is {*he*, t$_{her}$, *her*}. Once *he* and the position targeted by the movement of the object ([Spec,AgrOP]) are in the same MinD, both of them are equidistant from the object position, according to the notion of equidistance in (22). Therefore, movement of *her* to

[Spec,AgrOP] in (28b) is not blocked by the intervening subject in [Spec,VP], as desired.

Let's now examine the other potentially problematic case. After T merges with AgrOP, yielding T′ in (29), the subject should move [Spec,TP], crossing the moved object, as shown in (30).

(29)   [$_{T'}$ T [$_{AgrOP}$ her greeted$_v$ + AgrO [$_{VP}$ he [$_{v'}$ t$_v$ t$_{her}$]]]]

(30)   [$_{TP}$ he T [$_{AgrOP}$ her greeted$_v$ + AgrO [$_{VP}$ t$_{he}$ [$_{v'}$ t$_v$ t$_{her}$]]]]

The MinD(T) in (30), namely {*he*, AgrOP}, doesn't include the intervening *her* in [Spec,AgrOP], which belongs to MinD(AgrO) and MinD(*greeted$_v$*, t$_v$), as seen above. Once the target of movement and the intervening element are not in the same MinD, a minimality effect should obtain, contrary to fact.

As before, there is, however, a safe escape hatch. If AgrO in (29) adjoins to T, as shown in (31a) below, AgrO will extend its MinD, permitting the movement of the subject in (31b). That is, given that MinD(AgrO, t$_{AgrO}$) in (31b) is the set {*he, greeted, her*, VP}, the target of movement and the intervening element are equidistant from [Spec,VP] and no minimality arises.

(31)   a. [$_{T'}$ [$_{AgrO}$ greeted$_v$ + AgrO] + T [$_{AgrOP}$ her t$_{AgrO}$ [$_{VP}$ he [$_{v'}$ t$_v$ t$_{her}$]]]]
        b. [$_{TP}$ he [$_{AgrO}$ greeted$_v$ + AgrO] + T [$_{AgrOP}$ her t$_{AgrO}$ [$_{VP}$ t$_{he}$ [$_{v'}$ t$_v$ t$_{her}$]]]]

Finally, let's consider the further movement of the subject to [Spec,AgrSP] in order to check subject agreement, as shown in (32).

(32)   [$_{AgrSP}$ he AgrS [$_{TP}$ t$_{he}$ [$_{AgrO}$ greeted$_v$ + AgrO] + T [$_{AgrOP}$ her t$_{AgrO}$ [$_{VP}$ t$_{he}$ [$_{v'}$ t$_v$ t$_{her}$]]]]]

Notice that in this case there is no A-specifier intervening between [Spec,AgrSP] and [Spec,TP]. Thus, there is no minimality problem that would require raising T to AgrS. Of course, such movement may indeed take place for independent reasons; it simply is not required for the licensing of the movement from [Spec,TP] to [Spec,AgrSP].

Similarly, if the object in English actually doesn't move overtly to [Spec,AgrOP], the subject can move directly to [Spec,TP], even if the verb remains within VP, yielding the structure in (33) below. Once there is no filled A-specifier intervening between [Spec,VP] and [Spec,TP], and between [Spec,TP] and [Spec,AgrSP], each movement of the subject may proceed irrespectively of head movement (which, again, may indeed happen for other reasons).

(33)   [$_{AgrSP}$ he AgrS [$_{TP}$ t$_{he}$ T [$_{AgrOP}$ AgrO [$_{VP}$ t$_{he}$ [$_{V'}$ greeted her]]]]]

If the structure in (33) is the one obtained in English before Spell-Out, object movement to [Spec,AgrOP] in the covert component will, by contrast, necessarily require verb raising to AgrO; otherwise, a minimality violation should arise, induced by the intervening subject trace, as discussed above. After the verb adjoins to AgrO in the covert component, the trace of the subject and [Spec,AgrOP] fall within the extended MinD of the verb, as seen in the discussion of (28b), and the object may move to [Spec,AgrOP] in compliance with minimality.

This correlation between object shift and obligatory verb movement, which came to be known as Holmberg's Generalization, is attested in many languages. In Icelandic, for example, a direct object such as *flessar bækur* 'these books' may move out of VP in (34a), crossing the negation, but not in (34b).[6]

(34)   *Icelandic*
    a. [$_{CP}$ Ígær   las$_i$ ég$_j$ [þessar bækur]$_k$ ekki [$_{VP}$ t$_j$ t$_i$ t$_k$]]
         yesterday read   I   these books   not
       'Yesterday I didn't read these books.'
    b. *[$_{CP}$ Ígær   hefi$_i$ ég$_j$ [þessar bækur]$_k$ ekki [$_{VP}$ t$_j$ lesinn t$_k$]]
         yesterday have   I   these books   not   read
       'Yesterday I haven't read these books.'

The relevant difference between (34a) and (34b) regards movement of the main verb. Given that Icelandic is a V2 language, the main verb in (34a) and the auxiliary in (34b) move all the way to C^0. Assuming that object shift in (34) is movement to [Spec,AgrOP], the object is allowed to move out in (34a), because the movement of the verb to AgrO extends its MinD, rendering [Spec,AgrOP] and the intervening subject equidistant from the object position, as in (28b). In (34b), on the other hand, the participial verb remains *in situ*; therefore, [Spec,AgrOP] and [Spec,VP] are in different minimal domains and movement of the object across the subject violates minimality, as in (27).

To sum up, the combination of the notions of extended MinD in (21) and equidistance in (22) not only allows the derivation of simple transitive sentences, where the object and the subject cross each other, but also accounts for the correlation between head movement and object shift expressed by Holmberg's Generalization.

---

6 See Holmberg (1986, 1999) and Holmberg and Platzack (1995) for relevant discussion.

Exercise 5.6

Reexamine your answer to exercise 5.1 and discuss how the fact that Icelandic allows overt object shift may provide an account of the contrasts mentioned there in consonance with Relativized Minimality.

Exercise 5.7

Consider the definition of equidistance in (i) below. Does this definition suffice to accommodate the derivation of (ii)? Can this definition account for Holmberg's Generalization on the assumption that the shifted object sits in the accusative Case-marking position?

(i)   *Equidistance* (interim version)
      If α and β are in the same MinD, then α and β are equidistant from a target γ.

(ii) He greeted her.

5.4.1.2   Preventing overgeneration

Let's now return to the potential unwanted derivation of (35) with the meaning 'she greeted him', which would start with the VP in (36), where the external argument bears accusative and the internal argument bears nominative (cf. (13)/(14) above).

(35)   *He greeted her. [*with the intended meaning* 'She greeted him.']

(36)   [$_{VP}$ her [$_{V'}$ greeted he]]

Consider the stage after AgrO' in (37a) below is formed. *He* can't move to [Spec,AgrOP] due to Case incompatibility: *he* needs to check nominative Case and this is an environment of accusative Case-checking. Thus, only *her* can move to [Spec,AgrOP]. Note that such movement doesn't require movement of *greeted* to AgrO, for there is no intervening filled specifier between [Spec,AgrOP] and [Spec,VP]. Since raising the verb doesn't cause any problems, let's assume for concreteness that this happens, as illustrated in (37b), before the movement of the external argument in (37c).

(37)   a. [$_{AgrO'}$ AgrO [$_{VP}$ her [$_{V'}$ greeted he]]]
       b. [$_{AgrO'}$ greeted$_v$ + AgrO [$_{VP}$ her [$_{V'}$ t$_v$ he]]]
       c. [$_{AgrOP}$ her greeted$_v$ + AgrO [$_{VP}$ t$_{her}$ [$_{V'}$ t$_v$ he]]]

Next, T' is assembled, as shown in (38a) below. Suppose *he* moves to [Spec,TP] to check nominative Case, as shown in (38b).

(38)   a. [$_{T'}$ T [$_{AgrOP}$ her greeted$_v$ + AgrO [$_{VP}$ t$_{her}$ [$_{v'}$ t$_v$ he]]]]
       b. [$_{TP}$ he T [$_{AgrOP}$ her greeted$_v$ + AgrO [$_{VP}$ t$_{her}$ [$_{v'}$ t$_v$ t$_{he}$]]]]

Movement of *he* in (38b) crosses the A-specifiers filled by *her* and its trace. According to what we have seen thus far, this would be permitted only if the three Specs ([Spec,TP], [Spec,AgrOP], and [Spec,VP]) fell within the same MinD. But this is not the case, as made explicit in (39); in particular, MinD(*greeted*$_v$, t$_v$) includes [Spec,VP] (*t$_{her}$*) and [Spec,AgrOP] (*her*), but not [Spec,TP] (*he*).

(39)   a. MinD(T) = {*he*, AgrOP}
       b. MinD(*greeted*$_v$, t$_v$) = {*her*, t$_{her}$, t$_{he}$, }
       c. MinD(AgrO) = {*her*, *greeted*, VP}
       d. MinD(*greeted*) = {t$_{her}$, t$_{he}$}

Suppose we try to circumvent this problem by adjoining AgrO to T, before *he* moves, as illustrated in (40).

(40)   a. [$_{T'}$ [$_{AgrO}$ greeted$_v$ + AgrO] + T [$_{AgrOP}$ her t$_{AgrO}$ [$_{VP}$ t$_{her}$ [$_{v'}$ t$_v$ he]]]]
       b. [$_{TP}$ he [$_{AgrO}$ greeted$_v$ + AgrO] + T [$_{AgrOP}$ her t$_{AgrO}$ [$_{VP}$ t$_{her}$ [$_{v'}$ t$_v$ t$_{he}$]]]]

As seen in (41) below, the new minimal domain added to the list in (39) is MinD(AgrO, t$_{AgrO}$), which includes the members of MinD(AgrO) plus the members of MinD(T), excluding projections of AgrO. In (41), we find a MinD that includes [Spec,TP] and [Spec,AgrOP] (cf. (41a)) and a MinD that includes [Spec,AgrOP] and [Spec,VP] (cf. (41c)), but no MinD that includes the *three* Specs. Given that these three A-Specs are not equidistant from the object position, minimality blocks movement of *he* in (40b), as desired.

(41)   a. MinD(AgrO, t$_{AgrO}$) = {*he, her, greeted*, VP}
       b. MinD(T) = {*he*, AgrOP}
       c. MinD(*greeted*$_v$, t$_v$) = {*her*, t$_{her}$, t$_{he}$}
       d. MinD(AgrO) = {*her*, *greeted*, VP}
       e. MinD(*greeted*) = {t$_{her}$, t$_{he}$}

As a final remark, observe that according to the definition of extended minimal domain in (21), repeated below in (42), each instance of X^0 movement creates a new chain with its own minimal domain. Importantly, each successive adjunction doesn't extend the previous chain. In the case at hand, this means that after AgrO adjoins to T in (40a), MinD(AgrO) is extended, but the already extended MinD(*greeted*$_v$, t$_v$) is kept constant. If that were not the case, the three Specs in (40b) would fall within MinD(*greeted*$_v$, t$_v$)

after AgrO moves, and the "wild" derivation sketched above would be incorrectly ruled in. That extended MinDs should be so restricted is in fact a natural assumption. The element that actually moves in (40a), for instance, is AgrO; the adjoined verb is only a free rider.

(42)   *Extended Minimal Domain*
        The MinD of a chain formed by adjoining the head Y^0 to the head X^0 is the union of MinD(Y^0) and MinD(X^0), excluding projections of Y^0.

The notion of equidistance in (22) therefore seems to meet our needs. It relativizes minimality in such a way that it preserves the empirical coverage of the standard GB-account, while permitting subjects and objects to cross each other in the derivation of simple transitive sentences without giving rise to overgeneration.

Exercise 5.8

Assuming the definition of equidistance in exercise 5.7, repeated below in (i), discuss whether it suffices to block the derivation of (ii), starting with the structure in (iii).

   (i)   If α and β are in the same MinD, then α and β are equidistant from a target γ.

   (ii) *He greeted her. [*with the intended meaning* 'She greeted him.']

   (iii) [$_{VP}$ her [$_{V'}$ greeted he]]

5.4.1.3   Residual problems

Despite the considerable success of the approach taking minimality to be relativized with respect to minimal domains reviewed in the previous sections, it faces three related problems. The first one is that it's too restrictive in that it can't properly handle Case-checking involving ditransitive verbs. Let's consider why.

The null hypothesis regarding indirect objects is that their (structural) Case should be checked like the Case of subjects and direct objects, namely, in the Spec of some Agr-projection dominating VP. Evidence that this assumption may be correct is the fact that there are languages that exhibit agreement with indirect objects in addition to agreement with the subject and the direct object. Basque is one of them, as illustrated in (43), where the boldfaced morphemes of the auxiliary are the object agreement markers.[7]

---

7 This example is taken from Albizu (1997).

(43)   *Basque*
Azpisapoek etsaiari   misilak   saldu d-i-**zki-o**-te.
traitors.ERG enemy.DAT missiles.ABS sold PRES-AUX-*3.PL.ABS-*
                                                3.SG.DAT-3.PL.ERG
'The traitors sold the missiles to the enemy.'

Let's assume for purposes of discussion the original Larsonian structure in (44b) below, where the verb has raised from the lower VP-shell in (44a) (see section 3.3.2). Suppose we now try to accommodate the null hypothesis and the agreement pattern illustrated in (43) by adding to our inventory of functional categories the head *AgrIO*, which would be involved in checking indirect object agreement (and possibly dative Case). For concreteness, take AgrIO to be generated between TP and AgrOP, as depicted in the simplified structure in (45), in order to account for the basic word order subject – indirect object – direct object seen in (43).

(44)   a. [$_{VP}$ SU *e* [$_{VP}$ DO V IO]]
       b. [$_{VP}$ SU V [$_{VP}$ DO t$_V$ IO]]

(45)   [$_{AgrSP}$ AgrS [$_{TP}$ T [$_{AgrIOP}$ AgrIO [$_{AgrOP}$ AgrO [$_{VP}$ SU V [$_{VP}$ DO t$_V$ IO]]]]]]

Given the skeleton in (45), there is no derivation that allows the three arguments to check their Case, without violating minimality. Consider the details. There is no problem for the direct object to move to [Spec,AgrOP], skipping the subject in (46) below; after the verb adjoins to AgrO, its extended MinD is the set {DO, SU, t$_{DO}$, IO}, which renders [Spec,AgrOP] and [Spec,VP] equidistant from the position of the direct object, as discussed earlier. The problem arises with the movement of the indirect object. Suppose, for instance, that AgrO adjoins to AgrIO before the indirect object raises, as illustrated in (47).

(46)   [$_{AgrOP}$ DO V + AgrO [$_{VP}$ SU t$_V$ [$_{VP}$ t$_{DO}$ t$_V$ IO]]]

(47)   [$_{AgrIOP}$ IO [$_{AgrO}$ V + AgrO] + AgrIO [$_{AgrOP}$ DO t$_{AgrO}$ [$_{VP}$ SU t$_V$ [$_{VP}$ t$_{DO}$ t$_V$ t$_{IO}$]]]]

In (47), AgrO has its MinD extended so that it becomes the set {IO, V, DO, VP}, but MinD(V, t$_V$) remains constant ({DO, SU, t$_{DO}$, IO}); crucially, it's AgrO – not the verb – that is moving (see section 5.4.1.2). Thus, there is no MinD in (47), whether or not extended, that includes [Spec,AgrIOP] and the intervening specifiers (DO, SU, and t$_{DO}$); hence, movement of the indirect object should yield a minimality violation, contrary to fact.

It should be noted that if we change the order among the functional projections in (45), the same result obtains. Assume, for instance, that AgrIO intervenes between AgrS and TP, as illustrated in (48), which would also derive the canonical word order exemplified in (43).

(48)   [$_{AgrSP}$ AgrS [$_{AgrIOP}$ AgrIO [$_{TP}$ T [$_{AgrOP}$ AgrO [$_{vP}$ SU V [$_{VP}$ DO t_V IO]]]]]]

DO can move to [Spec,AgrOP] after the verb adjoins to AgrO, as shown in (49a) below, and SU can move to [Spec,TP] after AgrO adjoins to T, as shown in (49b). The indirect object, however, can't move to [Spec,AgrIOP] even if T adjoins to AgrIO, as shown in (49c); the target of movement, [Spec,AgrIOP], is within MinD(AgrIO) and MinD(T, t_T), but neither of these MinDs include OB, t_{SU}, and t_{OB} (the intervening specifiers). Again, movement of the indirect object out of VP for Case- and agreement-checking purposes should be blocked, which is an undesirable result.[8] We'll refer to this puzzle as *the three-agreement problem*.

(49)   a. [$_{AgrOP}$ DO V+AgrO [$_{vP}$ SU t_V [$_{VP}$ t_{DO} t_V IO]]]

    b. [$_{TP}$ SU [$_{AgrO}$ V+AgrO]+T [$_{AgrOP}$ DO t_{AgrO} [$_{vP}$ t_{SU} t_V [$_{VP}$ t_{DO} t_V IO]]]]

    c. [$_{AgrIOP}$ IO [$_T$ V+AgrO+T]+AgrIO [$_{TP}$ SU t_T [$_{AgrOP}$ OB t_{AgrO} [$_{vP}$ t_{SU} t_V [$_{VP}$ t_{DO} t_V t_{IO}]]]]]

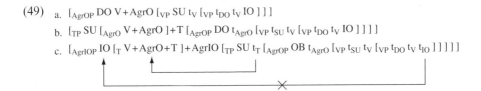

8 It's worth mentioning that languages that allow agreement with subjects, direct objects, and indirect objects in general exhibit person restrictions. Basque, for example, allows instances such as (43), in which all the arguments are third person, but not instances such as (i), where each argument is of a different person. The generalization is that three arguments are allowed as long as the absolutive argument is third person (Albizu 1997, 1998).

(i)   *Basque*
        Zuk   ni   etsaiari   saldu   na-i-o-zu.
        you.ERG   me.ABS   enemy.DAT   sold   1.ABS-AUX-3.DAT-2.ERG
        'You sold me to the enemy.'

Just why these person restrictions exist is not entirely clear – though note that they correlate with what can be observed in Spanish or Catalan clitic clusters, for example, an observation going back to Perlmutter (1971); see also Bonet (1991) for more recent discussion and Ormazabal and Romero (1998) with reference to Basque. One could take them to indicate that special requirements are in play when more than two arguments should leave the predicate and this is what we would expect if there is something problematic about moving so many arguments. However, given that the revised notion of equidistance to be discussed in the next section actually permits movement of three arguments from their θ-positions to their Case positions, we take the morphological restrictions exemplified by the contrast between (43) and (i) not to be directly associated with movement itself.

Another related problem has to do with linear word order. In chapter 7 we'll discuss linearity issues in some detail by examining Kayne's (1994) proposal, according to which all languages are underlyingly head-initial. Under such an approach, SOV order, for instance, is derived from a SVO structure through object movement to the left of the verb. Leaving the specifics of Kayne's proposal for section 7.3, let's assume that it's essentially correct and consider how we can derive SOV word order under the framework reviewed in the previous sections, where minimality is relativized with respect to MinDs.

Given the SVO order in (50a) below, the verb must raise to AgrO, as represented in (50b), in order for the object to move to [Spec,AgrOP], yielding (50c), as discussed earlier. By the same token, movement of the subject to [Spec,TP] requires that AgrO raise first, as shown in (50d–e).

(50)   a. [$_{VP}$ SU [$_{V'}$ V OB]]   (SVO order)
        b. [$_{AgrOP}$ V + AgrO [$_{VP}$ SU [$_{V'}$ t$_V$ OB]]]   (VSO order)
        c. [$_{AgrOP}$ OB V + AgrO [$_{VP}$ SU [$_{V'}$ t$_V$ t$_{OB}$]]]   (OVS order)
        d. [$_{TP}$ [$_{AgrO}$ V + AgrO] + T [$_{AgrOP}$ OB t$_{AgrO}$ [$_{VP}$ SU [$_{V'}$ t$_V$ t$_{OB}$]]]]
                                                                        (VOS order)
        e. [$_{TP}$ SU [$_{AgrO}$ V + AgrO] + T [$_{AgrOP}$ OB t$_{AgrO}$ [$_{VP}$ t$_{SU}$ [$_{V'}$ t$_V$ t$_{OB}$]]]]
                                                                        (SVO order)

The problem with such derivations is that we end up returning to our initial SVO order without ever passing through a stage that could yield SOV order. To put in general terms, if Kayne's universal SVO hypothesis is on the right track and if object movement in (a subset of) SOV languages is A-movement, the notion of equidistance we are exploring prevents the derivation of a structure compatible with SOV word order; crucially, in order for subjects and objects to cross each other, head movement is required to precede the movement of the relevant argument.

Finally, the definition of equidistance in (22), repeated below in (51), also faces a conceptual problem in that it basically stipulates that minimal domains have different properties depending on whether they are computed with respect to potential targets of movement or potential sources of movement.

(51)   *Equidistance* (first version)
        Say that α is the target of movement for γ. Then for any β that is in the same MinD as α, α and β are equidistant from γ.

The reason for this proviso is empirical. Without it, we can't prevent the unwanted derivation of the sentence in (52) below with the meaning 'she greeted him', starting with the VP in (53), with an accusative external argument and a nominative internal argument (see section 5.4.1.2). Consider why. MinD(*greeted*) in (53) is the set involving *her* and *he*. Thus, if elements in the same minimal domain counted as equidistant from any other position in the tree, *he* and *her* would be equidistant from both [Spec,TP] and [Spec,AgrOP]. Hence, *he* could move overtly to [Spec,TP] (and then to [Spec,AgrSP]), as shown in (54a), and the object could move to [Spec,AgrOP] covertly, as shown in (54b), without inducing minimality violations.

(52)   *He greeted her. [*with the intended meaning* 'She greeted him.']

(53)   [$_{VP}$ her [$_{V'}$ greeted he]]

(54)   a. [$_{AgrSP}$ AgrS [$_{TP}$ he T [$_{AgrOP}$ AgrO [$_{VP}$ her greeted t$_{he}$]]]]
         b. [$_{AgrSP}$ AgrS [$_{TP}$ he T [$_{AgrOP}$ her greeted$_V$ + AgrO [$_{VP}$ t$_{her}$ t$_V$ t$_{he}$]]]]

In order to rule out such unwanted result, the definition of equidistance in (51) doesn't take *he* and *her* to be equidistant from [Spec,TP] in (54a), because the position occupied by *he* in (53) is the source of movement and not the target of movement. Clearly, things work as desired. However, a minimalist mind would certainly ask *why* the system should be designed in this way. After all, the simplest – therefore most desirable – notion of equidistance should be valid for both targets and sources of movement. We return to this issue in the next section.

To sum up. Despite its virtues, the notion of equidistance given in (51) still has some room for improvement. In particular, it faces problems with respect to ditransitive predicates and SOV word order, and it stipulates an asymmetry between targets and sources of movement in relation to minimality.

Let's then consider an alternative approach.

5.4.2   Minimality and equidistance in an Agr-less system

The discussion above was rather technical, involving notions like (extended) minimal domains, which in turn serve to define some conception of equidistance able to prevent certain violations of minimality. However, the technicalia should not obscure the larger issue that the technical discussion should subserve. We want to hold three things true: (i) arguments are θ-marked within lexical projections (the PISH); (ii) DPs must check their (structural) Case outside their theta domains; and (iii) some notion of minimality holds to restrict movement operations. We have assumed to this point that the right way of implementing these ideas is in terms of

Agr-projections as defining Case domains. However, this is hardly obvious and, in fact, may well be incorrect, as shown by the three-agreement problem discussed in section 5.4.1.3. In this section we revisit the minimality issues raised in section 5.4.1, exploring an Agr-free system.[9] But before we proceed, let's pause for a while and consider a conceptual reason for doing away with Agr-projections.

Agr-projections have no obvious independent interpretation at the LF or PF interface. As such, their motivation is purely theory-internal. This makes it conceptually suspect for much the same reasons that S-structure is suspect: all things being equal, purely theory-internal entities are to be eschewed unless heavily favored on empirical grounds. This suggests that we should try to make do with functional projections that have some interpretation at the interface, most particularly the LF interface, that is, functional categories such as T, D, or C, but not Agr. The question is: can we do so?

5.4.2.1   Towards eliminating AgrO

With respect to AgrO, it's not particularly difficult to eliminate it and still retain the three desiderata noted above. What is required is that we rethink the structure of transitive clauses a little more closely and realize that they already have the ingredients we need. Take the reinterpretation of a transitive clause in terms of a Larsonian shell headed by a light verb, for instance. As discussed in section 3.4.1, there are several reasons to believe that the structure of a transitive predicate should be along the lines of (55), where the light verb is responsible for assigning the external θ-role (perhaps in conjunction with VP) and checking accusative Case.

(55)   [$_{vP}$ SU [$_{v'}$ v [$_{VP}$ V OB]]]

Given the structure in (55), we may pack the features that we used for checking in AgrO into the light verb and simply dispense with AgrO. Notice that if v can check accusative Case and object agreement, all we need is an adequate configuration for such checking to take place. As discussed in the previous chapters, we should always attempt to make do using just the structural configurations that come for free with the structure-building operations Merge and Move. Under an AgrO-based system, this is achieved by resorting to the Spec-head configuration. Suppose, then, that categories may have more than one specifier (see chapter 6 below for

---

9 This section is based on Chomsky's (1995: chap. 4) model.

discussion). If so, the object in (55) can move to the "outer" [Spec,*v*P] and participate in Case- and agreement-checking relations with the light verb either overtly, as shown in (56), or covertly.[10]

(56)   [$_{v}$P OB [$_{v'}$ SU [$_{v'}$ *v* [$_{VP}$ V t$_{OB}$]]]]

This clearly works and retains the desirable properties of the earlier AgrO-based story in that Case is checked outside the domain in which θ-roles are assigned.[11] It should be emphasized that the alternative sketched above is not simply a matter of terminology, renaming AgrO. The light verb is a "transitivizing" head, involved in the assignment of the external θ-role; in other words, *v*, unlike AgrO, is semantically active and therefore visible at the LF interface (see section 3.4.1).

We are still in need of an account of minimality, for the object in (56) is also moving across the subject. We could, of course, adopt the prior story and allow V to raise to the light verb, extending its MinD and rendering the two specifiers of *v*P in (56) equidistant from the object position. But we may do even better, completely dispensing with the notion of extended MinDs. The crucial difference under this approach to verbal shells is that the external and the internal arguments in (55) don't share the same MinD. This apparently small difference, which is independently motivated in terms of Theta Theory, has very interesting consequences. It not only allows subjects and objects to cross each other without overgeneration, but it considerably simplifies the theoretical apparatus discussed in section 5.4.1, by permitting the elimination of the notion of extended MinD and the removal of the stipulation in the definition of equidistance concerning targets of movement. Equidistance may now be simplified along the lines of (57).

(57)   *Equidistance* (final version)
         If two positions α and β are in the same MinD, they are equidistant from any other position.

Let's see the details. Given that both OB and SU are in MinD(*v*) in (56), they are equidistant from t$_{OB}$; hence, the object is allowed to cross the subject without violating minimality. Later, the subject moves to [Spec,TP] crossing OB, as shown in (58).

10 The notation in (56) should not mislead the reader: the object is not adjoined to *v*′, but sits in the outer Spec of *v*P. In section 6.3, we'll reexamine traditional X′-Theory and discuss a notation that makes the appropriate distinctions in instances such as (56).
11 Recall that from its moved position, the object may c-command into adjuncts previously adjoined to VP or *v*P, as discussed in section 4.4.1.

(58)   [$_{TP}$ SU T [$_{vP}$ OB [$_{v'}$ t$_{SU}$ [$_{v'}$ *v* [$_{VP}$ V t$_{OB}$]]]]]

Under the general definition of equidistance in (57), as the two Specs of *v*P in (58) are in MinD(*v*), they are equidistant from both targets *and sources* of movement. The subject can therefore cross the object in (58) without yielding a minimality effect, as desired.

Notice that the simplification of the notion of equidistance in (57) doesn't lead to overgeneration. Our usual suspect, the sentence in (59) below with the meaning 'she greeted him', is ruled out in a trivial manner. Given the structure in (60a), the external argument can move to the outer [Spec,*v*P] in order to check its Case outside its θ-position without any problems. By contrast, the internal argument crosses the two Specs of *v*P on its way to [Spec,TP] and they are neither in the MinD of the target of movement ([Spec,TP]) nor in the MinD of the source of the movement (the position occupied by t$_{he}$); hence, the movement depicted in (60c) is correctly ruled out by minimality.

(59)   *He greeted her. [*with the intended meaning* 'She greeted him.']

(60)   a. [$_{vP}$ her [$_{v'}$ *v* [$_{VP}$ V he]]]

        b. [$_{vP}$ her [$_{v'}$ t$_{her}$ [$_{v'}$ *v* [$_{VP}$ V he]]]]

        c. [$_{TP}$ he T [$_{vP}$ her [$_{v'}$ t$_{her}$ [$_{v'}$ *v* [$_{VP}$ V t$_{he}$]]]]]

Schematically, the effects of the absolute notion of equidistance in (58) can be illustrated as in (61), assuming that the relevant positions are of the same type.

(61)

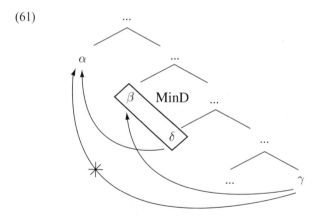

Given that β and δ in (61) are in the same MinD, neither of them induces minimality blocking with respect to the other. Hence, γ may move to the position of β, skipping δ, and δ may move to the position occupied by α, crossing β. By contrast, γ can't move directly to the position occupied by α: since the crossed elements are not in the same MinD as the target or the source of movement, they do induce minimality violations.

Consider now how this approach handles the three-agreement problem. Recall that under the Agr-based story, it was not obviously possible to derive ditransitive structures, due to minimality. Under the Agr-free approach, the simplified notion of equidistance in (57) allows for the relevant movements without the postulation of nontrivial provisos. The main difference between simple transitive and ditransitive structures on this story regards the number of features the light verb can check. All we have to say is that the light verb in ditransitive structures can also check (structural) dative Case and indirect object agreement. If so, the derivation of a sentence involving a ditransitive predicate where all the arguments move overtly, for instance, proceeds along the lines of (62).

(62)　　a. $[_{vP}$ SU $[_{v'} v$ $[_{VP}$ DO V IO $]]]$

　　　　b. $[_{vP}$ DO $[_{v'}$ SU $[_{v'} v$ $[_{VP} t_{DO}$ V IO $]]]]$

　　　　c. $[_{vP}$ IO $[_{v'}$ DO $[_{v'}$ SU $[_{v'} v$ $[_{VP} t_{DO}$ V t_{IO} $]]]]]$

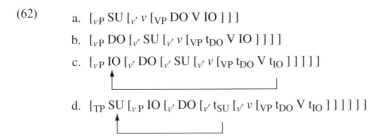

　　　　d. $[_{TP}$ SU $[_{vP}$ IO $[_{v'}$ DO $[_{v'} t_{SU}$ $[_{v'} v$ $[_{VP} t_{DO}$ V t_{IO} $]]]]]]$

In (62b) the direct object moves to the outer [Spec,vP], crossing the subject; since the two Specs of vP are in MinD(v), they are equidistant from t_{DO} and minimality is respected. In (62c), the indirect object moves to the outmost [Spec,vP] to check Case and agreement, crossing three Specs: [Spec,VP] and the two inner Specs of vP. Given that t_{DO} is in the same MinD as the source of the movement (the position occupied by t_{IO}), it doesn't induce a minimality blocking; DO and SU, in turn, are in the same MinD as the target of the movement (the outmost [Spec,vP]) and don't count as intervening either. Finally, the subject moves from its θ-position crossing the two outer Specs of vP; given that the crossed specifiers are in the same MinD as the source of the movement, minimality is again respected.

To put this in general terms, by sticking to projections motivated by interface considerations, we were able to simplify the notion of equidistance and broaden the empirical coverage by accounting for ditransitive structures. And, importantly, the "extralong" movements in (62c) and (62d) are allowed, while the unwanted long movement in (60c) is ruled out.

Assuming that equidistance is to be computed with respect to the source as well as the target of movement may also provide an account for the interesting contrast in (63) below, pointed out in Chomsky (1986a: 38). The pattern in (63) is unexpected, given that extraction of PPs out of *wh*-islands is in general worse than extraction of DPs, as exemplified in (64).

(63)   a. *$[_{CP}$ who$_i$ did you wonder $[_{CP}$ what$_k$ John [gave t$_k$ to t$_i$]]]
        b. ??$[_{CP}$ [to whom]$_i$ did you wonder $[_{CP}$ what$_k$ John [gave t$_k$ t$_i$]]]

(64)   a. ?$[_{CP}$ who$_i$ do you wonder $[_{CP}$ whether John gave a book to t$_i$]]
        b. ??$[_{CP}$ [to whom]$_i$ did you wonder $[_{CP}$ whether John gave a book t$_i$]]

All of the sentences in (63) and (64) are similar in that they involve a violation of minimality as the *wh*-movement to the matrix [Spec,CP] skips the embedded [Spec,CP]. Taking the paradigm in (64) to be the basic one, the reversal of the judgments in (63) is arguably due to crossings within the embedded VP. Let's then consider the lower VP-shell of *gave* in (63), as represented in (65).

(65)   [$_{VP}$ what [$_{V'}$ gave [$_{PP}$ to who(m)]]]

In (65), MinD(*gave*) is {*what*, PP}, whereas MinD(*to*) is {*who(m)*}. Thus, *what* doesn't induce a minimality violation for the movement of the PP, because they are in the same MinD; by contrast, since *what* is not in the same MinD as *who(m)*, it induces an additional minimality violation for the movement of *who(m)* to the matrix [Spec,CP]. The fact that (63a) is worse than (63b) can now be ascribed to the number of minimality violations each derivation involves: one in (63b) and two in (63a).

Exercise 5.9

As the reader can easily check, the analysis outlined above also allows movement of the indirect object to precede the direct object, yielding the order subject – direct object – indirect object. Given that the unmarked order in head-final languages is SU – IO – DO, what can ensure that the direct object moves first?

Exercise 5.10

In section 4.3.3, it was proposed that an element marked with oblique Case should be checked by moving to the specifier of the Agr-projection dominating the adposition it's related to. Given that regular ditransitive constructions in languages like English involve a preposition, as illustrated in (i), discuss whether dative Case in constructions such as (i) should also be analyzed along the lines of the derivation of Basque ditransitive constructions.

(i)   John gave a book to Mary.

What about double object constructions such as (ii) (see exercise 3.7)? How does Mary get its Case checked in (ii)?

(ii)   John gave Mary a book.

5.4.2.2 Towards eliminating AgrS

The approach explored above towards eliminating AgrO can clearly be extended to AgrS as well. In fact, we have been discussing subject movement thus far without resorting to AgrS. To be explicit, let's then assume that the head T, in addition to Case, may also check subject agreement. If so, we seem to have all the checking we need, without postulating a theory-internal projection such as AgrSP. This move actually returns us to the style of functional categories we had prior to Pollock's (1989) suggestion that we segregate each type of feature into its own headed projection.

Before we leave the topic of AgrSP, it should be mentioned that one type of empirical motivation that has been adduced in favor of AgrS, which finds its roots in Pollock's original argumentation, is that AgrS provides positions that are independently required universally or in some languages. In this regard, the so-called transitive expletive constructions, which present an expletive in addition to the regular subject, have become a hot topic. It has been argued that in constructions such as (66) from Icelandic, the expletive sits in [Spec,AgrSP], the subject sits in [Spec,TP], and the verb moves all the way to AgrS, yielding the word order expletive – verb – subject, as illustrated in (67).[12]

(66)   *Icelandic*
       Það   hefur   einhver   étið   hákarlinn.
       EXPL has   someone eaten shark.the
       'Someone has eaten the shark.'

(67)   [$_{AgrSP}$ Það hefur [$_{TP}$ einhver$_i$ t$_V$ [$_{vP}$ t$_i$ t$_V$ [$_{VP}$ t$_V$ étið hákarlinn]]]]

12 The literature on transitive expletive constructions is very rich. For data and relevant discussion, see, e.g., Bobaljik and Jonas (1996), Collins and Thráinsson (1996), Bobaljik and Thráinsson (1998), and Holmberg (2005) (source of (66)) for Icelandic and Zwart (1992) for Dutch.

It should be noted that the line of reasoning pursued here is *not* simply against the postulation of extra functional categories, but rather against categories that can't be motivated in terms of the interface levels. It could be the case, for instance, that the functional category above TP in (67) is indeed visible at LF, but it so happens that our theoretical tools are not yet sharp enough to detect its effects at LF. And, of course, it could also be the case that (66) really represents a departure from optimality and that we are forced to postulate an Agr-projection. As stressed in previous chapters, even the second result would be interesting. It would have shown that even if we started from different assumptions, we would be bound to reach a Pollockian system, with some Agr-projections that are not motivated in terms of the interface levels. The world would definitely not end with such a conclusion. We would then proceed to delimiting these failures of minimalist expectations and study why such failures exist. Given the heated ongoing debate in the literature about the structure and derivation of transitive expletive constructions such as (66), we'll not take side on the issue here and, rather, invite the reader to join the game. For expository purposes, we'll proceed assuming an Infl-system without AgrS.

5.4.2.3   Equidistance and word order

The reader might have noticed that all the relevant crossing discussed above did not require head movement. In other words, by dropping the notion of extended MinD, argument movement came to be dissociated from head movement. In fact, such dissociation may now allow an analysis of SOV languages compatible with Kayne's (1994) proposal that all languages are underlyingly SVO. As illustrated in (68), the SOV order can be cyclically generated without yielding a minimality violation: given that the two Specs of vP are in the same MinD, the object is allowed to cross the subject in (68b) and the subject is allowed to cross the moved object in (68c).

(68)   a. $[_{vP} \text{SU} [_{v'} v [_{VP} \text{V OB}]]]$ (SVO word order)
       b. $[_{vP} \text{OB} [_{v'} \text{SU} [_{v'} v [_{VP} \text{V } t_{OB}]]]]$ (OSV word order)
       c. $[_{TP} \text{SU} [_{T'} \text{T} [_{vP} \text{OB} [_{v'} t_{SU} [_{v'} v [_{VP} \text{V } t_{OB}]]]]]]$ (SOV word order)

The flip side of the coin is that if this approach is on the right track, we are unable to derive Holmberg's Generalization, which, as seen in section 5.4.1.1, ties object movement to verb movement. It's currently uncertain how serious a problem this is, given that the empirical standing of Holmberg's Generalization is somewhat unclear. If it fails to hold, then there is, of course, no problem with shifting to an Agr-less approach. Even if it does hold, it's worth pausing to observe that the Agr-less approach is not incompatible with Holmberg's Generalization; rather, it doesn't explain the correlation. Given the conceptual and empirical virtues of the Agr-less approach discussed above, we'll put further discussion of Holmberg's Generalization aside and proceed under the assumption that the Agr-less approach is indeed tenable.[13]

From this point onwards, we'll employ the clausal structure that arises from (68), that is, without recourse to Agr-projections and with TP as the subject/agreement projection.

Exercise 5.11

In this section, we saw some conceptual reasons for not postulating Agr-projections and discussed an alternative account of nominative, accusative, and dative Case-checking that did not rely on Agr-projections. Can the reasoning explored here also extend to oblique Case-checking? In other words, keeping the assumption that structural Case-checking takes place outside theta domains, how can we check the Case associated with the prepositions *about* and *for* in (i) without postulating an Agr-projection?

(i)   a. I read about it.
      b. For him to do it would be a surprise.

5.5   Relativizing minimality to features

The discussion above has redefined the locality part of Rizzi's (1990) classic Relativized Minimality in (69ii), leaving basically intact the description of the intervening element in (69i). That is, following Rizzi, we have tacitly assumed that A-positions count as a potential blockers for A-movement, A'-positions for A'-movement, and heads for head movement.

(69)   *Relativized Minimality*
        X α-governs Y only if there is no Z such that:
        (i) Z is a typical potential α-governor for Y and
        (ii) Z c-commands Y and does not c-command X.

---

13 See Chomsky (2001) and Bobaljik (2002), among others, for alternative accounts of Holmberg's Generalization that don't rely on head movement creating derived MinDs within which equidistance holds.

In this section we'll not attempt to identify the properties that characterize a position as A or A', which has become a murky business with the developments on clausal structure within GB. Rather, we'll show that minimality seems to be tuned to features rather than positions. In fact, we may find instances of intervening positions of the same type that don't induce intervention effects and, on the other hand, positions of different types that do count as intervening.

An example of the first case involves head movement. Koopman (1984) has argued that a focused verb in Vata moves to C^0, leaving behind a copy, as illustrated in (70) with the verb *li* 'eat' being focused.

(70)   *Vata*
      a. **li** à **li**-da zué saká.
         eat we eat-PAST yesterday rice
         'We ATE rice yesterday.'
      b. **li** O da saka **li**.
         eat s/he PERF.AUX rice eat
         'S/he has EATEN rice.'

The verb *li* moves to C^0 from the Infl-adjoined position in (70a) or from its base position in (70b). Leaving aside the reasons why the trace of such verb movement is phonetically realized,[14] what is relevant for our purposes is that in (70b), the main verb moves to C^0, crossing the auxiliary *da* in Infl, without giving rise to a minimality violation. That would be unexpected under the Head Movement Constraint, as subsumed under Relativized Minimality, for a head is moving to a head position skipping an intervening head position. If, on the other hand, minimality takes features rather than positions into consideration, the acceptability of (70b) receives a straightforward explanation, for auxiliaries can't be independently focalized in Vata (see Koopman 1984: 158). If the main verb in (70) is moving to check a focus feature, only elements with a similar feature would count as intervening; thus, the auxiliary in (70b) doesn't prevent movement of the main verb.

A similar case is found in verb topicalization constructions in Portuguese, as illustrated in (71).

---

14 See Koopman (1984), Nunes (1999, 2004), and section 7.5 below for discussion.

(71)   *Portuguese*
    a. Convidar, o   João   disse que   a   Maria   convidou
      invite.INF   the João   said   that   the Maria   invited
    o   Pedro (não o   Antônio).
    the Pedro not   the Antônio.
    'As for inviting [people], João said that Maria invited Pedro (not Antônio).'
    b. *Convidar, o   João discutiu com   a   mulher que
      invite.INF   the João discussed with   the woman that
    convidou o   Pedro (não o   Antônio).
    invited   the Pedro not the Antônio
    'As for inviting, João discussed with the woman that invited Pedro (not Antônio).'

Bastos (2001) argues that a topicalized verb in Portuguese must adjoin to a Top-head in the left periphery of the sentence. This is possible in (71a), where the verb moves from within a transparent domain, but not in (71b), where the verb moves from within a relative clause island. Again putting aside a discussion of why the trace of such verb movement is phonetically realized,[15] the relevant point for our purposes is that in (71a) the verb crosses many intervening heads without any problems. Crucially, none of these heads bears a topic-feature.

Classic instances of Superiority effects such as (72), on the other hand, exemplify the converse situation: positions of different types inducing intervention effects.

(72)   *What did who buy?

Under the standard assumption that [Spec,TP] is an A-position, movement of *what* to [Spec,CP], an A'-position, should be allowed, contrary to fact. However, if minimality is to pay attention to features rather than positions, movement of *what* to [Spec,CP] to check a *wh*-feature is correctly blocked by the intervening *who*, which also has a *wh*-feature.

To sum up, there seems to be good indication that minimality is in fact computed with respect to features rather than positions. This in itself is not an unnatural conclusion. After all, the properties of a given position are ultimately derived from the features it has. We'll therefore be assuming such conclusion in the chapters that follow.

---

15 See Bastos (2001), Nunes (2004), and section 7.5 below.

Exercise 5.12

In section 5.4.2.1, the contrast in (63), repeated below, was taken to show that the trace of *what* induces a minimality effect in (ia), but not in (ib). Discuss whether this contrast presupposes that minimality is to be relativized with respect to types of positions or types of features.

(i) a. *[$_{CP}$ who$_i$ did you wonder [$_{CP}$ what$_k$ John [gave t$_k$ to t$_i$]]]
     b. ??[$_{CP}$ [to whom]$_i$ did you wonder [$_{CP}$ what$_k$ John [gave t$_k$ t$_i$]]]

Exercise 5.13

In this chapter, we've considered minimality mainly from the perspective of the moving expression. However, we could also define it from the perspective of the targeted feature/head. In place of *Move*, assume that the grammar has a rule *Attract* and that a head with some feature F to be checked attracts the closest element able to check it. Define minimality for Attract and show how it operates in (70b), (71a), and (72) in the text. What feature is being attracted? What is doing the attracting? Why is Attract blocked in deriving (72), but not (70b) or (71a)? Assuming that this Attract-based approach should also be extended to checking Case and agreement, discuss if it's compatible with both the system with a single VP-shell and projections of Agr (see section 5.4.1) and the system with a double VP-shell and no projections of Agr (see section 5.4.2).

5.6   Conclusion

This chapter has explored a notion of locality that enables us to maintain the apparently conflicting conclusions reached in previous chapters. Recall that all arguments must receive their θ-role within the relevant lexical projection (see chapter 3), but must check their structural Case outside their θ-position (see chapter 4); hence, subjects and objects should cross each other in violation of the standard GB-notion of minimality. The specific proposal explored here is that the local configurations of a given head are computed as equidistant from the other positions in the tree, as encoded in (73) below. We have seen that (73) correctly allows subjects and objects to cross each other in the derivation of transitive clauses as well as "double" crossings in the derivation of ditransitive clauses, while at the same time preventing instances of overgeneration. Moreover, by taking minimality to be sensitive to features rather than positions, the empirical coverage got broadened.

(73)   *Equidistance*
         If two positions α and β are in the same MinD, they are equidistant from any other position.

Finally, we have also seen that the minimalist project to stick to functional projections motivated by interface conditions seems to be a viable goal also in empirical terms. In particular, we have discussed reasonable ways in which Agr-projections can be dispensed with. From now on, we'll thus assume the basic clausal structure in (74).

(74) $[_{CP}$ Spec C $[_{TP}$ Spec T $[_{vP}$ SU $[_{v'}$ *v* $[_{VP}$ V OB $]]]]]$

6 *Phrase structure*

6.1   Introduction

Recall from section 1.3 that one of the "big facts" regarding human
languages is that sentences are composed of phrases, units larger than
words organized in a specific hierarchical fashion. This chapter is devoted
to phrase structure. The starting point for our discussion will be
X′-Theory, the module of GB responsible for determining the precise
format of licit phrases and syntactic constituents in general.

One of the main motivations for the introduction of X′-Theory into
generative grammar was the elimination of a perceived redundancy in the
earlier *Aspects*-model. The *Aspects*-theory of the base included two kinds of
operations. First, there was a phrase-structure component based on a
variety of context-free phrase-structure rules (PS rules) such as those in (1)
below. (1a), for instance, states that a sentence S expands as (is formed by)
NP Aux VP and (1b) says that a VP expands as a V with optional NP, PP,
and S complements. The application of these sorts of rules generates phrase
markers (trees) with no lexical items at the terminals, as illustrated in (2).

(1)   *Basic phrase-structure rules*
      a. S   → NP Aux VP
      b. VP → V (NP) (PP) (S)
      c. NP → (Det) N (PP) (S)

(2)

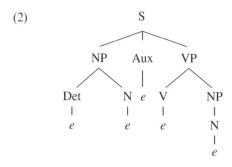

174

Lexical elements were then introduced into the empty terminal positions (designated by *e* in (2)) by a process of lexical insertion, yielding phrase markers like (3).

(3)

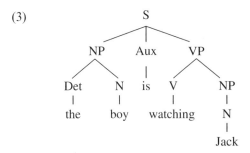

So dividing the task of building initial phrase markers contains an unfortunate redundancy.[1] To see this, consider what sorts of verbs can be inserted into the VP of (2), for instance. Only transitive verbs like *watch* and *kiss* yield an acceptable sentence if inserted. Intransitive verbs like *sleep* or *cough* don't take objects and so don't "license" enough of the available portions that the phrase structure affords, and ditransitive verbs like *give* or *put* are not provided with enough empty positions for all their arguments. In effect, the rules for lexical insertion must code the argument structure of the relevant lexical heads and match them to the possible phrase structure that the PS rules make available. In other words, the information about possible phrase structures is coded twice, once in the PS rules and a second time in the lexical entries.

X′-Theory was intended to eliminate this redundancy by dispensing with PS rules and construing phrase structure as the syntactic "projection" of the argument structure of a lexical head. It incorporates several distinctive claims, providing a recipe for how such "projection" from argument structure takes place. Under one of its more common formulations, the recipe has the general format along the lines of (4), where a head X projects a maximal constituent XP by being optionally combined with a complement, a number of modifiers (adjuncts), and a specifier that "closes off" the projection of X.

---

1 See, e.g., Chomsky (1965, 1970), Lyons (1968), and Jackendoff (1977).

(4)

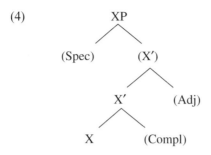

In the sections that follow we'll review the main properties encompassed by the general schema in (4), as well as the motivation for their postulation, and discuss if and how such properties can be derived or incorporated in a minimalist system. The chapter is organized as follows. In section 6.2 we review the main properties of phrase structure that X′-Theory intends to capture. In section 6.3, we discuss a "bare" version of phrase structure, according to which the key features of phrase structure follow from the internal procedures of the structure-building operation Merge, coupled with general minimalist conditions. Section 6.4 shows how structures formed by movement also fall under the bare-phrase-structure approach and introduce the copy theory, according to which traces are copies of moved elements. Finally, section 6.5 concludes the chapter.

6.2   X′-Theory and properties of phrase structure

6.2.1   *Endocentricity*

One of the key ingredients of the recipe for projecting phrases provided by X′-Theory is endocentricity. The general X′-schema in (4) embodies the claims that every head projects a phrase and that all phrases have heads. Support for this endocentric property of phrases comes from distributional facts. A single verb like *smile*, for instance, can be an adequate surrogate for the VP in (5) below, but the sequence adjective plus PP can't, as illustrated in (6). In other words, endocentricity imposes hierarchy of a specific kind onto linguistic structures, allowing for phrases structured as in (7a), but not as in (7b), for instance.

(5)   [John will [$_{VP}$ drink caipirinha]]

(6)   a. [John will [smile]]
          b. *[John will [fond of caipirinha]]

(7)   a. VP → V
          b. *VP → A PP

The endocentricity property coded by X′-Theory thus says that whenever we find phrases, we find morphemes that serve as heads of those phrases and that these heads are relatively prominent in not being further embedded within other phrases of a distinct type. It's not merely the case that verb phrases must contain verbs; they must *prominently* contain them. The phrase in (8a), for instance, contains the verb *like*, but it's a noun phrase rather than a verb phrase because the verb is too deeply buried within another phrase to serve as the head of the whole.

(8)   a. books that I like
         b. [[books [that I like]]]

Endocentricity also affords a local way of coding another interesting fact about natural languages: that words "go" with some words and not others. An example or two should make what we mean here clear. Consider a sentence like (9).

(9)   Rhinos were/*was playing hockey.

(9) displays subject-predicate agreement. The plural subject *rhinos* requires that the form of the past tense of *be* come out as *were*. In an example like (9), we can state the required relation very locally: the predicate immediately following or next to the subject must agree with it in number properties.

Consider now a slightly more complex case.

(10)   Rhinos playing on the same team were/*was staying in the same hotel.

Observe that the very same restriction witnessed in (9) holds in (10); that is, the verb agrees in number with *rhinos* and must be plural. However, in this instance, there is no apparent local linear relation mediating the interaction of *rhinos* and *were* as they are no longer linearly contiguous, at least not evidently. In fact, matters are much worse than this. Once we consider (9) and (10) together, it's easy to see that any number of words can intervene between the subject element coding number and the predicate, without altering the observed agreement requirement. How then can this restriction between subject and predicate be locally stated?

Endocentricity comes to the rescue. If we assume that phrases are projections of their heads as endocentricity mandates, then the number specification of an NP can be seen as a simple function of the number specification of its head. In the case of (10), for instance, the subject NP triggers plural agreement in virtue of the plural specification of its head *rhinos*, as illustrated in (11).

(11)   [[_{NP} [_{N'} *rhinos*] [playing on the same team]] *were* staying in the same hotel]

Observe that the NP projected from *rhinos* does abut *were* and hence the same locality requirement that holds between *rhinos* and *were* in (9) can be seen to be present in (10), as well, once some phrase structure is made explicit and we assume that there is a tight relationship between a phrase and its head, i.e. if we assume that phrases obey an endocentricity requirement.

Notice further that if agreement could peruse all the constituents of the subject, the verb *be* in (10) could in principle agree with *team*, which is actually linearly closer to it, and surface as *was*. The fact that this doesn't happen illustrates what may be called the *periscope property* induced by endocentricity: subject-predicate agreement is allowed to look into the subject NP and see its head, but nothing else.

Let's now consider the sentences in (12).

(12)   a. John ate bagels.
        b. *John ate principles.
        c. *John ate principles of bagel making.

(12b) is a funny sentence. Why? Presumably because principles are not things that one eats. This contrasts with (12a), since bagels are quite edible. Observe that the oddity of (12b) doesn't diminish if we add more elements to the phrase. Arguably, (12c) is odd for the same reason that (12b) is (principles are not edible). This in turn constitutes another example of the periscope property. Consider why. The object of a verb like *eat* should be something edible. To determine if an object denotes something edible, one need only look and examine its head. If the head is a food product like *bagels*, then all will go swimmingly. If the head is something like *principles*, then no matter what else edible we put in the phrase, the sentence will retain its oddity. Thus, the contrast between (12a) and (12c) is due to the fact that the head of the object NP is *bagels* in the former, and *principles* in the latter; crucially, *bagel* in (12c) is too buried to be seen by *ate*.

Accordingly, there are also no known cases where a syntactic relation cares about anything, but the head. For example, there are no verbs that select NPs with certain determiners, say *three* but not others, say *every*, or verbs that like some kinds of nominal modifiers for their complements, say PPs, but not others, say APs. Thus, although the verb *eat* imposes restrictions on the head of its complement, it seems to have no effect on what sorts of specifiers or modifiers this head may take, as illustrated in (13).

(13)   a. John *ate* [_{NP} Bill's/no/every *bagel*]
          b. I *ate* [_{NP} a big fat greasy luscious chocolate square *bagel* with no hole]

To sum up, endocentricity is a well-motivated property of the phrase structure of natural languages and is captured under the general X′-schema in (14).

(14)   XP → ... X ...

Before we move on, it's important to point out that endocentricity is not an intrinsic property of any phrase-structure system. The PS rule in (1a), repeated below in (15), for instance, is not endocentric. However, if endocentricity is an inherent property of all structures in natural languages, they should have no rules like (15). Research in the 1980s about functional heads both in the clausal and in the nominal domain indeed led to this conclusion and to the complete abandonment of PS rules. We return to this issue in section 6.2.5 below, where we discuss the structure of functional projections.

(15)   S → NP Aux VP

6.2.2   *Binary branching*

One further property of phrase structure incorporated into standard versions of the X′-schema is binary branching.[2] Within these versions of X′-Theory, multiple branching structures such as (16), for instance, came to be replaced by binary branching structures like (17).

(16)

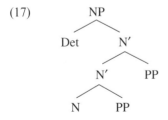

(17)

---

2 See especially Kayne (1984) on binary branching in phrase structure.

Binary branching was motivated for a mix of aesthetic and empirical reasons.[3] Let's consider one empirical argument. It's a standard assumption that syntactic processes and operations deal with syntactic constituents. Pronominalization is one such process. Consider the sentences in (18) below, for instance. In English, the pronoun *one* may replace *student of physics* in (18a) and *student of physics with long hair* in (18b).[4] Thus, each fragment that is pronominalized should be a syntactic constituent (a node in a syntactic tree) in the relevant NP structure. In other words, in order to capture the pronominalization facts in (18), there should be a node dominating only *student of physics* and excluding everything else and another node dominating *student of physics with long hair* and excluding everything else. These requirements are met in the binary branching structure in (17), as shown in (19a), but not in the multiple branching structure in (16), as shown in (19b).

(18)   a. John met this student of physics with long hair, and Bill met that one with short hair.
        b. John met this student of physics with long hair, and Bill met that one.

(19)   a.

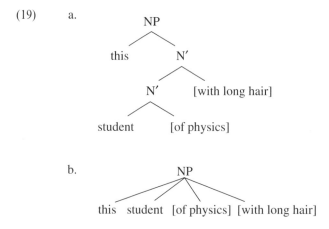

Research in the 1980s generalized binary branching to all lexical and functional projections, with very interesting empirical consequences.[5] Take double object constructions such as (20) below, for example. If their VP were to be assigned a *ternary* branching along the lines of (21), neither complement should be more prominent than the other, for

3 See Kayne (1984) for relevant discussion.
4 This test goes back to Baker (1978); see also Hornstein and Lightfoot (1981) and Radford (1981), among others, for early discussion.
5 See, e.g., Kayne (1984), Chomsky (1986a), and Larson (1988).

they c-command each other. However, binding and negative polarity licensing, which both require c-command, show that this can't be the case. Under the structure in (21), the anaphor in (22b), for instance, should be bound by *the boys* and the negative polarity item *anyone* in (23b) should be licensed by the negative quantifier *nothing*.

(20)   John gave Bill a book.

(21)

(22)   a. Mary showed [the boys]ᵢ [each other]ᵢ
         b. *Mary showed [each other] [the boys]ᵢ

(23)   a. John gave nobody anything.
         b. *John gave anyone nothing.

By contrast, if only binary branching is permitted, the contrasts in (22) and (23) can be accounted for if the phrase structure of double object constructions is actually more complex, with an extra layer of structure, as illustrated in (24).

(24)   a.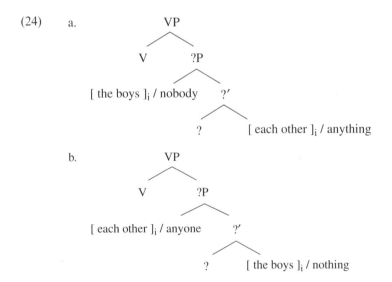

         b.

Given that in (24) the dative c-commands the theme, but not the opposite, the anaphor and the negative polarity item are licensed in (24a), but not in (24b); hence the contrasts in (22) and (23).

The assumption that all phrases are organized in terms of binary branching also led to the reevaluation of the clausal skeleton given in (25) below. We'll get back to this issue in section 6.2.5 below.

(25)

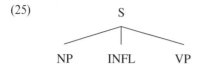

6.2.3   *Singlemotherhood*

Another property of phrase structure in natural languages is that syntactic constituents are not immediately dominated by more than one constituent. That is, syntactic constituents don't have multiple mothers. There seems to be no syntactic process that requires structures such as the ones below, for instance, where X in (26a) is the head of more than one phrase, and the complement of X in (26b) is also the specifier of Y.

(26)   a.

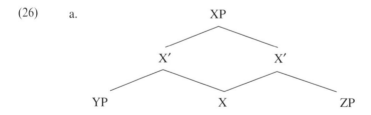

b.

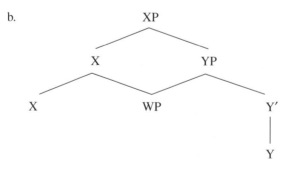

It's important to stress that there is nothing crazy about the structures in (26) by themselves.[6] Notice that they are endocentric and binary branching, like all the licit structures we have been examining thus far. One could even hypothesize that the structure in (26a), where X has two complements, would serve well to represent double object constructions, as shown in (27), or that the structure in (26b) would provide a nice account for the fact that in constructions involving headless relative clauses, the moved *wh*-phrase may function as the complement of a higher head (see section 2.3.2.3), as illustrated in (28).

(27)   a. John gave Mary a nice book.
        b.

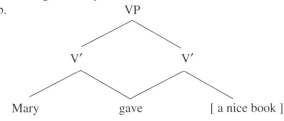

(28)   a. John always smiles at whoever he looks at.
        b.

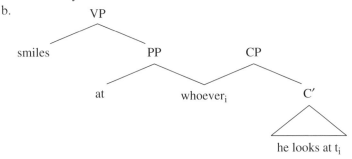

However, as discussed in section 6.2.2, facts regarding binding and negative polarity licensing show that in double object constructions, the dative must c-command the theme, which is not the case in (27b), where neither c-commands the other. In turn, if the structure in (28b) were allowed, VP-preposing should in principle leave CP stranded, contrary to fact, as illustrated in (29).

---

6 See McCawley (1981) for early discussion and Cann (1999), Starke (2001), Gärtner (2002), Abels (2003), and Citko (2005), among others, for more recent treatments of multi-dominance.

(29)   John said that he would smile at whoever he would look at, and
          a. smile at whoever he looked at, he did.
          b. *smile at whoever he did, he looked at.

   To sum up, despite the plausibility of multiple immediate dominance, it
seems to be a fact that human languages simply don't work this way, and
singlemotherhood is also a property of natural language phrases.

6.2.4   *Bar-levels and constituent parts*

Consider now the two possible representations for the phrase in (30) given
in (31).

(30)   this prince of Denmark with a nasty temper

(31)   a.

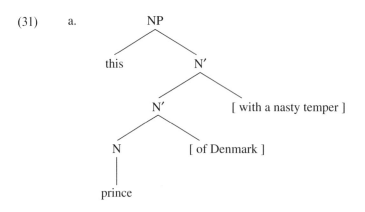

          b.

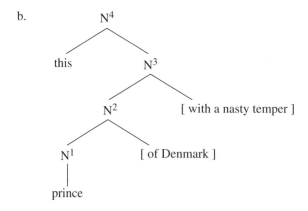

(31a) illustrates our familiar sandwich-like organization of X′-Theory: the bottom (the head), the top (the maximal projection), and the filling (the intermediate projections); in other words, three levels are encoded. (31b), on the other hand, differs in that it registers the total number of nominal projections (four in this case). At first sight, these appear to be just notational variants recording the same information. However, they actually make distinct empirical predictions when we also consider the two representations in the case of the simpler phrase in (32).

(32)   this prince

(33)   a.

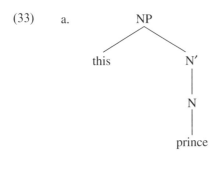

    b.

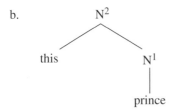

According to the counting approach, the constituent *prince* will always be of the same type (N^1), regardless of whether or not it occurs in more complex structures. By contrast, under the X′-approach, *prince* doesn't have the same status in (30) and (32); in (32), in addition to counting as an N, it's also an N′ as well (cf. (31a) and (33a)). In other words, the counting approach makes the prediction that if some syntactic process affects *prince* in (32), it may do the same in (30); the X′-approach, on the other hand, doesn't make such a prediction because *prince* doesn't necessarily have the same status in these phrases. Let's then see how the two approaches fare with respect to the *one*-substitution facts in (34).

(34)   a. John likes this prince and I like that one.
        b. *John likes this prince of Denmark and I like that one of France.

In (34a), *one* is a surrogate for *prince* and we have a well-formed sentence. Thus, under the counting approach, we should get a similar result in (34b), contrary to fact. Under the X'-approach, on the other hand, the contrast in (34) can be accounted for if *one* targets N'-projections; hence, it may replace the N'-projection of *prince* in (34a) (cf. (33a)), but there is no such projection in (34b) (cf. (31a)).[7] Facts like these require that an adequate theory of phrase structure in natural languages resort to the three-way bar-level system distinguishing heads, intermediate projections, and maximal projections.

In addition to encoding this three-way distinction, the general X'-schema in (35) also functionally identifies three constituent parts – complements, modifiers (adjuncts), and specifiers – which are mapped into their hierarchical positions according to the principles in (36).

(35)

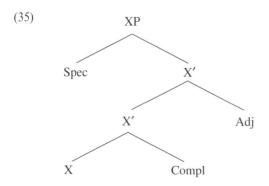

(36)   *Principles of phrase-structure relations*
        a. Complements are sisters to the head X.
        b. Modifiers are adjuncts to X'.
        c. Specifiers are daughters to XP.

That complements and modifiers are semantically distinct is easy to see. In the verbal domain, for instance, complements are generally obligatory, whereas adjuncts are optional, as illustrated in (37).

(37)   John fixed *(the car) (yesterday).

Furthermore, whereas the head and the complement form a single predicate, a modifier adds a further specification to an existing predicate. Compare the adjunct structure in (38a) with the complement structure in (38b) below,

---

7 These data get reanalyzed in section 6.2.6 below without the use of N'.

for example. (38a) says two things about Hamlet: that he is a prince and that he is from Denmark. (38b), on the other hand, says just one thing about him: that he has the property of being a prince of Denmark; in fact, it's quite meaningless to paraphrase (38b) by saying that Hamlet is a prince and is of Denmark.

(38)   a. Hamlet is a prince from Denmark.
         b. Hamlet is a prince of Denmark.

What X'-Theory does with the mapping principles is (36) is state that in addition to lexical information (the difference between *from* and *of* in (38), for instance), the hierarchical configuration is crucially relevant for the interpretation of complements and modifiers. This can be clearly seen by the contrast between (39) and (40).

(39)   a. the prince from Denmark with a nasty temper
         b. the prince with a nasty temper from Denmark

(40)   a. the prince of Denmark with a nasty temper
         b. *the prince with a nasty temper of Denmark

Whereas the adjuncts can freely interchange in (39), that is not the case of the complement and the adjunct in (40). This contrast in word order is accounted for by the mapping principles in (36). In (39), word order doesn't matter as long as (36b) is satisfied and each of the adjuncts is mapped as a sister of N', as shown in (41) below. In (40), on the other hand, only the order in (40a) can comply with both (36a) and (36b), as shown in (42a); the order in (40b) requires that *of Denmark* appears as a sister of N', as shown in (42b), yielding a conflict with the lexical specification of *of* and violating (36a).

(41)

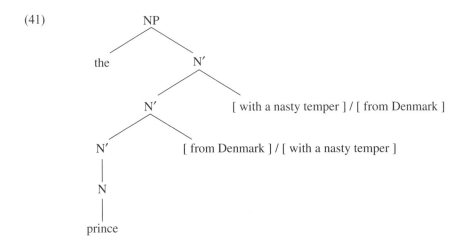

(42)   a.

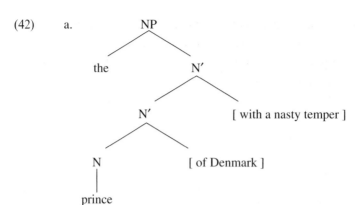

b.

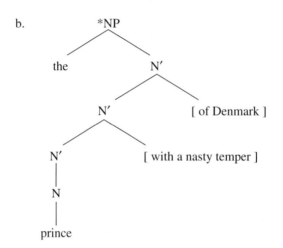

As for the functional identification of specifiers in (36c), the guiding intuition was that any head could project as many intermediate projections as there were adjuncts, but some specific projections would close off projections of that head. For instance, whereas one could keep indefinitely adding adjunct PPs to N′-projections and getting another N′, once a determiner was added, we would obtain an NP and no further projection from the relevant N head would further take place. Distributionally, this would explain why adjuncts can iterate, but determiners can't, as shown in (43).

(43)   a. the prince from Denmark with a nasty temper
        b. *this the prince from Denmark

To sum up, the key properties embodied in the X′-schema in (35) and the mapping principles in (36) are reasonably motivated and invite closer scrutiny from a minimalist perspective. We have already seen in section 5.4.2.1, for instance, that if *v*Ps allow more than one Spec, the system may get simpler. But before getting into a detailed discussion of phrase structure from a minimalist point of view, let's first briefly examine the consequences of assuming X'-Theory for the structure of functional heads.

Exercise 6.2

Try to build an argument based on syntactic constituency that VPs should also involve three bar-levels. Consider how VP ellipsis, VP fronting, and *do so* might be employed for collecting evidence.

Exercise 6.3

Some prepositions may be used to introduce both complements and adjuncts, as illustrated in (i). Based on this ambiguity, explain why (ii) has just one of the two potential readings it could have. (Assume the rough bracketing provided here.)

   (i) a. books on linguistics
        b. books on the floor

   (ii) books [on chairs] [on tables]

6.2.5   Functional heads and X'-Theory

As mentioned in section 6.1, one of the main motivations behind X'-Theory was the elimination of PS rules. Two such rules, however, still made their way into GB, namely, the rules for clausal structure in (44).

(44)   a. S' → Comp S
        b. S → NP Infl VP

(44a) was in fact more congenial to X'-Theory, in that it was endocentric (Comp was taken to be the head of S'[8]) and binary branching; its difference from the standard X'-schema was that it had just two levels: the head and the maximal projection. (44b), by contrast, was far from meeting X'-postulates: it was not endocentric, it had ternary branching and the issue of bar-levels was even worse, for S was not taken to be a maximal projection.

8 See Bresnan (1972).

Research in the mid-1980s led to the conclusion that PS rules could be completely eliminated from the grammar and that the clausal structure could be roughly organized along the lines of (45).[9]

(45)

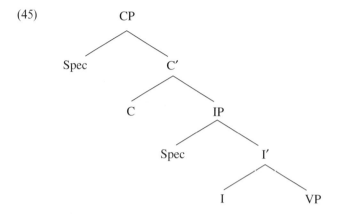

In (45), the complementizer C takes a projection of Infl (= I) as its complement and Infl, in turn, takes VP as its complement; [Spec,CP] is the position generally filled by moved *wh*-elements (or their traces) and [Spec,IP] is the position traditionally reserved for syntactic subjects.

Later research within **GB** has reexamined the structure in (45), suggesting that Infl (see section 4.3.1) and C should be split into several heads – such as T(ense), Agr(eement), Asp(ect), Top(ic), Foc(us), etc. – each of which projecting a distinct phrase.[10] Although there is disagreement with respect to the number of such phrases and the dominance relationship among them, researchers generally agree on one point: all of these phrases are in compliance with the postulates of X'-Theory.

A similar reevaluation took place with respect to nominal domains. At first sight, the traditional structure in (46a) below required just a minor readjustment: in order for a well-formed X'-structure to obtain, the determiner would have to project. (46b) should in principle fix this problem. However, by inspecting the projected structure of DP in (46b), one could not help but wonder what kind of complement a D head (= Det) could take or whether it could take a specifier.

---

9 See Fassi Fehri (1980), Stowell (1981), and Chomsky (1986a) for relevant discussion.
10 See Pollock (1989), Belletti (1990), Chomsky (1991), Rizzi (1997), Cinque (1999), and the more recent collections of papers in Cinque (2002), Belletti (2004), and Rizzi (2004).

(46)   a.

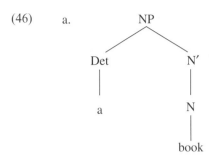

b.

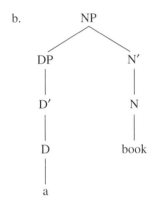

Addressing similar questions, research in the 1980s pointed to the conclusion that a better representation for a phrase such as *a book*, rather than (46b), should actually be along the lines of (47), where the determiner takes NP as its complement.[11]

(47)

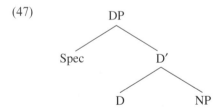

The structure in (47) receives support from very different sources. First, it still captures the old intuition that, in general, once a determiner is added to a structure, no further projections of N are possible. But it also has room to accommodate interesting cases such as (48) below, where a *wh*-element precedes the determiner and we are still in the "nominal"

---

11 See Brame (1982), Szabolcsi (1983), Abney (1987), and Kuroda (1988) for relevant discussion.

domain. (48) receives a straightforward analysis if we assume the structure in (47), with the *wh*-phrase in [Spec,DP].

(48)   [[how good] a story] is it?

The structure in (47) also captures the fact that in many languages determiners and clitic pronouns are morphologically similar or identical, as illustrated in (49) below with Portuguese.[12] Pronouns, under this view, should be D-heads without a complement.

(49)   *Portuguese*
         a. João viu   o   menino.
            João   saw   the   boy
            'João saw the boy.'
         b. João viu-o.
            João   saw-CL
            'João saw him.'

Further examination of the structure of DP, like what happened in the clausal domain, opened the possibility that there should be additional layers of functional projections between DP and NP.[13] Again, these ana-lyses generally agreed that the extra layers of functional structure were organized in compliance with X′-Theory.

Since a detailed discussion of the competing alternatives for clausal and nominal domains would derail us from our discussion of the general properties of phrase structure, from now on we'll assume the structures in (45) and (47) for concreteness.

Exercise 6.4

Try to build additional arguments for the structure in (45) and (47) in your language by using traditional tests for syntactic constituents.

Exercise 6.5

In section 6.2.1, we saw that the periscope property induced by endocentricity ensures that, for selectional purposes, a given head only sees the head of its complement and nothing else. Assuming the clausal structure in (45), that

---

12 See Postal (1966) and Raposo (1973) for early discussion.
13 Bernstein (2001) provides a recent overview of the "Clausal DP-Hypothesis" and plenty of references on the finer structure of DP developed in the wake of Brame (1982), Szabolcsi (1983), and Abney (1987).

would imply that a verb that selects a CP for a complement should see only the head C, and that should be it. However, the data in (i) and (ii) seem to show that the matrix verb is seeing more than the head of its complement. In (i) it seems to select the tense of the embedded clause, whereas in (ii) it appears to impose restrictions on the specifier of the embedded CP. How can these facts be reconciled with the periscope property?

(i) a. John wants Bill to win.
     b. *John wants that Bill will win.

(ii) a. John believes that Bill won.
      b. *John believes how Bill won.
      c. *John wonders that Bill won.
      d. John wonders how Bill won.

Exercise 6.6

In exercise 6.5, we saw that verbs appear to select the tense of their clausal complement. Things may seem more complicated in face of the following generalization: in English, if a verb requires that the [Spec,CP] of its complement be a *wh*-phrase, it imposes no restriction on the tense of the embedded clause. This is illustrated in (i) and (ii) below. Show how your answer to exercise 6.5 can also account for this generalization.

(i) a. *John wondered / asked that Bill won.
     b. John wondered / asked how Bill won.

(ii) a. John wondered / asked how Bill will win.
      b. John wondered / asked how to win.

Exercise 6.7

In section 6.2.1, we saw the effects of the periscope property induced by endocentricity in two different processes involving nominal domains: subject-verb agreement and selectional restrictions on complements. Reexamine these two processes assuming the DP structure in (47), showing what assumptions must be made in order for the DP-approach to capture the periscope property.

6.2.6   *Success and clouds*

X′-Theory became one of the central modules of GB as it made it possible to dispense with PS rules completely. This was particularly noticeable in its successful utilization in the analysis of functional projections. Interestingly, however, progress in the description of specific syntactic constituents under X'-Theory ended up somewhat clouding this bright and blue sky.

Consider, for example, the assumption that XPs don't have multiple specifiers. The main motivation behind it was distributional in nature. Determiners were analyzed as [Spec,NP] and negation as [Spec,VP], for instance, because once they were added in the structure, no further nominal or verbal projection would obtain. Notice, however, that this continues to be true even in the structures in (50) below, where D and Neg are heads that respectively take NPs and VPs as complements. In other words, what was seen as a requirement on the number of specifiers turned out to be a reflex of the fact that D and Neg, like any other head, project when they take a complement.[14]

(50)   a. [$_{DP}$ D NP]
        b. [$_{NegP}$ Neg VP]

Intermediate vacuous projections illustrate a similar case. It's reasonable to say that a given head, say the verb *smiled*, projects a VP, given that it may occupy VP slots, as exemplified in (51) below. However, why should it also project an intermediate V'- projection?

(51)   John [$_{VP}$ won the lottery]] / [$_{VP}$ smiled]

Vacuous V'-projections were taken to be useful in the characterization of mono-argumental verbs as unaccusative or unergative (see section 3.4.2), as shown in (52) below. However, with the introduction of light verbs in the theory (see section 3.3.3), the distinction can be made with no resort to vacuous projections, as shown in (53) (see section 3.4.2). The automatic projection in three bar-levels therefore has lost much of its appeal in the verbal domain.

(52)   a. unaccusative verbs: [$_{VP}$ V DP]
        b. unergative verbs: [$_{VP}$ DP [$_{V'}$ V]]

(53)   a. unaccusative verbs: [$_{VP}$ V DP]
        b. unergative verbs: [$_{vP}$ DP [$_{v'}$ v [$_{VP}$ V]]]

The same can be said with respect to the nominal domain. Recall from our discussion in section 6.2.4 that the pronoun *one* appears to be

---

14 In fact, as Chomsky (1999: 39, n. 66) puts it, "[i]t is sometimes supposed that [the possibility of multiple specifiers] is a stipulation, but that is to mistake history for logic."

a surrogate for N′-projections, explaining the adjunct-complement contrast between (54a) and (54b), for instance, which in turn requires that there be a vacuous N′-projection of *prince* in (54a).

(54)   a. John likes this prince from Denmark and I like that one from France.
        b. *John likes this prince of Denmark and I like that one of France.

Upon closer inspection, we can, however, see that this analysis crucially relies on two assumptions that now may not look as well grounded as before: first, that the determiner is the specifier of NP and second, that adjuncts are sisters of X′ (the mapping principle in (36b)). As mentioned in section 6.2.5, it has now become a consensus that determiners take NPs as their complements. Besides, as discussed in chapter 3, there are strong reasons to believe that external arguments are generated within their theta domains (the Predicate-Internal Subject Hypothesis), more precisely, as sisters of an intermediate projection. Under this picture, a phrase such as (55a), for instance, should be represented along the lines of (55b), where *John* is generated in [Spec,NP] and moves to [Spec,DP].

(55)   a. John's discussion of the paper
        b. [$_{DP}$ John$_i$ [$_{D′}$'s [$_{NP}$ t$_i$ [$_{N′}$ discussion of the paper]]]]

The question now is how the interpretive component distinguishes adjuncts from external arguments if they may be both sisters of N′. One can't simply say that specifiers are different in that they close off projections, for the distributional facts that motivated this assumption have received alternative explanations on more reasonable grounds. As mentioned above, determiners establish the upper boundary of a nominal projection, for instance, not because they are specifiers but because the merger of D and NP yields DP. Furthermore, we may need more than one specifier at least for *v*Ps, if the computation of locality is to be simplified, as discussed in section 5.4.2.1.

One possibility for accommodating these worries is to give up the mapping principle in (36b) (namely, that modifiers are adjuncts to X′) and assume that modifiers are actually adjoined to XP. This in effect provides a much more transparent mapping from structure to interpretation: arguments are dominated by XP and adjuncts are adjoined to XP. Under this scenario, the contrast in (54) may be accounted for without resorting to vacuous N′-projections, if *one* is a phrasal pronoun and can't replace simple lexical items. That is, it can't target *prince* in (56b), but it can in (56a), because in the latter *prince* is also an NP.

(56)   a. [$_{DP}$ this [$_{NP}$ [$_{NP}$ prince] [from Denmark]]]
       b. [$_{DP}$ this [$_{NP}$ prince of Denmark]]

The points above serve to show that much of the motivation for the initial postulates of standard X'-Theory got bleached as a deeper understanding of the structure of specific constituents was achieved. X'-Theory is therefore ripe for a minimalist evaluation.

Exercise 6.8

Check if the analysis of (54) along the lines of (56) can also be extended to (i) without resorting to vacuous N'-projections or making any other amendments.

(i)   John likes this prince from Denmark with the nasty temper, but I like that one with the sweet disposition.

6.3   Bare phrase structure

In this section, we will attempt to distinguish which of the properties of X'-Theory reflect true properties of phrase structure in natural languages and investigate if such properties may follow from deeper features of the language faculty. We will specifically review the minimalist approach to phrase structure known as *bare phrase structure*.[15]

6.3.1   *Functional determination of bar-levels*

Let's start our discussion with the qualm concerning bar-levels mentioned above.[15] Take the X'-schema in (57), which incorporates the assumption made in section 6.2.6 that modifiers are adjoined to maximal projections.

(57)

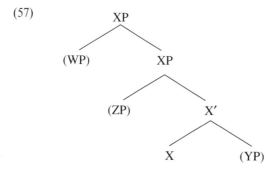

---

15 This section is primarily based on Chomsky (1995: sec. 4.3).

YP, ZP, and WP in (57) are, respectively, the complement, the specifier and an adjunct of the head X. Given that the actual realization of the projections of YP, ZP, and WP is regulated by other modules of the grammar (the Theta Criterion, for instance), they are in principle all optional. If none of them is realized, as illustrated by *John* in (58) below, then the three-bar-level distinction seems to be motivated just on theory-internal grounds, for independent empirical motivation for it has considerably dimmed, as discussed in section 6.2.6. The schema in (57) also invites a related question: *why* is it that only maximal projections can function as complements, specifiers, or modifiers?

(58)   Mary saw [$_{NP}$ [$_{N'}$ [$_N$ John]]]

These sorts of worries may be seen as different facets of the fundamental question of how to interpret the claim that a phrase consists of parts with various bar-levels. Abstractly speaking, one can conceptualize the difference between X, X′, and XP in two rather different ways. First, they may differ roughly in the way that a verb differs from a noun, that is, they have different intrinsic features. Alternatively, they can differ in the way that a subject differs from an object, namely, they differ in virtue of their relations with elements in their local environment, rather than inherently. On the first interpretation bar-levels are categorial features, on the second relational properties.

The three-bar-level analysis of *John* in (58) is clearly based on a featural conception of phrase structure. To compare it with a relational way of conceptualizing projections, let's assume the definitions in (59)–(61) and examine the structure in (62), for instance.[16]

(59)   *Minimal Projection: X^0*
        A minimal projection is a lexical item selected from the numeration.

(60)   *Maximal Projection: XP*
        A maximal projection is a syntactic object that doesn't project.

(61)   *Intermediate Projection: X′*
        An intermediate projection is a syntactic object that is neither an X^0 nor an XP.

---

16 These definitions are taken from Chomsky (1995: 242–43), who builds on work by Fukui (1986), Speas (1986), Oishi (1990), and Freidin (1992); the relational understanding of projection levels goes back to Muysken (1982). See also Chomsky (2000, 2001) for further discussion and, e.g., Chametzky (2000, 2003), Rubin (2002, 2003), Grohmann (2003b, 2004), Oishi (2003), and Boeckx (2004) for critical evaluation.

(62)

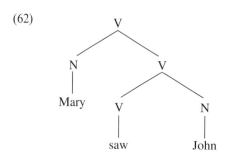

According to (59)–(61), *Mary*, *saw*, and *John* in (62) are each an X^0 (they are lexical items). The N-projection dominating *Mary* and the one dominating *John* are also interpreted as maximal projections since they don't project any further. The same can be said of the topmost V-projection; it's also a maximal projection. The V-projection exclusively dominating *saw* and *John*, on the other hand, is neither a minimal projection (it's not a lexical item), nor a maximal projection (it projects into another V-projection); hence, it's an intermediate projection. In other words, the definitions in (59)–(61) are also able to capture the fact that phrase structure may involve three levels of projection.

But it has additional advantages, as well. First, observe that there is simply no room for suspicious vacuous intermediate projections under this relational approach. In (62), for instance, the N-projection dominating *John* is both a minimal and a maximal projection; hence, it can't be an intermediate projection, according to (61).

The relational approach also derives the claim that complements, modifiers, and specifiers are maximal from a more basic assumption: an expression E will establish a local grammatical relation (either Spec-head, modification, or complementation relation) with a given head H only if E is immediately contained within projections of H. Let's call this assumption the *Strong Endocentricity Thesis*. According to this thesis, heads actually project structure via the complement, modifier, and specifier relations.[17] Thus, by being immediately contained by a projection of X, a complement, a specifier, or an adjunct of X are necessarily maximal according to (60), because they don't project further. To put this in

---

17 This would make a lot of sense if these relations were ultimately discharged in a neo-Davidsonian manner with specifiers, complements, and modifiers anchored to the semantic values of heads (see Parsons 1990, Schein 1993, and Pietroski 2004). Thus, verbs denote events, complements and specifiers are thematic relations to events, and modifiers are properties of events.

different words, the phrasal status of complements, specifiers, and adjuncts follows from the fact they enter into a local grammatical relation with a given head, and need not be independently postulated.

Bar-levels under the conception of phrase structure embodied in (59)–(61) are, therefore, not an inherent property of nodes in the tree, but rather the reflex of the position of a given node with respect to others. From a minimalist point of view, this is an interesting result. Recall that one of the features that ensure internal coherence to the minimalist project is the Inclusiveness Condition, which requires that LF objects be built from features of the lexical items in the numeration (see section 2.4). In order to encode maximal and intermediate projections, the featural approach to phrase structure in (57) tacitly relies on the theoretical primes expressed by the symbols " ^{0} ", " $^\prime$ ", and " P " (as in N^0, N', and NP, for instance), which can't be construed as lexical features. By contrast, under the relational approach, the double role played by *John* as a head and as a phrase in (62), for instance, is captured without the postulation of non-lexical features.

In fact, this observation may call into question the very distinction between terminal nodes and lexical items. In some sense, this distinction still keeps the same kind of redundancy perceived between PS rules and argument structure in the lexicon (see section 6.1). The lexical entry of *John*, for instance, arguably includes the information that *John* is a noun. That being so, what information does the categorical label N in (62) convey that *John* doesn't already convey? In other words, what piece of information would be lost if (62) were replaced by the structure in (63)?

(63)

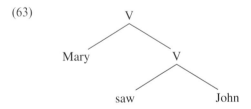

One could say that this redundancy between terminal nodes and lexical items could be tolerated, for categorial nodes appear to be independently required to specify the properties of projections other than heads. In (63), for instance, we need to register that *[saw John]* is a verbal rather than a nominal constituent. It should be observed that what is actually required is a labeling mechanism to encode the relevant properties of non-minimal projections; however, this doesn't imply that this mechanism should necessarily involve categorial features. The structure in (64), for instance, works pretty well in the sense that it encodes the fact that the constituents *[saw John]* and *[Mary saw John]* are of the same relevant type as *saw*.

(64)

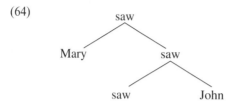

In the discussion that follows, we'll be assuming the projection-notation as in (64) instead of (62), guided by the intuition that we independently need lexical items, though we may not require categorial nodes.[18] But it's important to stress that the notation in (64) is just one way to encode the "projection" of the head. There are others conceivable that may as well do the job. We return to this issue below.

To summarize, the relational conception of bar-levels presents several advantages over a featural approach from a minimalist perspective: (i) it distinguishes different levels of projections in compliance with the Inclusiveness Condition; (ii) it doesn't have vacuous projections; (iii) it derives the fact that complements, specifiers, and adjuncts are maximal projections; and (iv) it allows the elimination of the distinction between terminal nodes and lexical items.

Assuming such a relational approach, we now turn to the mechanics of how phrase structure is built.

6.3.2   *The operation Merge*

As discussed in section 2.3.2.1, one of the "big facts" about human languages is that sentences can be of arbitrary length and within GB, this recursion property was encoded at D-Structure. It was shown, however, that grammatical recursion is not inherently associated with DS. One can ensure recursion in a system that lacks DS by resorting to an operation that puts lexical items together in compliance with X'-Theory. We referred to this operation as *Merge*. Given that DS was abandoned for conceptual and empirical reasons (see section 2.3.2) and that much of the motivation for

---

18 Some recent research in the framework of Distributed Morphology (see Halle and Marantz 1993, among others) pursues the idea that categorial information is defined relationally (see Marantz 1997 and subsequent work).

standard X′-Theory lost weight with later developments on phrase structure within GB (see section 6.2.6), it's now time to examine the details of
the operation Merge.

Building a phrase involves at least three tasks: combining diverse elements, labeling the resulting combination, and imposing a linear order
on the elements so combined. We'll leave the issue of linearization for
chapter 7 and concentrate on how we combine elements and how we label
the resultant combinations. For concreteness, take the derivation of the
VP in (65) below. We know that *at John*, for instance, is a PP. But how can
this be obtained from the independent lexical items *John* and *at*?

(65)   [$_{VP}$ Mary [$_{V'}$ looked [$_{PP}$ at John]]]

Let's start by bringing the Strong Endocentricity Thesis into the picture.
According to this thesis, local grammatical relations to a head X such as
Spec-head, complementation, and modification can only be established
under projections of X (see section 6.3.1). Furthermore, the Extension
Condition requires that such relations be established by targeting root
syntactic objects (see section 2.3.2.3). That is, if the computational system
establishes a head-complement relation between the lexical items *looked*
and *at* by combining them, the lexical item *John* will not be able to later
establish a head-complement relation with *at* by being combined with it.
Finally, let's invoke the general (substantive) economy guidelines of Last
Resort, according to which there are no superfluous steps in a derivation; in
other words, every operation must have a purpose (see section 1.3). Thanks
to this Last Resort property of syntactic computations, the combination of
Mary and *John* as a syntactic object, for instance, is not an option because
no local grammatical relation can be established between them.

With these considerations in the background, suppose that what the
operation Merge does is combine elements to form a set out of them, as
illustrated in (66).

(66)   {at, John}
                ⇑
        at ⇔$_{Merge}$ John

The set in (66) should be a new syntactic object with subparts that are
themselves syntactic objects. But this definitely can't be the whole story. *At*
and *John* in {at, John} are in too symmetrical a relation with respect to
each other (they are just members of a set) and such symmetry arguably

can't ground the asymmetric relations of Spec-head, complementation, and modification. Once no local grammatical relation can be established, economy should prevent the formation of the set in (66) from taking place. Notice that this reasoning also explains why *at* and *John* in (66) can't both project: again, if that happens, there will be no asymmetry between these elements to anchor the Spec-head, complementation and modification relations. In other words, a local relation can be established only if there is some asymmetry between the members of the set and such asymmetry may be reached if one of them labels the resulting structure. This is what is meant by projection of a head.

The question, then, is which of the constituents projects. Of course, we know the result: the head projects. But the question is *why* this is so, that is, why can *John* not project in (66), for instance? Although at this point we can't go much beyond speculation, this seems to be due to the fact that it's the head that has the information that it requires a Spec or a complement or is compatible with specific kinds of modifiers – and not the opposite. Thus, it's a property of *at* in (66) that it requires a complement, but it not a property of *John* that it requires a head to be the complement of. If something along these lines is correct, a head may project as many times as it has specifications to be met.

To put this in general terms, in addition to providing information regarding the immediate constituents of the syntactic object resulting from merger, the system must also signal the relevant properties of the new object, whether it's a VP or a PP, for instance. In other words, we need to label the resulting object. If the potential relation between *at* and *John* is such that the former may take the latter as complement (and not the opposite), *at* projects by labeling the structure as in (67) below. According to the functional determination of bar-levels discussed in section 6.3.1, the resulting syntactic object in (67) is a non-minimal maximal projection, *John* is both minimal and maximal, and *at* is a minimal non-maximal projection.

(67)   {at, {at, John}}

$$\Uparrow$$

at $\Leftrightarrow_{\text{Merge}}$ John

It's worth emphasizing that what is important here is that the constituent is labeled as having the relevant properties of its head and not how such labeling is annotated. We'll use the additional set notation in (67) because it's the one more commonly found in the literature, but it should be borne in mind that it would have been just as good for our purposes if *at* in (66) were underlined or received a star. This doesn't mean that the issue has no importance, but rather that at the moment it's not clear how exactly labeling should be technically implemented.

In fact, depending on its exact formulation, labeling may indeed be at odds with the Inclusiveness Condition in the sense that it may be adding features in the structure that may not be present in the numeration. In addition, given the Strong Endocentricity Hypothesis, the headness information encoded by a label is largely a function of the local grammatical relation being established (Spec-head, complementation, or modification). All of this brings the question of whether labels are really necessary.[19]

Even if the content of a label can be independently determined, it's still arguable that labels are required in the system as optimal design features. Let's consider why by examining the derivational steps in (68) and (69) below. In (68), the PP of (67) merges with *looked*, which projects under a complementation relation, yielding a verbal projection. In (69), such verbal projection merges with *Mary* and another verbal projection is obtained, this time in virtue of a Spec-head relation.

(68)   {looked, {looked, {at, {at, John}}}}
                        ⇧
         {at, {at, John}} ⇔ $_{Merge}$ looked

(69)   {looked, {Mary, {looked, {looked, {at, {at, John}}}}}}
                                ⇧
         {looked, {looked, {at, {at, John}}}} ⇔ $_{Merge}$ Mary

Notice that in both (68) and (69), the system doesn't need to compute the relations previously established in order to determine whether another local relation can be obtained. That is, by looking at the label of (67), the system has the information that this complex object is of a type that can enter into a complement relation with *looked*. Likewise, the label of the resulting object in (68) also allows the system to determine that such an object may enter into a local relation with *Mary*.

---

19 The whole set of issues that surround labeling (whether labels can be derived, if they are even necessary, whether they violate the Inclusiveness Condition, etc.) is currently a major focus of research. For relevant discussion, see Uriagereka (2000a), Boeckx (2002, 2004), and Collins (2002).

Now suppose we don't have labels. How does the system know that *Mary* may enter into a local relation with the relevant complex syntactic object in (68)? Or, putting this another way, if operations are carried out for some grammatical end, how does the system know that *Mary* can be merged with the label-less set {looked, {at, John}}? Apparently, by backtracking and determining first the kind of licensing/projection resulting from merging *at* and *John*, and then the kind of licensing/projection resulting from merging *looked* and the previously identified projection. This is obviously not very efficient, for the relation between *at* and *John*, for instance, in a sense gets repeatedly reestablished as more complex objects are formed. Besides, although such backtracking is manageable for simple objects such as the VP under discussion, recall that sentences in natural languages can have an unbounded number of recursions. Thus, the determination of the type of complex syntactic objects may be intractable if the constituent type is not encoded locally. Labels are in this regard a way of reducing the complexity of the task to a minimum: the system may simply check the label of a complex syntactic object to determine whether or not it can enter into a local relation with another syntactic object.

Consider in this regard an expression with a specifier, as well as a complement. What sort of locality could exist between *Mary* and *looked* in (65)/(69), for instance, without labeling? Note that the specifier and the head alone don't form a constituent and, assuming binary branching (see section 6.3.3 below), they are not immediate constituents of a larger object either. So, assuming that natural languages exploit at least two head-X relations (head-specifier and head-modifier) in addition to head-complement, such relations can be locally coded only if we allow the head to label all of its projections. In effect, labeling not only allows head-to-head relations to be locally stated, but also makes it possible to locally state *several* grammatical relations to the head, and this perhaps explains *why* natural languages have labeled constituents where the label codes information of the head.

Assuming that this suggestion is on the right track, we can also appreciate the role of the Inclusiveness Condition in the reasoning. The Inclusiveness Condition is more of a meta-theoretical condition in that it sets up boundaries for minimalist analyses; in particular, a minimalist analysis should refrain from adding theoretical entities that can't be construed as features of the lexical items that feed the derivation. An unavoidable violation of Inclusiveness can, however, serve to illustrate deeper properties of the system as it strives for optimal design. In the case at hand, despite the fact that labels may be at odds with Inclusiveness, they may also be the optimal way of allowing multiple relations with a head and determining the properties of a complex syntactic object, *all in a local manner*.

Let's recap. Minimalist commitments induce us to ask *why* each of the features found in phrase structure should hold true. What is it about language that gives it these features and not others? Why are constituents labeled? Why do heads project? These are tough questions and the suggestions above may well be on the wrong track. However, whatever the degree of our success in addressing these questions, it should not obscure the value and interest of the questions themselves. We noted in chapter 1 that one of the "big facts" about natural languages is that they have both words and phrases made up of words. Once this is noted, an operation like Merge, a grammatical operation that combines words into bigger and bigger units, is a natural feature of the system. What is less clear, however, is that labeling is also conceptually required given the "big facts" surveyed at the outset. Why do derived units need to have heads? We have suggested here that labeling is the optimal solution to a fact about words (they impose conditions on one another) and the basic relations among words (they enter into relations of specification, modification, and complementation to heads). The Strong Endocentricity Thesis amounts to saying that there are local grammatical bounds on the influence words can lexically exert on one another. We have conjectured that this, in turn, is possibly related to issues of computational efficiency as it puts a very local bound on word-to-word interactions. This looks like a good design feature. If this is indeed the case, then labeling can be seen as a solution to the following problem: allow words to interact but in a tractable manner.

So far, we have discussed complex syntactic objects involving complements and specifiers. What about adjuncts? How can they be distinguished from specifiers once the system allows as many specifiers as Spec-head relations licensed by a given head?

How to deal with adjunctions is a vexed problem within generative grammar, one that has never been adequately resolved. The properties of adjuncts are quite different from those of complements or specifiers. They don't enter into agreement relations, they appear to have different Case requirements from arguments, they are interpreted as conjuncts semantically, and they come in a very wide variety of category types. Thus, it's not clear what features, if any, are checked under merger by adjunction. Even more unclear is how exactly adjuncts syntactically relate to the elements that they modify. Recall that although forming a constituent with the modified projection, an adjunct is not dominated by the resulting syntactic object. This can be illustrated by head adjunction. Take V-to-T movement, for instance, which generates the structure in (70).

(70)

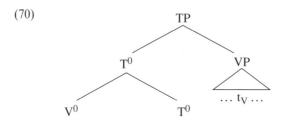

The verb and T in (70) clearly form a constituent, for T-to-C movement pied-pipes the verb adjoined to T. On the other hand, the moved verb can't be dominated by the structure resulting from adjunction; otherwise, it will fail to c-command its trace. That is why adjuncts are taken to be *contained* – not dominated – by the adjunction structure (see the discussion in section 5.4). Furthermore, we also want to say that adjunction of V to T doesn't disrupt the head-complement relation between T and VP. To borrow Haegeman's (1994) metaphor, being an adjunct is like being on a balcony: in some sense you are both inside and outside the apartment.

Translated in formal terms, being on a balcony amounts to saying that an adjunct doesn't change the label and bar-level of its target, though forming a constituent with it. To take a concrete example, if *hit John* in (71) is a non-minimal maximal projection labeled *hit*, the adjunction structure *hit John hard* in (72) should be characterized in the same way *and* – here comes the tricky part – preserve the previous bar-level specification about *hit John*; that is, *hit John* in (72) should remain a non-minimal maximal projection.

(71)   {hit, {hit, John}}

(72)   {?, {{hit, {hit, John}}, hard}}

If the label of (72) were just *hit*, the constituent in (71) would have projected, becoming an intermediate projection (a non-minimal non-maximal projection) with *hard* as its Spec. In other words, if the labels of adjunction structures were like the labels of projection structures, there would be no way to distinguish specifiers from adjuncts. We thus need another kind of label to make the appropriate distinctions. (73) below, which revives the old notation of Chomsky-adjunction, may well serve these purposes.[20]

(73)   {<hit, hit>, {{hit, {hit, John}}, hard}}

The pair <*hit, hit*> is taken to mean that the structure in (71), whose label is *hit*, determines the label of the structure in (73), but doesn't project. If (71) doesn't project in (73), it remains a non-minimal maximal projection, as desired.

Again, the notation above is nothing more than that: a notation. If it's not clear what the appropriate technical implementation of labeling under regular projection should be, labeling under adjunction gets even murkier.[21] However, the relevant questions about adjunction concern not the technology to get the empirical job done, but why it has the properties it has, rather than others. To date, no good answer has been forthcoming and we provide none here. For concreteness, we'll assume that the distinction between merger by projection and merger by adjunction in terms of their different labels reflects the different nature of the grammatical relations each operation establishes. In the sections that follow, we'll keep using the traditional bracket or tree notation, which are much easier to process visually, unless a substantial issue may be at stake.

To summarize, this section has reviewed the mechanics of phrase construction under the operation Merge. Merge is conceptually necessary given the obvious fact that sentences are composed of words and phrases. We have tried to provide some conceptual motivation for labeling as well. Whatever the insight gained by going down the road sketched above, many questions remain. For example, say we grant that labeling is in service of locality, *why* is it that we distinguish modifiers from specifiers and complements? Is this a semantic distinction projected into the syntax or is it an irreducibly syntactic categorization? Moreover, *why* are complements sisters of heads, while specifiers are sisters of intermediate projections, and not the opposite? What in the end distinguishes specifiers from modifiers? These are questions we have left to one side not because they

---

20 Whenever an expression is Chomsky-adjoined to an XP, the resultant structure bears the same label as the target of the adjunction. In (i), the adjunct *at six* is Chomsky-adjoined to the VP. Note that the constituent without *at six* is a VP as is the VP plus *at six*.

    (i)   John [VP [VP ate a bagel] [at six]]

21 For technical definitions of dominance, containment, and c-command using the set notations such as (71) and (73), see Nunes and Thompson (1998).

are unimportant, but because we currently have no compelling suggestions, let alone answers. Many questions remain open that we are confident that readers of this book will one day successfully address.

Exercise 6.9

Under traditional X′-Theory, the representation of multiple specifiers is indistinguishable from the notation of adjuncts to intermediate projections, as illustrated by the *v*P structure in (i), which is formed after the object moves to the outer [Spec,*v*P]. Provide the bare-phrase-structure representation of (i) and explain why it can't be confused with an adjunction structure.

(i)   [$_{vP}$ OB [$_{v'}$ SU [$_{v'}$ *v* [$_{VP}$ V t$_{OB}$]]]]

Exercise 6.10

Chomsky (1995) has suggested that what prevents the projection of two merged elements in a range of cases is that their features are such that they can't form a composite label, if we understand a label as being composite in the sense of the union or intersection of the features of merged elements. For example, under the assumption that a verb has the set of features {+V, −N} and a noun has the set of features {−V, +N}, if a verb and a noun merge and both project, the intersection of their features would be the null set and the union would be the set {+V, −N, −V, +N}, with incompatible properties. Notice, however, that this suggestion opens the possibility that if features don't conflict, double projection should in principle be possible.

  Having these observations as background, discuss if they could provide a viable way to explain periscope effects where a verb selects a noun buried within a DP-structure (see exercise 6.5). What would be the advantages and disadvantages of such an alternative analysis?

6.3.3   *Revisiting the properties of phrase structure*

Leaving aside the issue of bar-levels, which was addressed in section 6.3.1, let's now reconsider the other properties of phrase structure discussed in section 6.2 from the point of view of the "bare" phrase-structure approach reviewed in section 6.3.2. Let's start with binary branching.

  As discussed in section 6.2.2, the fact that phrase structure in natural languages displays binary branching is reasonably well motivated on empirical grounds. That being so, we should now face the question of *why* the language faculty should restrict syntactic objects this way. Minimalism may offer a possible answer. We noted that in building a sentence, we begin with lexical atoms and combine them via Merge to form larger and larger units. What is the nature of Merge? *If* it's an operation that combines at most two elements per operational step, then the fact that there is binary branching reflects the basics of this operation. Is there some reason why it should be that Merge involves at most two elements per step? Perhaps. Minimalism puts a premium on simple assumptions and asks that they be accorded methodological privilege in the sense of being shown to be inadequate before replaced. This has a potential impact on the specifics of the Merge operation as follows: What is the simplest instance of merger? What are the minimal specifications for a Merge operation that respect the "big facts" we know about natural language?

One thing we know is that Merge must be recursive. It can apply both to basic lexical items and to expressions that have themselves been formed via applications of Merge. This simply reflects the fact that there is no upper bound on sentence size. Second, it must be the case that Merge can combine *at least two* lexical items and form them into a constituent. We know this on two grounds. First, because this is the minimum required to get recursivity off the ground. We can't get larger and larger units unless we can repeatedly combine at least two units together again and again. Second, we have plenty of evidence that we need a two-place Merge operation to code some of the most basic facts, like the formation of unaccusative or transitive predicates, for instance. In other words, we need Merge to be able to form simple structures such as (74).

(74)   [$_{VP}$ arrived he]

Now for a minimalist maneuver. It's clearly necessary that Merge be able to take at least two arguments; all things being equal, it would be nice (on methodological grounds) if we could strengthen this, so that it's also true that Merge takes at most two arguments. In other words, seeing that two is the minimum required to meet the "big fact" of recursion in natural languages, it would be nice if it were the maximum as well. Note that this argument is very similar in form to the one that restricted levels to LF and PF (see chapter 2). We need at least these two to deal with sound/sign–meaning pairs; so, methodologically, we should try and make do with only these two. So too here: we need at least a two-place Merge operation; we should thus try and make do with at most a two-place Merge operation. That being so, binary branching follows straightforwardly. Consider the details.

Suppose we take three lexical items, α, β, and γ out of a numeration and try to form a ternary branching structure K as illustrated in (75), by simultaneously merging them.

(75)

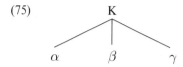

If Merge is a two-place operation, however, it can only manipulate two elements at a time, and a structure such as (75) can't be generated. Merge should first target two of the lexical items, say α and β, forming K, and then combine K with the remaining lexical item, as shown in (76) below. But notice that only binary branching structures are yielded.

(76)   a.

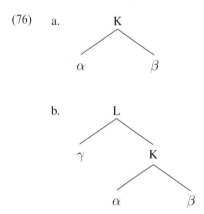

So it's perhaps plausible that binary branching is a reflection of the simplicity of language design: a two-place Merge operation is the minimum required to allow recursion (a "big fact"). Methodologically, it would be best if that were all that was required. Binary branching suggests that, at least in this respect, we live in the best of possible worlds. Pangloss be praised!

As for endocentricity (see section 6.2.1), it arguably follows from the interaction between Last Resort and the asymmetric nature of the local grammatical relations of head-complement, Spec-head, and modification. The Last Resort condition demands that every operation must serve a grammatical purpose. In the case at hand, if two elements are combined by Merge, either a head-complement, Spec-head, or modification relation must obtain in order for it to be licensed. Having one of these elements label the resulting structure creates an asymmetry between them that may ground these asymmetric relations. In fact, given the suggestion in section 6.2.2 regarding the inherent features of the head and their role in projection, the constituent containing the head will always project. Thus, any complex syntactic object will have its properties determined by one of its immediate constituents; that is, syntactic objects are always endocentric.

Finally, let's consider the singlemotherhood property, according to which a syntactic constituent can't have multiple mothers. Suppose, for instance, that after having merged α and β, forming K, we try to merge γ with β, forming L, as illustrated in (77).

(77)   a.

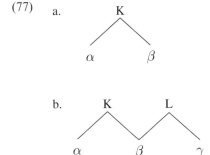

The step illustrated in (77b) is, however, precluded by the Extension Condition, which requires that Merge target root syntactic objects. That is, once K is formed in (77a) its constituents are no longer available for further merger. Addition of γ in the structure will have to be through merger with K, as seen in (76b).

Notice that it might also be possible to conceive of the Extension condition as a reflex of simplicity in the system. If only root syntactic objects can be merged, as in (76), the search space for the computational system is considerably reduced, for the pool of potential mergers is narrowed down to a minimum.

To summarize, the discussion above suggests that many of the properties of phrase structure in natural languages captured by X′-Theory can receive a more principled account if we assume a two-place structure-building operation such as Merge, coupled with general minimalist principles of economy and methodological simplicity.

Exercise 6.11

Discuss whether vacuous intermediate projections can be generated if structures are built by applications of Merge as described in section 6.2.2. In particular, what prevents an element from merging with itself?

Exercise 6.12

Consider the structure in (i), where the verb has adjoined to T in violation of the Extension Condition. Lay out the problem and discuss possible scenarios under which such movement could comply with the Extension Condition.

(i)

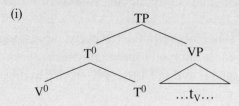

6.4   The operation Move and the copy theory

To this point, we have mainly discussed what we might term the "base configurations" of phrases, those formed by a series of Merge operations. Let's now address the question of how structures formed by movement are generated. Recall that within GB, movement proceeds by filling empty positions projected at DS or adjoining to structures projected at DS, in accordance with the Structure Preservation Condition. In section 2.3.2, however, we saw not only that there is no need for all the structure-building operations to precede movement, but also, and more importantly, that there is empirical evidence showing that structure-building and movement operations should actually be interspersed (see sections 2.3.2.3 and 2.3.2.4). Having these considerations in mind, how should we understand the operation Move under the context of the bare phrase structure discussed in the previous sections?

Take the movement illustrated in (78) below, for instance. Part of the description of the movement in (78) is identical to the Merge operation depicted in (79). In both cases, the syntactic object labeled TP in (78a) and (79a) merges with another syntactic object, *a man* in (78b) and *there* in (79b), establishing a Spec-head relation and further projecting, thus becoming an intermediate projection.

(78)   a. [TP T [VP arrived [DP a man]]]
        b. [TP [DP a man]i [T' T [VP arrived ti]]]

(79)   a. [TP T [VP arrived [DP a man]]]
        b. [TP there [T' T [VP arrived [DP a man]]]]

In other words, a movement operation appears to take Merge as one of its components.[22] Under this view, then it's not at all that surprising that Merge and movement can alternate.

What are then the other components? Well, we have to say that somehow a trace is inserted in the object position of *arrived* in (78b) and this seems to put us in a corner. On the one hand, the empirical motivation for traces is overwhelming, as any cursory look in the GB-literature can show. On the other hand, traces are by definition theoretical primes inserted in the course of the computation and are not present in the numeration, which is at odds with the Inclusiveness Condition.

Upon closer inspection, it may be that the size of the problem is actually related to the way in which it was presented. In fact, we don't have overwhelming evidence for *traces* and, for that matter, not even for *movement*. After all, nobody would bother to check if the speed of the DP in (78b) was within legal limits ... In other words, what we actually have is an amazing set of facts that show that elements that appear in one position may get interpreted in a different position, the so-called *displacement property* of human languages (one of the "big facts"). The question that we have to address then is: can we account for this property within the bounds of minimalist desiderata?

The structure-building part of movement, as we have seen, can be naturally captured by Merge. What we have to come up with is a solution for the "residue" of movement that is congenial to Inclusiveness. A conceivable way to meet this requirement is to assume that a trace is actually a copy of the moved element.[23] As a copy, it's not a new theoretical primitive; rather, it is whatever the moved element is, namely, a syntactic object built based on features of the numeration. In other words, if traces are copies, Inclusiveness is pleased. Under this view, the movement depicted in (78) should actually proceed along the lines of (80), where the system makes a copy of *a man* and merges it with TP in (80a).

(80)   a. $[_{TP}$ T $[_{VP}$ arrived $[_{DP}$ a man $]]]$
        b. *Copy DP* $\rightarrow$
           $[_{DP}$ a man $]$
        c. *Merge DP and TP* $\rightarrow$
           $[_{TP}$ $[_{DP}$ a man $]$ $[_{T'}$ T $[_{VP}$ arrived $[_{DP}$ a man $]]]]$

22 See section 10.2.2 for potential consequences for economy computations.
23 See Chomsky (1993), Nunes (1995, 1999, 2001, 2004), Bošković (2001), and Bošković and Nunes (2004), among others.

Note that treating movement as simply the sequence of operations Copy
and Merge leads us to expect that whatever principles apply when Merge
alone (i.e. without Copy) obtains should also hold when movement (Copy
and Merge) takes place. Consider, for example, the fact that Merge alone is
subject to Last Resort, that is, it must serve some purpose. The same
is observed with respect to movement. The merger in (80c), for instance, is
licensed by Last Resort in that it allows the strong feature of T and the Case
feature of both T and *a man* to be checked.

Now consider the issue of how the label of the constituent resulting from
movement is determined. In particular, one wonders *why* the whole expression in (80c), for instance, is labeled TP, or put more generally, *why* the
target of movement projects. Well, what else could it be? Recall that the
Strong Endocentricity Thesis requires that in order for a local grammatical
relation (Spec-head, head-complement, or head modifier) to be established, the head of the constituent must project. In the case of (80c), the
checking relations mentioned above should take place under a Spec-head
relation with T; hence, the head T projects and the resulting projection is a
TP. According to a suggestion made in section 6.3.2, this is arguably related
to the fact that it makes sense to say that T in (80a) needs a specifier, but it
doesn't make any sense at all to say that *a man* in (80a) needs a head to be the
specifier of. The important thing is that this is not different in essence from
the (simple) merger in (79): the Strong Endocentricity Thesis requires that T
projects, as shown in (79b), in order for the Spec-head relation afforded by
Merge to be established, and this is again arguably due to the fact that it's an
inherent property of T that it requires a specifier, but it's not an inherent
property of *there* that it requires a head to be the specifier of.

If we assume that the grammar only looks at what it has in deciding what
to do next and doesn't "remember" earlier operations (in other words, if
tree building is Markovian), then the fact that what is merged in movement
is a copy is irrelevant to the Merge operation applied. As far as the
grammar is concerned, both applications of Merge are identical and so
should be subject to identical principles. Recall the suggestion in section
6.3.2 that labeling could be understood as a feature of optimal design of the
system in that it allows structure building to work with the current information available, with no need to backtrack to earlier stages of phrase-
structure building. That this line of reasoning also yields the desired
empirical outcomes in the context of movement is quite pleasing and
buttresses the assumption that movement is not a primitive operation,
but the combination of the operations Copy and Merge.

At this point, the reader might, however, ask if this way of satisfying Inclusiveness is not too extravagant: the cost being the introduction of a new operation, Copy, and a new problem: why is the structure in (80c) not pronounced as (81), with the two links of the DP-chain phonetically realized or, to put in general terms, why can a trace not be phonetically realized?

(81)   *A man arrived a man.

As it turns out, the alternative sketched above seems to be neither theoretically costly, nor empirically problematic. First, it seems that we independently need an operation like Copy.[24] To see this, let's examine what we mean when we say that we "take" an item from the lexicon. Clearly, this is not like taking a marble from a bag containing marbles. In the latter case, after taking the marble, the bag contains one less marble. In contrast, consider the (simplified) numeration that feeds (80) given in (82) below, for instance. When we say that we took those four items from the lexicon to form N in (82), we definitely don't mean that the lexicon has now shrunk and lost four items. Rather, what we are tacitly assuming is that numerations are formed by *copying* items from the lexicon. Thus, once the system independently needs such a copying procedure, it could as well use it in the syntactic computation, as illustrated in (80).

(82) $N = \{arrived_1, a_1, man_1, T_1\}$

Second, we do indeed find instances where traces are pronounced, as illustrated in (83), where the intermediate traces of *met wie* 'with who' are realized.[25]

(83)   *Afrikaans*
          Met wie het   jy nou weer gesê met wie het Sarie
          with who have you now again said with who did Sarie
          gedog   met wie gaan Jan trou?
          thought with who go   Jan marry
          'Who(m) did you say again that Sarie thought Jan is going to marry?'

Cases such as (83) suggest that the realization of copies is more a matter of the phonological component, rather than syntax *per se*. We'll return to this issue in chapter 7 and discuss a plausible explanation for why in general a chain doesn't surface with all *of* its links phonetically realized, as shown by (81).

---

24 See Hornstein (2001).
25 The Afrikaans datum is taken from du Plessis (1977).

Finally, by assuming that traces are actually copies, we may be able to account for binding facts within minimalist boundaries. Consider the sentence in (84), for instance, which should be represented as in (85), under the trace theory of movement.

(84)   Which picture of himself did John see?

(85)   [[which picture of himself]$_i$ did [John see t$_i$]]

In (85), the anaphor is not bound by *John*, but the sentence in (84) is nevertheless acceptable. In order to account for cases like this, GB requires additional provisos. For instance, Binding Theory should be checked at DS, prior to movement of *which picture of himself*, or at LF, after the moved element is "reconstructed," that is, put back in its original position; alternatively, the notion of binding should be modified in such a way that *John* in (85) gets to bind *himself* in virtue of its c-commanding the trace of the element containing *himself*.[26]

Leaving a more detailed discussion of Binding Theory to chapter 8 below, what is relevant for our purposes is that the copy theory accounts for (84), without extra machinery. As seen in (86), the copy of *himself* in the object position is appropriately bound by *John*, as desired.

(86)   [[which picture of himself] did [John see [which picture of himself]]]

To summarize, the copy theory of movement seems to be an approach to the displacement property of human languages worth pursuing, in that it's tuned to minimalist worries and has some empirical bite both on the PF and LF sides. In the chapters that follow, we'll examine several other issues that also point to the conclusion that movement is just the result of applications of Copy and Merge.

Exercise 6.13

In section 2.3.2.2, it was proposed that the TRAP, as defined in (i), would prevent a derivation of (ii) along the lines of (iii), with raising to a thematic position. As seen in this section, the copy theory takes movement to be the combination of the operations Copy and Merge. If this is so, how is the derivation in (iii) to be blocked? Or, to put it in more general terms, given the theoretical framework developed thus far, should it be blocked? If so, why?

---

26 See Barss (1986), for instance, for a proposal along these lines.

(i)   *Theta-Role Assignment Principle (TRAP)*
      θ-roles can only be assigned under a Merge operation.

(ii) Mary hoped to kiss John.

(iii) [Mary$_i$ hoped [t$_i$ to kiss John]]

6.5   Conclusion

Generative grammar has had many illuminating things to say about phrase structure. Minimalism has adopted the main results of these earlier approaches, largely encompassed by X′-Theory, and has tried to rationalize and explain the various properties of phrase structure on grounds of economy, simplicity, and optimal design. This, in turn, has led to very interesting questions and minimalism has raised them to prominence even if it has not yet offered fully compelling answers.

This chapter has argued in particular that the key properties of phrase structure follow from the inner workings of the structure-building operation Merge, coupled with general minimalist conditions, yielding what was referred to as a bare phrase structure. In addition, it was proposed that Move is not a primitive operation of the system, but the result of the interaction between the operations Copy and Merge (the copy theory of movement). Recent developments in the theory of movement strengthen the theoretical appeal of such an approach with very interesting empirical evidence, as we'll see in the chapters that follow.

7   *Linearization*

7.1   Introduction

To this point we have left the issue of linear word order aside and have concentrated exclusively on structural properties. This focus reflects the widely accepted and long-held belief within the generative tradition that grammatical operations are structure-dependent and do not (by and large) exploit linear dependencies. The study of grammar has been, until very recently, the study of hierarchical dependencies and their alterations. Linear properties were taken to be of secondary interest (if of any interest at all) to grammarians.

Under this traditional view, English and Japanese VPs, for instance, are structurally the same (their dominance and sisterhood relations are identical), their difference residing only in the order of constituents, with the verb preceding its object in English, but following it in Japanese, as respectively represented in (1) and (2).

(1)   Norbert [$_{VP}$ ate bagels]

(2)   *Japanese*
       Jiro-ga [$_{VP}$ sushi-o   tabeta]
       Jiro-NOM   sushi-ACC   ate
       'Jiro ate sushi.'

The type of superficial difference illustrated in (1) and (2) was captured by directionality parameters that stated the order between heads and complements and heads and specifiers for the constituents of a given language.[1] In the case at hand, for instance, English was taken to set the option *VO* and Japanese was taken to set the option *OV* for the parameter regarding the order between the verb and its complement.

---

1 For early discussion, see Chomsky (1981), Stowell (1981), Koopman (1984), and Travis (1984).

In this chapter, we'll address the question of how to deal with linear order within minimalism, based on Kayne's (1994) influential work, which takes word order to piggyback on hierarchical structure. But before getting to the details proper, we should first ask the following minimalist question: *why* do we have linear order?

One interesting answer to this question is that linearization is what we get when we try to force a two-dimensional structure through a one-dimensional channel. Phrase-markers are 2D-objects: their lexical items are organized in terms of the sisterhood and the dominance relation; that is, phrase-markers have breadth and depth. The organization of PF outputs is, however, one-dimensional: a string of sounds or signs. Linearization can thus be conceived as the process required to get phrase-markers ready for manipulation by the Articulatory-Perceptual (*A-P*) system, which interfaces with the PF level (see section 1.3). In other words, linearization is the price one pays for "losing" a dimension, for having to plug a square peg into a round hole.

If this is correct, then linearization is essentially a PF-affair: an interface requirement imposed by the A-P system. Without linearization, the A-P system would not be able to "read" grammatical objects. Under the assumption that grammatical derivations only converge if they are legible at *both* the LF and PF interfaces (see section 1.5), linearization thus exists because it is required for PF legibility, therefore for convergence.

If linearization can be justified along these lines, then it is not a quirk in the system, but rather a response to interface conditions. The next minimalist question we can then ask is: how *optimal* is such a response? This is what we'll be discussing in the next sections. In section 7.2 we point out some undesirable features of the approach to linear order in terms of directionality parameters and in section 7.3 we discuss an alternative approach in terms of Kayne's Linear Correspondence Axiom, which takes precedence at PF to be determined by asymmetric c-command. Section 7.4 discusses how the LCA captures correlations between syntactic phenomena and word order and section 7.5 shows how the LCA may be indirectly responsible for the fact that traces (in general) are not phonetically realized. Finally, section 7.6 concludes the chapter.

7.2   Imposing linear order onto X′-Theory templates

As mentioned above, the traditional GB-approach to word order is that linear relations are *added* to the structural relations of a phrase-marker and that cross-linguistic variation with respect to word order is captured by directionality parameters that specify the order of complements and specifiers with respect to the relevant heads. That is, given the structural relations established by X'-Theory, such directionality parameters would fix one of the options available in (3) and (4).

(3)   a. X' → X Compl
        b. X' → Compl X

(4)   a. XP → Spec X'
        b. XP → X' Spec

There are two kinds of problems with this approach, as pointed out by Kayne (1994). The first one is that it appears to overgenerate in predicting structures that are not found in natural languages. Take the options in (4) applied to CP projections, for instance. If [Spec,CP] could either precede or follow C', we should in principle expect *wh*-movement in natural languages to explore both options. This is not the case, however. Languages massively take option (4a), with *wh*-movement to a left [Spec,CP], instead of (4b), with *wh*-movement to a right [Spec,CP]. There are just a few languages that allegedly allow *wh*-movement to a right [Spec,CP] reported in the literature, and even for these, the evidence is not very clear.[2]

Another interesting gap in this approach in terms of parameters of directionality regards "anti-V2 structures." V2 languages such as German are standardly analyzed as involving movement of a finite verb to C and movement of some XP to [Spec,CP], under the options in (3a) and (4a) for projections of C.[3] The sentence in (5a), for instance, is assigned the simplified structure in (5b).

(5)   *German*
        a. Gestern   hat   Joachim   eine   leckere   Bratwurst   gegessen.
           yesterday has   Joachim   a   tasty   bratwurst   eaten
           'Yesterday, Joachim ate a tasty bratwurst.'

---

2 As Sabel (1998) discusses, Bergvall (1987) entertains such a proposal for Kikuyu. However, these right-peripheral *wh*-phrases show different properties from left-peripheral landing sites; for example, Tuller (1992) shows for Tangale, Ngizim, and Kanakuru (all Afro-Asiatic/Chad languages) that postverbal *wh*-phrases sit in a focus position which is not filled by rightward movement. See also Petronio and Lillo-Martin's (1997) reanalysis of the American Sign Language (ASL) data that Neidle, Kegl, Bahan, Aarons, and MacLaughlin (1997) analyzed in terms of *wh*-movement to a right [Spec,CP].

3 This long-standing tradition goes back to Bach (1962), Koster (1975), den Besten (1977, 1989), and Thiersch (1978) and constitutes the standard analysis still today (but see Zwart 1993, 1997).

b. [$_{CP}$ Gestern$_k$ [$_{C'}$ hat$_i$ + C^0 [$_{TP}$ Joachim t$_k$ eine leckere Bratwurst gegessen t$_i$]]]

If languages could freely choose among the options of (3) and (4) with respect to matrix C, we should in principle expect to find the mirror-image of German, that is, a language that explores the options (3b) and (4b) and whose last constituents would be a finite verb and an XP, as illustrated in (6). However, no such languages seem to exist.

(6)   [[$_{C'}$ [$_{TP}$ ... t$_V$ t$_{XP}$] [V + T] + C^0] XP]

It should be pointed out that these gaps across languages are not by themselves a knockout argument against the directionality-parameter approach. After all, it could perfectly be the case that the apparent non-existence of rightward movement to [Spec,CP] and "anti-V2 structures" could be independently explained by principles yet to be discovered. These unexpected gaps are nonetheless interesting enough to stimulate minimalist thought.

A more serious problem in this regard is the fact that the directionality-parameter approach has nothing to say about robustly attested correlations between word order and syntactic phenomena. Consider the options for the order between a head and its complement in (3), for instance. Given that the syntactic relations are the same in both orders, we should expect them never to differ in syntactic terms.

This is clearly not the case, however. Take the difference between prepositions and postpositions, for instance. Under the directionality-parameter approach, these adpositions just reflect the two options in (3). If a language chooses (3a), we have a prepositional system, as shown in (7a); if it chooses (3b), we have a postpositional system instead, as in (7b).

(7)   a. [$_{PP}$ P DP]
         b. [$_{PP}$ DP P]

However, the two options do differ in terms of agreement possibilities. As mentioned in section 4.3.3, adpositions may agree with their argument in languages that employ postpositions, but not in languages that use prepositions.[4] And this asymmetry may even be attested within the same language if it admits both prepositions and postpositions. As seen in

---

4 See Kayne (1994: 49), citing Ken Hale in personal communication.

section 4.3.3, in Hungarian, for instance, one may find the order P-DP only with adpositions that don't permit agreement with their argument, as shown in (8) below. Under the standard assumption that agreement phenomena are syntactic in nature, why they should be influenced by word order is a mystery within the directionality-parameter approach.

(8)   *Hungarian*
    a. én-mögött-em
       I-behind-POSS.1.SG
    b. *mögött-em   én
       behind-POSS.1.SG I
       'behind me'
    c. *a   hídon   át
       the bridge.SUP over
    d. át   a   hídon
       over the bridge.SUP
       'over the bridge'

Another correlation between the options in (3) with syntactic phenomena is illustrated by extraction. In Basque, for instance, a clausal complement may follow or precede the subcategorizing verb, as illustrated in (9). Under the options in (3), that amounts to saying that Basque may allow either of the structures in (10).

(9)   *Basque*
    a. Jonek   uste du [Mirenek   bera   maite duela]
       Jon.ERG think AUX Miren.ERG he.ABS love   AUX.COMP
    b. Jonek [Mirenek   bera   maite duela] uste du.
       Jon.ERG Miren.ERG he.ABS love AUX.COMP think AUX
       'Jon thinks that Miren loves him.'

(10)   a. $[_{VP}$ V $[_{CP} \dots]]$
    b. $[_{VP} [_{CP} \dots]$ V $]$

If this is all there is to this alternation, the question then is why the order in (10a) allows extraction from within the embedded clause, but the order in (10b) doesn't, as respectively illustrated in (11).[5]

---

5 This argument was first raised by Ormazabal, Uriagereka, and Uribe-Etxebarria (1994). We use double embedding since Basque *wh*-movement enforces a kind of inversion in which nothing may intervene between the overtly moved *wh*-phrase and the verbal element. See Ormazabal (1995) and Uriagereka (1999d) for relevant discussion.

(11)   *Basque*
    a. Nor$_i$ uste du Jonek [esan duela   Mirenek [Aitorrek t$_i$
    who.ABS think AUX Jon.ERG said   AUX.COMP Miren.ERG Aitor.ERG
    maite duela]]?
    love   AUX.COMP
    b. ?? Nor$_i$ uste du   Jonek [[Aitorrek t$_i$ maite duela]   esan
       who.ABS think AUX   Jon.ERG   Aitor.ERG   love AUX.COMP said
    duela   Mirenek]?
    AUX.COMP   Miren.ERG
    'Who does Jon think that Miren said that Aitor loves?'

To summarize, though satisfying the requirements of the A-P system, the mere addition of linear order to phrase-markers doesn't leave much room to account for correlations between syntactic relations and word order – and this is a very unfortunate state of affairs. Let's then consider an alternative.

7.3   The Linear Correspondence Axiom (LCA)

In section 7.1, it was suggested that the A-P system requires that the object it receives has linear order properties. However, the discussion in section 7.2 indicates that if we just add linear order as an independent property of grammatical objects, we will not be able to capture some interesting correlations between syntactic relations and word order. Conceivably, it could be the case that the mere addition of a linear order relation is not the optimal way to satisfy the requirements of the A-P system. Suppose this is so. Then the question is whether there is a more optimal way to meet such requirements.

Well, recall from our discussion of projections and labeling (section 6.3.2) that the asymmetric nature of head-complement, Spec-head, and head-modifier relations arguably imposes an asymmetry on the simple combination of syntactic objects, leading one of the objects to project and label the resulting constituent. Perhaps something of that sort is what goes on with linear order business. The precedence relation among lexical items that is detected at PF is also an asymmetric relation: if a lexical item α precedes a lexical item β, it must be the case that β doesn't precede α. Given that the mere addition of precedence in the system was not very satisfactory, as we have just seen in section 7.2, another possibility is to look for an asymmetric relation already existing within syntactic objects that could be mapped onto precedence. With this in mind, consider the syntactic relations of an abstract structure such as (12), for example, where α and β are lexical items.

(12)

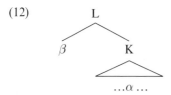

The sisterhood relation between β and K is symmetrical (i.e. they c-command each other), therefore irrelevant for our purposes. The dominance relation between L and β and L and α, for instance, is by contrast asymmetric (neither β nor α dominate L); however, it alone doesn't seem very useful to establish a precedence relation between α and β, given that both of these lexical items stand in the same relation with respect to L (namely, they are both dominated by L). Now consider the combination of sisterhood and dominance, namely C-Command, as defined in (13).[6]

(13)   *C-Command*
        α c-commands β iff
        (i) α is a sister of β or
        (ii) α is a sister of γ and γ dominates β.

According to (13), β and K in (12) c-command each other in virtue of being sisters, a symmetrical relation that is again irrelevant for our purposes. The c-command relation between β and α is, however, asymmetric: β c-commands α in virtue of being the sister of an ancestor of α (namely, K), but α doesn't c-command β; that is, β asymmetrically c-commands α. Let's then consider the possibility that asymmetric c-command is the optimal structural relation to be mapped onto precedence. That is, assuming that two-dimensional syntactic objects have to be flattened out into strings of lexical items, the phonological system, rather than adding the precedence relation onto phrasal objects, should be able to "read" precedence off the syntactic tree, by focusing on asymmetric c-command relations.

This is in essence the intuition behind Kayne's (1994) proposal that linear order is established based on asymmetric c-command relations, in accordance with an algorithm he referred to as the *Linear Correspondence*

---

6 For relevant discussion of c-command within the bare phrase-structure system, see Epstein (1999) and Chomsky (2000, 2001, 2004).

Axiom (LCA). In order to discuss the details of such a mapping algorithm, we must first make it explicit what kind of phrase structure one is assuming. Kayne's original formulation of the LCA was based on (a version of) X′-Theory. We will, however, discuss the LCA in the context of the bare phrase-structure system, given its promising results reviewed in chapter 6. As a starting point, let's assume the preliminary version of the LCA given in (14) and examine the structure in (15b).

(14)   *Linear Correspondence Axiom (LCA)* (preliminary version)
         A lexical item α precedes a lexical item β iff α asymmetrically c-commands β.

(15)   a. Norbert will eat the big bagel.
         b. [$_{TP}$ Norbert$_i$ [$_{T'}$ will [$_{VP}$ t$_i$ [$_{V'}$ eat [$_{DP}$ the [$_{NP}$ big [$_{NP}$ bagel]]]]]]]

For the sake of discussion, let's assume that an adjunct asymmetrically c-commands the target of adjunction. If so, the structure in (15b) can be mapped on to the sequence *Norbert >will >eat >the >big >bagel*, where ">" may be read as either 'asymmetrically c-commands' or 'precedes'. In other words, as stated in (14), the LCA correctly predicts that the structure in (15b) will surface at PF with the order seen in (15a).

The reader might have noticed that in (15b) we used a trace rather than a copy of *Norbert* (see section 6.4). We return to this issue below in section 7.5. For now, it suffices to assume that lower copies are phonologically empty for some reason, and that only phonologically visible elements are relevant for linearization purposes. The last assumption makes a lot of sense. It's simply a fact that in the flow of speech or signing, we don't find "empty beats" (momentary interruptions of speech or signing) corresponding to empty categories. It's true that that would have made the theoreticians' lives much easier, but theoreticians' happiness doesn't appear to be a factor in how biology makes grammars.

The neat correspondence between asymmetric c-command and precedence seen in (15) suggests that a mapping along the lines stated in (14) may indeed be an optimal way to meet the linearization requirements of the A-P system. However, when a sentence such as (16a) is considered, we see that things can't be that simple.

(16)   a. The man from Toledo will visit Mary.
         b. [$_{TP}$ [$_{DP}$ the man from Toledo]$_i$ [$_{T'}$ will [$_{VP}$ t$_i$ [$_{V'}$ visit Mary]]]]

The structure in (16b) presents two distinct problems with respect to the formulation of the LCA in (14). First, the complex subject. Note that none of the lexical items inside the complex subject enter into an asymmetric c-command relation with any of the lexical items in the rest of the sentence. As such, (14) can't order the lexical items inside the subject with respect to the remaining lexical items. *Toledo* and *will*, for instance, don't stand in an asymmetric c-command relation and therefore they can't be linearized with respect to one another, given (14). Second, take a look at the foot of the structure. *Visit* and *Mary* c-command each other; hence, according to (14), no order could be established between them either. Let's consider each of these problems in turn, starting with the complex subject.

Let's first reconsider a less problematic case. Given that *will* in (16b) asymmetrically c-commands *Mary*, the LCA mandates that the former precedes the latter. This of course entails that the phonemes of *will* also precede the phonemes of *Mary*. However, this result doesn't follow from the LCA, since phonemes don't enter into c-command relations. Rather, the relevant precedence among the phonemes of *will* and *Mary* is a byproduct of the fact that these phonemes are integral parts of the lexical items that undergo linearization. Now suppose for the sake of reasoning that we could consider *the man from Toledo* in (16b) as a kind of complex lexical item. If this were true, the linear order between such a complex element and *will*, for instance, would pose no problems; once the postulated complex lexical item would asymmetrically c-command *will*, it should precede *will*. Now, still following this reasoning, if *Toledo* is part of such a complex lexical item, it should also precede *will* just by being part of the complex item *the man from Toledo*, in a way similar to the case of the precedence relation among phonemes of different lexical items just mentioned. Given that it doesn't appear to make sense to say that *the man from Toledo* in (16a) is a complex lexical item, another possibility compatible with the reasoning being entertained is to allow this phrase to be independently computed by the LCA and have the order between *Toledo* and *will*, for instance, piggyback on the linearization of the complex subject as a whole.[7]

---

7 Of course, whether or not these remarks make sense depends exactly on what is meant by *complex lexical item*. In fact, Uriagereka (1999c) explores an approach along these lines in an attempt to keep the LCA as simple as (14). In order to linearize complex subjects and complex adjuncts with respect to the rest of the clause while still sticking to (14), Uriagereka proposes that Spell-Out may apply as many times as necessary. In particular, it may apply independently to complex subjects and adjuncts, shipping them to the phonological

Consider the reformulation of the LCA in (17) in this regard.

(17)   *Linear Correspondence Axiom (LCA)* (final version)
         A lexical item α precedes a lexical item β iff
         (i) α asymmetrically c-commands β or
         (ii) an XP dominating α asymmetrically c-commands β.

According to the condition (ii) of (17), *Toledo* must precede *will* in (16b), because the DP *the man from Toledo*, which dominates *Toledo*, asymmetrically c-commands *will*. The lexical items buried within a complex subject will therefore get ordered with respect to the remaining lexical items of the clause in virtue of the linearization of the complex subject itself. To put it in more general terms, *all* the parts of an XP precede whatever that XP precedes.

Before addressing the second puzzle, notice that the second condition of (17) makes specific reference to an XP, not to any syntactic object dominating α. In particular, intermediate projections are disregarded for the purposes of linearization. This is in fact crucial. Consider T' in (16b), for instance. Unless explicitly stipulated, T' does asymmetrically c-command the lexical items dominated by the complex subject. Thus, if intermediate projections were not excluded from (17), no order could be established among the lexical items dominated by the subject and the ones dominated by T'. For instance, *Toledo* would be required to precede *will* in virtue of the fact that the subject asymmetrically c-commands *will*, but *will* would also be required to precede *Toledo* in virtue of the fact that T' asymmetrically c-commands *Toledo*. The contradictory requirement that *Toledo* and *will* should precede each other doesn't arise, however, if the LCA only takes into consideration heads and maximal projections but ignores intermediate projections, as stated in (17ii).

So, empirically, we must restrict the LCA to lexical items and XPs. But is there a conceptual reason for the LCA to be restricted to only XPs among the relevant phrasal syntactic objects? Perhaps. Recall that linearization is at the service of the phonological component and it appears that phonology looks at heads and maximal projections, but not at intermediate projections

component and converting them into complex lexical items of sorts, which are then linearized with respect to the clause by (14). As argued by Nunes and Uriagereka (2000), if something along these lines is correct, it may explain why extraction out of subjects and adjuncts is not allowed (see Huang 1982, for instance): once complex subjects and adjuncts are spelled out, their constituents are not visible for syntactic purposes anymore. For further details, see the discussion in Uriagereka (1999c) and Nunes and Uriagereka (2000).

or "segments" of adjunction structures.[8] In other words, if one thinks of
linearization as "preparing" the phrase marker for phonological processes,
then it makes sense that what gets linearized is what the phonology cares
about. Recall that we used this reasoning to put the linearization of traces
and empty categories in general outside the LCA; as they are not present at
the PF-level, they need not be linearized. Similarly, if, as seems to be the
case, the phonology disdains intermediate projections, then they should
not fall under the auspices of the LCA. Put positively, the LCA should
order what the phonological system manipulates. The latter works on
heads and maximal phrases; hence, these are what the LCA should handle
before shipping the phrase-marker to the PF-interface.

Let's now turn our attention to the second problem, the lack of asymmetric c-command between *visit* and *Mary* in (16b). The problem is in fact
quite general. It arises every time we have a syntactic node that only dominates lexical items. In the abstract structure in (18), for instance, the problem
shows up with respect to the pair of lexical items *a* and *b*, *d* and *e*, and *g* and *h*.

(18)

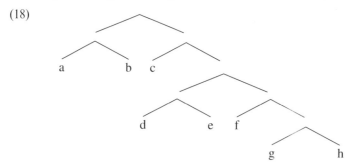

Notice that in the case of (16b), if we had an NP and an N-node dominating
Mary, as shown in (19), the verb would asymmetrically c-command N, and
therefore *visit* would be required to precede *Mary*, as desired.

(19)

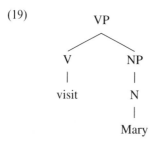

---

8 On the mapping from syntax to phonology and the keen interest that this mapping has in X^0 and
   XP, see, e.g., work by Selkirk (1984, 1986), Inkelas and Zec (1995), and Truckenbrodt (1995,
   1999) as well as much of the material in Inkelas and Zec (1990), and references cited therein.

However, as we have discussed in section 6.3.1, the two nodes dominating *Mary* in (19) are just an artifact of the X′-Theory template and it would not be desirable to reintroduce the distinction between terminals and lexical items or the "P"-feature of NP in (19) to annotate that *Mary* is a maximal projection.

We need not go in that direction, though. There are indeed three possible solutions to the linearization problem sketched in (18) within the bounds of the bare-phrase-structure approach, and languages may differ with respect to the specific solutions they may choose to employ. For instance, the problem in (16b) can be easily circumvented if we take into consideration the fact that, in many languages, a name may be preceded by a definite article, as illustrated by the Portuguese sentence in (20).

(20)   *Portuguese*
        A   Maria   saiu.
        the   Maria   left
        'Maria left.'

Given (20), it could be the case that English, too, uses a determiner together with a proper noun, but a null one. That is, the appropriate representation of the lower VP in (16b) should be along the lines of (20), where *visit* asymmetrically c-commands *Mary* and, according to the LCA, should precede it.

(21)   [$_{VP}$ visit [$_{DP}$ D Mary]]

Crucial in this approach is the assumption that phonologically empty categories are ignored by the LCA; otherwise, the problem detected in (16b) would just be pushed one layer down, for the empty D head and *Mary* in (21) also stand in a mutual c-command relation. This, however, is a reasonable assumption to make, given that the A-P system seems to disregard phonologically empty material (such as traces; see the discussion following (15) above). If on the right track, this suggests the following speculation: maybe phonetically empty functional heads exist because they allow syntactic objects to be linearized.[9]

To consider this, let's step back a little. One minimalist question that we could have raised earlier is *why* not every lexical item has phonological features. From a naïve point of view, it seems that the interpretation of

---

9 This is similar in spirit to Kayne's (1994: 29–30) conjecture that the existence of Agr-heads in UG may be motivated by the need to linearize more than one specifier/adjunct.

the pair (LF, PF) would be more transparent if each lexical item with LF-content were assigned a representation at PF. If this were true, however, no syntactic object would ever be linearizable, for any complex syntactic object has lexical items in mutual c-command, as illustrated in (18). So, lacking a more transparent relation between LF and PF may be a small price to pay if the language faculty is to be legible at all by the A-P system.

Regardless of whether or not this speculation is on the right track, languages do seem to use functional heads without phonological content as a way to get around the mutual c-command problem. Such heads may be particularly useful in the nominal domain. Notice, for instance, that if the DP in (20) has the structure in (22), it faces the same kind of problem noticed in (16b): the overt determiner and the name are not in an asymmetric c-command relation and can't be linearized in compliance with the LCA.

(22)   [$_{DP}$ a   Maria]
          the   Maria

However, if there is at least one extra layer of projection between DP and NP headed by a phonologically null head, as illustrated in (23), the determiner will then asymmetrically c-command the name, allowing the structure to be linearized. Of course, whether X in (23) is a number or gender head, for instance, is something that one should also try to motivate independently.[10]

(23)
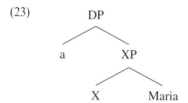

This strategy for finessing the problem of mutually c-commanding lexical items is, we believe, unlikely to be the whole story. It's very likely that there are cases where no postulation of empty heads can be independently justified and we actually find two overt lexical items in mutual c-command. Fortunately, there remain at least two further ways of overcoming this problem. The first one has to do with movement. If one of the lexical items in question moves, it will asymmetrically c-command the

---

10 In the wake of Abney (1987) and Ritter (1991), for example, a lot of research on nominal structure has looked at finer articulation; see, e.g., Bernstein (2001) for an overview and a range of papers in Cinque (2002) for further discussion.

other item from its new position and its trace, being phonetically null, will be disregarded by the LCA. Uriagereka (1998: 220–21) suggests that this is a plausible explanation for the paradigm in (24), for instance.[11]

(24)   a. *an atom split
         b. an atom split in three pieces
         c. split atom

If *atom* and *split* are in a mutual c-command relation, as shown in (25a) below, no order can be established. The contrast between (24a) and (24b) should then be due to the fact in (25b), *atom* asymmetrically c-commands *split* and a linear order can be established between the two, in accordance with the LCA. (25a) can be rescued, however, if *split* moves to a position from where it asymmetrically c-commands *atom*, as illustrated in (25c), yielding the order in (24c).

(25)   a.

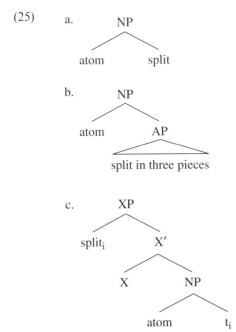

     b.

     c.

A third way of solving the mutual c-command problem is to hide one of the lexical items from sight of the LCA. How can this happen? Well, we are working under the assumption that the LCA deals with heads and phrases. In particular, it doesn't operate below the word level; it doesn't play a role in ordering morphemes, for example. Thus, if a given head gets morphologically integrated

---

11 See also Moro (2000) for relevant discussion.

into another head, it will be invisible to the LCA and will be indirectly ordered by the linearization of the complex item that contains it. To illustrate, consider pronouns. We mentioned in section 6.2.5 that pronouns may be conceived as intransitive Ds, that is, Ds that don't take NPs for complements. The VP of the sentence in (26a), for instance, should be represented along the lines of (26b), where the verb and the pronoun c-command each other and as a consequence no linear order can be established under the LCA.

(26)   a. I like it.
        b. [$_{TP}$ I$_i$ [$_{T'}$ T [$_{VP}$ t$_i$ [$_{V'}$ like it]]]]

It's interesting to observe that the object pronoun in (26) is actually phonologically cliticized to the verb (*like't*). Suppose that this cliticization is actually a reflex of a morphological reanalysis converting the verb and its object in (26b) into a complex lexical item, as represented in (27) below. Assuming that linearization follows morphological computations, the LCA "sees" just two lexical items to be linearized in (27), *I* and the complex item *#like-it#*, and mandates that *I* precede *#like-it#*, given the asymmetric c-command relation between the two.

(27)   [$_{TP}$ I$_i$ [$_{T'}$ T [$_{VP}$ t$_i$ [$_{V'}$ #like-it#]]]]

To summarize, the LCA can be conceived as an optimal response to satisfy the linearization requirements of the A-P system in that precedence is just read off the asymmetric c-command relations in a syntactic tree. The potential linearization problem involving two lexical items in mutual c-command can be circumvented, allowing the structure to be linearized in compliance with the LCA and in consonance with the bare-phrase-structure approach, in three different scenarios: (i) one of the lexical items is phonologically empty; (ii) one of the lexical items moves; or (iii) the two lexical items are morphologically fused so that only the resulting complex item is subject to the LCA, not its internal parts. These are the options available in a minimalist system and the intrinsic properties of the lexical items or the languages in question will determine which option is chosen. It should be mentioned that we are not contending that the specific analyses suggested above are correct. Rather, our point is simply that if correct, they would illustrate how each of these options could be instantiated.

Before we move on, one word about our familiar troublemakers: adjuncts. At this point, there is no consensus in the literature on whether or not adjuncts should also be ordered by the LCA, which is, of course, related to lack of consensus on the structural representation of adjuncts (see section 6.3.2).[12] We will not attempt take a side on this hotly debated issue here. For the purpose of exposition, we will assume that adjuncts may either precede or follow the target of adjunction.

Exercise 7.1

Assuming for concreteness that adjuncts asymmetrically c-command the target of adjunction, linearize the structure in (ii) below, using the definition of the LCA in (14), repeated here in (i).

(i) *Linear Correspondence Axiom*
   α precedes a lexical item β iff α asymmetrically c-commands β.

(ii) [$_{TP}$ Norbert$_i$ [$_{T'}$ [$_{VP}$ t$_i$ [$_{v'}$ [$_{DP}$ the [$_{NP}$ [$_{NP}$ bagel] big] eat] will]]]]

Exercise 7.2

In exercise 7.1, the adjective *big* was adequately ordered by the version of the LCA in (14), under the assumption that an adjunct asymmetrically c-commands the element it is adjoined to. Keeping this assumption constant, discuss whether the versions of the LCA in (14) and (17), repeated below in (i) and (ii), would also be successful in ordering complex adjuncts. For concreteness, what if *big* in exercise 7.1 were replaced by *very big*?

(i) *Linear Correspondence Axiom* (preliminary version)
   A lexical item α precedes a lexical item α iff β asymmetrically c-commands β.

(ii) *Linear Correspondence Axiom* (final version)
   A lexical item α precedes a lexical item β iff α asymmetrically c-commands β or an XP dominating α asymmetrically c-commands β.

Exercise 7.3

Assume that LCA does not "see" intermediate projections. If so, must the definition of the LCA in (17), repeated below in (i), make reference to maximal projections? Given the functional determination of bar-levels discussed in section 6.3.1, are there reasons to suppose that intermediate projections are computationally invisible?

(i) *Linear Correspondence Axiom* (final version)
   A lexical item α precedes a lexical item β iff α asymmetrically c-commands β or an XP dominating α asymmetrically c-commands β.

---

12 For relevant discussion, see Kayne (1994), Chomsky (1995), Alexiadou (1997), Laenzlinger (1998), Cinque (1999), Ernst (2001), Uriagereka (2001), and Rubin (2002), among others.

Exercise 7.4

In section 6.2 we saw that three crucial properties of phrase structure are endocentricity, binary branching, and singleheadedness. Endocentricity excludes objects such as (i), binary branching disallows structures such as (ii), and single-headedness, structures like (iii). Discuss if these three properties may be derived from the LCA, by examining how these structures should be linearized.

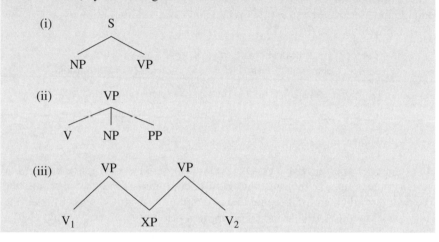

Exercise 7.5

The sentence in (i) below can be phonetically realized in two ways, with distinct meanings. The reduced form, represented in (iia), is associated with an unmarked reading, whereas the stressed form in (iib) is associated with focus. How can these two possibilities in (ii) be accounted for in terms of linearization and their meaning differences?

(i)   Mary likes him.

(ii) a. Mary likes'm.
      b. Mary likes HIM.

Exercise 7.6

Consider the contrast between *John* and *him* in (i) and (ii) below. Could it be accounted for in terms of linearization?

(i) a. Mary called up John.
    b. Mary called John up.

(ii) a. *Mary called up him.
     b. Mary called him up.

Exercise 7.7

Assuming that an object pronoun like *him* or *her* can be linearized with respect to a mutual c-commanding verb by being morphologically realized with the verb and becoming invisible to the LCA, as exemplified in (i), what predictions do you make with respect to the sentence in (ii) if either object is pronominalized, or if both objects are pronominalized?

  (i) a. John likes'm.
      b. John likes'er.

  (ii) John showed Bill the new actress.

Exercise 7.8

In exercise 7.4 you discussed the question of whether the LCA could derive the binary branching property of phrase structure, by examining (abstract) ditransitive predicates involving indirect objects. Now consider a double object construction where each of the arguments is realized by a pronoun. Can your conclusions in exercise 7.7 still be maintained?

Exercise 7.9

(26a), repeated below in (i), was discussed and analyzed under the single-VP-shell approach. Would the analysis be substantially different if we had instead assumed a double VP-shell, with a projection of a light verb?

  (i) I like it.

Exercise 7.10

Look for other potential cases of lexical items in mutual c-command in your language and check which options are chosen to circumvent the linearization problem.

7.4   The LCA and word order variation

Section 7.3 explored the conjecture that the optimal way to meet the linearization demands of the A-P system is not simply by adding precedence to phrase structure, but rather by reading precedence off the phrase structure through asymmetric c-command (the LCA). This provides a natural explanation for the correlations between word order and syntactic phenomena: under this view, word order is not dissociated from syntactic structure but is rather determined by it. Let's then see how well the LCA fares with respect to the phenomena discussed in section 7.2.

Under the standard assumption that prepositions and postpositions don't differ in terms of θ-marking, let's reconsider the contrast in (8), repeated below in (28).

(28)   *Hungarian*
      a. én   mögött-em
          I   behind-POSS.1.SG
      b. *mögött-em   én
          behind-POSS.1.SG   I
          'behind me'
      c. *a   hídon   át
          the bridge.SUP   over
      d. át   a   hídon
          over   the   bridge.SUP
          'over the bridge'

According to the LCA, the adpositions in (28) differ not only in terms of their order with respect to their arguments, but also in structural terms. If an adposition precedes the lexical items of its argument, it must be the case that it asymmetrically c-commands them, as abstractly represented in (29a) below. By the same token, if the argument of an adposition precedes it, the argument should asymmetrically c-command the adposition; in other words, the argument must have moved past the adposition, as shown in (29b).

(29)   a. [P [$_{DP}$ ...]]
      b. [[$_{DP}$ ...]$_i$ ... [P t$_i$]]

Thus, given that prepositions and postpositions involve different structural configurations, the fact they differ in terms of agreement, as in (28), comes as no surprise. In fact, as mentioned in section 4.3.3, the existence of agreement in postpositional but not with prepositional structures mimics the agreement contrast between SV and VS word orders in many languages. In Brazilian Portuguese, for instance, subject verb agreement is obligatory in SV, but not in VS structures, as respectively illustrated in (30).

(30)   *Brazilian Portuguese*
      a. Alguns   problemas   apareceram.
          some   problems   appeared.PL
      b. Apareceu   alguns   problemas.
          appeared.SG   some   problems
          'Some problems appeared.'

Contrasts such as (30) have been standardly analyzed as following from the different structural configurations involving the verb and the subject in each of the sentences. The subject and the verb are presumably in a Spec-head configuration in (30a), as illustrated in (31a) below, but not in (30b), as illustrated in (31b). It is thus arguably the case that postpositions – but not prepositions – also stand in a Spec-head relation with their argument, triggering agreement. That is, the DP in (29b) has moved to [Spec,PP], or P adjoins to some higher functional head and the DP moves to the specifier of that head.

(31)   a. $[_{TP}$ DP $[_{T'}$ V + T $[_{VP}$ ...]]]
         b. $[_{TP}$ V + T $[_{VP}$ ... DP]]

This approach to the difference between prepositions and postpositions in structural terms may also account for some unexpected asymmetries regarding the kinds of constituents that may appear to the left or to the right of an adposition. Take the alternation in (32) and (33) below, for example.[13]

(32)   a. They looked up the number.
         b. They looked the number up.

(33)   a. They left out this part.
         b. They left this part out.

One plausible way to analyze these sentences is that Modern English preserved some of its archaic postpositional structures. If so, under the directionality-parameter approach, these sentences should be represented as in (34) and (35), respectively, with the adposition preceding or following its argument.

(34)   a. [they looked $[_{PP}$ up [the number]]]
         b. [they looked $[_{PP}$ [the number] up]]

(35)   a. [they left $[_{PP}$ out [this part]]]
         b. [they left $[_{PP}$ [this part] out]]

The question that arises under the directionality-parameter approach is why a similar alternation can't take place in (36) and (37), with the PP and the CP argument freely preceding or following the relevant adposition.

(36)   a. [they ganged $[_{PP}$ up [on John]]]
         b. *[they ganged $[_{PP}$ [on John] up]]

---

13 See den Dikken (1995a) for extensive discussion.

(37)   a. [they found [$_{PP}$ out [that they were wrong]]]
        b. *[they found [$_{PP}$ [that they were wrong] out]]

By contrast, the difference between (32) and (33), on the one hand, and (36) and (37), on the other, may actually be expected under the LCA-based approach. In the postpositional structures in (32b), (33b), (36b), and (37b), the argument of the adposition must have moved to some specifier position from where it can asymmetrically c-command the adposition, as represented in (29b). The impossibility of (36b) and (37b) is then due to independent restrictions on PPs and CPs in specifier positions in English, as illustrated in (38).

(38)   a. *[John wondered why [$_{TP}$ [$_{PP}$ behind the bushes] [$_{T'}$ sat a rabbit]]]
        b. *[John asked if [$_{TP}$ [$_{CP}$ that Bill left] [$_{T'}$ is true]]]

Let's now consider the correlation between word order and extraction. Recall that Basque allows extraction from an embedded clause when the clausal complement follows the verb, but not when it precedes it, as shown in (11), repeated here in (39) (see note 5).

(39)   *Basque*
        a. Nor$_i$ uste   du   Jonek   [esan   duela   Mirenek   [Aitorrek t$_i$
            who.ABS think AUX Jon.ERG   said AUX.COMP Miren.ERG   Aitor.ERG
            maite   duela]]?
            love   AUX.COMP
        b. ??Nor$_i$ uste   du   Jonek   [[Aitorrek t$_i$ maite duela]   esan
            who.ABS   think AUX Jon.ERG   Aitor.ERG   love   AUX.COMP said
            duela   Mirenek]?
            AUX.COMP   Miren.ERG
        'Who does Jon think that Miren said that Aitor loves?'

According to the LCA, the difference in word order in (39) should reflect a difference in structure. In particular, under the assumption that the clausal complement of both sentences is θ-marked in the same configuration, the CP-V order in (39b) should be derived from the structure in (40a) by moving the complement CP to some specifier position higher than the verb, as represented in (40b).

(40)   a. [$_{VP}$ V [$_{CP}$ ...]]
        b. [[$_{CP}$ ...]$_i$ ... [$_{VP}$ V t$_i$]]

The contrast between (39a) and (39b) now follows from the general ban on extraction from specifiers,[14] independently illustrated in (41), where

---

14 This is known as the Condition on Extraction Domain (CED), first proposed by Huang (1982). See also note 7 above.

extraction of *who* is permitted from within the object position, but not from within [Spec,TP].[15]

(41)   a. [who$_i$ did [$_{TP}$ you [$_{VP}$ take [a picture of t$_i$]]]]
       b. *[who$_i$ was [$_{TP}$ [a picture of t$_i$]$_k$ [$_{VP}$ taken t$_k$]]]

As for the possibility of *wh*-movement to a right [Spec,CP] or anti-V2 structures pointed out in section 7.2, which are in principle allowed by the directionality-parameter approach, they are simply blocked in the LCA-based approach to linear order. If licit movement is always to an (asymmetrically) c-commanding position, the moved element will always precede the target of movement.[16] Hence, there should be no such thing as moving to positions that are to the right of the launching site. One should not be misled by notation in this regard. Once we give up on the directionality parameter, the two structures in (42) below are just notational variants of the same representation. In particular, XP and V asymmetrically c-command, and therefore must precede, the lexical items dominated by TP (see exercise 7.1).

(42)   a.   b.

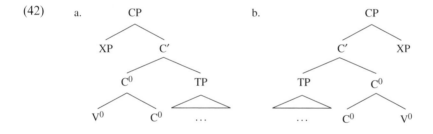

To summarize, the LCA-approach to linear order is empirically superior to the approach in terms of directionality parameters in that it not only carves the system in an appropriate way so that correlations between syntactic phenomena and word order can be accounted for, but also provides an explanation of the non-existence of certain word orders in natural languages.

---

15 For further discussion on the differences between VO and VO languages from the perspective of the LCA, see, e.g., Zwart (1993, 1997) and the collection of papers in Svenonius (2000).
16 In section 8.3.5.2 we'll discuss cases that involve licit movement that is "sideward" instead of "upward," but the existence of such cases doesn't affect the point being made here.

Exercise 7.11

Discuss whether (42a) and (42b) are notational variants of the same representation by using the bare phrase-structure notation discussed in section 6.3.

7.5   Traces and the LCA

Let's now reconsider our proposal that traces should be disregarded by the LCA. The reason for this, we conjectured in section 7.3, is that the LCA is introduced in the system in order to satisfy the linearization requirements of the A-P system, which only seems to care about elements with phonetic matrices; if traces don't have phonetic matrices, they should then be ignored by the LCA. Assuming that this reasoning is on the right track, we are now in a position to pose a deeper minimalist question: *why* are traces phonologically empty? Again, from a naïve point of view, it seems that if traces were indeed phonetically realized, the interpretation of the pair (LF, PF) would seem to be more transparent in that elements with LF-content would be assigned an interpretation at PF.

The GB-answer to this question amounts to "*Because!*": it is stipulated that traces be phonetically null. Within minimalism, the question posed above becomes even harder once we adopt the copy theory of movement (see section 6.4), according to which movement is just Copy plus Merge and a trace is a copy of the moved element. For instance, if the relevant structure of (43) is (45), where superscript annotates copies, rather than (44), what is the problem with pronouncing the copy of *he* in [Spec,VP] in (45), yielding the sentence in (46)?

(43)   He must like Mary.

(44) $[_{TP}$ he$_i$ $[_{T'}$ must $[_{VP}$ t$_i$ $[_{V'}$ like $[_{DP}$ D Mary $]]]]]$

(45) $[_{TP}$ he^i $[_{T'}$ must $[_{VP}$ he^i $[_{V'}$ like $[_{DP}$ D Mary $]]]]]$

(46)   *He must he like Mary.

Interestingly, if we explore the null hypothesis that if traces are copies, they should be subject to the same principles that the "original" elements are subject to, we may have a plausible answer.[17] Let's consider how. A derivation consists of two sorts of operations: taking elements from

17 See Nunes (1995, 1999, 2001, 2004) for detailed discussion.

the lexicon and combining these into grammatical structures. In the case of the derivation of (43), for instance, the computational system first forms the numeration N in (47) below, specifying which lexical items and how many instances of each of them can be used by the syntactic component (see section 2.3.2.6). The lexical items of N are then culled and applications of Merge and Copy to these lexical items and syntactic objects formed out of them finally yield the structure in (45).

(47) $N = \{he_1, like_1, D_1, must_1, Mary_1\}$

The structure in (45) should then be assigned interpretations at the LF and PF levels. As discussed in section 7.3, in order to be legible by the A-P system, the structure in (45) must be linearized and we have argued that the LCA is an optimal response to this requirement. To say that a lexical item must be linearized in accordance with the LCA amounts to saying that it should be assigned one position in a PF-string, based on its position in the syntactic tree. But now we have a problem with copies: if we have more than one copy of a given lexical item in the structure, this lexical item doesn't have a single position in the tree but as many positions as there are copies. Take (45), for instance. Given that the copy of *he* in [Spec,TP] asymmetrically c-commands *must*, the LCA requires that *he* precede *must*; by the same token, *must* is required to precede the copy of *he* in [Spec,VP] because it asymmetrically c-commands it. The problem is that the two instances of *he* relate to the same lexical item of N in (47); in other words, the LCA requires that *must* should both precede and be preceded by the same lexical item, *he*, and this is not a possible linear order. The same kind of problem is noted between the two copies: given that the higher copy asymmetrically c-commands the lower one, *he* is required to precede itself, which again can't be possible in a linear order. This thus explains why a chain can't surface with all of its links phonetically realized. The attempted derivation of (46) from the structure in (45) is doomed because (45) can't be linearized and, as such, it is not legible at PF.

So, if we assume that movement involves copies and that in order for a derivation to converge, the elements in the numeration must be assigned linear positions in accordance with the LCA, then a structure involving movement can only be linearized if every copy but one disappears. In other words, the reason traces are phonetically null is that this allows the structure to be linearized and be readable by the A-P system. Phonetically null elements don't need to be linearized; so when movement takes place, to ensure convergence, all the copies but one must become phonetically null, i.e. "delete."

There are still two questions to answer, however: which copies delete, and why? We have been assuming that whenever an element moves, it checks features. Leaving a more detailed discussion of feature checking to chapter 9 below, let's then assume that such feature checking renders a moved copy more digestible at the interfaces, in the sense that it has fewer (if any) features that need to be further checked. If so, the higher a copy is, the more optimal it is in terms of the interfaces, for it will have checked more features. In the case of (45), for example, the higher copy of *he* has its Case-feature checked, but the lower copy does not. Hence, the lower copy is deleted and the structure can be linearized, yielding the sentence in (43). We may thus explain *why* not every copy is phonetically realized, as well as which copies will surface as phonetically null traces.

A crucial feature of this reasoning is that it doesn't stipulate that the lower copies are the ones that are deleted. And this is important, for we would otherwise risk reintroducing the notion of a trace as a theoretical primitive, in violation of the Inclusiveness Condition (see the discussion in section 6.4). Even more importantly, the reasoning above leaves open a very interesting possibility; if the phonetic realization of the highest copy causes problems in the phonological component, a lower copy (a trace) can be realized instead.

With this in mind, consider the contrast between (48) and (49) below.[18] (48) illustrates the well-known fact that Romanian is a multiple *wh*-fronting language; hence the unacceptability of the *wh-in situ* in (48b). (49), on the other hand, seems to be an exception to the paradigm illustrated in (48), in that a *wh*-element *in situ* is allowed.

(48)   *Romanian*
    a. Cine   ce   precede?
       who   what   precedes
    b. *Cine   precede   ce?
       who   precedes   what
       'Who precedes what?'

(49)   *Romanian*
    a. *Ce   ce   precede?
       what what   precedes
    b. Ce   precede   ce?
       what   precedes   what
       'What precedes what?'

---

18 See Bošković (2001, 2002a), Nunes (2004), and Boškovic and Nunes (2004), for further discussion.

Bošković (2002a), however, argues that the appearances here are deceiving. The unacceptability of (49a) is related to a restriction in the phonological component prohibiting adjacent occurrences of *ce* 'what'. That is, from a syntactic point of view, there is no difference between (48) and (49); we have multiple *wh*-fronting in both cases. It just happens that if the higher copy of the moved object of (49) is realized, it will violate this ban on adjacent identical words, which is found in several languages.[19] The phonological system then deletes the higher copy of the object *ce* 'what', as sketched in (50) below, allowing the structure to both be linearized and comply with the adjacency restriction. Independent evidence that the object in (49) has undergone overt movement in the syntactic component is the fact that it patterns like moved *wh*-objects in being able to license a parasitic gap, as shown in (51), something that an *in situ* *wh*-object can't do, as shown in (52).[20]

(50)   [ce$_{SU}$ [~~ce$_{OB}$~~ [~~ce$_{SU}$~~ precede ce$_{OB}$]]]

(51)   *Romanian*
         Ce   precede   ce   fără   să   influenţeze?
         what   precedes   what   without   SUBJ-PRT   influence.3.SG
         'What precedes what$_i$ without influencing it$_i$?'

(52)   *Who bought what after finding?

Let's finally consider one further consequence of analyzing deletion of traces in terms of the LCA. We have seen in section 7.4 that a given lexical item may fall beyond the visual field of the LCA if it gets morphologically fused with another lexical item. In this case, the reanalyzed lexical items behave like morphemes of the complex lexical item in the sense that they are linearized as a byproduct of the LCA applying to the complex item. If undergoing morphological fusion is a way for a given element not to be computed by the LCA, we predict that phonetic realization of multiple copies may be allowed if some of the copies undergo morphological fusion.[21]

---

19 See Golston (1995) for a discussion of many such cases and Richards (2002) for some related issues.

20 The fact that a parasitic gap cannot be licensed by an *in situ* *wh*-phrase was first observed by Engdahl (1983). For recent perspectives on parasitic gaps, see, e.g., Nunes (1995, 2001, 2004), Nissenbaum (2000), Hornstein (2001), and the articles in Culicover and Postal (2001).

21 See Nunes (1999, 2004), Boškovic and Nunes (2004), Boeckx, Hornstein, and Nunes (2004) for examples and further discussion.

With this in mind, consider verb focalization in Vata again, as illustrated in (53) below,[22] where a focalized verb is doubled by an identical verb in the regular position occupied by verbs (see section 5.5). If the two instances of *li* 'eat' in (53) are actual copies, the derivation should in principle have crashed because the structure could not be linearized: the pronoun *à* 'we', for instance, would have been required to precede and be preceded by the same lexical item, *li*.

(53)   *Vata*
    li à **li**-da   zué   saká.
    eat *we* *eat-PAST* *yesterday* *rice*
    'We ATE rice yesterday.'

There is an alternative, however. Let's assume that the focalization illustrated in (53) involves movement of the verb to a focus position preceding TP, as sketched in (54) below. Now suppose that the verb and the focus head get morphologically fused in the phonological component, as represented by "#" in (54). Assuming as before that linearization follows morphological computations, the topmost copy of the verb in (54) will then become invisible to the LCA after the proposed morphological reanalysis. That is, the LCA will consider just the two lower copies and given that the copy adjoined to T^0 is the one with more features checked, it will be retained and the lowest copy will be deleted, yielding sentences such as (53).

(54)

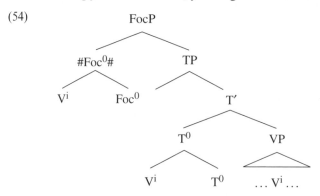

Two pieces of evidence indicate that something along these lines might be correct. First, none of the particles that occur in Infl (T^0) may appear with the fronted verb, as exemplified in (55) below with boldface.

---

22 The Vata data are taken from Koopman (1984). The analysis reported here is based on Nunes (2004).

This suggests that such particles make the verb morphologically heavy enough so that the morphological fusion with the focus head is blocked.

(55)   *Vata*
        a. (***ná`**)  **le**  wa  ná`-le-ka.
              NEG *eat they* NEG-*eat*-FT
           'They will not EAT.'
        b. **li(*-wa)** wà li-wa zué.
              eat TP   *they eat*-TP *yesterday*
           'They ATE yesterday.'

Second, and perhaps more interestingly, the only verbs that can't undergo duplication under focus in Vata are auxiliaries, the defective verb *na/la/lO* 'to say', and the verbs *lÈ* 'to be' and *kà* 'to have', exactly the set of verbs that are not subject to independent morphological processes that affect other verbs in the language (see Koopman 1984: 158). If these verbs independently resist morphological operations, it is then natural that they can't be duplicated under focus, for such duplication would require the morphological reanalysis sketched in (54).

To summarize, in section 6.4 we discussed conceptual and empirical reasons for the adoption of the copy theory of movement within minimalism. Despite its promising features, the copy theory left us with a puzzle: if traces are really copies, what is the problem with pronouncing them? This section has shown that we need not stipulate that traces can't be phonetically realized. The LCA coupled with optimality considerations determine that in the general case, only the highest link can be phonetically realized. But depending on specific properties of the phonological component, we may find traces pronounced instead of the head of the chain, or even cases of multiple copies being phonetically realized. Again, we see that the conceptual concerns of minimalism may lead to interesting results, with a substantial broadening of empirical coverage.

Exercise 7.12

Consider the "*wh*-copying" construction illustrated with German in (i) below (see among others McDaniel 1986, 1989), which appears to have two copies of the moved *wh*-element. *Wh*-copying constructions have the following properties: (a) they are subject to island effects, as shown in (ii); (b) the *wh*-element can't be a full *wh*-phrase, as illustrated in (iii); and (c) although intermediate traces may be allowed to be phonetically realized, as seen in (i), the lowest *wh*-copy must be deleted, as shown by the contrast between (i) and (iv). Is it possible to account for these properties with an analysis similar to the one applied to verb focalization in Vata?

German

(i) **Wen**   glaubt   Hans, **wen**   Jakob gesehen hat?
     whom   *believes* *Hans*   *whom Jakob seen   has*
     'Who does Hans believe Jakob saw?'

(ii) *__Wen__ glaubt Hans die Tatsache, **wen**   (dass) Jakob gesehen hat?
     whom believes Hans the fact   *whom that   Jakob seen   has*
     '*Who does Hans believe the fact (that) Jakob saw?'

(iii) *__Wessen Buch__ glaubst du, **wessen Buch** Hans liest?
      whose   book *believe   you whose   book   Hans reads*
      'Whose book do you believe Hans is reading?'

(iv) *__Wen__ glaubt   Hans, **wen**   Jakob **wen**   gesehen hat?
     whom   believes   Hans   whom Jakob   whom   seen   has
     'Who does Hans believe Jakob saw?'

7.6   Conclusion

This chapter started by asking why we have linear order properties in natural languages and raised the hypothesis that this follows from requirements of the A-P system in that it apparently takes for input a string of sounds or signs. The question then was how to satisfy these requirements. The GB-approach in terms of directionality parameters added precedence into the system but failed to capture recurrent correlations between syntactic relations and word order. We have then explored an alternative approach: precedence should not be added to the system, but be read off the syntactic tree through the LCA. This alternative approach proved to be empirically more successful in that it provides ways to account for the correlations between hierarchical structure and word order. It addition, it paved the way for the elimination of the (empirically incorrect) stipulation that traces must be phonologically empty. At the end of the day, we have reached a conceptually more appealing picture of the relation between structure and word order, while at the same time broadening empirical coverage.

8   *Binding Theory*

8.1   Introduction

Chapters 6 and 7 considered some empirical and methodological reasons for treating movement as the combination of two simpler operations: Copy and Merge. So construing movement allowed us to eliminate traces as grammar-internal formatives (a methodological plus) and forced us to consider why the traces are phonetically null. According to the proposal discussed in chapter 7, if copies are not deleted in the phonological component, they may cause the derivation to crash at PF, as they induce contradicting linearization requirements (for instance, that a given syntactic object A must precede and be preceded by another syntactic object B).

We supported this reasoning empirically in two different ways. First, we observed that there are cases where what gets phonologically realized is not the antecedent of a trace but the trace itself. Second, we reviewed evidence suggesting that multiple copies can be pronounced if they are able to evade the conditions that force their deletion. Either case is not even a descriptive possibility if traces are defined as phonetically null, as is the case in GB-style accounts. By contrast, if traces are construed as copies, both cases can be properly handled, as we demonstrated in section 7.5.

This chapter considers binding theoretic evidence for the same conclusion, by exploring a suggestion made in section 6.4 regarding the interpretive properties of traces under the copy theory of movement. We'll see that the copy theory allows us to rebut empirical arguments for the postulation of DS and SS based on binding considerations. As we discussed in chapter 2, the elimination of DS and SS is minimalistically desirable on methodological grounds. The copy theory lets us advance towards this goal, as it provides an account of certain "connectedness" effects that have long been of interest within generative grammar.

The chapter is organized as follows. In section 8.2, we review some binding theoretic arguments within GB that favor the postulation of DS and SS. In section 8.3, we then show how the copy theory can be pressed into service to circumvent this conclusion. We then proceed to examine other cases related to these examples and review an argument by Chomsky (1993) that a theory incorporating levels like DS and SS is empirically *worse off* than one that eschews them. We end with some additional evidence tying binding effects with movement. Section 8.4 concludes.

8.2   Binding Theory phenomena as potential arguments for DS and SS

8.2.1   *Warming up*

Let's start our discussion by reviewing the workings of a standard GB-version of the Binding Theory, which invokes principles along the lines of (1) and the auxiliary definitions in (2) and (3).[1]

(1)   *Binding Theory*
    (i) *Principle A:*
        An anaphor (e.g. a reflexive or reciprocal) must be bound in its domain.
    (ii) *Principle B:*
        A pronoun must be free (not bound) in its domain.
    (iii) *Principle C:*
        An R-expression (e.g. a name, a variable) must be free (everywhere).

(2)   *Domain*
    α is the domain for β iff α is the smallest IP (TP) containing β and the governor of β.

(3)   *Binding*
    α binds β iff α c-commands and is coindexed with β.

Assuming (1)–(3), let's examine the data in (4).[2]

(4)   a. *[Mary$_i$ said that [$_{TP}$ Joe liked these pictures of herself$_i$]]
      b. [Mary$_i$ said that [$_{TP}$ Joe liked these pictures of her$_i$]]
      c. *[He$_i$ said that Mary likes these pictures of Joe$_i$]

---

1 These are standard definitions. For a fuller discussion of the nuances see Chomsky (1986b), van Riemsdijk and Williams (1986), Haegeman (1994), and Harbert (1995).
2 There is considerable variation among English speakers concerning the acceptability of examples like (4a), which involve complex NPs that contain reflexives, so-called *picture-NPs*. For purposes of discussion, we'll assume that this variation can be independently explained and focus on the judgments reported in the text.

The domain of the anaphor *herself* in (4a) is the embedded TP as it is the smallest TP that contains *herself* and its governor (*of*).[3] Since this domain does not contain its antecedent (*Mary*), *herself* is not bound in its domain; hence, the unacceptability of (4a) should be attributed to a violation of Principle A. As Principle B is the converse of Principle A, (4b) is fine: the pronoun *her* is free (not bound) in its domain, the embedded TP. Lastly, (4c) is unacceptable as *Joe* is subject to Principle C, which prohibits R-expressions from being bound at all.

Note that data such as (4) do not shed the light on the question of where Binding Theory applies, for the DS, SS, and LF representations of the sentences in (4) will be essentially the same and the relevant binding domains won't change from one level to the other. Once we have a tie, we should then analyze the sentences in (4) in LF terms, given that LF is independently necessary.

In the next sections, we will, however, discuss some more complex binding phenomena that appear to provide evidence for saying that the Binding Theory must apply at DS or SS, and not exclusively at LF, where our minimalist hearts would desire.

Exercise 8.1

Assuming that Case-features are checked in a Spec-head configuration (see chapter 3):

a. provide the LF representation of the sentences in (4) both under the split Infl-approach (with TP and Agr-projections) and the approach based on an unsplit Infl (TP only) associated with a light verb projection (with multiple vP-specifiers); and

b. discuss if the definition of domain in (2) needs to be reformulated under either approach in order to capture the data in (4).

8.2.2 Principle A

In section 2.3.1.2, we discussed and reanalyzed some data involving covert *wh*-movement that at face value appeared to indicate that Principle C should be computed at SS, and not at LF. Comparable data involving Principle A are subject to the same reanalysis. Let's see the details.

---

3 Recall that complements are governed by the heads that they are sisters to. One might treat *of* here not as a governor, but as a kind of dummy Case-marker (see Chomsky 1981, for instance). In this scenario, *picture* is the actual governor of *herself*, but according to (2), the embedded TP is still the domain of *herself*. For expository purposes, we will henceforth assume that the preposition is the relevant governor in *picture*-NPs.

Consider the sentence in (5) below, for instance. If covert movement moves the whole *wh*-phrase, as standardly assumed within GB, the LF structure of (5) should be along the lines of (6), after the *in situ wh*-phrase moves in the covert component and forms a complex operator with *which woman* (see section 2.3.1.2).

(5)   *John$_i$ wondered which woman liked which pictures of himself$_i$.

(6)   LF:
       [$_{TP}$ John$_i$ wondered [[which pictures of himself$_i$]$_k$ + [which woman]$_j$ [$_{TP}$ t$_j$ liked t$_k$]]]

In (6), the domain of *himself* is the matrix TP and it is bound by *John* in this domain. Thus, if Principle A were to apply to the LF structure in (6), we would wrongly predict that (5) should be an acceptable sentence. Hence, the conclusion seems to be that Principle A should not apply at LF, but at SS or DS, prior to covert *wh*-movement.

This conclusion is not forceful, though. It is valid only if the LF structure of (5) is as in (6), that is, if covert *wh*-movement targets the *whole wh*-phrase. If, instead, covert *wh*-movement targets only the *wh*-element, as proposed in section 2.3.1.2, (5) should actually have the LF representation in (7).

(7)   LF:
       *[$_{TP}$ John$_i$ wondered [which$_k$ + [which woman]$_j$ [$_{TP}$ t$_j$ liked [t$_k$ pictures of himself$_i$]]]]

Given the LF structure in (7), it now makes no difference if Principle A is computed at DS, SS, or LF, for *himself* fails to be bound in its domain (the embedded TP) at all these levels (see exercise 2.3). Again, in case of a tie, an analysis in LF terms is the default winner, for LF is required by bare output conditions.

Although the reanalysis of covert *wh*-movement discussed in section 2.3.1.2 also proved successful in handling Principle A cases such as (5), other cases seem less prone to a reinterpretation in LF terms. Consider, for instance, the sentence in (8a), with its DS, SS, and LF representations given in (8b–c) (irrelevant details omitted).

(8)   a. John$_i$ wondered which picture of himself$_{i/k}$ Fred$_k$ liked.
       b. DS:
          [$_{TP}$ John$_i$ wondered [$_{CP}$ [$_{TP}$ Fred$_k$ liked [which picture of himself$_{i/k}$]]]]
       c. SS/LF:
          [$_{TP}$ John$_i$ wondered [$_{CP}$ [which picture of himself$_{i/k}$]$_m$ [$_{TP}$ Fred liked t$_m$]]]

(8a) is ambiguous. The reflexive *himself* can have either *John* or *Fred* as its antecedent. We can account for the first reading by assuming that the Binding Theory applies at SS or at LF; in (8c), the smallest TP that contains the anaphor and its governor is the matrix one and *himself* is indeed bound by *John* in this domain. If SS does not exist as a level (recall the arguments for the conceptual desirability of this in chapter 2), we should then account for the matrix subject reading of (8a) in terms of LF, by assuming that Principle A applies at this level. However, if this is where Principle A applies and if (8c) is the correct LF structure for (8a), we can't derive the reading where *Fred* is the antecedent of *himself*; in (8c), *Fred* can't bind the reflexive as it doesn't c-command it. The question then is how to derive this reading.

Notice that the embedded subject reading for *himself* could be captured if the structure in (8b) were computed, that is, if we allowed Principle A to apply at DS as well. But this isn't a welcome theoretical move from a minimalist perspective. Recall, we have argued that a methodologically optimal theory would dispense with *both* DS and SS. Hence, getting the indicated reading by applying Principle A at DS is not an attractive option.

Another possibility is to license binding throughout the derivation rather than apply the binding principles only at levels. So, for concreteness, say that we let binding apply anywhere in the course of the derivation.[4] We could then either let *Fred* bind *himself* prior to the movement of the *wh*-phrase that contains *himself* or let *John* bind it after *wh*-movement. Note that this process does not advert to levels like DS or SS, as binding is not done *at* a level but applies throughout a derivation.

Postponing further discussion to section 8.3.4, it should be observed that sentences such as (9) below pose obstacles to such an approach.[5] If the reciprocal *each other* could be bound in the course of the derivation, it should be licensed by the matrix subject after the *wh*-movement represented in (10). However, this is not clearly the case; Chomsky (1993) reports that the reciprocal in (9) can only take the embedded subject for its antecedent.[6]

(9)   The students asked what attitudes about each other the teachers had.

4 Such approaches to binding were proposed, for example, by Belletti and Rizzi (1988) and Lebeaux (1995). For relevant discussion, see, e.g., Epstein, Groat, Kawashima, and Kithara (1998).
5 See Chomsky (1993) and the discussion in section 8.3.4 below.
6 Some native speakers find this data somewhat subtle. We will assume for the time being that Chomsky's (1993) description is correct.

(10)   [$_{TP}$ [the students]$_k$ asked [what attitudes about [each other]$_{i/*k}$]$_m$ [$_{TP}$ [the teachers]$_i$ had t$_m$]]]

Thus, allowing Binding Theory to apply everywhere may lead to over-generation at least with respect to Principle A. We'll see below that such an approach is not tenable for Principles B and C either. We are then left with the impression that resorting to DS is the only viable alternative to deal with the downstairs reading of the anaphors in (8a) and (9), and that the LF licensing of the upstairs reading of (8a) seems to be an exceptional case.

Exercise 8.2

Given the definitions of Principle B in (1ii) and domain in (2), discuss if the sentence in (i) provides evidence for or against the analysis of covert *wh*-movement we resorted to in order to account for the unacceptability of (5) in LF terms.

(i)   John$_i$ wondered which woman liked which pictures of him$_i$.

8.2.3   *Principle B*
Let's now consider (11).

(11)   John$_i$ wondered which picture of him$_{i/*k}$ Fred$_k$ liked.

(11) is identical to (8a) except that we have substituted a pronoun for the reflexive. Given that Principle B is the reverse of Principle A, we should in principle expect that the readings that were available in (8a), should be impossible in (11). In other words, given that in (8a) the anaphor can take either *John* or *Fred* as its antecedent, we would predict that the pronoun in (11) could take neither of them as its antecedent. However, this is not exactly the case. Although coreference between *him* and *Fred* is not possible, coreference between *him* and *John* is.

This seems to strongly suggest that Principle B should also be computed at DS, prior to *wh*-movement, as shown in (12a) below, and not at SS or LF, as represented in (12b). In (12a), the domain of the pronoun is the embedded TP and coindexation with *Fred* violates Principle B, but coindexation with *John* is allowed, which is the correct result. By contrast, if the input to the computation of Principle B were the structure in (12b), the domain for the pronoun would be the matrix TP; the pronoun would be prevented from taking *John* but allowed to take *Fred* as its antecedent, exactly the opposite of what we want to obtain.

(12)   a. <u>DS</u>:
         [$_{TP}$ John$_i$ wondered [$_{CP}$ [$_{TP}$ Fred$_k$ liked [which picture of him$_{i/k}$]]]]
         b. <u>SS/LF</u>:
         [$_{TP}$ John$_i$ wondered [$_{CP}$ [which picture of him$_{i/k}$]$_m$ [$_{TP}$ Fred$_k$ liked t$_m$]]]

Even if we explore the possibility that Principle B applies in the course of
the derivation and not to a particular level, it seems that we still need
something like DS, that is, a phrase marker in which all the lexical elements
have been merged. Let's see why.

Recall from chapter 2 that we build phrase markers in a bottom-up
fashion, through a series of applications of Merge and Move. Recall, too,
that we build these structures cyclically. In particular, we adhere to the
Extension Condition in building (overt) structures (see section 2.3.2.4).
With this in mind, consider how to construct (11). We first build the
embedded TP, leaving *John* and *wondered* in the numeration, as illustrated
in (13) (irrelevant traces and functional categories omitted; *Q* stands for an
interrogative complementizer).

(13)   a. N = {John$_1$, T$_1$, wondered$_1$, Q$_1$, Fred$_0$, liked$_0$, which$_0$, picture$_0$, of$_0$,
            him$_0$}
         b. [$_{TP}$ Fred liked [which picture of him]]

At this point, we could try to coindex *Fred* and *him*, but Principle B would
forbid this (a good result). It's not clear if at this point we could also try to
coindex *him* and *John*, as the latter has not yet been introduced into the
derivation. But even if we could, Principle B would allow it (another good
result), since such coindexation would not leave the pronoun bound in its
domain.

Let's proceed, by selecting and merging the interrogative complementizer Q and moving the *wh*-phrase to [Spec,CP] to check its strong feature, as
shown in (14) below. Given the definition of domain in (2), the pronoun in
(14b) doesn't have a domain, for no TP dominates it. Let's assume that
Principle B is inapplicable in such circumstances.[7] The computation then
proceeds to selecting and merging the remaining lexical items, yielding the
TP in (15), and Principle B may now apply.

(14)   a. N' = {John$_1$, T$_1$, wondered$_1$, Q$_0$, Fred$_0$, liked$_0$, which$_0$, picture$_0$, of$_0$,
            him$_0$}
         b. [$_{CP}$ [which picture of him]$_i$ Q [$_{TP}$ Fred liked t$_i$]]

---

7 Notice that if we allow Principle B to apply vacuously in absence of a TP dominating the
relevant pronoun, coindexation between *him* and *Fred* in (13b) would be incorrectly
permitted.

(15)   a. N'' = {John$_0$, T$_0$, wondered$_0$, Q$_0$, Fred$_0$, liked$_0$, which$_0$, picture$_0$, of$_0$, him$_0$}

   b. [$_{TP}$ John wondered [$_{CP}$ [which picture of him]$_i$ Q [$_{TP}$ Fred liked t$_i$]]]

Let's first try to coindex *Fred* and *him* in (15b). This time we succeed. Once *Fred* doesn't c-command the pronoun in (15b), the coindexing doesn't run afoul of Principle B and the embedded subject reading for the pronoun is incorrectly permitted. So, in order to prevent this undesirable result, we must assume that once one has tried to coindex two expressions in a previous step of the derivation and this attempted indexation has failed, then we cannot try to license the indexation again later on. Furthermore, we must assume that for pronouns, *one must try to coindex at the first opportunity*. In other words, one cannot refrain from applying Principle B to the coindexation between *Fred* and *him* in (13b) and then apply it in (15b), after the *wh*-phrase has moved. (Recall that this was the move that we explored to accommodate the ambiguity of the reflexive in (8a).)

There's still another problem. Observe that the domain of the pronoun in (15b) is the matrix clause. Thus, if we coindex *him* and *John*, we will violate Principle B as the pronoun is now bound in its domain. As before, we incorrectly predict that this reading isn't possible.

The upshot is this: even if we allow binding principles to apply throughout the derivation to derive the ambiguity of reflexive cases like (8a) without invoking DS and SS, we can't apply this trick to analogous Principle B examples like (11). To capture Principle B effects adequately, we seem to need DS, that is, a level at which syntactic constituents have not undergone movement and *all* the elements that will be used in the sentence have been integrated into the phrase marker.

Exercise 8.3

In this section, we saw that an approach that applies coindexation and Principle B in the course of the derivation does not succeed in eliminating the need of DS. Suppose that instead of coindexing, we use contraindexing, that is, we assign an index *i* to a given pronoun and a different index to each DP that *cannot* be the antecedent for the pronoun. Can DS now be dispensed with if contraindexing and Principle B apply in the course of the derivation? In other words, can we derive the possible and impossible readings of (11)?

8.2.4   Principle C

Principle C cases point to the same conclusion reached in section 8.2.3. Consider the sentence in (16), for instance, where neither pronoun can take *John* as its antecedent.

(16)   He wondered which picture of John he liked.

The DS, SS, and LF representations of (16) are given in (17) (irrelevant details omitted).

(17)   a. <u>DS</u>:
         [$_{TP}$ he wondered [$_{CP}$ [$_{TP}$ he liked [which picture of John]]]]
         b. <u>SS/LF</u>:
         [$_{TP}$ he wondered [$_{CP}$ [which picture of John]$_m$ [$_{TP}$ he liked t$_m$]]]

In (17a), both pronouns c-command *John*. Thus, if Principle C is computed at DS, coreference between *John* and either pronoun is correctly blocked. In (17b), on the other hand, only the pronoun in the matrix clause c-commands *John*. Thus, if Principle C is computed at SS or LF, we get the correct result that *John* can't be the antecedent of the matrix subject, but we incorrectly predict that the pronoun in the embedded clause can take *John* as its antecedent.

Allowing Principle C to apply in the course of the computation is not helpful either; in the end, something like DS must be resorted to. In order to prevent *John* from being the antecedent of the embedded subject in (16), Principle C must evaluate the coindexation between these two elements *only before* wh-*movement*; if it does after *wh*-movement, this coindexation will be incorrectly permitted. Again, the conclusion seems to be that DS must be kept in the system for empirical reasons.

8.2.5   Summary

We started our discussion with some data involving covert *wh*-movement that appeared to suggest that Principle A should apply prior to LF, and showed that the analysis of covert movement discussed in section 2.3.1.2 provides us with an alternative account of these data in terms of LF, in consonance with our minimalist guidelines. However, consideration of additional data didn't seem to leave much reason for minimalist optimism. We have seen that Principles A, B, and C seem to unavoidably require DS and that Principle A may also apply later than DS. In other words, not only does this fit ill with minimalist desires to eliminate DS and SS as grammatical levels, but it also points to what appears to be an inelegant property of grammar: that Binding Theory cannot receive a uniform treatment, for its principles apply in different ways.

Bad as this may be, things actually seem to be still worse. Recall that headless relative clauses and *tough*-movement constructions constitute strong arguments against DS, in that they couldn't be derived if all operations of lexical insertion must precede all instances of movement; that is, they could be derived only if applications of Merge and Move were interspersed (see sections 2.3.2.3 and 2.3.2.5). The data reviewed in the previous sections, in contrast, require that lexical insertion precede movement in order to get the binding facts correctly. So, we seem to have arrived at an impasse: if we don't allow applications of Merge and Move to mix, we can't build phrase markers bottom-up in a cyclic manner – but if we allow them to mix, we don't get the binding facts right.

The aim of the next section is to show that we can get out of this impasse if we assume the copy theory of movement, coupled with some conventions concerning the format of LF phrase markers which relate to our earlier reinterpretation of covert *wh*-movement.

Exercise 8.4

The coreference possibilities in (16) can be accounted for if we assume first that Principle C applies repeatedly in the course of the derivation, and second that, once it excludes a given coreference possibility at a given derivational step, such coreference possibility is struck out for consideration at later steps. Discuss if such an approach can account for (i), and if (i) presents problems for the conclusion in the text regarding the necessity of DS.

(i)   Which picture of John$_i$ did he$_{*i}$ say that he$_i$ liked?

8.3   The copy theory to the rescue

The binding data discussed in section 8.2 suggest that at least DS is empirically indispensable. In this section, we show that there is a way around this conclusion if movement is reduced to the more primitive operations Copy and Merge, as proposed in chapters 6 and 7. Before getting into details, however, a minimalist interlude.

From a methodological perspective, grammars without internal levels like DS and SS are better than those with such. Thus, *all things being equal*, if a grammar G without DS and SS can duplicate the empirical results of a grammar G′ that use such levels, then G is superior to G′. This bit of minimalist wisdom has the consequence that a minimalist reanalysis of the data in section 8.2 need not cover more empirical ground to be preferable: a tie goes to the minimalist! Why is this so? Because DS and SS are not independently required by the interfaces and therefore should be postulated only when every possibility within minimalist boundaries has been tried and failed.

This said, the mechanisms that we shall use to get the desired empirical coverage had better not go (too far) beyond what is needed in a DS/SS-based account; otherwise, it will become considerably less clear whether or not a theory without DS/SS levels is truly methodologically preferable. In other words, if in order to meet the empirical challenge posed by G′, G must introduce hokey mechanisms that go beyond those a theory like G′ requires, then we are just trading one set of methodological undesirables for another. Thus, as we proceed, we'll always pause and compare each step forward with the GB-mechanics in order to make sure that the mechanisms we invoke to solve the empirical problems are natural and/or analogous to those that a DS/SS-based analysis requires.

8.3.1   *Reconstruction as LF deletion*
The presentation in section 8.2 strictly followed GB in assuming that movement operations leave coindexed traces. As discussed in section 6.4, the Minimalist Program has, instead, adopted the copy theory of movement, according to which a trace is actually a copy of the moved element that (in general) gets deleted in the phonological component (see section 7.5). Let's then reexamine our problematic data under the copy theory, starting with the sentence in (8a), repeated below in (18).

(18)   John$_i$ wondered which picture of himself$_{i/k}$ Fred$_k$ liked.

In the derivation of (18), the *wh*-phrase moves, leaving a copy behind, as represented in (19) below (irrelevant details omitted). Let's assume that the copy left behind is deleted in the phonological component for the linearization reasons suggested in section 7.5 and put the issue of phonetic realization aside. What is relevant for our purposes is that (19) is the structure that Spell-Out ships to the covert component.

(19)   [$_{TP}$ John wondered [$_{CP}$ [which picture of himself] [$_{TP}$ Fred liked [which picture of himself]]]]

The interesting property of (19) is that it contains two copies of *himself*, each of which in a different domain. Thus, if the higher copy were chosen for interpretation, *himself* in (18) should take *John* as its antecedent; if the lower copy were chosen, *Fred* should be the antecedent. Crucially, it seems that the two copies can't both be selected for interpretation, for although *himself* in (18) can mean 'John' *or* 'Fred', it can't mean 'John' *and* 'Fred' simultaneously. Thus, in order to get the right interpretation for (18), what we need is to convert (19) into a structure that has an operator-variable format and get rid of one of the copies of *himself*.

In a GB-style theory, *wh*-traces are interpreted as variables and the *wh*-elements in [Spec,CP] are understood as quantificational operators. Let's then assume, on a par with the GB-account, that the copy inside the embedded TP in (19) is interpreted as a variable, while the material in [Spec,CP] is interpreted as a quantificational operator. Let's further assume that we must "reduce" the *wh*-chain in (19), deleting the repeated material so that only a single copy of each expression gets interpreted. This assumed, a potential reduction of (19) is given in (20) below, which is assigned the logical structure in (21). Given (20), the copy of *himself* that is available for interpretation must be bound in its domain (the matrix TP), and we derive the matrix subject reading of (18).

(20)   LF:
       [$_{TP}$ John wondered [$_{CP}$ [which picture of himself] [$_{TP}$ Fred liked ~~[which picture of himself]~~]]]

(21)   John wondered which *x*, *x* a picture of himself, Fred liked *x*

If, on the other hand, the *wh*-chain in (19) were reduced as in (22) below, we would be able to derive the interpretation of *himself* as 'Fred', but no operator-variable frame would be generated, for the *wh*-element – the quantificational material – is not in [Spec,CP]. The question then is how to derive an adequate LF structure that allows the embedded subject reading for *himself* in (18).

(22)   LF:
       *[$_{TP}$ John wondered [$_{CP}$ ~~[which picture of himself]~~ [$_{TP}$ Fred liked [which picture of himself]]]]

Recall that we have seen cases of overt *wh*-movement where (part of) the non-quantificational material is left behind, as illustrated in (23)–(25) below (see section 2.3.1.2). Moreover, in order to provide an LF account of the unacceptability of (26a) and (27a), we have assumed that covert *wh*-movement targets the *wh*-element alone, as represented in (26b) and (27b) (see sections 2.3.1.2 and 8.2.1).

(23)   *French*
       Combien$_i$ a-t-il   consultés [t$_i$ de livres]?
       how.many has-he consulted   of books
       'How many books did he consult?'

(24)   *German*
       Was$_i$ hast du [t$_i$ für Bücher] gelesen?
       what have you   for books   read
       'What books did you read?'

(25)   [which portrait]$_i$ did he buy [t$_i$ that Harry likes]

(26)   a. *Which man said he$_i$ liked which picture that Harry$_i$ bought?
       b. <u>LF</u>:
          *[$_{CP}$ which$_k$ + [which man]$_m$ [$_{TP}$ t$_m$ said he$_i$ liked [t$_k$ picture that Harry$_i$ bought]]]

(27)   a. *John$_i$ wondered which woman liked which pictures of himself$_i$.
       b. <u>LF</u>:
          *[$_{TP}$ John$_i$ wondered [which$_k$ + [which woman]$_j$ [$_{TP}$ t$_j$ liked [t$_k$ pictures of himself$_i$]]]]

Thus, we already have the relevant ingredients to derive the downstairs reading of *himself* in (18). All we need to say is that a possible reduction of a *wh*-chain may leave only the quantificational material in [Spec,CP]. That is, (19) may be converted into the structure in (28).

(28)   <u>LF</u>:
       [$_{TP}$ John wondered [$_{CP}$ [which ~~picture of himself~~] [$_{TP}$ Fred liked [~~which~~ picture of himself]]]]

(28) is parallel to (23)–(27) in that the semantic restriction appears not on the operator, but on the variable. Assuming that (28) is indeed a possible reduction of (19), it may be assigned the well-formed logic structure in (29) and the available copy of *himself* must be bound in its domain by *Fred*; hence the embedded subject reading for *himself* in (18).[8]

(29)   John wondered which *x*, Fred liked *x* picture of himself

An analogy might help make the intuitive content of the two methods of semantic restriction illustrated in (21) and (29) more lively. Think of the operator as a flashlight and the variable as the objects it can shine on. Putting the restrictor on the operator acts to change the beam that flashlight emits, say by allowing it to illuminate only blue objects. The restrictor on the variable leaves the beam unaffected but restricts the objects that the beam can be pointed at, say it removes all but the blue objects from view. In both cases, the only visible objects will be the blue ones. But this will be so for two different reasons; either because of the limited quality of the emitted light or because of the restrictions on the objects available for illumination.

---

8 See Fox (1999) for further discussion of the semantics of (29).

Wrapping up, the possibilities afforded by the copy theory allow the ambiguity of (18) to be traced to the two options outlined in (21) and (29). If we choose the first, then at LF only the higher copy of *himself* survives and it will have to be bound by *John*. The second interpretation comes from retaining the lower one, thereby making *Fred* the antecedent. Note that once we allow these mechanisms, we are able to account for the two readings of (18) exclusively at LF. That is, we have now encountered our proverbial tie, and the minimalist LF-based analysis may be declared the winner.

But before we leave for celebrations and move on to inspect how to incorporate the other data discussed in section 8.2, we should ask ourselves whether the technology introduced here is too exotic and/or goes far beyond what a GB-analysis would require. Recall that if this is the case, the methodological advantages of the minimalist alternative recede.

The technology required for our minimalist alternative involves two parts: the copy theory and "deletions" required to get LF into the right format for interpretation. As discussed in sections 6.4 and 7.5, the copy theory is a methodological improvement on trace theory, both conceptually and empirically. On the conceptual side, the copy theory explores operations that are already part of the computational system (Merge and Copy) and complies with the Inclusiveness Conditions in that it does not introduce new kinds of theoretical entities (namely, traces) that are not present in the numeration (see section 6.4). On the empirical side, it accounts for cases where "traces" (lower copies) are pronounced instead of the head of the chain and cases where more than one copy gets pronounced (see section 7.5). So, this change from trace theory to the copy theory is a plus.

The deletions, on the other hand, might be seen as a minus, for no deep motivation for them was provided.[9] Two things are worth pointing out, though. First, the kind of quantificational structure with the restriction on the variable, which was used to account for the downstairs reading of *himself* in (18), seems to be independently required to deal with instances of overt movement such as (23)–(25), both in GB and in minimalism. And second, GB also employs mechanisms similar to the sort of deletions discussed here to account for some "reconstruction" phenomena.

Consider the data in (30) and (31), for instance.

(30)   a. Whose mother did you see?
       b. <u>SS</u>:
          $[_{CP}$ [whose mother $]_i$ did $[_{TP}$ you see t_i]]

---

9 For some attempts to motivate these deletions, see Martin and Uriagereka (1999), Hornstein (2001), and Grohmann (2003b).

(31)   a. To who(m) did you talk?
        b. <u>SS</u>:
           $[_{CP} [$ to who(m) $]_i$ did $[_{TP}$ you talk $t_i]$ $]$

The semantics of questions is generally assumed to be revealed by the appropriate answers they elicit.[10] More specifically, it is assumed that the *form* of an appropriate response is provided by the logical form of a sentence, as the set of appropriate answers is determined by "filling" in the gap left by *wh*-movement. Given that the sentences in (32), for example, are appropriate answers to the questions in (30a) and (31a), their logical form should be along the lines of (33).

(32)   a. I saw *Bill's* mother and *Frank's* mother.
        b. I talked to *Bill* and I talked to *Frank*.

(33)   a. who$_x$ you saw x's mother
        b. who$_x$ you talked to x

    Now, under the assumption that these logical forms should be derivable from compatible LF structures, the LF representations of the sentences in (30a) and (31a) can't be isomorphic with their SS representations in (30b) and (31b). Note that the trace left in (30b) is a DP trace and the one in (31b) is a PP trace. If answers are determined by just filling in the gap with an expression of the relevant type, we should be able to put any DP in the first and any PP in the second, once the selectional properties of the verbs are satisfied. But clearly, the "answers" for (30a) and (31a) given in (34) are not wrong, but beside the point.

(34)   a. I saw Mary.
        b. I talked about Fred.

    To overcome this problem of dissimilarity between logical forms and the syntactic representations that underlie them, the GB trace-based account must be supplemented with rules that reconfigure structure at LF. The standard assumption is that in the covert component, one can "reconstruct" complex *wh*-phrases to their trace positions and then raise just the simplex *wh*-operators (cf. section 2.3.1.2). In the case of (30a) and (31a), for instance, the LF representations resulting from such a reconstruction process should be as in (35b) and (36b), which are now compatible with the logical forms in (33) and the answers in (32).

---

10 This is the classic approach going back to Hamblin (1973) and Karttunen (1977).

(35)   a. <u>SS</u>:
            [CP [whose mother]i did [TP you see ti]]
       b. <u>LF</u>:
            [CP whosej did [TP you see [tj mother]]]

(36)   a. <u>SS</u>:
            [CP [to who(m)]i did [TP you talk ti]]
       b. <u>LF</u>:
            [CP who(m)j did [TP you talk [to tj]]]

The copy theory replaces this process of reconstruction with the deletion operations we surveyed above. In the case of (30a) and (31a), the structures shipped to the covert component are as in (37a) and (38a), and after deletion, their LF representations are as in (37b) and (38c), which can be appropriately translated into the logical forms in (33).

(37)   a. [CP [whose mother] did [TP you see [whose mother]]]
       b. <u>LF</u>:
            [CP [whose ~~mother~~] did [TP you see [~~whose~~ mother]]]

(38)   a. [CP [to who(m)] did [TP you talk [to who(m)]]]
       b. <u>LF</u>:
            [CP [~~to~~ who(m)] did [TP you talk [to ~~who(m)~~]]]

It's fair to say that these deletion rules are no more cumbersome or exotic than the reconstruction processes they replace. In fact, one might argue that they are more natural. Be that as it may, so long as they are no worse, it suffices for our minimalist purposes.

It's also worth mentioning that not only *wh*-chains, but also A-chains must be subject to this process of covert "chain reduction," in the sense that repeated material within different links must be deleted. Consider the data in (39), for example.

(39)   a. *[it seems to themi that [John and Mary]i were angry]
       b. [[John and Mary]i seem to [each other]i to have been angry]

The unacceptability of (39a) suggests that the preposition *to* preceding the experiencer is just a morphological marking of oblique Case, which doesn't prevent the pronoun *them* from c-commanding *John and Mary*, inducing a Principle C violation. That being so, the structure in (40a) below, which underlies the raising construction in (39b) under the copy theory, should also yield a Principle C violation, for the anaphor c-commands the lower copy of *John and Mary*. However, this undesirable result is correctly excluded if chain reduction also applies to A-chains, yielding the LF structure in (40b), which complies with Principle C. Again, the assumption that A-chains must also undergo chain reduction in the covert component is at least comparable to the GB-assumption that reconstruction is optional in the case of A-movement.

(40)   a. [$_{TP}$ [John and Mary] seemed to [each other] [$_{TP}$ [John and Mary] to have been angry]]
       b. <u>LF</u>:
          [$_{TP}$ [John and Mary] seemed to [each other] [$_{TP}$ ~~[John and Mary]~~ to have been angry]]

To conclude. With the help of the copy theory, we have been able to provide a comparable LF-based analysis of the ambiguity in sentences such as (18), repeated below in (40), which is at least as adequate as the ones found within GB in terms of traces, reconstruction, and/or non-interface levels of representation. We therefore have a flashing green light to proceed to reexamining the remaining data of section 8.2.

(41)   John$_i$ wondered which picture of himself$_{i/k}$ Fred$_k$ liked.

Exercise 8.5

Assuming the analysis of (41) given in the text, explain how the ambiguity of (i) can be captured.

(i)   Which picture of himself$_{i/k}$ did John$_i$ say that Fred$_k$ liked?

Exercise 8.6

Given the analysis of the data in (39), consider the data in (i)–(ii) below (see Lebeaux 1991). The unacceptability of (i) under the indicated reading suggests that like the dative *to* of raising predicates, the passive *by* in (i) does not prevent *her* from c-commanding *Mary*, inducing a Principle C violation. Assuming this to be so and assuming further that a pronoun can only be interpreted as a bound variable if it is c-commanded by a quantified expression, provide the LF structures of the sentences in (ii) and explain why one is acceptable and the other isn't.

(i)   *It is known by her$_i$ that Mary$_i$'s bread is the best there is.

(ii) a. [His$_i$ mother]$_k$'s bread seems to [every man]$_i$ to be known by her$_k$ to be the best there is.
      b. *[His$_i$ mother]$_k$'s bread seems to her$_k$ to be known by [every man]$_i$ to be the best there is.

8.3.2   The Preference Principle

Let's now reconsider the problematic cases involving Principles B and C discussed above in sections 8.2.3 and 8.2.4, which are repeated below in (42).

(42)   a. John$_i$ wondered which picture of him$_{i/*k}$ Fred$_k$ liked.
         b. He$_{i/*j}$ wondered which picture of John$_j$ he$_{i/k/*j}$ liked.

As the reader may have already anticipated, getting the right configurations won't be problematic. What will be more troublesome is to prevent overgeneration. First, let's turn to the required structures. Assuming the copy theory, the relevant structures that feed the covert component are the ones given in (43) below. If we apply to (43) the second strategy to reduce *wh*-chains discussed in section 8.3.1, we derive the LF representations in (44), which in turn can be converted into the logical forms in (45).

(43)   a. [$_{TP}$ John wondered [$_{CP}$ [which picture of him] [$_{TP}$ Fred liked [which picture of him]]]]
         b. [$_{TP}$ he wondered [$_{CP}$ [which picture of John] [$_{TP}$ he liked [which picture of John]]]]

(44)   a. LF:
            [$_{TP}$ John wondered [$_{CP}$ [which ~~picture of him~~]
            [$_{TP}$ Fred liked [~~which~~ picture of him]]]]
         b. LF:
            [$_{TP}$ he wondered [$_{CP}$ [which ~~picture of John~~] [$_{TP}$ he liked [~~which~~ picture of John]]]]

(45)   a. John wondered which x Fred liked x picture of him
         b. he wondered which x he liked x picture of John

Importantly, if Principles B and C apply to the LF representations in (44), we correctly account for coreference possibilities in (42). The pronoun in (44a) can't be bound in its domain by *Fred*, but it can be bound outside its domain by *John*; in (44b), on the other hand, coindexation of either pronoun with *John* violates Principle C.

The problem is that there is another possibility for reducing the *wh*-chain of (43) (see section 8.3.1), namely, the one in which the whole *wh*-phrase is interpreted upstairs and the downstairs copy is deleted, as represented in (46).

(46)   a. LF:
            [$_{TP}$ John wondered [$_{CP}$ [~~which picture of him~~]
            [$_{TP}$ Fred liked ~~which picture of him~~]]]

b. <u>LF</u>:
[$_{TP}$ he wondered [$_{CP}$ [which picture of John]
[$_{TP}$ he liked ~~which picture of John~~]]]

If the Binding Theory is applied to the LF representations in (46), we would incorrectly predict that in (42a), the pronoun could take *Fred* but not *John* as its antecedent and that in (42b), the embedded subject could take *John* as its antecedent.

The question then is how to enforce that the system will implement chain reduction along the lines of (44) and not (46). Chomsky (1993: 209) proposes that this is a matter of economy, suggesting the *Preference Principle* in (47).

(47)   *Preference Principle*
         Try to minimize the restriction in the operator position.

Given the chain-reduction possibilities in (44) and (46), the Preference Principle will choose the derivations that employ (46), where the non-quantificational material in the operator position is deleted, and we obtain the correct results. We thus have an adequate LF-based account of the problematic data in (42).

However, the postulation of the Preference Principle raises two questions. First, why a preference rather than an absolute requirement? Second, what motivates it?

It is a preference rather than an absolute requirement for empirical reasons. Recall that the ambiguity of sentences such as (48) below was accounted for in terms of the two kinds of chain reduction represented in (49). If minimization of material in the operator position were an absolute requirement, the system should only resort to (49b) and only the embedded subject reading should be derived.

(48)   John$_i$ wondered which picture of himself$_{i/k}$ Fred$_k$ liked.

(49)   a. <u>LF</u>:
            [$_{TP}$ John wondered [$_{CP}$ [which picture of himself]
            [$_{TP}$ Fred liked ~~[which picture of himself]~~]]]
         b. <u>LF</u>:
            [$_{TP}$ John wondered [$_{CP}$ [which ~~picture of himself~~]
            [$_{TP}$ Fred liked [~~which~~ picture of himself]]]]

The question now is what differentiates Principle A cases, where both kinds of chain reduction can be used, from cases involving Principles B and C, which do comply with the Preference Principle. Chomsky tries to account for this difference by assuming that anaphors move covertly to a position where they can be licensed by their antecedents.[11] The intuition behind these proposals is that anaphors can only refer if they agree with their antecedents; under the assumption that agreement involves a local relation, anaphors must then move prior to LF to a position where they can establish such an agreement. That being so, the actual choice between the two possibilities of chain reduction will then depend on covert anaphor movement.

Suppose that after the structure in (50) is shipped to the covert component, the lower anaphor moves to a position closer to its binder, as represented in (51).

(50)   [$_{TP}$ John wondered [$_{CP}$ [which picture of himself] [$_{TP}$ Fred liked [which picture of himself]]]]

(51)   [$_{TP}$ John wondered [$_{CP}$ [which picture of himself] [$_{TP}$ Fred + himself liked [which picture of himself]]]]

Reduction of the *wh*-chain in (51) in compliance with the Preference Principle deletes the non-quantificational material from [Spec, CP], yielding (52a) below. Given that anaphor movement displays the locality characteristic of A-movement, let's then assume that it is indeed A-movement. If so, the anaphor chain in (52a) must also undergo chain reduction (see section 8.3.1), yielding the final LF representation in (52b), which derives the embedded subject reading for *himself*.

(52)   a. [$_{TP}$ John wondered [$_{CP}$ [which ~~picture of himself~~] [$_{TP}$ Fred + himself liked [~~which~~ picture of himself]]]]
        b. [$_{TP}$ John wondered [$_{CP}$ [which ~~picture of himself~~] [$_{TP}$ Fred + himself liked [~~which~~ picture of ~~himself~~]]]]

Let's now examine the scenario where the upper copy of *himself* in (50) is the one that moves, as shown in (53) below. If the *wh*-chain in (53) is reduced in compliance with the Preference Principle, we obtain the structure in (54). However, such chain reduction arguably causes the derivation to crash. Unlike what happens in (52a), the chain reduction in (54) "breaks" the anaphor chain, by deleting one of its links, and this result may be interpreted as a Theta-Criterion violation. In addition, the two surviving copies of *himself* in (54) aren't in a local configuration and can't be interpreted as a chain; hence, they cannot undergo chain reduction.

11 For early proposals, see Lebeaux (1983) and Chomsky (1986b).

Under the assumption that only a single copy of a given expression can be legible at the interface (see section 8.3.1), the structure should then violate Full Interpretation at LF as well (see sections 1.3 and 1.5).

(53)   [$_{TP}$ John + himself wondered [$_{CP}$ [which picture of himself]
        [$_{TP}$ Fred liked [which picture of himself]]]]

(54)   LF:
        *[$_{TP}$ John + himself wondered [$_{CP}$ [which ~~picture of himself~~]
        [$_{TP}$ Fred liked [~~which~~ picture of himself]]]]

In either scenario, once the optimal option for the reduction of the *wh*-chain in (54) doesn't lead to a convergent derivation, we are allowed to consider the other chain-reduction possibility. Recall that only convergent derivations can be compared for economy purposes (see section 1.5). If the derivation of (54) doesn't converge, then it doesn't block the derivation illustrated in (55), which employs the less preferred option for reducing *wh*-chains.

(55)   a. [$_{TP}$ John + himself wondered [$_{CP}$ [which picture of himself]
           [$_{TP}$ Fred liked ~~[which picture of himself]~~]]]
        b. LF:
           [$_{TP}$ John + himself wondered [$_{CP}$ [which picture of ~~himself~~] [$_{TP}$ Fred
           liked ~~[which picture of himself]~~]]]

In (55a), the whole *wh*-phrase is kept in [Spec,CP] and its lower copy is deleted; the anaphor chain is subsequently reduced in (55b) and the matrix subject reading for *himself* is derived.

The inherent referential differences between anaphors, on the one hand, and pronouns and R-expressions, on the other, thus provide us with a conceptual basis to account for the fact that the Preference Principle always applies to constructions involving Principle B and C, but not Principle A. As an economy principle, the Preference Principle only chooses among convergent derivations.

Let's take stock. Our LF-based account of the potentially problematic data has the following ingredients: (i) the copy theory; (ii) chain reduction in the covert component; (iii) covert movement of anaphors; and (iv) the Preference Principle. As discussed in section 8.3.1, the copy theory is very welcome from a minimalist perspective and chain reduction is at least comparable to the GB-assumptions regarding reconstruction. As for the idea that anaphors move covertly, it is also assumed by many GB-theories and so does not choose between the two alternatives. This leaves the

Preference Principle. Though it works, it is not clear why it holds and, as such, it raises questions for the minimalist. At present, no particularly good motivation has been advanced for this principle and to some extent, this just reflects the general incipient stage of investigations concerning derivational economy.

Be that as it may, it's interesting to observe that something like the Preference Principle must also be assumed within GB, when we expand our data set. Consider, for instance, the GB-analysis of the sentences in (56)–(58).

(56)   a. *He$_i$ greeted Mary after John$_i$ walked in.
        b. DS/SS/LF:
           *[he$_i$ [greeted Mary [after John$_i$ walked in]]]

(57)   a. After John$_i$ walked in, he$_i$ greeted Mary.
        b. DS:
           *[he$_i$ [greeted Mary [after John$_i$ walked in]]]
        c. SS/LF:
           [[after John$_i$ walked in]$_k$ [he$_i$ [greeted Mary t$_k$]]]

(58)   a. *Which picture of John$_i$ did he$_i$ like?
        b. DS:
           *[he$_i$ did like [which picture of John$_i$]]
        c. SS:
           [[which picture of John$_i$]$_k$ he$_i$ did like t$_k$]
        d. LF:
           *[which$_k$ he$_i$ did like [t$_k$ picture of John$_i$]]

Recall that the contrast between (56a) and (57a) was taken to show that Principle C should not apply at DS (see section 2.3.1.2); otherwise, both sentences should be unacceptable as they have the same DS representation, as seen in (56b)/(57b), where *John* is c-commanded by *he*. If that is so, the unacceptability of (58a) should then be attributed not to a Principle C violation at DS, but at LF, after part of the *wh*-phrase is reconstructed back to its original position, as shown in (58d). But why is reconstruction obligatory in (58), but not in (57)? Crucially, if the moved adverbial clause of (57c) were reconstructed at LF, (57a) should pattern like (56a), contrary to fact. The answer seems to be that A′-movement involving operators, as in the case of (58a), must reconstruct if possible; in order words, something like the Preference Principle must hold even within GB.

To conclude, we have been able to provide an LF-based analysis of Binding Theory that has at least the same empirical coverage as alternatives that need DS and SS, and we have achieved this result by resorting to machinery that is either superior or at least comparable to the machinery assumed in GB. As such, though there remains some work to do, our minimalist project has not clearly met its Waterloo in the domain of binding.

Exercise 8.7

In the discussion above, the ambiguity of (ia) was indirectly attributed to anaphor movement in the covert component. Thus, if the higher instance of *himself* in (ib) moves, only the matrix subject reading is available; if the lower instance does, only the embedded subject reading can be derived. Assuming this to be so, what would go wrong if *both* instances of *himself* move in (ib)?

(i) a. John$_i$ wondered which picture of himself$_{i/k}$ Fred$_k$ liked.
  b. [$_{TP}$ John wondered [$_{CP}$ [which picture of himself] [$_{TP}$ Fred liked [which picture of himself]]]]

Can your answer to the previous question also apply to the analysis of (ii)? If not, what blocks covert movement of two instances of *himself* in the structure associated with (ii)?

(ii) Which picture of himself$_{i/k}$ did John$_i$ say that Fred$_k$ liked?

Exercise 8.8

Assuming the approach given in the text, explain why the sentences in (i) are unacceptable with the intended reading.

(i) a. *Whose$_i$ girlfriend did he$_i$ send flowers to?
  b. *Which picture of [which man]$_i$ did he$_i$ see?

Exercise 8.9

Assuming the analysis explored in this section, explain how the contrast in (i) can be derived and discuss if it can be captured by an approach that says that Principle C must apply repeatedly in the course of the derivation (see section 8.2.4).

(i) a. *Which picture of John$_i$ did he$_i$ like?
  b. Which picture of John$_i$ did Mary say he$_i$ liked?

Exercise 8.10

Discuss if and how anaphor movement, as discussed in this section, satisfies the Uniformity Condition (see section 2.4).

8.3.3   Indices and inclusiveness (where does Binding Theory apply, after all?)
Let's examine the economy argument developed in section 8.3.2 more closely. Consider the sentence in (59) below, for instance. Given the two possibilities in (60) for reducing the *wh*-chain associated with (59), the Preference
Principle is assumed to choose (60a), where the non-quantificational
material is deleted in the operator position, yielding the Principle B effect
registered in (59).

(59)   Mary wondered which picture of him$_{i/*k}$ Fred$_k$ liked.

(60)   a. <u>LF</u>:
           [$_{TP}$ Mary wondered [$_{CP}$ [which ~~picture of him~~]
           [$_{TP}$ Fred liked [~~which~~ picture of him]]]]
        b. <u>LF</u>:
           [$_{TP}$ Mary wondered [$_{CP}$ [which picture of him]
           [$_{TP}$ Fred liked ~~[which picture of him]~~]]]

However, there seems to be a loose end with this argument.[12] If the
Preference Principle, as an economy principle, only chooses among convergent derivations, as we saw in the discussion of Principle A, shouldn't
the computational system then disregard (60a) and choose the less preferred option in (60b)? After all, coindexation between *him* and *Fred*
violates Principle B in (60a), but not in (60b). In other words, shouldn't
violations of the Binding Theory cause the derivation to crash? What's
wrong with this reasoning?

The problem is that it treats indices as *parts* of syntactic objects. Note
that (60a) is unacceptable *only with that indexation*. That aside, it's a well-
formed LF structure. So what we must now ask is whether indices are true
grammatical formatives. More pointedly, in a minimalist system, *should*
they be? Chomsky (1995: 228) suggests not:

> A "perfect language" should meet the condition of inclusiveness: any
> structure formed by the computation [...] is constituted of elements
> already present in the lexical items selected for [the numeration] N;
> no new objects are added in the course of the computation apart from
> rearrangement of lexical properties (in particular, **no indices**, bar levels in
> the sense of X′-theory, etc. [...]).   [our emphasis – NH, JN, and KKG]

Under the reasonable assumption that referential indices, the ones standardly used for Binding Theory computations, can't be conceived of in

---

12 See Ferreira (2000) for discussion of this point.

terms of lexical features, the Inclusiveness Condition should ban their postulation as grammatical entities (see section 2.4).[13]

We discussed the Inclusiveness Condition in chapters 6 and 7, where we reanalyzed the properties of phrases and traces. It was used to argue for a relational understanding of bar-levels and for a replacement of traces with copies. The idea seems computationally very natural: what grammars do is relate lexical atoms; they do not create new kinds of objects. If we adopt this perspective, then the potential problem mentioned above is only apparent, for it relies on computing convergence relative to alternative *indexations*. If there are no indices, the two possible reductions of the *wh*-chain in (60) then lead to convergent derivations and the Preference Principle does apply, choosing (60a).

Assuming that this is the right way of thinking of things, where should we then compute Principle B, if it doesn't apply to the LF structure represented in (60a)? Well, what we want to say is that (59) cannot be interpreted with *Fred* and *him* coreferential and we want to say this without mentioning indices. Why then not simply say that a structure like (60a) converges with a perfectly fine interpretation, but it's not one that allows the pronoun to be anaphorically dependent on *Fred*? This requires a very slight emendation to the binding principles.

For instance, we could adopt Chomsky and Lasnik's (1993) version of the Binding Theory given in (61), which perfectly fits our needs in that it's stated in terms of interpretive principles, without resorting to indices.

(61)   *Binding Theory*
   (i) *Principle A:*
       If α is an anaphor, interpret it as coreferential with a c-commanding phrase in its domain.
   (ii) *Principle B:*
       If α is a pronoun, interpret it as disjoint from every c-commanding phrase in its domain.
   (iii) *Principle C:*
       If α is an R-expression, interpret it as disjoint from every c-commanding phrase.

Given this formulation of the Binding Theory, we may take (60a) to converge and block (60b), and the Principle B in (61ii) will require that *him* in (60a) be interpreted as disjoint from *Fred*, as desired.

---

13 But see Kural and Tsoulas (2005) for a proposal to capture indices under Inclusiveness.

To conclude, if indices can't be syntactic primitives, as entailed by the Inclusiveness Condition, the Binding Theory should be formulated along the lines of (61), with interpretive principles operating not at LF, but at the Conceptual-Intentional interface (the interface where LF touches the other cognitive systems). It's worth noting that this *is* a result compatible with minimalist expectations.

Recall that the hypothesis that the minimalist project explores is that there should be no grammar-internal levels such as DS or SS, not that *all* properties related to language must be stated at LF or PF or that *all* the reasons for the unacceptability of sentences must be captured at these interface levels. Thus, it's a perfectly sound result that phenomena that were previously analyzed in terms of the syntactic component *stricto sensu* get reanalyzed in terms of the other cognitive systems that interface with the language faculty. In fact, we may take the discussion in this section as providing a criterion for one to decide if a given phenomenon belongs to syntax proper or to the interfaces. The idea is that if two derivations compete in terms of economy and the computational system chooses one that does not result in an acceptable sentence, the source of such unacceptability can't be a matter of convergence at LF. In the case of (59), for example, its unacceptability under the index k for the pronoun cannot be viewed as failure to converge at LF.

Exercise 8.11

We've seen in this section that if the Inclusiveness Condition holds, Principle B violations *must* be accounted for in terms of the C-I interface, rather than LF. Discuss if similar conclusions can be reached in the case of Principles A and C, by examining the sentences in (i).

(i)   a. *Which picture of John$_i$ did he$_i$ like?
      b. John wonders which picture of himself Mary liked.
      c. *She wonders which picture of himself she liked.

8.3.4   Idiom interpretation and anaphor binding

We saw in section 8.3.2 that as regards binding, we could dispense with DS and SS without losing empirical coverage. The technology required to gain this coverage is either superior or analogous to what is assumed in GB. As ties favor the minimalist alternative, we could conclude that we are done. However, it would be nice to find an argument that showed not only that the minimalist proposal could do *as well* empirically as the standard, but that it could do better. Chomsky (1993: 206ff.) offers such an argument and we will review it here.

Consider the sentence in (62).

(62)   John wondered which picture of himself Bill took.

(62) involves two kinds of ambiguity. First, it can have a literal or "idiomatic" interpretation; that is, *take* can be interpreted as a regular verb meaning 'snatch away' or as a light verb that forms a complex predicate with *picture*, meaning 'photograph'. Focusing now on the non-idiomatic 'snatch'-reading; the sentence is still ambiguous in the way we discussed in section 8.3.2 above; either *John* or *Bill* can be the antecedent of the reflexive. Recall, this ambiguity hinges on anaphor movement in the covert component. If the lower instance of the reflexive moves, we obtain the LF representation in (63a), which derives the embedded subject reading in (64a); on the other hand, if the higher copy moves, we get the LF structure in (63b), which underlies the matrix subject reading in (64b).

(63)   a. LF:
         [$_{TP}$ John wondered [$_{CP}$ [which ~~picture of himself~~] [$_{TP}$ Bill + himself took [~~which~~ picture of ~~himself~~]]]]

         b. LF:
         [$_{TP}$ John+himself wondered [$_{CP}$ [which picture of ~~himself~~] [$_{TP}$ Bill took ~~[which picture of himself]~~]]]

(64)   a. John wondered which$_x$ Bill+himself$_y$ took [x picture of y]
         b. John+himself$_y$ wondered [which picture of y]$_x$ Bill took x

Chomsky observes that this ambiguity is missing for the idiomatic reading of *take picture*. Under this interpretation, only the binding analogous to (64a) is available; in other words, only *Bill* can be interpreted as the antecedent of the reflexive.[14] This can be explained if we require that idioms reconstruct to their base positions as a precondition for having the idiomatic reading. Hence, the structure in (63a) allows both the idiomatic and the non-idiomatic reading, whereas (63b) allows only the latter.

This obligatory reconstruction for the idiom makes sense in the context of a theory without DS. It's generally assumed that idioms are not

---

14 This is a contentious claim. Many native speakers of English don't share this judgment, which weakens the force of the conclusion to be drawn. Since we are mainly concerned with the logic of the argument, we'll abstract away from this potential problem and proceed under the assumption that the judgments reported in the text are correct.

compositional and that they are listed as single items in the lexicon. In a theory with DS, an idiom is inserted into DS as a unit. In a theory without DS, the unitary nature of the idiom must be captured at some other level. In a minimalist theory, the *only* level available for this is LF, as only this level affects semantic interpretation. Note too, that phonetically, the idiom in (62) does not form a unit; *picture* is nowhere near *take*. So, LF is the only place where the idiomatic reading is checked and it is also the representation that feeds Binding Theory. In other words, *the two interpretive options are determined by the same phrase marker*. Thus, we expect the reading of one to determine that of the other and this is what we see in (63a): the reconstruction that licenses the idiom forbids the reflexive from having the matrix subject as antecedent.

This coincidence of interpretive options can't be reduplicated in a theory with optional SS binding or in a theory in which binding options are determined throughout the course of the derivation. Why not? Consider a theory with DS and optional binding throughout the derivation. Say that on this account, we code the idiomatic restriction at DS and allow reflexive binding at SS. Given these assumptions, it should be possible to bind the reflexive in (65b) below, after having determined the idiomatic reading in (65a). This will thus incorrectly permit the reading in which the reflexive in (62) is bound by *John* and the predicate *take picture* is idiomatically interpreted.

(65) a. <u>DS</u>:
        [John wondered [Bill took [which picture of himself]]]
      b. <u>SS</u>:
        [John wondered [[which picture of himself]$_i$ [Bill took t$_i$]]]

(62) also presents problems for a theory where reconstruction of the idiom is required at LF, but binding is allowed at both SS and LF, as illustrated in (66).

(66) a. <u>SS</u>:
        [John wondered [[which picture of himself]$_i$ [Bill took t$_i$]]]
      b. <u>LF</u>:
        [John wondered [which$_k$ [Bill took [t$_k$ picture of himself]]]]

In this case, the reflexive can be bound in (66a) and reconstruction in (66b) licenses the idiomatic reading. Once again, *John* is incorrectly interpreted as the antecedent of *himself* under the idiomatic reading of *take picture*.

Both alternatives fail for the same reason. What Chomsky's observations require is that reflexive binding be determined at the same place as idiomatic interpretation. This is only possible in a theory that rejects DS and SS interpretation, concentrating all interpretation at LF. Only if this is assumed can the *coincidence* of the interpretive options be accommodated. Thus, it is precisely because the other options have the grammar affect interpretation at more than one point that they cannot account for the correlation discussed above. A minimalist account, in contrast, must consolidate all interpretation at LF because it rejects DS and SS, and this permits an appropriate account of the noted semantic correlation between binding and idiomatic readings.

One point is worth emphasizing. If this analysis is on the right track, then it provides an *empirical* argument for the minimalist approach. As we have noted earlier, an empirical tie would favor a minimalist account as it is conceptually superior given that it dispenses with DS and SS and eliminates traces and indices as grammatical formatives. The argument here adds an empirical reason for preferring the minimalist option; it gets a semantic correlation that the other approaches cannot!

Exercise 8.12

In section 8.2.2, we observed that in (ia) below, the reciprocal can only be interpreted as the embedded subject, as confirmed by the sentence in (ib). Given the discussion in this section, provide the LF representation of (ia) and explain why the matrix subject reading is not allowed. In addition, discuss what we can conclude with respect to the unacceptability of (ib); does it result from lack of convergence at LF or from computations at the Conceptual-Intentional interface (see section 8.3.3)?

    (i) a. The students asked what attitudes about each other the teachers had.
        b. *The students asked what attitudes about each other Mary had.

Exercise 8.13

The data in (i) below show that two quantifiers may alternate their scope if they are in the same clause, but not if they are in different clauses (see May 1985, for instance). Hence, the sentence in (ia) is ambiguous in that it can either describe a scenario where a certain student attended all courses (with wide scope for *some student*) or a scenario where no courses were empty of students (with wide scope for *every course*); by contrast, (ib) only has the interpretation where *some student* has wide scope. With this background information, provide the LF structures of the sentences in (ii) and explain why (iia) is scope ambiguous, whereas (iib) only has the reading where *someone* has wide scope (see Aoun 1982). What conclusion can we draw with respect to computations of Binding Theory and scope interaction?

(i)   a. Some student attended every course.   (∃∀: OK; ∀∃: OK)
      b. Some student said that Mary attended every course.   (∃∀: OK; ∀∃: *)

(ii) a. Some student seems to have attended every course. (∃∀: OK; ∀∃: OK)
      b. Some student seems to himself to have attended every course.

                                                           (∃∀: OK; ∀∃: *)

Exercise 8.14

Determine which readings the sentences in (i) have and derive them on the basis of
the discussion in this section (see Chomsky 1986b).

(i)   a. The boys wondered which jokes about each other the girls told.
      b. The boys wondered which jokes about each other the girls heard.

8.3.5   *Further issues*

8.3.5.1   Binding into complement and adjunct clauses

There is one more kind of argument for the relevance of DS to the Binding
Theory that we need to consider before wrapping up this chapter. Consider
the contrast in (67).

(67)   a. *Which claim that John$_i$ was asleep did he$_i$ discuss?
         b. Which claim that John$_i$ made did he$_i$ discuss?

These two sentences have different binding properties. The pronoun cannot be coreferential with *John* in (67a), though it can be in (67b).[15] This is
quite unexpected, for the Preference Principle should in principle require
that the structures in (68) be converted into the ones in (69), where *John*
should be interpreted as distinct from *he* in both structures; hence, we
obtain a correct result for (67a), but not for (67b).

(68)   a. [[which claim that John was asleep] did [he discuss [which claim that
             John was asleep]]]
         b. [[which claim that John made] did [he discuss [which claim that John
             made]]]

(69)   a. LF:
             [[which ~~claim that John was asleep~~] did [he discuss [~~which~~ claim that
             John was asleep]]]

15 For relevant discussion, see among others van Riemsdijk (1981), Freidin (1986), Lebeaux
    (1988, 1991, 1995), Speas (1991), Chomsky (1993), Heycock (1995), and Lasnik (1998).

b. <u>LF</u>:
[[which ~~claim that John made~~] did [he discuss [~~which~~ claim that John made]]]

The problem then is how to distinguish (67a) from (67b). One difference between them is clear: (67a) involves a noun complement clause, (67b) involves a relative clause and so an adjunct. Lebeaux (1988) tied the contrast between (67a) and (67b) to the complement/adjunct difference by assuming that complements must be present at DS, but adjuncts may be introduced in the course of the derivation. That is, although there is a single possibility for the noun complement clause of (67a) to be introduced into the derivation, namely at DS (prior to *wh*-movement, as illustrated in (70)), the introduction of the relative clause of (67b) may be introduced either before or after *wh*-movement, as illustrated in (71) and (72).

(70)   a. <u>DS</u>:
[he did discuss [which [claim [that John was asleep]]]]
        b. <u>SS</u>:
[[which [claim [that John was asleep]]]$_i$ did he discuss t$_i$]

(71)   a. <u>DS</u>:
[he did discuss [[which claim] [OP$_k$ that John made t$_k$]]]
        b. <u>SS</u>:
[[[which claim] [OP$_k$ that John made t$_k$]]$_i$ did he discuss t$_i$]

(72)   a. <u>DS</u>:
[he did discuss [which claim]]
        b. <u>SS</u>:
[[[which claim]$_i$ [OP$_k$ that John made t$_k$]]$_i$ did he discuss t$_i$]

The unacceptability of (67a) can now be accounted for in terms of (70) if Principle C applies at DS or at LF after reconstruction. That being so, (67b) should also be unacceptable if (71) were the only way to derive this sentence. The acceptability of (67b) is thus attributed to the additional derivation available in (72), where the relative clause is adjoined after *which claim* moves to [Spec,CP]. Regardless of whether one computes Principle C at DS or at LF after reconstruction, *he* won't c-command *John* in (72) and Principle C will be satisfied.

Chomsky (1993) assumes the gist of Lebeaux's proposal and implements an alternative that doesn't invoke DS. More specifically, he proposes that the introduction of complements into the structure must satisfy the Extension Condition in (73), whereas the introduction of adjuncts need not do so. Let's consider the details.

(73)   *Extension Condition* (preliminary version)
        Overt applications of Merge and Move can only target root syntactic objects.

Recall that the Extension Condition ensures cyclicity in a minimalist system by preventing overt instances of Merge and Move from targeting the "middle" of a given syntactic structure (see section 2.3.2.4). Given that Move has been reanalyzed as Copy and Merge under the copy theory of movement, (73) can now be simplified along the lines of (74).

(74)   *Extension Condition* (revised preliminary version)
        Overt applications of Merge can only target root syntactic objects.

According to (74), the structure in (68a) is built by a series of applications of Merge, always targeting the root. The relevant steps are illustrated in (75).

(75)   a. *several applications of Merge* →
           [$_{CP}$ that John was asleep]
        b. CP + $_{Merge}$ *claim* →
           [$_{NP}$ claim that John was asleep]
        c. NP + $_{Merge}$ *which* →
           [$_{DP}$ which claim that John was asleep]
        d. DP + $_{Merge}$ *discuss* →
           [$_{VP}$ discuss [which claim that John was asleep]]
        e. *additional applications of Merge* →
           [$_{CP}$ did he discuss [which claim that John was asleep]]
        f. *Copy and Merge the* wh-*phrase* →
           [$_{CP}$ [which claim that John was asleep] did he discuss [which claim that John was asleep]]

The structure in (75f) is converted into (69a), preventing coreference interpretation for *he* and *John*, as discussed above.

If the introduction of adjuncts need not satisfy the Extension Condition, as proposed by Chomsky, (67b) may be derived in a way analogous to (75), but there is also another derivation available, as sketched in (76).

(76)   a. *several applications of Merge* →
           [$_{CP1}$ OP$_i$ that John made t$_i$]
        b. *several applications of Merge* →
           [$_{CP}$ did he discuss [which claim]]

    c. *Copy and Merge* wh-*phrase* →
       [$_{CP2}$ [which claim] did he discuss [which claim]]
    d. *Merge (by adjunction) CP$_1$ to the* wh-*phrase* →
       [$_{CP2}$ [[which claim] [$_{CP1}$ OP$_i$ that John made t$_i$]] did he discuss [which
       claim]]
    e. *Deletion in the phonological component* →
       [$_{CP2}$ [[which claim] [$_{CP1}$ OP$_i$ that John made t$_i$]] did he discuss [~~which~~
       ~~claim~~]]
    f. *Deletion in the covert component* →
       <u>LF</u>:
       [$_{CP2}$ [[which] [$_{CP1}$ OP$_i$ that John made t$_i$]] did he discuss [~~which~~ claim]]

Observe that in (76d), we have adjoined the relative clause to the *wh*-phrase
after the *wh*-phrase has moved, and this should be possible if adjunction is
exempt from the Extension Condition. Thus, the acceptability of (67b) under
coindexation between *he* and *John* is due to the additional derivation in (76).
Crucially, *he* does not c-command *John* in the LF representation in (76f).

    Again, we have been able to attain the same empirical coverage as GB by
employing comparable technology, but without resorting to non-interface
levels of representation. It should also be noted that from a conceptual
point of view, the minimalist reinterpretation reviewed here seems to be
more natural. First, the assumption that adjunction is not subject to the
Extension Condition seems to be independently required in order to derive
head movement. Given the structure in (77a), for instance, verb movement
does not target the root TP projection, but rather a subpart of TP, namely,
T, as shown in (77b).

(77)   a. [$_{TP}$ T^0 [$_{VP}$ ... V ...]]

      b.

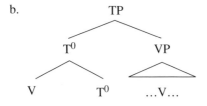

And second, addition of relative clauses in the course of the derivation
can be seen as a stab at DS. Recall that as a starting point for the derivation
within GB, DS should be the unique root syntactic object available to the
computation. If relative clauses may be assembled independently, this
undermines the role of DS within GB (see sections 2.3.1.3 and 2.3.2.5).

To put it broadly, the interpretation contrast between (67a) and (67b), rather than providing an argument for DS, actually calls into question DS's own existence *even within GB*. Needless to say that minimalists won't get depressed with this result.

8.3.5.2   The Extension Condition and sideward movement

The contrast between complement and adjunct clauses reviewed in the previous section relies on the assumption that adjunction structures are not subject to the Extension Condition and this seems to be independently required for head movement. That being so, our minimalist-inclined minds should now be asking *why* this should be the case.

Given that adjunction is our perennial troublemaker, one could say that the exceptionality of adjunction with respect to the Extension Condition is just another unavoidable stipulation regarding adjunction. Upon close inspection, it seems that such stipulated exceptionality is undesirable not only on conceptual, but on empirical grounds as well.

Take the unacceptable sentence in (78) below, for instance, which is a canonical example of the impossibility of extraction out of an adjunct island.[16] Under the copy theory, the derivation of (78) should involve copying *which book* in (79) and merging it in the matrix [Spec,CP].

(78)   *Which book did you leave the library without finding?

(79)   [did you [$_{VP}$ [$_{VP}$ leave the library] [$_{PP}$ without PRO finding [which book]]]]

For the purposes of discussion, let's just translate the ban on movement from within an adjunct island in terms of the copy theory, by saying that an element within an adjunct cannot be a target for copying.[17] That is, once the computation has reached the stage in (79), where PP is adjoined to VP, the contents of PP are unavailable for copying; hence, *which book* cannot be copied and the derivation crashes because the strong *wh*-feature of the interrogative complementizer cannot be checked.

This being so, we now need to block the derivation sketched in (80)–(84).

(80)   a. K = [$_{PP}$ without PRO finding [which book]]
        b. L = [did you [$_{VP}$ leave the library]]

---

16 See Cattell (1978) and Huang (1982).

17 For relevant discussion of adjunct islands from a minimalist perspective, see Takahashi (1994), Nunes and Uriagereka (2000), Hornstein (2001), Nunes (2001, 2004), and Boeckx (2003a).

(81)   a. K = [_PP_ without PRO finding [which book]]
         b. L = [did you [_VP_ leave the library]]
         c. M = [which book]

(82)   a. K = [_PP_ without PRO finding [which book]]
         b. N = [[which book] did you [_VP_ leave the library]]

(83)   [[which book] did you [_VP_ [_VP_ leave the library] [_PP_ without PRO finding
         [which book]]]]

(84)   [[which book] did you [_VP_ [_VP_ leave the library] [_PP_ without PRO finding
         [~~which book~~]]]]

In (80) we have two independent syntactic objects that were formed by
cyclic applications of Merge. Given that the interrogative complementizer
has a strong *wh*-feature that must be checked overtly, the computational
system can then make a copy of *which book*, as shown in (81c), and merge it
with L, yielding N in (82b). If adjunction is not subject to the Extension
Requirement, K can then be adjoined to the VP in (82b), yielding the
structure in (83). Further computations involve the deletion of the lower
copy of *which book* in (83) in the phonological component (see section 7.5),
as represented in (84), incorrectly ruling in the sentence in (78).

Notice that we cannot rule out copying *which book* from K based on the
ban on copying from adjuncts alluded to above. Like the notions of
specifier and complement, the notion of adjunct is relational. That is, a
given constituent becomes the specifier, the complement, or the adjunct of
X only when it merges with X (see section 6.3.1); before that, we have just
independent syntactic objects. Crucially, in the derivation sketched in
(80)–(84), *which book* was copied *before* the PP became an adjunct by
merging with VP in (83).

One could think that the problem resides in the steps sketched in
(80)–(84), where *which book* moves "sideways," from one tree to the other.
This may be a reasonable objection in a system like GB, which assumes that
Move is an operation and that there is only a single root syntactic object
throughout the derivation, namely, the one provided by DS. However, such
objection has no place in the framework being explored here, which allows
syntactic structures to be built in parallel and takes movement to be just the
application of Copy and Merge. Blocking the steps in (80)–(84) by stipulat-
ing that a copied element can only merge with the tree that contains the
"original" would actually amount to resurrecting DS.

A more promising approach is to explore the null hypothesis under
the framework assumed here, allowing sideward movement, and resort

to the Extension Condition in (74) to rule out the unwanted derivation in
(80)–(84). Once the merger between PP and VP in (82)–(83) is non-cyclic
(VP is not a root syntactic object in (82b)), it would be prohibited by the
Extension Condition. The advantage is that we may now be able to derive
the exceptional cases of non-cyclic merger discussed above in cyclic manner by relying on sideward movement.

The derivation of overt V-to-T (i.e. the traditional V-to-I) movement,
for instance, can proceed along the lines of (85)–(88).

(85)   a. $K = T^0$
        b. $L = [_{VP} \ldots V \ldots]$

(86)   a. $K = T^0$
        b. $L = [_{VP} \ldots V \ldots]$
        c. $M = V$

(87)   a. $N = [_{T^0} V + T^0]$
        b. $L = [_{VP} \ldots V \ldots]$

(88)

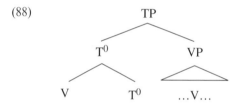

Given the syntactic objects in K and L in (85), the computational system
makes a copy of the verb, as shown in (86c), and adjoins it to Infl, to check
its strong V-feature. The resulting adjunction structure in (87a) then
merges with VP, yielding the structure in (88), which is obviously the
same object in (77b). However, the crucial point here is that at no point
in the derivation of (85)–(88) was the Extension Condition violated.[18]

Similar considerations apply to apparent instances of non-cyclic adjunction of relative clauses. The relevant derivation of (67b), for instance,
repeated below in (89), can proceed along the lines of (90)–(93), where
the *wh*-phrase is copied from K, as shown in (91c), and merges with the
relative clause (say, to license the null operator), yielding N in (92b).
N then merges with K, yielding the object in (93), which is identical to

18 For further discussion, see Bobaljik (1995a), Nunes (1995, 2001, 2004), Bobaljik and
   Brown (1997), Uriagereka (1998), Nunes and Uriagereka (2000), Hornstein and Nunes
   (2002), Boeckx (2003b), and Agbayani and Zoerner (2004).

(76d). The only difference is that (93) was built in consonance with the Extension Condition.[19]

(89)   Which claim that John$_i$ made did he$_i$ discuss?

(90)   a. K = [did he discuss [which claim]]
         b. L = [OP$_k$ that John made t$_k$]

(91)   a. K = [did he discuss [which claim]]
         b. L = [OP$_k$ that John made t$_k$]
         c. M = [which claim]

(92)   a. K = [did he discuss [which claim]]
         b. N = [[which claim] [OP$_k$ that John made t$_k$]]

(93)   [[[which claim] [OP$_k$ that John made t$_k$]] did he discuss [which claim]]

Couldn't we use a similar sideward-movement approach to derive a representation of (67a), repeated below in (94), in which the noun complement clause is attached after the *wh*-phrase has moved to [Spec,CP]? No! Why not? Because sideward movement in this case *would* violate the Extension Condition. Given the derivational steps in (95)–(96), CP$_1$ can't merge non-cyclically with *claim* in (96c) and the attempted derivation fails.

(94)   Which claim that John$_i$ was asleep did he$_i$ discuss?

(95)   a. K = [$_{CP1}$ that John was asleep]
         b. L = [did he discuss [which claim]]

(96)   a. K = [that John was asleep]
         b. L = [did he discuss [which claim]]
         c. M = [which claim]

The only alternative is along the lines of (97), where the noun complement clause merges with *claim* prior to *wh*-movement, and coreference between he and *John* is prevented by Principle C, as discussed in section 8.3.5.1.

(97)   a. [did he discuss [which [claim [that John was asleep]]]]
         b. [[which [claim [that John was asleep]]] did he discuss [which [claim [that John was asleep]]]]
         c. LF:
            [[which ~~[claim [that John was asleep]]~~] did he discuss [~~which~~ [claim [that John was asleep]]]]

19 For further discussion, see Nunes (1995, 2001, 2004).

In summary, the distinction between relative clauses and noun complement constructions can be traced to how it is that these two structures are derived. The latter requires that the clausal complement be merged prior to merging the DP that contains it within the complement of V. The relative clause, in contrast, can be merged after the *wh*-phrase moves without violating the Extension Condition either if this condition specifically excludes adjunction or, in a more principled manner, if relative clauses can be adjoined via sideward movement later in the derivation.

Exercise 8.15

Consider the derivation sketched in (ii)–(vi) below, which would incorrectly rule in the sentence in (i) (see Nunes 2004). The crucial property of this derivation is that a copy of *which book* is made prior to the adjunction of K to L in (iva); that is, the derivation below is in compliance with the Extension Condition. Discuss how it can still be ruled out within the bounds of minimalist guidelines.

(i)   *Which book did you leave the library without finding?

(ii)   a. K = [$_{PP}$ without PRO finding [which book]]
       b. L = [$_{VP}$ leave the library]

(iii) a. K = [$_{PP}$ without PRO finding [which book]]
       b. L = [$_{VP}$ leave the library]
       c. M = [which book]

(iv)   a. N = [did you [$_{VP}$ [$_{VP}$ leave the library] [$_{PP}$ without PRO finding [which book]]]]
       b. M = [which book]

(v)   [[which book]^{i} did you [$_{VP}$ [$_{VP}$ leave the library] [$_{PP}$ without PRO finding [which book]^{i}]]]

(vi)   [[which book]^{i} did you [$_{VP}$ [$_{VP}$ leave the library] [$_{PP}$ without PRO finding [which book]^{i}]]]

Exercise 8.16

Nunes (1995, 2001, 2004) and Hornstein (2001) argue that a parasitic gap like (i), for instance, should be derived via "sideward movement," along the lines of (ii)–(vi).

(i)   Which paper did you file without reading?

(ii)   a. K = [without reading [which paper]]
       b. L = file

(iii) a. K = [without reading [which paper]]
       b. L = file [which paper]

(iv) [$_{VP}$ [$_{VP}$ file [which paper]] [$_{PP}$ without reading [which paper]]]

(v) [did you [$_{VP}$ [$_{VP}$ file [which paper]] [$_{PP}$ without reading [which paper]]]]

(vi) a. [[which paper] did you [$_{VP}$ [$_{VP}$ file [which paper]] [$_{PP}$ without reading [which paper]]]]

   b. *Deletion in the phonological component:*
   [[which paper] did you [$_{VP}$ [$_{VP}$ file ~~[which paper]~~] [$_{PP}$ without reading ~~[which paper]~~]]]

Assuming this to be correct, discuss how the illicit parasitic gap in (vii) can be excluded, given the potential derivation in (viii)–(x).

(vii) *Who did you file which paper without reading?

(viii) a. K = [without reading [which paper]]
   b. L = file

(ix) a. K = [without reading [which paper]]
   b. L = file [which paper]

(x) a. [who [$_{VP}$ [$_{VP}$ filed [which paper]] [$_{PP}$ without reading [which paper]]]]

   b. *Deletion in the phonological component:*
   [who [$_{VP}$ [$_{VP}$ filed [which paper]] [$_{PP}$ without reading ~~[which paper]~~]]]

8.4 Conclusion

In this chapter we have shown that the copy theory of movement can be pressed into service to solve problems for minimalism in the domain of binding. Using copies and conventions on how to interpret them, we were able to develop an approach to reconstruction that permitted all binding effects to be consolidated to the single level of LF, an allowable level given minimalist sensibilities. The theory that emerges also dispenses with indices. All in all, it appears that the copy theory carries a broad empirical load both in PF and LF matters and seems to be an indispensable part of an empirically adequate minimalist approach to language.

9 *Feature interpretability and feature checking*

9.1 Introduction

This chapter focuses on the checking procedure that has been relied upon thus far, and on the traditional distinction between overt and covert movement. We'll take the analyses developed in previous chapters as a starting point, discussing their consistency with the general architectural features of the model and raising further minimalist questions.

Section 9.2 reviews aspects of checking theory and throws up a number of major questions; we will examine each of these questions in the sections that follow. In section 9.3 we discuss the hypothesis that feature checking is actually triggered by the need to eliminate [−interpretable] features from the computation. Section 9.4 examines two reanalyses of covert movement that are compatible with the Uniformity Condition: the Move-F and the Agree approaches. Finally, section 9.5 concludes the chapter.

9.2 Some questions concerning checking theory

Let's first review the initial motivation for the introduction of checking within the system. As seen in section 2.3.1.1, the standard view within GB that Case Theory should apply at SS rests upon two technical assumptions: first, that Case is *assigned* and second, that such assignment takes place under a *government* configuration. We've shown that an equally plausible implementation of Case Theory could cover the core set of Case-related phenomena without resorting to SS as a level of representation. Specifically, nominal elements could enter the derivation with their Case-features already specified, and the appropriateness of a particular Case-bearing element in a given structure would be enforced by a checking procedure matching such Case-feature with the Case-feature of a local head. If no appropriate matching is possible, the derivation then crashes at LF.

Consider the derivations in (1) and (2), for instance.

(1)   a. [$_{TP}$ she$_i$ [$_{T'}$ T^0 [$_{VP}$ was seen t$_i$]]]
        b. *[$_{TP}$ her$_i$ [$_{T'}$ T^0 [$_{VP}$ was seen t$_i$]]]

(2)   a. *[John expects [$_{TP}$ she$_i$ [$_{T'}$ to [$_{VP}$ t$_i$ win]]]]
        b. [John expects [$_{TP}$ her$_i$ [$_{T'}$ to [$_{VP}$ t$_i$ win]]]]

According to this checking approach, both *her* and *she* in (1) and (2) enter the derivation with their Case-features specified and move to [Spec, TP]. Since finite T in (1) is associated with nominative Case, *she* can have its Case-feature checked in this configuration, but *her* can't; hence, the contrast in (1) is due to the fact that *her* doesn't have its Case-feature checked, causing the derivation to crash at LF. In (2), on the other hand, the embedded T isn't associated with a Case-feature; the pronouns must then move covertly to the next Case-checking position, say [Spec,AgrOP], for concreteness. Given that AgrO is associated with accusative Case, it can check the Case of *her*, but not the Case of *she*, which then causes the derivation of (2a) to crash at LF.

Such an analysis is congenial to general minimalist guidelines in that it resorts to the conceptually necessary level of LF and to a local configuration made available by the structure-building operation Merge (in this particular case, a Spec-head configuration). Importantly, we have also seen that this alternative is actually empirically superior to the standard GB-approach in that it's able to account for existential constructions such as (3) or binding facts such as (4), for instance, without special provisos.

(3)   [Mary thinks that [$_{TP}$ there is [a cat] on the mat]]

(4)   [Mary [$_{VP}$ [$_{VP}$ entertained [the men]] [$_{PP}$ during each other's vacations]]]

The DP *a cat* in (3) can have its Case-requirements met after it moves covertly to a position where it can have its Case-feature checked (see section 2.3.1.1), say, by creating an additional [Spec,TP]. Similarly, after *the men* in (4) moves covertly to [Spec,AgrOP] to have its Case-feature checked, it'll be able to c-command and license the anaphor inside the adjunct PP (see section 4.4.1).[1]

---

1 As we've seen in section 4.4.2, an alternative analysis of (4) is to say that *the men* overtly moves to its Case-checking position, followed by overt movement of the verb to a higher position. For purposes of discussion, here we only take the covert movement analysis into consideration.

This checking approach was further generalized in order to account for cross-linguistic variation regarding movement, without relying on SS parameters (see section 2.3.1.3). Take the difference in verb movement between French and English, and in *wh*-movement between English and (Mandarin) Chinese (see section 2.3.1.3), as illustrated by (5) and (6).

(5) a. *French*
      Jean bois   souvent du vin.
      Jean drinks often   of wine
      'Jean often drinks wine.'
     b. John often drinks wine.

(6) a. What did Bill buy?
     b. *Mandarin Chinese*
      Bill mai-le   shenme?
      Bill buy-ASP what
      'What did Bill buy?'

It was proposed that the relevant difference in each pair of languages has to do with strong features, features that cause a derivation to crash at PF unless they are overtly checked. The contrast in (5) and (6), for instance, can be captured if French T has a strong V-feature and the English interrogative complementizer has a strong *wh*-feature.

To summarize, the checking procedure seems to be an interesting technical device from a minimalist point of view in that it makes it possible to account for the relevant facts by means of filter conditions at LF, as in the case of Case Theory, or at PF, as in the case of movement parameters. This being so, it sets up the stage for a series of minimalist questions. The first one is *why* checking exists to begin with. Notice that in the case of movement parameters, we have the sketch of an answer: if movement doesn't occur, an illegitimate object will reach PF. However, this line of reasoning can't be trivially extended to Case Theory. If the pronouns of (1) and (2) have all their relevant features specified as they enter the derivation, *why* should these features further require licensing through checking?

Another related question has to do with *when* such licensing obtains. Take (5) and (6), for instance. What would go wrong if verb movement in English and *wh*-movement in Chinese proceeded overtly? In section 2.3.1.3, these unwanted movements were excluded by the economy principle Procrastinate (see also section 2.3.1.5), according to which covert movement is more economical than overt movement. But one of course wonders *why* this is so, *why* covert operations are of a different nature than overt operations. Notice that from a minimalist perspective, the problem goes beyond the fact that such a distinction between overt and covert operations is stipulative. Stipulations must almost always be made in order to deepen investigations. But in this case, the stipulation that an operation is subject to different conditions depending on whether or not its application is overt or covert may have undesirable consequences for the whole architecture of the system. In particular, it may violate the Uniformity Condition, which requires that the operations available in the covert component be also available in the overt component (see section 2.4). Let's see why exactly such violation may be problematic.

Recall that the metatheoretical role of the Uniformity Condition is to keep us alert in face of luring statements like "such and such operations must apply before/after Spell-Out." Consider the case at hand under this light. If there's a single operation of movement, it doesn't make sense to say that overt movement is inherently more costly than covert movement. Thus, by assigning different economy values to overt and covert movement without independent motivation, the Procrastinate proposal is tacitly assuming that they are in fact *two* different operations. That being so, we should now ask what would happen if the system "mistakenly" applies the operation of "covert movement" in overt syntax.

Suppose, for instance, that verb movement in English or *wh*-movement in Chinese have taken place overtly. The structures resulting from either of these movements are definitely consistent with LF requirements (after all, these are the structures that are assumed to feed LF) and there seems to be no obvious reason why these structures should cause the derivation to crash at PF. One could then propose that these unwanted structures should actually be ruled out by Spell-Out, that is, "covert movement" cannot take place before Spell-Out. The problem with this proposal is that if there's no independent reason for why Spell-Out should be unable to apply to structures resulting from "covert movement," it's being tacitly treated as an intermediate level of representation: it's working as a filtering device with properties that can't be derived in terms of LF or PF.

To put it in general terms, in order to prevent SS from haunting us disguised in different terminology, the Uniformity Condition requires that minimalist proposals take the inventory of syntactic operations available to the computational system to remain constant throughout the whole syntactic computation. Thus, in the case under discussion, the apparent preference for covert movement over overt movement shouldn't be ensured by brute force through Procrastinate but should be derived from independent considerations.

Similar considerations apply to the difference between overt and covert movement with respect to cyclicity. Notice, for instance, that covert movement of the "associate" of the expletive in (3) and covert movement of the direct object to [Spec,AgrOP] in (4) both target the "middle" of the tree; that is, the relevant mergers in (3) and (4) don't take two root syntactic objects as input. This state of affairs is in fact consistent with the revised formulation of the Extension Condition given in (7) (see section 8.3.5.1), since it's stipulated to apply only to overt operations.

(7)   *Extension Condition* (revised preliminary version)
        Overt applications of Merge can only target root syntactic objects.

However, the question is again *why* this is so. And again, given that this unmotivated distinction between overt and covert movement violates the Uniformity Condition, Spell-Out is tacitly being understood as a level of representation: it's being responsible for filtering out structures that would arguably be allowed by LF and PF.

In the sections that follow, we'll discuss a possible answer for the question of why checking should exist and outline two different scenarios under which the syntactic relations captured through covert movement can be analyzed in a way consistent with the Uniformity Condition, with respect to both economy and extension.

9.3   Feature interpretability and Last Resort

As pointed out in section 1.3, one of the "big facts" about human languages is that sentences show displacement properties in the sense that expressions that appear in one position may be interpreted in another position. We may now ask *why* this is so, *why* natural languages have movement. It's worth mentioning, incidentally, that this question is not new; it has been raised since the early days of generative syntax,[2] but the general perception was that the theoretical frameworks then available were not developed enough to properly address this question.

9.3.1   *Features in the computation*
Although still in an embryonic stage, minimalism may offer new insights on this issue, as it provides a completely new view of the language faculty. By exploring the hypothesis that properties of the language faculty may be

---

2 See Miller and Chomsky (1963) and Chomsky (1965), for instance.

an optimal response to the demands of the other systems of the mind, minimalism raises the possibility that movement exists because it's required by the interface systems. The obvious question then is what these requirements are. Addressing related issues, research in the past decade has suggested that the existence of movement is somehow tied to the role lexical features play at the interfaces.[3] Let's then consider such features in more detail, under the assumption that lexical items are comprised of sets of phonological, semantic, and formal (syntactic) features.

Phonological features are readable at PF, but not at LF; conversely, semantic features are readable at LF, but not at PF. Thus, in a convergent derivation, it must be the case that these features are appropriately teased apart during the computation. Given the architecture of the model adopted here, Spell-Out is a good candidate to play this role, stripping phonological features from the computation that proceeds from the numeration to LF and shipping them to the phonological component (see section 2.3.1.6).

Now, if PF can only handle phonological features, formal features must also be eliminated before they reach PF even if they are shipped to the phonological component. That is, if formal features are required for morphological computations in the phonological component, for example, they must be deleted after fulfilling their role in order for the derivation to converge at PF.[4] The lexical item *dogs*, for instance, has the formal feature [plural], which is associated with the phoneme /z/; both pieces of information can arguably be manipulated by morphology, but after such morphological computations are concluded, only /z/ should proceed to PF. In other words, although the phonological features correlated with formal features can receive an interpretation at PF, the formal features themselves can't.

So far, we have witnessed an all-or-nothing scenario: semantic and formal features are not legible at PF and phonological features are not legible at LF. The issue of the legibility of formal features at LF is more complex, though. Consider agreement within DP in (8) and subject-predicate agreement in (9), for instance.

(8)   *Portuguese*
       a. **o**   gat**o**   bonit**o**
          the.MASC.SG   *cat.MASC.SG*   *beautiful.MASC.SG*
          'the beautiful tomcat'

---

3 See Chomsky (1995, 2000, 2001, 2004) and Uriagereka (1998) for relevant discussion.
4 See Chomsky (1995: 230–31) and Nunes's (1995: 231) FF-Elimination.

b. **a**   gata   bonita
   the.FEM.SG   cat.FEM.SG   beautiful.FEM.SG
   'the beautiful cat'

c. **os**   gat**os**   bonit**os**
   the.MASC.PL   cat.MASC.PL   beautiful.MASC.PL
   'the beautiful tomcats'

d. **as**   gat**as**   bonit**as**
   the.FEM.PL   cat.FEM.PL   beautiful.SFEM.PL
   'the beautiful cats'

(9)   she$_{[3.SG]}$ is$_{[3.SG]}$ nice

It's obvious that at LF, the information conveyed by the features [MASC/FEM] and [SG/PL] in (8) and [3.SG] in (9) must be assigned the interpretation 'masculine/feminine', 'singular/plural', and 'third person singular', respectively. What is not at all obvious is that these pieces of information should be stated multiple times at LF. (8d), for instance, does not mean that the cat is three times feminine or three times plural. Further indication that agreement information seems to be disregarded at LF is suggested by the fact that it's ignored for purposes of ellipsis interpretation, as illustrated in (10), where the masculine plural *bonitos* 'beautiful' licenses the ellipsis of the feminine singular *bonita*.

(10)   *Portuguese*
        Os   gatos   são   bonit**os**   e
        the.MASC.PL   cat.MASC.PL   are$_{[3.PL]}$ beautiful.MASC.PL   and
        a   gata   também   é.
        the.FEM.SG   cat.FEM.SG   also   is$_{[3.SG]}$
        'The tomcats are beautiful and so is the cat.'

If the repeated information in (8) and (9) is computed only once at LF, then it's plausible to assume that just one piece of the relevant information is actually legible by LF. In other words, although these features appear to convey the same information, some of them are interpretable at LF, while others are not. Let's call these different features [+interpretable] and [−interpretable], respectively. If so, according to the logic of the system, the [−interpretable] features must be eliminated before they reach LF; otherwise, Full Interpretation will be violated and the derivation should crash at LF (see sections 1.3 and 1.5). Of course, this in turn raises the more fundamental question of why lexical items should have [−interpretable] formal features to begin with.

To summarize, the discussion so far has revolved around two different mysteries: first, why does the language faculty have movement? And second, why does the language faculty have [−interpretable] (formal) features? One of the most interesting ideas developed within minimalism is that these two mysteries are but two faces of the same coin. Thus, if we can get a grasp on one, we will have found the key to the other.

Let's then consider one instantiation of this idea, according to which the existence of [−interpretable] formal features is in fact the major puzzle to be explained. Under this view, movement is just a response to overcome this lack of optimality.[5] In other words, [−interpretable] features remain mysterious; in the best of possible worlds, they shouldn't exist, period. But once they exist (for whatever reasons), the language faculty had to resort to some mechanism to eliminate them; otherwise, LF would not be able to read the objects formed by the computational system. And here comes movement to the rescue: it's through movement operations that [−interpretable] features get eliminated. From this perspective, the checking operation that is licensed by movement is actually elimination of [−interpretable] formal features. Furthermore, given that every operation must be licensed, movement must then comply with the Last Resort condition in (11).[6]

(11)   *Last Resort*
        A movement operation is licensed only if it allows the elimination of [−interpretable] formal features.

In the next section, we examine some consequences of this idea.

9.3.2   *To be or not to be interpretable, that is the question*

If the same kind of information may or may not receive an interpretation at LF, as illustrated by the ϕ-features (person, gender, and number) in (8) and (9), then the first question that comes to mind is how to distinguish them. Interestingly, part of the story has already been unveiled by traditional grammars. It has been a standard assumption for centuries that the predicate agrees with the subject and not the opposite. In other words, the

---

5 See Chomsky (1995) for this approach and Chomsky (2000, 2001, 2004) for a different one.
6 Last Resort has been technically implemented either in terms of *Greed* (see Chomsky 1993), according to which movement is licit only if some feature of the moved element is checked/ deleted, or in terms of *Enlightened Self-Interest* (see Lasnik 1995d, 1995e, 1999 and the discussions in Chomsky 1995, Collins 1996, Bošković 1997, Kitahara 1997, and Hornstein 2001), according to which movement is licensed as long as some feature gets checked/ deleted, regardless of whether it's a feature of the moved element or the target of movement. In the following discussion, we'll be assuming the Enlightened Self-Interest interpretation of Last Resort.

relation is not symmetrical; rather, the subject determines the specification of the predicate. We may naturally interpret such an asymmetry as indicating that the relevant φ-features of subjects (and of arguments, in general) are [+interpretable], whereas the φ-features of predicates are [−interpretable]. If so, the simplified derivation of a sentence like (12) below may proceed along the lines of (13).

(12)   Mary loves John.

(13)   a. $[_{TP}$ -s$_{\{\phi-\}}$ $[_{VP}$ Mary$_{\{\phi+\}}$ $[_{V'}$ love- John $]$ $]$ $]$
        b. $[_{TP}$ Mary$_{\{\phi+\}}$ $[_{T'}$ -s$_{\{\phi-\}}$ $[_{VP}$ t $[_{V'}$ love- John $]$ $]$ $]$ $]$

Assuming that φ-features of verbal predicates are generated in T, after *Mary* raises to [Spec,TP] in (13b), its [+interpretable] φ-features enter into a checking relation with the [−interpretable] φ-features of T and delete them. Deletion of the φ-features of T licenses the movement of *Mary*, in accordance with Last Resort (see (11)), and allows the derivation to converge at LF. Similar considerations should extend to feature checking within DP.[7]

Resorting to intuitions found in traditional grammars doesn't always provide us with useful insight, though. Structural Case, for instance, is also traditionally treated as an asymmetrical relation: some elements assign Case to some other elements. However, it's not very obvious what kind of interpretation structural Case receives at LF, if any at all. Under the checking approach, *Mary* in (13b), for example, checks its Case-feature against the Case-feature of the finite T. If checking amounts to the elimination of [−interpretable] features upon matching, at least one of these Case-features should be [−interpretable]. The question then is which one.

---

7 However, things may not be as straightforward as suggested in the text and a more detailed semantic analysis may be required in order to determine which features within DPs are [+interpretable] and which ones are not. Take the DP in (i), for instance.

(i)   *Portuguese*
       a   gata   bonita
       the.FEM.SG cat.FEM.SG beautiful.FEM.SG
       'the beautiful cat'

Whereas it's very plausible to say that gender is [+interpretable] on the noun, but [−interpretable] on the determiner and the adjective, it's not so obvious whether number should be [+interpretable] on the noun or on the determiner. Languages may in fact vary in marking overt number on either of them, as illustrated in (ii) and (iii).

(ii)   the books
(iii) *(Colloquial) Brazilian Portuguese*
       os   livro
       the.PL   book.SG

Let's consider an indirect way to determine whether or not a feature is [+interpretable]. If a given feature is [+interpretable], traditional considerations regarding recoverability of deletion will require that such a feature does not get deleted upon checking; that is, checking only deletes [−interpretable] features. If so, we reach the following conclusion: [−interpretable] features cannot participate in more than one checking relation, whereas [+interpretable] features are free to participate in multiple checking relations. The reason is that a [−interpretable] feature gets deleted after checking, whereas a [+interpretable] feature is unaffected by a checking relation. Hence, a [+interpretable] feature is free to participate in multiple checking relations, whereas a [−interpretable] one is knocked out after participating in a single checking relation.

With these considerations in mind, let's reexamine our conclusion that the φ-features on the subject are [+interpretable]. According to the reasoning laid out above, they should then be able to participate in multiple checking relations. That this is indeed true is shown by raising constructions such as (14).

(14)   *Portuguese*
a. **As**   alun**as**   **parecem** ter sido contratad**as**.
   the.FEM.PL   student.FEM.PL   seem.3.PL have been hired.FEM.PL
   'The (female) students seem to have been hired.'
b. [TP [as alunas]i [T′ -**m**|3.PL| [vP parece- [TP ti [T′ ter [vP sido
   [TP ti -**das**|FEM.PL| [vP contrata- ti]]]]]]]]]

In (14b), *as alunas* 'the (female) students' is generated as the internal argument of the passive verb and moves successive-cyclically to the specifier of the participial TP, to the specifier of the infinitival TP, and, finally, to the specifier of the matrix TP. The interesting point for our discussion is that the φ-features of *as alunas* enter into a checking relation with the φ-features of both the participial T and the matrix T. This multiple checking thus confirms our previous conclusion that the φ-features of arguments are [+interpretable].

The derivation in (14b) also tells us something regarding the EPP. Recall from section 2.3.1.3 that the EPP was reinterpreted as a strong D/N-feature in T, forcing its specifier to be filled before Spell-Out. Given that the strong feature of each of the three Ts in (14b) was successfully checked by *as alunas*, we are led to the conclusion that the relevant feature of *as alunas*, say the categorial feature of the determiner, is also [+interpretable] as it was able to participate in more than one checking relation.

Returning to the issue of whether or not structural Case is [+interpretable], we have to inspect the Case-feature of both the "assigner" and the "assignee." Let's start with the former, by examining the contrast in (15).

(15)   a. Mary gave a book to John.
        b. *Mary gave a book John.

For purposes of discussion, let's assume that in (15a), *a book* covertly checks its Case against the Case of the light verb and *John* covertly checks its Case against the Case of the preposition (cf. section 4.3.3). If the Case-feature of the light verb were [+interpretable], it should be able to participate in more than one checking relation. In particular, it should be able to check the Case of both *a book* and *John* in (15b). Given the unacceptability of (15b), we are led to the conclusion that the Case-feature of the light verb (and, in general, of other structural "Case-assigners") is [−interpretable] and is rendered inert once it participates in a checking relation.

Just for the sake of completeness, it should be mentioned that the problem with (15b) cannot be simply due to mismatch between the (abstract) oblique Case of *John* and the accusative Case of the light verb; the sentence is out even under a derivation in which *John* enters the numeration specified for accusative, rather than oblique Case. Also, the derivation of (15b) has no problem with respect to minimality; as shown in (16), *a book* and *John* are in the same minimal domain (the minimal domain of *gave*) and therefore should be equidistant from the light verb (see section 5.4.2.1).

(16)   [$_{vP}$ Mary [$_{v'}$ v [$_{VP}$ [a book] [$_{V'}$ gave John]]]]

Let's now consider the Case-feature of the "assignee," by examining the contrast between (17) and (18).

(17)   a. John seems to love Mary.
        b. [$_{TP}$ John$_i$ [$_{T'}$ -s [$_{VP}$ seem- [$_{TP}$ t$_i$ to [t$_i$ love Mary]]]]]

(18)   a. *John seems that loves Mary.
        b. *[$_{TP}$ John$_i$ [$_{T'}$ -s [$_{VP}$ seem- [$_{CP}$ that [$_{TP}$ t$_i$ -s [t$_i$ love Mary]]]]]]

As discussed above, the φ-features and the categorial feature of arguments are [+interpretable] and may participate in multiple checking relations. This entails that *John* can check the EPP-feature of the embedded and the matrix T of both (17b) and (18b), and the φ-features of the two Ts in (18b) as well. Given that one of the differences between the two structures is that the embedded T in (18b) has a Case-feature to check, the contrast between

(17) and (18) can then be taken to show that the Case-feature of the "assignee" is also [−interpretable]. If so, when *John* enters into a checking relation with the embedded T in (18b), its Case-feature is deleted and unable to enter into another checking relation with the matrix T; the derivation then crashes at LF because the [−interpretable] Case-feature of the matrix T was not deleted through checking. In (17b), on the other hand, the embedded T has no Case-feature and *John*, therefore, reaches the matrix [Spec,TP] with its Case-feature unchecked; upon checking, the Case-features of both *John* and the finite T are deleted and the derivation converges, as desired.

To sum up, the existence of movement operations is justified from the perspective described above as the means to computationally fix a departure from optimality existing in the lexicon: the presence of [−interpretable] formal features. It's worth pointing out that such an approach need not invoke global computations; that is, the computational system need not look ahead to see whether or not a given feature will be assigned an interpretation at LF in order to decide whether or nor to apply deletion at a given derivational step. Lexical redundancy rules already divide formal features in the two relevant flavors: [+interpretable] or [−interpretable]. If a given item is a verb, for instance, its ϕ-features are lexically specified as [−interpretable]; hence, at any given derivational step, the computational system has the information that such features must be deleted upon checking.

One technical question that arises is what exactly we mean by "deletion under checking." Suppose it means elimination from the structure; let's then examine its consequences for the derivation of (19), for instance.

(19)   a. *It seems that was told John that he would be hired.
       b. *[$_{TP}$ it$_i$ [$_{T'}$ -s [$_{VP}$ seem- [$_{CP}$ that [$_{TP}$ t$_i$ [$_{T'}$ was [$_{VP}$ told John [that he would be hired]]]]]]]]

In (19b), the expletive is inserted in the embedded clause and checks its Case-feature. Given that this feature is [−interpretable], it should then be eliminated from the structure and the expletive should be unable to check the Case-feature of the matrix [Spec,TP]. That by itself cannot be the source of the ungrammaticality of the resulting structure. Since *John* has not checked its Case-feature, it could perfectly move in the covert component and check it against the unchecked Case-feature of the matrix T. Crucially, relativized minimality within minimalism is computed with respect to features (see section 5.5) and the trace of the expletive would have no Case-feature to induce an intervention effect if deletion were interpreted as removal from the structure; in other words, the sentence in (19a) would in fact be incorrectly ruled in, under such a scenario.[8]

Suppose, by contrast, that what deletion does is just render a given feature invisible for LF computations. It's as if deletion makes features inert by painting them blue and LF doesn't see painted features because it wears blue glasses.[9] Under this technical implementation, the unwanted derivation of (19b), for instance, is correctly ruled out. Although inert for further checking and invisible at LF, the deleted Case-feature of the trace of the expletive in (19b) is present in the structure and correctly blocks the movement of *John*. In other words, what is relevant for purposes of computing locality is just whether there are any intervening features of the relevant sort, regardless of whether or not they are deleted, that is, invisible at LF. Also, given that we've been assuming that strong features can't be eliminated in the phonological component and cause the derivation to crash at PF unless they are overtly checked (see section 2.3.1.3), we may now extend this notion of deletion to strong features as well. Thus, checking a strong feature overtly amounts to rendering it invisible at both LF *and* PF.

It's worth pointing out that the conception of deletion as making a given feature invisible at the relevant interface – rather than removing it from the structure – is consistent with the fact that the morphological computations of the phonological component manipulate formal features, regardless of whether or not they are [+interpretable] at LF. If [−interpretable] features were removed from the structure after being checked, morphology wouldn't be able to access them. We'll henceforth assume this technical implementation of deletion and use it in the next section as a tool to probe into the feature composition of expletives in English.

Exercise 9.1

Within GB it was generally assumed that *pro* was licensed by rich verbal agreement morphology (see Rizzi 1982, for instance). How can this intuition be captured if we adopt the distinction between [+interpretable] and [−interpretable] features presented in the text? (See Kato [1999] for relevant discussion.)

---

8 For further discussion, see Nunes (1995, 2000, 2004).
9 We borrowed this metaphor from Bob Frank (personal communication).

Exercise 9.2

We've seen that the unacceptability of (ia) indicates that structural Case of a light verb is [−interpretable]. That being so, how should the double object construction in (ib) be analyzed with respect to its Case properties?

(i)   a. *Mary gave a book John.
       b. Mary gave John a book.

Exercise 9.3

The data in (i) below seem to mimic the pattern of (17a) and (18a), repeated in (ii). That is, successive-cyclic A-movement is not possible if launched from a Case-position, whereas successive-cyclic *wh*-movement is not possible if launched from the specifier of an interrogative complementizer. Discuss what assumptions must be made if (i) is to receive an analysis along the lines of the one offered in the text to account for (ii).

(i)   a. $[_{CP}$ what$_i$ did you say $[_{CP}$ t$_i$ that Mary bought t$_i$]]
       b. *$[_{CP}$ what$_i$ do you wonder $[_{CP}$ t$_i$ Mary bought t$_i$]]
(ii) a. $[_{TP}$ John$_i$ seems $[_{TP}$ t$_i$ to $[_{vP}$ t$_i$ love Mary]]]
       b. *$[_{TP}$ John$_i$ seems that $[_{TP}$ t$_i$ $[_{vP}$ t$_i$ loves Mary]]]

Exercise 9.4

In this section we've discussed two possible interpretations of deletion under checking: removal from the structure and invisibility at the relevant interface. Given your answer to exercise 9.3, discuss which of these interpretations is supported by the unacceptability of (i).

(i)   *[how$_i$ do you wonder [what$_k$ Mary fixed t$_k$ t$_i$]]

9.3.3   *A case study of expletives*

Given the conclusions reached in section 9.3.2, let's examine the paradigm in (20).

(20)   a. $[_{TP}$ there$_i$ seems $[_{TP}$ t$_i$ to be $[_{PP}$ a man in the room]]]
         b. *$[_{TP}$ there$_i$ seems $[_{TP}$ t$_i$ to be $[_{PP}$ many people in the room]]]
         c. $[_{TP}$ there$_i$ seem $[_{TP}$ t$_i$ to be $[_{PP}$ many people in the room]]]
         d. *$[_{TP}$ there seem that $[_{TP}$ [many people]$_i$ are $[_{PP}$ t$_i$ in the room]]]

In (20a), *there* successfully checks the EPP-feature of both the embedded and the matrix clause. Since [−interpretable] features are deleted after checking, it should have at least a [+interpretable] feature capable of doing that. Let's then assume that this feature is its categorial D-feature.

At first sight, *there* could also have φ-features, more specifically [3.SG], given that the [−interpretable] φ-features of the matrix clause in (20a) must have been appropriately checked. If that were true, however, *there* should also be able to check the φ-features of the matrix T in (20b), and the corresponding sentence should be acceptable, contrary to fact. Besides, the contrasts between (20a) and (20b), on the one hand, and between (20b) and (20c), on the other, further indicate that the element that triggers agreement with the matrix predicate is in fact the "associate" of the expletive (*a man* in (20a) and *many people* in (20b, c)). Hence, we are led to the conclusion that *there* does not have φ-features.

Let's now consider Case. If *there* had a Case-feature, it should be able to check the Case-feature of the matrix T in all of the structures in (20) and we would then be lacking an explanation for the unacceptability of the sentence corresponding to (20d); crucially, given that the φ-features of *many people* are [+interpretable], *many people* could move in the covert component to check the [−interpretable] φ-features of the matrix T in (20d), as presumably happens in (20c). By contrast, if *there* does not have Case, we are able to account for the contrast between (20c) and (20d). In (20d), *many people* checks its Case-feature against the Case-feature of the embedded T and is therefore unable to enter into another checking relation; the derivation then crashes at LF because the [−interpretable] Case-feature of the matrix T wasn't checked. In (20c), on the other hand, the associate has not checked its Case-feature and can therefore move covertly to check the Case-feature of the matrix T, allowing the derivation to converge at LF.

The expletive *it*, in turn, has a different feature specification, as indicated by (21).

(21)   [$_{TP}$ it seems that [$_{TP}$ [many people]$_i$ are [$_{PP}$ t$_i$ in the room]]]

Given that the sentence corresponding to (21) is acceptable, it must be the case that the matrix T has all of its [−interpretable] features appropriately checked. This means that *it* must at least have a feature that is able to check the EPP, say, its categorial D-feature. We have also seen that in a configuration such as (21), *many people* has already checked its Case and cannot enter into a further checking relation with the Case-feature of the matrix T (cf. (20d)). Thus, it must be that *it* also has a Case-feature. Finally, given the agreement mismatch between the matrix T and *many people*, it must also be the case that it's the expletive that is checking the φ-features of T; more precisely, *it* should be specified as [3.SG]. The unacceptability of (22) under this analysis should be due to the fact that *many people* cannot have its Case-feature checked, for the expletive checks the Case-feature of the matrix T.

(22)   *[it$_i$ seems [$_{TP}$ t$_i$ to be [$_{PP}$ many people in the room]]]

To summarize, the discussion above leads to the conclusion that the configurations where *there* and *it* are licensed are different due to their different feature composition. More specifically, the expletive *there* is lexically specified as having a categorial feature, but no Case- or ϕ-features, whereas the expletive *it* is fully specified with categorial, Case, and ϕ-features (see Chomsky 1995).

As mentioned earlier, expletive constructions constitute one of the toughest syntactic puzzles yet to be properly accounted for and the analysis above should only be seen as an exercise into the mechanics associated with feature interpretability.[10] Like the analyses currently available, it's still very descriptive in the sense that it begs the more fundamental question of *why* expletives should exist to begin with, or *why* a language like English may in fact have two such creatures. (Is two the upper limit on the number of expletives a given language may have?) However, it's certainly a virtue of minimalism that it more explicitly exposes the areas for which we may have technical descriptions, but not a deep understanding. As always, raising meaningful questions is the first step to finding meaningful answers.

Exercise 9.5

In this section we've been assuming that existential *be* in English plays no specific role in licensing the associate of the expletive. If this is so, how can we account for the contrast in (i) (see Lasnik 1992a)?

(i)   a. I expect there to be many people at the party.
       b. *I expect there many people at the party.

Exercise 9.6

As Chomsky (1995: 273) has observed, agreement with the associate seems to correlate with the feature composition of the expletive: the relevant verb agrees with the associate if the expletive lacks Case- and ϕ-features, like English *there*,

---

10 For discussion and alternative analyses see Chomsky (1993, 1995, 2000), Chomsky and Lasnik (1993), and Lasnik (1999); see also note 14 of chapter 2 for further references and the discussion in sections 10.2 and 10.3. For a very different perspective, see the predicate-inversion analysis of Moro (1989, 1997) and related work.

but not if the expletive is fully specified, like French *il*, as illustrated in (i). If *il* in (ib) has a Case-feature, discuss how the associate *trois hommes* can have its Case-feature checked.

(i)   a.   There are three men in the room.
      b.   *French*

Il	y	a	trois	hommes	dans	la	salle.
EXPL	LOC	*has*	*three*	*men*	*in*	*the*	*room*

      'There are three men in the room.'

Exercise 9.7

Can the analysis presented in this section account for the contrast in (i)? If not, what extra assumptions must be made?

(i)   a.   There arrived a man in the park.
      b.   *There a man kissed Mary.

Exercise 9.8

Discuss if and how the contrast in (i) below can be accounted for under the analysis suggested in the text.

(i)   a.   *There is many people in the room.
      b.   There's many people in the room.

Exercise 9.9

If your native language is not English, discuss what the feature composition of its expletive(s) is.

9.4   Covert movement

9.4.1   *Some problems*

Although the proposal sketched in section 9.3 gives some steps towards answering why movement operations exist, we are still left with some of the problems raised in section 9.2. Take the expletive construction in (23), for instance.

(23)   [Mary said that [$_{TP}$ there were three students in the room]]

According to the analysis developed in section 9.3.3, *three students* in (23) should move covertly to a position where it can check (that is, delete) its

Case and the Case and φ-features of the embedded T. Assume, for concreteness, that it creates another [Spec,TP], as shown in (24) below (see
chapter 5 on multiple specifiers of *v*P, for example). Two questions then
arise with respect to this movement: first, why can't it proceed overtly?
And second, why is it allowed to proceed non-cyclically, targeting the
"middle" of the tree?

(24)   [Mary said that [$_{TP}$ [three students]$_i$ [$_{T'}$ there were t$_i$ in the room]]]

The answer to the first question is that movement is regulated by the
economy principle Procrastinate, according to which covert movement is
more economical than overt movement (see sections 2.3.1.3 and 2.3.1.5).
Thus, if the movement depicted in (24) need not take place overtly (to
check some strong feature), Procrastinate determines that it must take
place in the covert component, after the application of Spell-Out. As for
the second question, covert movement is taken to be exempt from the
Extension Condition, as stated in (25) (see sections 2.3.2.4 and 8.2.3).

(25)   *Extension Condition* (revised preliminary version)
         Overt applications of Merge can only target root syntactic objects.

It's clear that these are just brute force answers that stipulate the results
we want to obtain, without explaining them. Furthermore, as pointed out
in section 9.2, both Procrastinate and the Extension Condition in (25) are
inconsistent with the Uniformity Condition on the mapping from the
numeration to LF, and this has the undesirable consequence of reintroducing SS-like constraints disguised in different formulations. Given that the
structure in (24), for instance, is assumed to be a well-formed object at LF
and that there is no obvious reason for why it should be excluded at PF,
Spell-Out is tacitly playing the role of SS in ruling it out.

Notice, incidentally, that the problem regarding Procrastinate involving
(24) is harder than the comparable violation of Procrastinate in (26), where
the main verb moved overtly in English.

(26)   *John reads often books.

Recall that overt movement is triggered by the need to eliminate strong
features, given that these features are indigestible at PF. Thus, in French
the verb must move overtly in order to knock out the strong V-feature of T.
In section 2.3.1.3, we assumed that the V-feature of T is weak in English
and sentences such as (26), although corresponding to licit LF objects,
were ruled out by Procrastinate.

304 Understanding Minimalism

There is an equally plausible alternative that need not invoke Procrastinate, though. Suppose that movement parameters are to be accounted for
not in terms of the strength of a given feature (strong or weak), but in terms
of presence or absence of strong features.[11] That is, instead of saying that the
V-feature of T is strong in French and weak in English, let's simply assume
that French T has a strong V-feature, whereas English T doesn't. If so, (26) is
to be ruled out by Last Resort (see (11)): movement of *reads* is not required
because it feeds no feature checking; hence, it's prevented from taking place
since it serves no purpose.

However successful this approach may be for cases such as (26), it
cannot be extended to (24). There, movement of the associate is indeed
required to check [−interpretable] Case- and φ-features, regardless of
strong features. So, an alternative account of the facts captured under
Procrastinate is still called for.

In the next two sections we present two alternative approaches to covert
movement, which circumvent the Procrastinate and the cyclicity problems
mentioned above in different ways. As things stand right now, it's not clear
that one should be preferred over the other and we won't attempt to make
a choice here. We'll rather present potential arguments for each of them,
highlighting the fact that both proposals find their roots in the idea
discussed in section 9.3 that feature checking is somehow tied to deletion
of [−interpretable] formal features.

9.4.2   Alternative I: Move F

If movement operations are triggered by the need to delete [−interpretable]
formal features in the mapping from the numeration to LF through
checking, as proposed in section 9.3, minimalist considerations should
lead us to expect movement to operate just with formal features, rather
than categories. This expectation seems to be contrary to fact, however. A
core property of human languages is that they place categories (lexical
items and phrases) in positions different from the ones where they are
interpreted. The question then is why the language faculty departs from
optimality in such a way.

9.4.2.1 The operation Move F

Chomsky (1995) suggests that this departure is actually illusory. Movement
(still understood as Copy and Merge) does indeed target formal features.

---

11 See Chomsky (1995) and Lasnik (2001b), for instance.

However, properties of the phonological component (yet to be made fully explicit) may require that when the formal features of a lexical item or phrase move, all the other features of that category be pied-piped. If so, overt movement of the set of formal features F has the appearance of movement of a category containing F.

Let's examine the logic of this *Move F* approach in more detail by considering the movement of the *wh*-phrase in (27) below. Take the derivational step after the computational system has built the object in (28) and assume that, spelling aside, the structure of *whose book* is along the lines of (29).[12]

(27)   Whose book did you read?

(28)   [did + Q [you read [whose book]]]

(29)

```
              DP
           ┌───┴────┐
          who       D′
                 ┌──┴───┐
                's     book
```

In (28), the interrogative complementizer Q has a strong *wh*-feature that must be overtly checked; otherwise the derivation crashes at PF (see section 2.3.1.3). Thus, if the formal features of *who* move overtly and adjoin to Q, a feature checking would be established and the relevant [−interpretable] *wh*-features would be deleted (in the technical sense; see section 9.3.2). That is, the sentence corresponding to (28) should be acceptable, contrary to fact.

Let's then assume that one defining morphological property of strong features is that they can only be checked by lexical items or projections of lexical items, but not by sets of formal features that by themselves don't constitute a lexical item. Furthermore, let's assume that economy considerations dictate that the smallest of such projections be copied for purposes of strong feature checking (see section 2.3.1.3 for related discussion). If so, movement of the formal features of *who* in (28) doesn't suffice to check the strong *wh*-feature of Q; a projection containing such features must move, instead. Let's then move *who*, which is the smallest projection containing the *wh*-feature, as illustrated in (30).

---

12 For relevant discussion see Janda (1980), Fabb (1984), Abney (1987), and Corver (1990), among others.

(30)   a. [~~who~~ did + Q [you read [~~who~~ ['s book]]]]
        b. *Who did you read's book?

The problem with (30) can't be feature checking; the strong *wh*-feature of Q is appropriately checked. However, (30) arguably violates the morphological requirements on the possessive suffix, which must attach to the genitive element.[13] That being so, one wonders why the sentence in (31), which would allow the possessive suffix to have its requirements satisfied, is not acceptable either.

(31)   *Whose did you read book?

The problem with (31) is that there is no licit syntactic derivation for it, because *whose* (= *who's*) alone is not a syntactic constituent, as can be seen in (29), and therefore cannot undergo movement.

The derivation in (32) below, where the whole object DP is moved to [Spec,CP], is therefore the only one that can satisfy all the relevant requirements. In other words, (i) the strong *wh*-feature of Q can be appropriately checked; (ii) the possessive suffix can be morphologically licensed; (iii) movement is operating with a syntactic object; and (iv) the phrase *whose book* is the smallest syntactic object that can allow all of these requirements to be met, in consonance with economy guidelines.

(32)   [[who ['s book]]^i did + Q [you read [who ['s book]]^i]]

This analysis predicts that in languages where the possessive determiner doesn't have affixal requirements, the sentences corresponding to (30b) should actually be well formed. To a first approximation, this prediction seems to be borne out. It has long been observed that languages that don't have overt determiners in general admit "left branch" extraction of the sort illustrated in (30b), as illustrated in (33).[14]

(33)   a. *Latin*
        Cuiam$_i$ amat   Cicero   [t$_i$ puellam]?
        whose   loves   Cicero   girl
        'Whose girl does Cicero love?'

---

13 See Lasnik's (1981) Stranded Affix Filter, for instance.
14 The Left Branch Condition was proposed by Ross (1967), who already noted the "exceptional" behavior of (determinerless) Russian and Latin. For relevant discussion, see among others Uriagereka (1988) (the source of (33a)), Corver (1990), and, more recently, Bošković (2003) (the source of (33b)).

b. *Serbo-Croatian*
   Čijeg$_i$ si   vidio [t$_i$ oca]?
   whose   are   seen   father
   'Whose father did you see?'

The contrast between (30b) and the sentences in (33) can receive a natural explanation if the null possessive determiner of the relevant phrases in (33) does not need to be affixed to the genitive phrase. That is, the only relevant requirement at stake is that the strong *wh*-feature of the interrogative complementizers of (33) be checked.

Under this view, overt movement of categories is thus understood as movement of formal features, combined with pied-piping triggered by morphological requirements of the phonological component. Given that economy considerations require that only material needed for convergence be pied-piped, covert movement need not (and therefore must not) resort to pied-piping, because it does not feed morphology. In other words, covert movement would be the optimal form of movement and should involve only sets of formal features.

Indirect evidence for this asymmetry between overt and covert movement is provided by contrasts such as the one in (34), for instance.

(34)   *Brazilian Portuguese*
        a. Que   fotografia de [si   mesmo]$_{i/k}$ [o   João]$_k$ disse que
           which   picture   of   self own   the   João   said that
           [o   Pedro]$_i$ viu?
           the   Pedro   saw
        b. [O   João]$_k$ disse que   [o   Pedro]$_i$ viu   que   fotografia
           the João   said that   the   Pedro   saw which   picture
           de   [si   mesmo]$_{i/*k}$?
           of   self   own
           'Which picture of himself did João say that Pedro saw?'

As discussed in section 2.3.1.4, *wh*-movement to the matrix clause is optional in Brazilian Portuguese and this optionality was associated to the matrix interrogative complementizer: if it has a strong *wh*-feature, overt *wh*-movement is obligatory; otherwise, overt *wh*-movement is blocked by Procrastinate. (34a) shows that, as in English, an anaphor embedded in the moved *wh*-phrase can be coreferential with either the matrix or the embedded subject (see section 8.2.2). If covert *wh*-movement in (34b) involved movement of the whole *wh*-phrase, we should in principle expect that the anaphor should also be ambiguous. However, this is not the case; the anaphor in (34b) can only have the embedded subject reading. If, on the other hand, the relevant covert movement involves only formal features of the interrogative determiner *que* 'which', as illustrated in (35), then the local anaphor *si mesmo* 'himself' must be interpreted as coreferential with the embedded subject, as desired (see section 8.3.1).

(35)   [**FF(*que*)** + Q [o João]$_k$ disse que [o Pedro]$_i$ viu que fotografia de [si mesmo]$_{i/*k}$]

Similar considerations apply to existential constructions such as (36).[15]

(36)   a. [[many students]$_i$ seemed to each other [t$_i$ to have been in trouble]]
       b. *[there$_i$ seemed to each other [t$_i$ to have been many students in trouble]]

(36a) shows that a subject moved overtly can license a higher anaphor. If covert movement of the associate in (36b) involved the whole phrase *many students* (say, by creating an extra [Spec,TP]), the licensing of the anaphor in (36a) and (36b) should pattern alike, which is not the case. By contrast, if only the relevant set of formal features of *many students* move and adjoin to T, as illustrated in (37), the contrast in (36) can be accounted for if the licensor of the anaphor must have semantic features, which is the case in (36a), but not in (36b).

(37)   *[there$_i$ FF(*many students*) + I^0 seemed to each other [t$_i$ to have been many students in trouble]]

Another kind of potential evidence for the Move-F approach has to do with the phenomenon referred to as *vehicle change*, which is illustrated in (38).[16]

(38)   a. *Mary admires John$_i$, but he$_i$ doesn't.
       b. Mary admires John$_i$, but he$_i$ doesn't think Susan does.

(38a) seems to be unproblematic. Assuming for concreteness that ellipsis resolution involves some sort of (post-)LF-copying, copying the VP of the first conjunct of (38a) into the second conjunct, as represented by boldface in (39a) below, should yield a Principle C violation. However, this cannot be the whole story; otherwise, VP-copying in (38b), as illustrated in (39b), should also give rise to a Principle C effect, contrary to fact.

15 See Lasnik and Saito (1992) and den Dikken (1995b) for discussion.
16 See Fiengo and May (1994) on vehicle change, and Aoun and Nunes (1997) for the analysis of vehicle change effects in terms of Move F.

(39)   a. *Mary admires John$_i$, but he$_i$ doesn't **[admire John$_i$]**
       b. *Mary admires John$_i$, but he$_i$ doesn't think Susan does **[admire John$_i$]**

Let's consider the VP-structure of the first conjunct under the Move-F approach. After the main verb adjoins overtly to the light verb (see section 3.3.3) and the formal features of *John* move covertly to check its Case-feature and the Case- and the φ-features of the light verb, we obtain the simplified structure in (40).

(40)   [$_{TP}$ Mary [$_{vP}$ FF(*John*) + admires + v^0 [$_{VP}$ admires John]]]

Now suppose that in addition to copying the whole VP into the second conjunct of (38), we may also copy just the v^0-structure, with the main verb and the formal features of the object adjoined to it, as illustrated in (41).

(41)   a. *Mary admires John$_i$, but he$_i$ doesn't
          [FF(*John$_i$*) + admire + *v*]
       b. Mary admires John$_i$, but he$_i$ doesn't think Susan does
          [FF(*John$_i$*) + admire + *v*]

Recall that under the Move-F approach, covert movement leaves semantic features behind. Thus, FF(*John*) in (40) basically involve the features [nominal], [ACC], and [3.SG.MASC]. Notice that this feature specification is not different from the feature specification of the pronoun *him*; in other words, *John* involves all formal features of *him* plus additional semantic features. If FF(*John*) should pattern like a pronoun for purposes of the Binding Theory in virtue of its deficient pronominal-like feature specification, the structures in (41) should then pattern like the ones in (42), where Principle B is violated in (42a) but complied with in (42b); hence, the surprising contrast in (38).[17]

(42)   a. *Mary admires John$_i$, but he$_i$ doesn't admire him$_i$
       b. Mary admires John$_i$, but he$_i$ doesn't think Susan admires him$_i$

We'd like to stress that we are not claiming that this is the best way to analyze the data in (34), (36), and (38). The important thing to bear in mind is that the logic of the Move-F approach leads us to expect asymmetries between overt and covert movement of the kind illustrated by these data.

---

17 See Aoun and Nunes (1997) for this suggestion and further discussion.

Exercise 9.10

If pied-piping is actually triggered by morphology, discuss what kind of morpho-logical requirements may trigger movement of the whole DP from [Spec,vP] to [Spec, TP], as shown in (ia), instead of moving just one of its lexical items, as shown in (ib) and (ic).

(i)   a. That boy is smiling.
      b. *That is boy smiling.
      c. *Boy is that smiling.

Exercise 9.11

In section 4.4.2, it was pointed out that the anaphor in (i) below (see also section 9.2) could be licensed by either overt or covert movement of the direct object. Show why only one of these approaches is compatible with the Move-F analysis of (36) sketched in the text.

(i)   Mary entertained the guests during each other's vacations.

Exercise 9.12

Under the Move-F approach, movement targets the set of formal features of a given lexical item. Would there be a difference if Move F actually targeted individual formal features? Discuss the potential advantages and disadvantages of allowing individual features to undergo movement.

9.4.2.2   Move F and Procrastinate
Assuming that interpretation asymmetries such as the ones in (34), (36), and (38) may put some empirical flesh on the conceptual bones relating movement and feature checking, we are now in a position to address the conceptual problems regarding Procrastinate.

As noted in section 9.4.1, since Procrastinate stipulates that covert movement is inherently more economical than overt movement, it's at odds with the Uniformity Condition on the mapping from the numeration to LF, according to which the operations available in the covert compon-ent should also be available in the overt component as well. Notice that the Uniformity Condition doesn't require that the operations be necessarily the same. If there are independent reasons for a given covert operation not to apply overtly, that is consistent with the Uniformity Condition, for such a covert operation would *in principle* be available in overt syntax. In other words, the mapping from the numeration to LF must be uniform in the sense that in principle it may resort to the same set of operations, regardless of whether the computation is pre- or post-Spell-Out.

The Move-F approach has exactly the format described above. Movement for purposes of feature checking *does* target sets of formal features both overtly and covertly. However, if just a set of formal features moves overtly to check a strong feature, the morphological requirements of the strong feature won't be met; a lexical item or a projection of a lexical item containing such a set of features will then have to move instead. Notice that the difference between covert and overt movement now corresponds to the difference between movement of formal features and movement of categories. Thus, we may push this idea to its limits and simply drop the covert component of syntactic computations altogether. In other words, we may assume that all movement operations proceed overtly and the question of whether we have feature movement or category movement will depend on the presence or absence of strong features, coupled with economy computations that determine that movement (Copy) should target the smallest number of features that may satisfy all the relevant requirements.

Consider *wh*-movement in this regard, for instance. If all movements must take place overtly, movement to check *wh*-features may in principle yield one of the structures sketched in (43), before Spell-Out.

(43) a. *$[_{CP}$ FF([*wh*-constituent]) + Q_{strong} $[_{TP}$ ... [*wh*-constituent] ...]]
      b. $[_{CP}$ [*wh*-constituent] Q_{strong} $[_{TP}$ ... [*wh*-constituent] ...]]
      c. $[_{CP}$ FF([*wh*-constituent]) + Q $[_{TP}$ ... [*wh*-constituent] ...]]
      d. *$[_{CP}$ [*wh*-constituent] Q $[_{TP}$ ... [*wh*-constituent] ...]]

In all of the derivations outlined in (43), the *wh*-feature of the interrogative complementizers can be appropriately deleted under feature checking; so, Full Interpretation at LF can't be the problem in (43a) and (43d). (43a) is nevertheless ruled out because a strong feature can only be checked by lexical items or projections of lexical items; hence, overt movement of *wh*-phrases, illustrated in (43b), must be chosen in a language like English, for instance, whose interrogative complementizer has a strong feature. The choice of (43c) over (43d), on the other hand, is determined by economy. If moving (copying) just the set of formal features of the *wh*-constituent is enough to check the *wh*-feature of a complementizer lacking strong features, pied-piping (extra copying) is unnecessary and should therefore be blocked by economy computations. (43c) thus represents the Chinese-type of *wh*-constructions, where the *wh*-constituent as a whole remains *in situ* and only its formal features move.

To sum up, once the Move-F approach postulates an independently motivated asymmetry between overt and covert movement in terms of movement of categories vs. movement of features, there is no reason for us to still keep movement before and after Spell-Out. The computational system employs as many instances of movement as necessary and finally applies Spell-Out to the resulting object. The interpretation asymmetries that were analyzed in terms of *when* a movement operation has taken place are now captured in terms of the *kind of element* that is undergoing movement. In such a scenario, where there is no covert movement, Procrastinate effects are appropriately derived from plausible economy considerations that basically say that moving (copying) less material is better than moving (copying) more material; in other words, feature movement should be preferred over category movement, all things being equal.[18]

The picture of the grammar that emerges from this discussion is represented in (44).

(44)   *The computational system under the Move-F approach*

$$N = \{A_i, B_j, C_k \dots\}$$

Select and Merge and Copy

LF $\longrightarrow$ PF

Spell-Out

Given a numeration N, the computational system selects its lexical items and forms syntactic objects out of them by applying Merge and Copy (recall that Move has been reanalyzed as Copy + Merge; see sections 6.4 and 7.5). LF is formed after the numeration has been exhausted, all possible features have been checked, and a single root syntactic object (a single tree) is assembled. Spell-Out then applies to the LF object and ships the relevant information to the phonological component, deriving PF after further computations.

Exercise 9.13

In the discussion of (43), it was tacitly assumed that the [−interpretable] *wh*-feature of an interrogative complementizer Q may be strong or weak. In section

---

18 For relevant discussion, see Nunes (1995, 2001, 2004), Oishi (1997), and Simpson (2000). For an opposing view that argues for covert phrasal movement, see, e.g., Pesetsky (2000).

9.4.2.1, we however mentioned the possibility that the parameter may simply be whether or not Q has a strong *wh*-feature. Discuss if this possibility changes our previous conclusions regarding the abstract paradigm in (43).

Exercise 9.14

Consider the sentences in (i) below, where the strong wh-feature of the interrogative complementizer can be successfully checked by either the *wh*-word or the whole *wh*-phrase (see sections 2.3.1.2 and 8.3.1). At first sight, economy considerations should block (ib), given that movement of the *wh*-word alone would suffice to check the strong *wh*-feature, as shown in (ia). Discuss what kind of provisos should be made in order for the two sentences of (i) to be correctly ruled in.

(i) *French*
    a. Combien   as   tu   acheté de livres?
      how.many have you bought of books
    b. Combien de livres as   tu   acheté?
      how.many of books have you bought
      'How many books did you buy?'

9.4.2.3 Move F and the Extension Condition

Let's now return to the problem of cyclicity. In (43c), repeated below in (45), for instance, the formal features of the *wh*-constituent move overtly and adjoin to the interrogative complementizer Q. At first sight, such an operation is bound to be non-cyclic, since Q is not the top of the tree (it's not a root syntactic object).

(45) $[_{CP}$ FF($[$ *wh*-constituent $]$) + Q $[_{TP} \ldots [$ *wh*-constituent $] \ldots]]$

But notice that this scenario is not different from the one involving head movement discussed in section 8.3.5.2. Recall that under the sideward-movement analysis made available by the copy theory of movement, V-to-T movement, for instance, could proceed as in (46)–(49) below. That is, once the computational system has built VP and selected from the numeration a T head that has a strong V-feature (cf. (46)), the verb within VP can be copied (cf. (47)) and merged with T (cf. (48)), and the resulting adjunction structure then merges with VP (cf. (49)). The important point is that the syntactic object in (49) is assembled without resort to non-cyclic merger.

(46)   a. $K = T^0_{\{STRONG\text{-}V\}}$
      b. $L = [_{VP} \ldots V \ldots]$

(47)   a. $K = T^0_{\{STRONG-V\}}$
        b. $L = [_{VP} \ldots V \ldots]$
        c. $M = V$

(48)   a. $N = [_{T^0} V + T^0]$
        b. $L = [_{VP} \ldots V \ldots]$

(49)

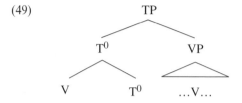

Movement of formal features can also proceed along the same lines, without violating the Extension Condition. The derivation of a *wh-in situ* construction such as (43c) can unfold as in (50)–(53).

(50)   a. $K = Q$
        b. $L = [_{TP} \ldots [wh\text{-constituent}] \ldots]$

(51)   a. $K = Q$
        b. $L = [_{TP} \ldots [wh\text{-constituent}] \ldots]$
        c. $M = FF([wh\text{-constituent}])$

(52)   a. $N = [_Q FF([wh\text{-constituent}]) + Q]$
        b. $L = [_{TP} \ldots [wh\text{-constituent}] \ldots]$

(53) $[_{CP} FF([wh\text{-constituent}]) + Q [_{TP} \ldots [wh\text{-constituent}] \ldots]]$

Given the derivational stage in (50), where the interrogative complementizer Q has a *wh*-feature to be checked but has no strong feature, the computational system makes a copy of the formal features of the *wh*-constituent in (50b), as shown in (51c), and adjoins it to Q, as shown in (52a). Further merger between N and L in (52) yields the structure in (53) ($=$(43c)). Again, every single instance of merger operates with root syntactic objects in compliance with the Extension Condition.

Put in more general terms, the Move-F approach also allows the removal of the stipulation that only overt operations are subject to the Extension Condition, as stated in (54) below. Once all applications of merger and movement apply overtly, the Extension Condition can be reformulated as in (55).

(54)   *Extension Condition* (revised preliminary version)
        Overt applications of Merge can only target root syntactic objects.

(55)   *Extension Condition* (final version)
        Applications of Merge can only target root syntactic objects.

9.4.2.4 Move F and checking domains

The Move-F story still has an interesting conceptual consequence. Recall from section 5.4 that the checking domain of a given head H typically involves the elements adjoined to H and the specifiers of H. We should now raise our minimalist eyebrows and ask *why* this is so, why we have *two* basic checking configurations rather than one. To put things in a different way, if a given element moves to check features of H, the closest possible configuration for such checking to be established is adjunction to H; a Spec-head configuration doesn't seem to be an optimal configuration in the sense that it can be reached only after the head merges with its complement, but the complement is not participating in the checking relation between the specifier and the head.

According to the Move-F approach, head adjunction is the optimal checking configuration. However, adjunction to a given head may not yield a well-formed morphological object. Morphology has many restrictions on what can appear under an X^0-element, among which is the general ban on complex phrases under X^0.[19] If head adjunction does not lead to convergence because of morphological restrictions, the system then resorts to the second most optimal configuration, which is the Spec-head configuration.

For purposes of illustration, let's ignore cyclicity and consider the potential continuations of (56) under this perspective.

(56)   [TP will_strong-D [VP [the boy] [eat [a bagel]]]]

Given that *will* has a strong D-feature to be checked (the EPP), movement of just FF([*the boy*]) will not suffice to check it. Economy considerations then dictate the minimal projection containing the D-feature should be moved. This projection is the determiner *the*. However, if *the* has some affixal properties that can only be satisfied within DP, adjunction of *the* alone to *will* will not be tolerated by morphology. The next option then is to move the DP *the boy*, as shown in (57) below. Now, the strong feature of *will* can be checked and *the* can have its affixal requirements satisfied.

---

19 But see Grohmann (2003b: chap. 5) on a reformulation of this ban in terms of a PF-constraint.

(57)

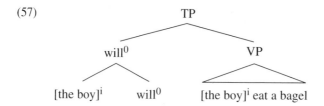

The problem with (57) is that, again, morphology will not be pleased due to the presence of the complex phrase *the boy* within an X⁰-element, namely, *will*. The computational system then exploits the other remaining closer relation to *will*, namely the specifier, as illustrated in (58) below (where we mark the checked feature by embossing). In other words, the system will resort to a Spec-head relation just in case the optimal option of head adjunction doesn't lead to a convergent result in the phonological component.[20]

(58)   [$_{TP}$ [the boy]^i [$_{TP}$ will$_{strong-D}$ [$_{VP}$ [the boy]^i [eat [a bagel]]]]]

9.4.2.5 Summary

Exploring the consequences of the relation between feature checking and elimination of [−interpretable] features, the Move-F approach raises some interesting minimalist questions – *Why* does the computational system move features rather than categories? *Why* does it resort to Spec-head configurations for feature checking in additional to the optimal configuration of head adjunction? – and outlines a very appealing picture of syntactic computations, which is able to capture some remarkable interpretation asymmetries involving covert and overt movement. Under this view, all syntactic operations take place overtly and in a cyclic manner; the decision of what to move (features vs. categories) is determined by the morphological requirements of strong features plus economy consideration regarding the amount of material being moved (copied). Finally, the computational system always attempts to explore the optimal configuration of head adjunction, but if the result of such adjunction yields a morphologically illicit object, the system then resorts to the nonoptimal Spec-head configuration. This approach is able to derive Procrastinate effects without postulating an asymmetry on the mapping from the numeration to LF and analyze covert movement in a way consistent with the Extension Condition. Under this view, what was previously analyzed

---

20 See Nunes (1995, 1998) for further discussion.

as covert movement should be understood as overt (sideward) movement of formal features.

9.4.3   Alternative II: Agree

The Move-F approach reviewed in section 9.4.2 rests on the lexicalist assumption that lexical items enter the derivation fully inflected. Lexical redundancy rules provide the computational system with the information of whether a given formal feature is [+interpretable] or not (see section 9.3.2) and [−interpretable] features are then deleted through feature checking.

9.4.3.1   The operation Agree

An interesting nonlexicalist alternative to this view of encoding feature interpretability in the lexicon is to assume that only [+interpretable] features are fully specified in the lexicon, whereas [−interpretable] features acquire their values in the course of the derivation. Take the attribute [person], for instance. Under this view, it's lexically assigned a value (1st, 2nd, 3rd) when associated with a pronoun, but no value when associated with a verb. But, of course, morphology requires that the feature [person] on a verb be appropriately specified and Full Interpretation requires that [−interpretable] formal features be deleted. The proposal is that this double role is played by *Agree*, a new operation of the computational system. Given the appropriate configuration for feature matching, Agree assigns values to unvalued features for morphological reasons, while at the same time deleting such [−interpretable] features for purposes of LF.[21]

Under this approach, overt movement is still a property of strong features. Movement of formal features, on the other hand, is replaced by Agree, and the locality and Last Resort conditions on feature movement are appropriately translated as requirements on the matching relation between a *probe* and a *goal*. A probe is a head with [−interpretable] features and a goal is an element with matching [+interpretable] features. In order to have its [−interpretable] features deleted for LF purposes and specified for morphological purposes, a given probe peruses its c-command domain in search of a goal. A goal is accessible to a given probe only if there is no intervening element with the relevant set of features; that is, relativized minimality holds (see chapter 5).

---

21 See Chomsky (2000, 2001, 2004) for discussion.

Furthermore, in order for a goal to be active for purposes of Agree, it must have some [−interpretable] feature unchecked. Once a given element has all of its [−interpretable] features checked, it becomes inactive; it's still in the structure and may induce minimality effects, but it can't participate in any other agreement relation.

Finally, based on the fact that Case is morphologically realized only on the "assignee" and not the "assigner," it's assumed that nouns have Case-features, but "Case assigners" don't. Case-checking/specification under this view is analyzed as the reflex of the agreement relation involving the [+interpretable] φ-features of the noun and the [−interpretable] φ-features of the relevant Case checker. For instance, a given Case-feature will be specified as accusative under φ-feature agreement with a light verb, but as nominative under φ-feature agreement with a finite T.[22]

Let's consider some examples in order to make these key notions clearer. Take the derivation of the sentence in (59), for instance, after successive applications of Merge yield the structure in (60).[23]

(59)   She loves him.

(60) $[_{vP}\ v_{\{\textbf{p:?};\ \textbf{N:?}\}}\ [_{VP}\ \text{love pro}_{\{P:3;\ N:SG;\ G:MASC;\ \textbf{CASE:?}\}}\ ]\,]$

In (60), the light verb has [−interpretable], therefore unvalued, φ-features. It then probes its complement in search of a suitable goal and finds it in the object pronoun: it has [+interpretable] φ-features capable of valuing the φ-features of the light verb; it's local (there is no intervening element with φ-features); and it's active for agreeing purposes, for it has a

---

22 What seems to be crucial for Case-checking is the feature [person], as will be shown below. For the purposes of exposition, we will be assuming that light verbs (*v*) and finite tense (T) in English only have person and number features. Nothing would substantially change, however, if they also had an abstract gender feature. Cross-linguistic variation in this regard would then be only a matter of the morphological realization of this feature (phonetically realized in Arabic finite T, for instance, but not in English finite T).

23 For purposes of readability, we'll be using the following abbreviations and conventions:

    (i) • G: [gender]; MASC: [masculine]; FEM: [feminine]
        • N: [number]; SG: [singular]; PL: [plural]
        • P: [person]; 1: [first]; 2: [second]; 3: [third]
        • STRONG: strong feature ("EPP")
        • φ⁻: [−interpretable] φ-features
        • φ⁺: [+interpretable] φ-features
        • ?: no value specified
        • **boldface**: unchecked [−interpretable] feature
        • embossed: valued and deleted [−interpretable] feature

[−interpretable] Case-feature to be valued. Upon matching through Agree, the φ-features of the light verb are then valued for purposes of morphology and deleted for purposes of LF and, as a byproduct of this agreeing relation, the Case-feature of the object is specified as accusative for morphological purposes and deleted for LF purposes, as represented in (61).

(61)   [$_{vP}$ $v$$_{\{P:3;\ N:SG\}}$ [$_{VP}$ love pro$_{\{P:3;\ N:SG;\ G:MASC;\ CASE:ACC\}}$]]

The next steps involve merger of another pronoun and of the inflectional head:

(62)   [$_{TP}$ T$_{\{\textbf{P:?;}\ \textbf{N:?;}\ \textbf{STRONG}\}}$ [$_{vP}$ pro$_{\{P:3;\ N:SG;\ G:MASC;\ \textbf{CASE:?}\}}$
         [$_{v'}$ $v$$_{\{P:3;\ N:SG\}}$ [$_{VP}$ love pro$_{\{P:3;\ N:SG;\ G:MASC;\ CASE:ACC\}}$]]]]

Due to its [−interpretable] φ-features, T peruses its complement searching for a suitable goal. The object pronoun is neither accessible (the subject pronoun intervenes) nor active (it has no unchecked [−interpretable] features). The subject pronoun is, on the other hand, both accessible and active. Agree then applies to T and the pronoun in [Spec,vP], valuing their [−interpretable] features and making them invisible at LF, as represented in (63).

(63)   [$_{TP}$ T$_{\{P:3;\ N:SG;\ \textbf{STRONG}\}}$ [$_{vP}$ pro$_{\{P:3;\ N:SG;\ G:MASC;\ CASE:NOM\}}$
         [$_{v'}$ $v$$_{\{P:3;\ N:SG\}}$ [$_{VP}$ love pro$_{\{P:3;\ N:SG;\ G:MASC;\ CASE:ACC\}}$]]]]

What about the strong feature of T in (63)? Recall that under the Move-F approach, it was assumed that strong features can be checked only by lexical items or projections of lexical items. Thus, in order for a head H to have its strong feature checked, a category containing the relevant feature must then merge with either H itself or with a projection of H (head adjunction and Spec-head configurations, respectively). This assumption is kept in its essence within the Agree approach: a strong feature of a probe P must be checked by a local constituent C that contains a feature that matches it.

Thus, the strong feature of T (the EPP-feature) in (63) must be checked by a nominal element (see section 2.3.1.3) either by simple merger in the case of an expletive (see section 9.3.3) or by movement. In the absence of an expletive in the derivational step in (63) (see section 10.3.1 below for detailed discussion), the strong feature of T triggers the movement of the closest pronoun, yielding the structure in (64).

(64)   [$_{TP}$ pro$_{\{P:3;\ N:SG;\ G:MASC;\ CASE:NOM\}}$ [$_{T'}$ T$_{\{P:3;\ N:SG;\ STRONG\}}$
         [$_{vP}$ pro$_{\{P:3;\ N:SG;\ G:MASC;\ CASE:NOM\}}$ [$_{v'}$ $v$$_{\{P:3;\ N:SG\}}$
         [$_{VP}$ love pro$_{\{P:3;\ N:SG;\ G:MASC;\ CASE:ACC\}}$]]]]]

After deletion of traces and insertion of the phonological features associated with morphological specification, (64) is converted into (65), which then surfaces as (59), repeated here as (66), after further computations in the phonological component.

(65)   [$_{TP}$ she [$_{T'}$ -s [$_{vP}$ v [$_{VP}$ love him]]]]

(66)   She loves him.

Once the pronoun in [Spec,TP] in (64) doesn't have an unchecked [−interpretable] feature, it's inert for further agreeing relations. Thus, if (64) is embedded under a raising predicate, as shown in the simplified representation in (67) below, the subject pronoun won't be able to value the [−interpretable] φ-features of the matrix T even if it moves to check the strong feature. In other words, "hyperraising" constructions such as (68) simply cannot be generated under this system.[24]

(67)   [$_{TP}$ T$_{\{\phi^-;\ \text{STRONG}\}}$ seem [that [$_{TP}$ she$_{\{\phi^+;\ \text{CASE:NOM}\}}$ loves him]]]

(68)   *[she$_i$ seems that [t$_i$ loves him]]

Now consider the acceptable sentence from Arabic in (69a) below. It has some resemblance with (68) in the sense that its subject is involved in agreement relations with two different inflectional heads, as shown in the simplified structure in (69b). The question then is how (68) and (69a) can be appropriately teased apart.

(69)   *Standard Arabic*
   a. l-banaant-u   kunna   waaqif-aat.
      the-girls-NOM   were.3.FEM.PL   standing-FEM.PL
      'The girls were standing.'
   b. [$_{TP}$ l-banaant-u$_i$ [$_{T'}$ T$_{\{P:3;\ N:PL;\ G:FEM;\ \text{STRONG}\}}$ [$_{vP}$ kunna [$_{TP}$ t$_i$
      [$_{T'}$ T$_{\{N:PL;\ G:FEM;\ \text{STRONG}\}}$ [$_{vP}$ t$_i$ waaqif-aat]]]]]]

In the GB-model, the difference between (68) and (69a) can be stated in terms of Case: the unacceptable "hyperraising" construction in (68) involves A-movement from a Case-marked position, whereas the acceptable participial sentence in (69a) involves A-movement from a Caseless position. In order to capture this distinction in the Agree-based system, we have to determine what features are involved in Case valuation. The logic of the system tells us

---

24 See Ura (1994), Ferreira (2000), and Rodrigues (2004) for relevant discussion.

that the Case-feature of the external argument in (69b) did not get valued after the φ-features of the participial T agreed with the φ-features of the external argument; otherwise, the pronoun would not be active for purposes of further agreement.[25] From this, we may conclude that the features [number] and [gender] by themselves are not capable of valuing a Case-feature. That leaves us with the feature [person], present in the embedded TP of (67), but absent in the embedded TP of (69b). We may therefore conclude that it's the feature [person] that is crucial for Case-valuing under φ-feature agreement.[26] Hence, the pronoun in (67) has its Case-feature valued after it values the φ-features of the embedded finite T, which contains the feature [person]. On the other hand, the agreeing relation between the participial T and the external argument in (69b) leaves the Case-feature of the subject unaltered, allowing it to enter into further agreement with the matrix T.

The similarity between A- and A′-movement shown in (70) and (71) below (see also exercise 9.3) suggests that the logic of the analysis sketched above may also be extended to A′-relations: in the same way a DP can't enter into agreement relations with more than one Case-valuing head (cf. (71a)), a *wh*-phrase cannot participate in checking relations with more than one interrogative complementizer (cf. (71b)).

(70)   a. [John$_i$ T seems [t$_i$ to [t$_i$ love Mary]]]
        b. [what$_i$ did + Q you say [t$_i$ that John bought t$_i$]]

(71)   a. *[John$_i$ seems that [t$_i$ T [t$_i$ loves Mary]]]
        b. *[what$_i$ do you wonder [t$_i$ Q John bought t$_i$]]

Suppose, for instance, that interrogative complementizers have a [−interpretable] F that is valued by a *wh*-feature and that *wh*-elements have a [−interpretable] feature F′ that is valued as a reflex of A′-agreement with an interrogative complementizer.[27] In the derivation of (70b), the required checking relations are obtained without problems, as sketched in (72).

---

25 Especially since Kayne (1989), Belletti (1990), and Chomsky (1991), participial structures have enjoyed quite a lot of attention by syntacticians (see Belletti 2004 for a recent survey of participial issues and further references). Whether or not participials head their own AgrPartP doesn't concern us here; what counts is the impact on inflectional syntax, thus allowing for a T-like head to enter the derivation as sketched in (69b). For more on case and agreement patterns in Arabic, see Sultan (2002). We also thank Jamal Ouhalla for discussion.

26 Note that, while teasing apart the different φ-features that make up agreement was not in the limelight of GB, Bashir (1987) already offered arguments from Kashmiri to the effect that [person] plays a crucial role for determining finiteness of a clause (in terms of opacity), but not [number] or [gender] (cf. Rudin 1988b: 49, n. 4).

27 See Chomsky (2001, 2004) and Hornstein (2001: 118–19).

(72)   a. [$_{CP}$ that$_{\{STRONG\}}$ [John bought what$_{\{WH;\ F'\}}$]]

b. [$_{CP}$ what$_{\{WH;\ F'\}}$ that$_{\{STRONG\}}$ [John bought t]]

c. [$_{CP}$ did + Q$_{\{F:?;\ STRONG\}}$ you say [$_{CP}$ what$_{\{WH;\ F'\}}$ that$_{\{STRONG\}}$ [John bought t]]]

d. [$_{CP}$ what$_{\{WH;\ F'\}}$ did + Q$_{\{F:WH;\ STRONG\}}$ you say [$_{CP}$ t that$_{\{STRONG\}}$ [John bought t]]]

By contrast, in the derivation of (71b) sketched in (73), *what* cannot agree with the matrix interrogative complementizer when the stage in (73c) is reached, because it has become inactive for further computations as it doesn't have [−interpretable] feature unchecked anymore. The derivation then crashes, as desired.

(73)   a. [$_{CP}$ Q$_{\{F:?;\ STRONG\}}$ [John bought what$_{\{WH;\ F'\}}$]]

b. [$_{CP}$ what$_{\{WH;\ F'\}}$ Q$_{\{F:WH;\ STRONG\}}$ [John bought t]]

c. [$_{CP}$ do + Q$_{\{F:?;\ STRONG\}}$ you wonder [$_{CP}$ what$_{\{WH;\ F'\}}$ Q$_{\{F:WH;\ STRONG\}}$ [John bought t]]]

Putting aside the fact that the feature composition proposed above for the *wh*-elements and interrogative complementizers is rather sketchy, the attempt to analyze (70) and (71) in a uniform way has an interesting consequence worth exploring. According to the suggestion outlined above, what makes a *wh*-phrase interrogative may not be its *wh*-feature alone, but its agreement relation with an interrogative complementizer. Evidence that something along these lines is on the right track is the fact that many languages use the same words for indefinite and interrogative pronouns, as illustrated in (74) from Mandarin Chinese.[28] The instantiation of one meaning rather than the other depends on whether the expression is in the scope of an interrogative or declarative complementizer, which suggests that some sort of A′-agreement is at stake.[29]

---

28 This example is taken from Cheng (1991: 113), who provides a list of homophonous and derivative forms for indefinite quantifiers and *wh*-expressions across a variety of languages, as illustrated in (i) and (ii) (see Cheng 1991: 79–81).

(i)   a. Korean: *nwukwu*   'who'/'somebody'
       b. Japanese: *dare*   'who'/'someone'
       c. Diyari: *mina*   'what'/'something'

(ii)   a. Polish: *kto/ktoś*   'who'/'someone'
       b. Hungarian: *hol/valahol*   'where'/'somewhere'

29 For other instances of A′-agreement, see, e.g., Georgopoulos (1991) on Palaun, Chung (1998) on Chamorro, McCloskey (2002) on Irish, and Adger and Ramchand (2005) on Scottish Gaelic.

(74)   *Mandarin Chinese*
        guojing mei-you   mai   sheme
        Guojing   not-have   buy   what
        'Guojing didn't buy anything.'
        or 'What didn't Guojing buy?'

Exercise 9.15

In the derivations of (69a), (70), and (71b) we've put aside the details of the overt adjunction of the main verb to the light verb and the overt adjunction of T to the interrogative complementizer (see, for example, sections 3.3.3, 5.5, and 7.2). Discuss what sort of assumptions would be necessary for these movements to be properly accounted for under the analysis outlined in the text.

Exercise 9.16

Provide the relevant steps of the derivation of (i) and show how it is to be excluded within the Agree-based approach.

   (i)   *John$_i$ seems to t$_i$ that Mary has left.
         'It seems to John that Mary has left.'

Exercise 9.17

Discuss how the analysis of the distribution of PRO in terms of null Case seen in section 4.3.4 is to be interpreted under the Agree-system, by examining the derivations of the structures in (i).

   (i)   a. [it is rare [PRO$_i$ to be elected t$_i$ in these circumstances]]
         b. *[it is rare [PRO$_i$ to seem to t$_i$ that the problems are insoluble]]
         c. *[PRO$_i$ is rare [t$_i$ to be elected t$_i$ in these circumstances]]

Exercise 9.18

Agree may apply in a "long distance" fashion affecting elements that are not in a head-complement or Spec-head configuration. Can't the conceptual objections raised against government also apply to the structural configuration required for Agree to apply? If not, why not?

9.4.3.2   Expletive constructions in the Agree-based system

Let's now consider the derivation of an expletive construction such as (75) under this approach.

(75)   There seem to be three men in the room.

Given that the embedded clause of (75) doesn't have a Case-checking light verb, the first relevant agreeing possibility arises when the embedded TP in (76a) below is formed. Under the assumption that the infinitival *to* only has a strong feature to be checked, the expletive *there* is inserted and checks it, as shown in (76b). After the syntactic object in (76c) is formed, the matrix T probes its complement to value its [−interpretable] features and check its strong feature (the EPP). Agree then values the φ-features of T and specifies the Case-feature of *three men* as nominative, as shown in (76d). After *there* moves in (76e), the EPP-feature of the matrix T is checked and the derivation converges.

(76)   a. $[_{TP}$ to$_{\{STRONG\}}$ $[_{VP}$ be [[three men $]_{\{P:3; N:PL; G:MASC; CASE:?\}}$ in the room]]]

   b. $[_{TP}$ there $[_{T'}$ to$_{\{STRONG\}}$ $[_{VP}$ be [[three men $]_{\{P:3; N:PL; G:MASC; CASE:?\}}$ in the room]]]]

   c. $[_{TP}$ T$_{\{P:?; N:?; STRONG\}}$ seem $[_{T'}$ there $[_{T'}$ to$_{\{STRONG\}}$ $[_{VP}$ be [[three men] $_{\{P:3; N:PL; G:MASC; CASE:?\}}$ in the room]]]]]

   d. $[_{TP}$ T$_{\{P:3; N:PL; STRONG\}}$ seem $[_{T'}$ there $[_{T'}$ to$_{\{STRONG\}}$ $[_{VP}$ be [[three men] $_{\{P:3; N:PL; G:MASC; CASE:NOM\}}$ in the room]]]]]

   e. $[_{TP}$ there$_i$ $[_{T'}$ T$_{\{P:3; N:PL; STRONG\}}$ seem $[_{T'}$ t$_i$ $[_{T'}$ to$_{\{STRONG\}}$ $[_{VP}$ be [[three men $]_{\{P:3; N:PL; G:MASC; CASE:NOM\}}$ in the room]]]]]]

Note that the intervening *there* in (76c) doesn't prevent T from entering into an agreeing relation with *three men* because it doesn't have [+interpretable] φ-features to value the φ-features of T (see section 9.4.3.1). By contrast, it's able to check an EPP-feature and does block the movement of the associate, as shown in (77).

(77)   *Three men seem there to be in the room.

Exercise 9.19

Show if and how the structures in (i) can be analyzed under the Agree-based approach outlined in the text.

(i)   a. *[there$_i$ seems [t$_i$ to be many people in the room]]

   b. *[there$_i$ seem that [[many people]$_i$ are t$_i$ in the room]]

   c. *[there seem [there to be many people in the room]]

   d. [I believe [there$_i$ to be expected [t$_i$ to be many people in the room]]]

   e. [it seems that [[many people]$_i$ are t$_i$ in the room]]

Exercise 9.20

One difference between the Move-F and the Agree approaches is that in the former a [−interpretable] feature may be checked against another [−interpretable] feature, whereas in the latter a [−interpretable] feature must be checked by a [+interpretable] feature. Discuss the consequences of this difference, by examining the derivation of the sentence in (i) under the Agree approach.

(i)   It seems that it has rained a lot.

9.4.3.3   Interpretation asymmetries in the Agree-based system

As the reader can easily check, the Agree-based approach has basically the same empirical coverage as the Move-F approach. This is due to the fact that the alternative to "covert" relations each approach proposes (movement of features or agreement) is subject to the same conditions of Last Resort, minimality, and economy.

Take the contrasts in (36) and (34), for instance, repeated below as (78) and (79).

(78)   a. [[many students]$_i$ seemed to each other [t$_i$ to have been in trouble]]
         b. *[there$_i$ seemed to each other [t$_i$ to have been many students in trouble]]

(79)   *Brazilian Portuguese*
         a. Que   fotografia   de   [si   mesmo]$_{i/k}$ [o   João]$_k$ disse   que
            which picture   of   self own   the João   said   that
            [o   Pedro]$_i$ viu?
            the   Pedro   saw
         b. [O   João]$_k$ disse   que   [o   Pedro]$_i$ viu   que
            the João   said   that   the Pedro   saw   which
            fotografia   de   [si   mesmo]$_{i/*k}$?
            picture   of   self own
            'Which picture of himself did João say that Pedro saw?'

Since there is no covert movement in the Agree-based approach, the associate in (78b) and the *wh*-phrase in (79b) remain *in situ* and have their [−interpretable] features valued for morphological purposes and deleted for LF purposes through "long distance" agreement: ϕ-feature agreement with the matrix T in (78b) and A′-agreement with the matrix interrogative complementizer in (79b). Once these elements remain *in situ* throughout the derivation, the anaphor in (78b) won't be properly bound and the local anaphor of (79b) must be bound by the embedded subject, as desired.

The crucial difference between the Move-F and the Agree approaches actually resides in the way they analyze [−interpretable] features, which ultimately depends on whether or not the lexicalist approach to feature specification is correct. For instance, if ellipsis is interpreted as PF-deletion, the Agree-based approach will have some advantages over the Move-F approach. Consider the sentences in (80) and (81), for instance.

(80)   *Portuguese*
Os   gatos   são   bonitos   e
the.MASC.PL ***cat.MASC.PL*** ***are*[3.PL]** *beautiful.MASC.PL*   *and*
a   gata   também é.
the.FEM.SG *cat.FEM.SG*   *also*   *is*[3.SG]
'The tomcats are beautiful and so is the cat.'

(81)   John does not have any money, but Bill does.

If ellipsis involves some sort of PF-deletion under identity, the lexicalist view adopted by the Move-F approach would fail to account for the elliptical constructions in (80) and (81), given that their non-elliptical counterparts do not show identity, as illustrated in (82) and (83).

(82)   *Portuguese*
Os   gatos   são   **bonitos**   e
the.MASC.PL *cat.MASC.PL* *are*[3.PL] *beautiful.MASC.PL*   *and*
a   gata   também   é   **bonita**.
the.FEM.SG *cat.FEM.SG*   *also*   *is*[3.SG]   *beautiful.FEM.SG*
'The tomcats are beautiful and so is the cat.'

(83)   John does not **have any** money, but Bill **has some** money.

By contrast, under the Agree-based approach, ellipsis could apply at a derivational step before the relevant [−interpretable] features were assigned a value and became morphologically distinct. Consider, for instance, the structures in (84) and (85) below. Before φ-feature agreement for the adjectival predicate in (84) and T in (85) and (A′-)agreement for the determiner in (85), the predicates are identical and should thus permit ellipsis, yielding the sentences in (80) and (81).[30]

(84)   [[[os gatos]{G:MASC; N:PL} são **bonit-**{G:?S; N:?}] e [[a gata] {G:FEM, N:SG} também é **bonit-**{G:?; N:?}]]

(85)   [[John T{P:?; N:?} not **have-DET**{F:?} **money**] but [Bill T{P:?; N:?} **have-DET**{F:?} **money**]]

---

30 See Zocca (2003) and Nunes and Zocca (2005) for relevant discussion.

We are not contending here that this is the best analysis of the mismatches found in ellipsis constructions. Our point is simply that given that the main difference between the Move-F and the Agree approaches regards feature specification, any piece of evidence for feature specification throughout the derivation is in principle more congenial to Agree than to Move-F.

Exercise 9.21

Discuss if and how the vehicle changes effects illustrated in (i) (see section 9.4.2.1) can be accounted for under the Agree-based approach.

(i) a. *Mary admires John$_i$, but he$_i$ doesn't.
   b. Mary admires John$_i$, but he$_i$ thinks Susan doesn't.

9.4.3.4 Procrastinate and Cyclicity in the Agree-based system

Let's get back to the Procrastinate and cyclicity problems that the traditional analysis of covert movement faces and examine how the Agree-based system circumvents them.

Given that "covert" relations are reinterpreted as overt agreement, there is no need for a covert component in the Agree approach and, therefore, no need for a principle such as Procrastinate, which evaluates applications of a given operation in the overt and covert components. All checking operations proceed overtly. Procrastinate effects again follow from the presence of strong features: in their absence, agreement takes place without movement. Once there is no covert movement, overt movement may always proceed in a cyclic manner (given the possibility of sideward movement), in compliance with the Extension Condition, as shown in section 8.3.5.2.

9.4.3.5 Summary

The Agree-based approach also captures "covert" relations without violating the Uniformity Condition on the mapping from the numeration to LF: given that there is no covert component in this approach, the computation is vacuously uniform. The general picture of the grammar under the Agree-based approach shown in (86) below is, therefore, not substantially different from the one seen under the Move-F approach (cf. (44)). The only relevant difference is the addition of Agree to the inventory of operations of the computational system. This shows that the choice of the Agree-based system instead of the Move-F approach must be justified on empirical grounds. All things being equal, the approach that does not increase the number of primitives in the model is the one to be preferred.

(86)   *The computational system under the Agree approach*

$N = \{A_i, B_j, C_k \dots\}$

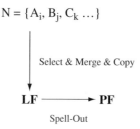

Select & Merge & Copy

LF ──────▶ **PF**

Spell-Out

9.5   Conclusion

This chapter has discussed two major problems that the standard GB idea of covert movement entails within minimalism. First, it requires the conceptually dubious principle Procrastinate, which stipulates that covert movement is intrinsically more economical than overt movement; and second, it allows for non-cyclic merger, being at odds with the Extension Condition on phrase-structure building. Both of these aspects constitute violations of the Uniformity Condition on the mapping from the numeration to LF and, as a consequence, we face the possibility that S-Structure is being resurrected under the technical rubbish.

The discussion of these problems has led us to consider deeper questions such as *why* movement operations should exist to begin with. As mentioned earlier, this question has been in linguists' minds since the onset of the generative enterprise. Minimalism comes to offer a fresh look at this old problem, by paying closer attention to the role lexical features play in the computation. A very promising idea is that the existence of movement in natural languages is somehow related to the fact that natural languages, for yet unexplained reasons, have formal features that are legible neither at LF nor at PF.

One instantiation of this idea is that the existence of [−interpretable] formal features in the lexicon is a departure from optimality and that movement is an optimal solution to this problem in that it allows these illegible features to be appropriately deleted, allowing the interface to read the objects built by the computational system. In this chapter, we've considered two different implementations of this conception of movement: the Move-F and the Agree approaches. The interesting consequence that each approach has is that they allow the relations that were previously captured in terms of covert movement to be reinterpreted in terms of overt cyclic operations: movement of features or agreement. In other words, neither approach faces the problems related to Procrastinate and the Extension Condition, which the earlier analysis in terms of covert category movement faced.

It's too early to see which of these alternative approaches to covert movement is on the right track and we should not let the new technical aspects found in each approach obscure a more fundamental fact: that the minimalist hypothesis that the language faculty is an optimal solution to interface requirements has led to the empirical discovery that feature interpretability and syntactic computation are intricately connected. The moral of the story is that even if neither of the alternative approaches to covert movement proves to be correct, we will have significantly broadened the domain of empirical research by scrutinizing GB with minimalist lenses.

10 *Derivational economy*

10.1   Introduction

All generative approaches to grammar have included conditions limiting
movement in various ways. Ross (1967) is an early (and still an outstand-
ing) example of how to constrain movement via locality conditions of
various kinds.[1] The minimality idea in chapter 5 that moves must be "the
shortest possible" to be licit is a modern descendant of Ross's earlier
progeny. This chapter reviews other kinds of rather different restrictions
on movement and grammatical relations, in general.

Island conditions and minimality restrictions act to limit the reach of
an operation (i.e. a given rule can't relate A and B because they are too
distant from one another). The restrictions we'll be examining, by
contrast, don't restrict the reach of a rule, but its applicability (i.e.
although a given rule could relate A and B *if applied*, it simply can't
apply in the cases considered). For example, we'll contrast movement
with other available grammatical options, exploring the idea that movement is permitted just in case these other options aren't. Thus, in
contrast to minimality where the locality issues are entirely local (*Can
I go from here to there without violating minimality?*), the considerations
laid out in the following require a comparison among alternative derivational options (*Is this grammatical option the best among the various
ones at my disposal?*).

---

1 Traditionally, locality is taken to be an upper-bound limit on how far a dependency can
  stretch (after Ross 1967, see, e.g., Koster 1978, Culicover and Wilkins 1984, Rizzi 1990,
  Manzini 1992, Sabel 1996, Starke 2001, or Boeckx 2003a); Lasnik (2001a), Svenonius
  (2001), and Grohmann (2003c) provide recent overviews and further references, and
  Hiraiwa (2003) discusses various conceptions of locality within phase-based syntax (the
  approach we present in section 10.4 below). Grohmann (2000b, 2003b) proposes that the
  opposite condition also holds, namely that there is a lower bound on locality, or *anti-
  locality*.

This kind of comparative non-local reasoning has recently become fashionable in a variety of areas.[2] We outline how a version of this intuition has been developed within minimalism. In section 10.2, we review the general assumptions regarding economy we've made so far. Section 10.3 deals with existential constructions and discusses the proposal that there's an economy preference for operations of merger over operations of movement. Section 10.4 lays out the proposal that derivations are to be computed in a piecemeal fashion, by resorting to the notion of phases and subarrays. Section 10.5 presents another kind of economy: economy of lexical resources. Section 10.6 concludes this final chapter.

10.2   Economy computations: preliminary remarks

We have assumed that a derivation is a syntactic computation that operates with syntactic objects (lexical items and phrases built from them) and yields the pair (π, λ), where π is a PF object and λ is an LF object (see section 1.5). If π and λ comply with Full Interpretation (i.e. all [−interpretable] features have been appropriately checked), the derivation is said to converge at PF and LF, respectively, and a derivation is taken to be convergent only if it converges at both PF and LF. Furthermore, we've been assuming that two derivations can be compared for economy purposes only if they are both convergent and if they both take the same numeration as a starting point (see sections 1.5 and 2.3.2.6). Before we proceed to refinements on this picture of derivational economy, let's review why we need to make these assumptions.

Let's start by asking what the most economical syntactic computation we can think of is, given the general picture outlined above. For sure, it's the one in which no syntactic operation is employed and, consequently, no pair (π, λ) is formed; in other words, the potentially most economical syntactic computation is the one in which nothing happens. However, if such computation were taken into consideration for economy purposes, it would rule out any syntactic computation that employed some syntactic operation. In this scenario, the language faculty would simply consist of a lexicon and that should be it. Hence, we must assume that the set of syntactic derivations is a subset of the set of conceivable syntactic

2 Optimality Theory uses it in a big way (see Archangeli and Langendoen 1997, Legendre, Grimshaw, and Vikner 2001, and Müller 2003 among others) as does Representation Theory in Williams (2003), for example.

computations. More concretely, we may assume that a syntactic computation is a derivation only if it forms the pair (π, λ). By assuming that only derivations can compete in terms of economy, the unwanted scenario sketched above doesn't arise, for a computation where nothing happens doesn't qualify itself as a derivation and can't be taken into consideration for economy purposes (see sections 1.3 and 1.4).

The pool of comparable derivations should be further restricted to the convergent ones. Take the derivations that yield the structures in (1), for instance.

(1)   a. *[$_{TP}$ was [arrested John]]
           b. [John$_i$ was [arrested t$_i$]]

A natural economy criterion is that shorter derivations (that is, derivations that employ fewer operations) should block longer ones. However, if economy was computed solely on the basis of the number of operations, the derivation of (1a) should incorrectly block the derivation of (1b), which involves an additional operation of movement. If, on the other hand, economy only takes convergent derivations into account, the derivation of (1a) isn't considered for purposes of economy computations, for the strong feature of T (the EPP-feature) hasn't been checked, causing the derivation to crash at PF.

Finally, convergence alone is not enough to exclude all the unwanted comparisons. Take the derivations of the sentences in (2), for example.

(2)   a. The boy cried.
           b. The boy with a toy cried.

Both derivations are convergent. However, the derivation of (2b) appears to be less economical than (2a), for it employs more syntactic operations to build the PP *with a toy* and merge it in the structure. Thus, if the derivations of (2a) and (2b) were allowed to enter into competition for economy purposes, (2a) would incorrectly rule (2b) out. To put it in general terms, if the computational system had direct access to the lexicon and economy were only restricted to convergent derivations, the language faculty would definitely encompass more than a lexicon. However, it would only permit very simple sentences, for it would basically exclude adjuncts and recursion in general because they would require "unnecessary" derivational steps.

At first sight, this potential problem is remedied by assuming that the computational system doesn't have direct access to the lexicon, but takes a numeration as the repository for the items that will feed the derivation (see section 2.3.2.6). This is not enough, though. Given that the lexical items of

(2a) form a subset of the lexical items of (2b), both derivations could in principle have the (simplified) numeration in (3) below as their starting point. That is, the computational system could use all of the lexical items of the numeration, yielding (2b), or only some of them, yielding (2a). Under this scenario, we would again obtain the incorrect result that the derivation of (2a) should be more economical than (2b), blocking it.

(3) $N = \{the_1, boy_1, with_1, a_1, toy_1, cried_1\}$

We thus need to further assume that a syntactic computation only counts as a derivation if it exhausts the numeration that feeds it (see section 2.3.2.6). That being so, (3) will only be associated with the derivation of (2b) and the derivation of (2a) will have to start from the (simplified) numeration in (4).

(4) $N = \{the_1, boy_1, cried_1\}$

We can now prevent the unwanted competition between the derivations of (2a) and (2b) if we further restrict economy computations to convergent derivations that start with the same numeration. If so, the derivations of (2a) and (2b) simply don't interfere with one another for purposes of economy and it doesn't even make sense to ask if one is more economical than the other.

Below we'll examine cases that point to further refinements with respect to how derivational economy is to be computed.

10.3   Derivational economy and local computations

10.3.1   *Existential constructions: the problem*
Consider the derivation of the sentence in (5), as sketched in (6).[3]

(5)   There seems to be someone here.

(6)   a. [$_{TP}$ to$_{\{STRONG\}}$ [$_{VP}$ be [someone$_{\{P:3;\ N:SG;\ CASE:?\}}$ here]]]
        b. [$_{TP}$ there [$_{T'}$ to$_{\{STRONG\}}$ [$_{VP}$ be [someone$_{\{P:3;\ N:SG;\ CASE:?\}}$ here]]]]
        c. [$_{TP}$ T$_{\{P:?;\ N:?;\ STRONG\}}$ seem [$_{T'}$ there [$_{T'}$ to$_{\{STRONG\}}$ [$_{VP}$ be [someone$_{\{P:3;\ N:SG;\ CASE:?\}}$ here]]]]]
        d. [$_{TP}$ T$_{\{P:3;\ N:SG;\ STRONG\}}$ seem [$_{T'}$ there [$_{T'}$ to$_{\{STRONG\}}$ [$_{VP}$ be [someone$_{\{P:3;\ N:SG;\ CASE:NOM\}}$ here]]]]]
        e. [$_{TP}$ there$_i$ [$_{T'}$ T$_{\{P:3;\ N:SG;\ STRONG\}}$ seem [$_{T'}$ t$_i$ [$_{T'}$ to$_{\{STRONG\}}$ [$_{VP}$ be [someone$_{\{P:3;\ N:SG;\ CASE:NOM\}}$ here]]]]]]

---

3 For purposes of presentation, we'll be assuming the Agree-based approach to covert relations (see section 9.4.3) throughout the chapter.

The expletive *there* merges with the structure in (6a) checking the EPP-feature of the embedded T, yielding (6b), and after further computations, the structure in (6c) is formed. The matrix T then probes its complement and enters into an Agree relation with *someone*, which values the ϕ features of T and the Case of *someone*, as shown in (6d). Crucially, *there* in (6d) only has a D-feature and induces no minimality effect with respect to the agreeing relation between the matrix T and *someone*. *There* may, however, raise to check the matrix EPP-feature, yielding (6e).

Consider now the derivation of the analogous sentence in (7) below, shown in (8). Assuming that the numeration that feeds (8) doesn't contain the expletive *there*, *someone* raises all the way to the matrix [Spec,TP] and all the [–interpretable] features are appropriately checked.

(7)   Someone seems to be here.

(8)   a. [TP to{STRONG} [VP be [someone{P:3; N:SG; CASE:?} here]]]
       b. [TP someone{P:3; N:SG; CASE:?}i [T′ to{STRONG} [VP be [ti here]]]]
       c. [TP T{P:?; N:?; STRONG} seem [T′ someone{P:3; N:SG; CASE:?}i
          [T′ to{STRONG} [VP be [ti here]]]]]
       d. [TP T{P:3; N:SG; STRONG} seem [T′ someone{P:3; N:SG; CASE:NOM}i
          [T′ to{STRONG} [VP be [ti here]]]]]
       e. [TP someone{P:3; N:SG; CASE:NOM}i [T′ T{P:3; N:SG; STRONG} seem [T′ ti
          [T′ to{STRONG} [VP be [ti here]]]]]]

Once (5) and (7) are acceptable sentences in English, one then wonders why (9) below is unacceptable, given the availability of the derivation sketched in (10).

(9)   *There seems someone to be here.

(10)   a. [TP to{STRONG} [VP be [someone{P:3; N:SG; CASE:?} here]]]
       b. [TP someone{P:3; N:SG; CASE:?}i [T′ to{STRONG} [VP be [ti here]]]]
       c. [TP T{P:?; N:?; STRONG} seem [T′ someone{P:3; N:SG; CASE:?}i
          [T′ to{STRONG} [VP be [ti here]]]]]
       d. [TP T{P:3; N:SG; STRONG} seem [T′ someone{P:3; N:SG; CASE:NOM}i
          [T′ to{STRONG} [VP be [ti here]]]]]
       e. [TP there [T′ T{P:3; N:SG; STRONG} seem [T′ someone{P:3; N:SG; CASE:NOM}i
          [T′ to{STRONG} [VP be [ti here]]]]]]

The EPP-feature of the embedded clause in (10b) is checked by *someone* (as in (8b)), and the EPP-feature of the matrix clause in (10e) is checked by *there* (as in (6e)); all the other [–interpretable] features in (10) are checked under the agreeing relation between the matrix T and *someone*, also in the same way we see it in (6d) and (8d). Given that the derivations in (7) and (8) converge, the unacceptability of (9) is therefore rather puzzling. The only apparent difference between (5) and (9) is that the associate is closer to the matrix T in (9) than it is in (5). However, it's hard to see why this should disrupt anything.

Notice that the problem is not inherent to the specific minimalist approach to existential constructions sketched above. (9) is also mysterious from a GB-perspective. In Chomsky's (1986b) influential analysis, for instance, the associate of the existential construction in (5), for example, must move covertly to replace the expletive. But given that *someone* arguably can move through the embedded [Spec, TP] in the derivation of (7), it should in principle be able to remain in this position at SS and replace the expletive in the covert component, incorrectly ruling (9) in.[4]

The problem might be harder for GB-approaches, though. Recall that in GB all operations apply freely as long as the resulting structures satisfy the filters postulated at different levels. And the problem with (9) is that it seems to comply with such filters. From a minimalist perspective, on the other hand, syntactic objects must not only satisfy output conditions imposed by the interfaces, but also be built in an optimal way. That is, among the class of convergent derivations, some are better than others in that they manage to converge more efficiently or economically. There is thus the possibility that although (9) results from a convergent derivation, it isn't the most economical derivation available to the system. This is the line we'll explore in the next section.

> **Exercise 10.1**
>
> Discuss if the unacceptability of the sentence in (9), repeated below in (i), also poses problems for a Move-F approach to covert movement.
>
> (i) *There seems someone to be here.

10.3.2   *Preference for Merge over Move*

Let's reexamine the derivations of (5) and (9), repeated below in (11), in detail.

(11)   a. There seems to be someone in the room.
         b. *There seems someone to be in the room.

The derivation of these two sentences arguably start from the same numeration: N_0 in (12) below. Given N_0, the computational system selects *someone* and *here* and merges them, as shown in the derivational step in (13).

---

4 For further discussion within GB, see Raposo and Uriagereka (1990), who analyze cases such as (9) in terms of a recursive definition of government.

Subsequent selection and merger of *be* (cf. (14)) and *to* (cf. (15)) reduce the numeration to N_3 and form the syntactic object M in (15b).

(12) $N_0 = \{\text{there}_1, T_1, \text{seem}_1, \text{to}_1, \text{be}_1, \text{someone}_1, \text{here}_1\}$

(13)   a. $N_1 = \{\text{there}_1, T_1, \text{seem}_1, \text{to}_1, \text{be}_1, \text{someone}_0, \text{here}_0\}$
        b. K = [someone here]

(14) $N_2 = \{\text{there}_1, T_1, \text{seem}_1, \text{to}_1, \text{be}_0, \text{someone}_0, \text{here}_0\}$
        L = [be someone here]

(15)   a. $N_3 = \{\text{there}_1, T_1, \text{seem}_1, \text{to}_0, \text{be}_0, \text{someone}_0, \text{here}_0\}$
        b. M = [to be someone here]

So far, the derivations of (11a) and (11b) have been identical. However, they differ from the next derivational step on. The derivation of (11a) uses the expletive to check the EPP-feature of *to*, as shown in (16), and after *seem* and T are selected and merged (cf. (17)–(18)), the numeration has been exhausted and *there* moves to check the matrix EPP-feature, yielding S in (19b).

(16)   a. $N_4 = \{\text{there}_0, T_1, \text{seem}_1, \text{to}_0, \text{be}_0, \text{someone}_0, \text{here}_0\}$
        b. P = [there to be someone here]

(17)   a. $N_5 = \{\text{there}_0, T_1, \text{seem}_0, \text{to}_0, \text{be}_0, \text{someone}_0, \text{here}_0\}$
        b. Q = [seem [there to be someone here]]

(18)   a. $N_6 = \{\text{there}_0, T_0, \text{seem}_0, \text{to}_0, \text{be}_0, \text{someone}_0, \text{here}_0\}$
        b. R = [T seem [there to be someone here]]

(19)   a. $N_7 = \{\text{there}_0, T_0, \text{seem}_0, \text{to}_0, \text{be}_0, \text{someone}_0, \text{here}_0\}$
        b. S = [there$_i$ T seem [t$_i$ to be someone here]]

By contrast, the next step following (15) in the derivation of (11b) involves movement of *someone* to check the EPP-feature of *to*, as shown in (20) below. Further selection and merger of *seem*, *to* and *there* in (21)–(23) finally yield S′ in (23b).

(20)   a. $N_{3'} = \{\text{there}_1, T_1, \text{seem}_1, \text{to}_0, \text{be}_0, \text{someone}_0, \text{here}_0\}$
        b. P′ = [someone$_i$ to be t$_i$ here]

(21)   a. $N_{4'} = \{\text{there}_1, T_1, \text{seem}_0, \text{to}_0, \text{be}_0, \text{someone}_0, \text{here}_0\}$
        b. Q′ = [seem [someone$_i$ to be t$_i$ here]]

(22)   a. $N_{5'} = \{\text{there}_1, T_0, \text{seem}_0, \text{to}_0, \text{be}_0, \text{someone}_0, \text{here}_0\}$
        b. R′ = [T seem [someone$_i$ to be t$_i$ here]]

(23)   a. $N_{6'} = \{\text{there}_0, T_0, \text{seem}_0, \text{to}_0, \text{be}_0, \text{someone}_0, \text{here}_0\}$
        b. S′ = [there T seem [someone$_i$ to be t$_i$ here]]

As seen in section 10.3.1, both derivations of the sentences in (11) converge (they both check all [–interpretable] features) and start from the same numeration N_0 in (12). They are then eligible for comparison in terms of economy and, given the contrast in (11), we should expect the derivation of (11a) to be more economical than (11b). The obvious question then is what the relevant economic metric will be. Clearly, it can't be derivational length. As the reader can verify, both derivations involve the same number of steps. Also, it can't be simply the types of operations employed in the derivation as a whole, for the same number of merges and movements (and agreeing relations) were used in the two derivations, as the reader can easily check.

Once a global metric evaluating the two derivations as a whole doesn't provide us with the means to distinguish the derivations of (11a) and (11b), let's then pursue a more local approach proposed by Chomsky (1995). In the case under discussion, the two derivations share not only the same initial numeration N_0, but also the same derivational history up to the derivational step in (15). Since they differ from then on, the key to the puzzle may reside exactly at the point where the two derivations split, namely, (16) and (20). Notice that here we appear to have a true option in the sense that either step may lead to a convergent result. The steps that follow either of these steps, by contrast, do not have such freedom. Once *there* is inserted in (16), for instance, the checking of the matrix EPP-feature is deterministic: it must be checked by *there*, as shown in (19); movement of *someone* to check it, as shown in (24), is blocked by the intervening expletive (see section 9.4.3.2).

(24)   *[someone$_i$ T seem [there to be t$_i$ here]]

So, the puzzle revolves around the two options for checking the EPP-feature of *to* available at the derivational step in (15): merger of *there*, as in (16), or movement of *someone*, as in (20). Chomsky's suggestion is that movement is a more costly option than merger. If so, at the derivational step in (15), the computational system takes the derivational route sketched in (16)–(20), and the derivation of (11b) is correctly ruled out.

Let's examine some features of this suggestion more closely. First, in what sense is movement less economical than merger? Well, recall that we have adopted the copy theory of movement (section 6.4). On this conception, movement is actually a composite operation made up of two more primitive processes, Copy and Merge. If this is so, then there is a very clear sense in which "Move" is more complex (hence less economical) than Merge: it contains Merge as a proper subpart! Thus, if the grammar aims to minimize complexity, then there's a good sense in which it'll try to execute Merges rather than "Moves."

This part/whole relation imposes an intrinsic metric of complexity between "Move" and Merge and fully justifies the assumption that "Move" is the more complex operation. This said, it is worth observing that economy reasoning does not require this sort of intrinsic ordering; an extrinsic ordering can also serve. However, what the part/whole relation provides is a strong rationale for the ordering; one that makes sense and this would be missing from the unvarnished assertion that Merge is cheaper than "Move."

This cost accounting, however, is not sufficient. Note that the *total* number of Merges and Moves is the same in the derivations of (11a) and (11b). In particular, the two derivations employ one application of the costly option of movement: movement of *someone* in the derivation of (11b) (cf. (20b)) and movement of *there* in the derivation of (11a) (cf. (19b)). The only difference is the *timing* of the application of movement: in the derivation of (11b), the computational system resorted to movement in an earlier derivational step than in the derivation of (11a). This distinction makes a big difference, however, *if* we assume that the calculation of cost is *local*. In other words, given the derivational step in (15), the *next* available option is to either Merge *there* or move *someone*. As "Move" (consisting of the two operations Copy plus Merge) is more costly than Merge, the most economical option *at this point* is to Merge *there* rather than move *someone*. So, Merge *there* it must be!

The assumption that derivations must be identical at the point where they are compared makes sense. Comparing derivations is not that desirable from a computational perspective. As such, if we must do it, then we should limit it to the degree possible. One way of drastically cutting down comparisons is by limiting them to derivations that are identical at the point that they are being compared. This implies that two sentences with different numerations are never compared. Similarly, derivations that start with the same numeration will cease to be compared if at any point they access different items from the numeration, thereby defining different lexical arrays for the next derivational step. These assumptions limit the amount of derivational comparisons that the grammar exploits and therefore reduces the computational complexity of the comparison procedure. In short, the numeration is a key technical element in making economy work.[5]

---

5 For further discussion of comparison of derivations, see among others the collection of papers in Wilder, Gärtner, and Bierwisch (1997).

Take the derivation of (7), repeated below in (25a), for instance. The fact that (25a) results from a convergent derivation involving movement of *someone* to check the EPP-feature of *to*, as illustrated in (25b), is not at all problematic. The derivation of (25a) can't be compared with the derivation of (11a), for instance, because its initial numeration N in (26) is different from N_0 in (12) in that it doesn't contain *there*. Hence, when the computational system reaches the derivational step in (27), there's no option of merging *there*, as *there* isn't available in the numeration; movement of *someone* is thus the only option that leads to a convergent result and economy is not an issue.

(25)   a. Someone seems to be here.
        b. [someone$_i$ [t$_i$ to [be t$_i$ here]]]

(26)   N = {T$_1$, seem$_1$, to$_1$, be$_1$, someone$_1$, here$_1$}

(27)   a. N′ = {T$_1$, seem$_1$, to$_0$, be$_0$, someone$_0$, here$_0$}
        b. K = [to be someone here]

To conclude. This section started out by discussing an empirical puzzle. Given a standard set of assumptions concerning the analysis of existential constructions, there was no obvious reason for the unacceptability of (28) below. Following Chomsky (1995), we presented an analysis according to which the derivation of (28) converges but is less economical than an alternative derivation built based on the same array of lexical items. The key idea is that derivations compete with one another in a limited way and that those that locally exploit superior operations are preferred. In particular, merger should be preferred to movement if the two options lead to convergent results. In what follows we consider some potential problems for this sort of account and review some of the mechanisms and principles advanced to save it.

(28)   *There seems someone to be here.

Exercise 10.2

According to the proposal reviewed in the text, "Move" is less economical than Merge in the sense that it's more complex, involving the primitive operations Copy and Merge. Could this rationale be maintained if the computational system could access the lexicon directly, without the mediation of a numeration? If so, how? If not, why not?

Exercise 10.3

Another possible way to rationalize the difference between lexical insertion and movement and account for the contrast in (11), repeated below in (i), is to say that the system attempts to maximally exploit the lexical resources that are still available to the computation, given that it'll have to exhaust the numeration anyway. Discuss whether this reasoning is conceptually or empirically superior to Chomsky's (1995) suggestion that the difference is couched on the part/whole relationship between Merge and "Move."

(i) a. There seems to be someone here.
    b. *There seems someone to be here.

Exercise 10.4

Under the Agree-based approach, *John* and *Mary* in the sentences of (i) below don't have their Case-features valued as they enter the derivation; that is, both sentences arise from the same initial numeration. Given that both sentences are acceptable, we should reach one of the following conclusions: that the two derivations are not comparable for purposes of economy (hence, the derivation of one sentence doesn't block the derivation of the other) or that they are comparable, but equally economical. According to the discussion in this section, which conclusion is correct?

(i) a. John loves Mary.
    b. Mary loves John.

Exercise 10.5

The discussion of the contrast in (i) below given in this section tacitly assumed that derivations proceed in a step-by-step fashion in the sense that lexical items are merged to the available structures as they are selected from the numeration. Would there be a problem if, instead, the computational system selected all the lexical items of the numeration before starting to build structures? Could the analysis of the contrast in (i) presented in the text be maintained in this scenario? If so, show how. If not, discuss how such flow of uninterrupted selections can be prevented.

(i) a. There seems to be someone here.
    b. *There seems someone to be here.

Exercise 10.6

Can the approach reviewed in this section also account for the contrast in (i)? If not, what assumptions must be made in order for (i) to be accounted for, as well?

(i) a. There was a man arrested.
    b. *There was arrested a man.

10.3.3 *θ-relations and economy computations*

Consider the (simplified) derivation of (29), sketched in (30)–(35).

(29)   John expected someone to be here.

(30) $N_0 = \{John_1, T_1, v_1, expected_1, to_1, be_1, someone_1, here_1\}$

(31)   a. $N_1 = \{John_1, T_1, v_1, expected_1, to_0, be_0, someone_0, here_0\}$
          b. [$_{TP}$ to be someone here]

(32)   a. $N_1 = \{John_1, T_1, v_1, expected_1, to_0, be_0, someone_0, here_0\}$
          b. [$_{TP}$ someone$_i$ to be t$_i$ here]

(33)   a. $N_2 = \{John_1, T_1, v_0, expected_0, to_0, be_0, someone_0, here_0\}$
          b. [$_{vP}$ v [$_{VP}$ expected [$_{TP}$ someone$_i$ to be t$_i$ here]]]

(34)   a. $N_3 = \{John_0, T_1, v_0, expected_0, to_0, be_0, someone_0, here_0\}$
          b. [$_{vP}$ John [$_{v'}$ v [$_{VP}$ expected [$_{TP}$ someone$_i$ to be t$_i$ here]]]]

(35)   a. $N_4 = \{John_0, T_0, v_0, expected_0, to_0, be_0, someone_0, here_0\}$
          b. [$_{TP}$ John$_k$ T [$_{vP}$ t$_k$ [$_{v'}$ v [$_{VP}$ expected [$_{TP}$ someone$_i$ to be t$_i$ here]]]]]

Starting from the (simplified) numeration N_0 in (30), the computational system selects some lexical items and assembles the TP in (31b). *Someone* then moves to check the EPP-feature of *to*, as shown in (32), and further computations form the *v*P structure in (33b). *John* then merges with this structure, receiving the external *θ*-role, and finally moves to the matrix [Spec,TP], yielding the structure in (35b), which surfaces as (29).

At first sight, this derivation appears to contradict the economy-based analysis reviewed in section 10.3.2. Here's the problem: why is *someone* allowed to move at the derivational step after (31) if the reduced numeration N_1 contained an element that could check the EPP-feature of *to*, namely, *John*? Don't we have a violation of "Merge over Move" here? Notice that the sentence in (36a), which results from merger of *John* in the embedded [Spec,TP], as illustrated in (36b), is not acceptable.

(36)   a. *John expected to be someone here.
          b. [$_{TP}$ John$_k$ T [$_{vP}$ t$_k$ [$_{v'}$ v [$_{VP}$ expected [$_{TP}$ t$_k$ to be someone here]]]]]

Upon close inspection, the contrast between (29) and (36a) need not be contradictory with what we saw earlier, though. Recall that less economical operations are permitted *if* the more economical options don't lead to a convergent result. In this case, then, the relevant question is whether the derivation in (36b) converges.

Chomsky (1995) suggests that it doesn't, due to problems regarding Theta Theory. Let's assume, as we did in previous chapters, that a DP obtains a θ-role by merging into a θ-position (see section 2.3.2.2). Let's further assume that an argument must enter a derivation through a thematic door. In other words, an argument's *first* merge must be into a thematic slot. With these two assumptions, the derivation underlying (36) can't converge as *John* first merges into the embedded [Spec, TP] and this is not a thematic position. Say that this is correct. Then it suffices to explain why (29) is an acceptable sentence. The cheaper option in (36b) leads to a crashing result; as crashing derivations don't block less economical options, the movement of *someone* in (32b) is allowed.

This account, however, raises an interesting conceptual question: *why* must an argument first merge into a θ-position? Note that this requirement is similar to the old GB-requirement that all elements begin their derivational lives in D-Structure, a level that requires all and only θ-positions to be filled. Isn't this a problem if we hope to eliminate DS from the grammar? Not necessarily. As we already remarked in section 2.3.2.2, the absence of DS doesn't imply the absence of DS-like conditions. The proposal here is that "first Merge" be into a thematic slot and this can be stated without mentioning a DS *level*. Chomsky, for instance, suggests that this restriction might follow if θ-roles were not features. Recall that according to Last Resort, a movement operation is licit only if it allows the elimination of [–interpretable] formal features (see section 9.3). If θ-relations don't involve ([–interpretable]) formal features, then movement into a θ-position will not comply with Last Resort and will be barred. If a DP is to receive a θ-role, it must then merge – and not move – into a thematic slot. In other words, if θ-roles are not feature-like, then the "first Merge" requirement follows.

These remarks necessarily raise another question: If θ-roles are not features, then what are they? There is a long tradition, going back to Frege and Russell, that considers θ-roles as positional or relational facts about an argument, i.e. you are the logical subject if you are in this position, object if in that one.[6] If this is right, then having a θ-role is not a matter of bearing a certain feature, but being in a certain position. If this is so, then θ-roles are not features and so movement into θ-positions should be barred by Last Resort and the "first Merge" of an argument would have to be into a thematic slot.

---

6 See e.g. Dowty (1991), Bouchard (1995), Williams (1995), Ackerman and Moore (2001), Salo (2003), and Reinhart (2004) for critical discussion and further references.

This line of reasoning is very contentious and currently the subject of a lot of debate.[7] To help understand why this might be so, consider the following. Under the view presented above, Case contrasts with θ-roles in being a feature. How is Case-quality determined? In other words, what gets nominative, what gets accusative in English? The DP in relation to tensed T gets nominative and objects of V get accusative. But doesn't this suggest that Case is just a relational property? If so, should movement to check Case also violate Last Resort? In fact, most every feature is assigned/checked in a configurational context and so marks a relation. If this fact suffices to eliminate θ-roles as features, why not these others?

We won't further pursue these questions here. Rather, we'll explore another alternative that is able to account for the contrast between (29) and (36a) regardless of whether or not movement to θ-positions should be licit.[8] Note that since these sentences involve ECM structures, the embedded argument should get its Case checked by the matrix predicate. With this in mind, let's examine the relevant derivational steps in (37)–(40) in more detail.[9]

(37)   a. $N_1 = \{John_1, T_1, v_1, expected_1, to_0, be_0, someone_0, here_0\}$

       b. $[_{TP} \text{ to}_{\{STRONG\}} [_{VP} \text{ be someone}_{\{P:3; N:SG; CASE:?\}} \text{ here }]]$

(38)   a. $N_2 = \{John_0, T_1, v_1, expected_1, to_0, be_0, someone_0, here_0\}$

       b. $[_{TP} \text{ John}_{\{P:3; N:SG; CASE:?\}} \text{ to}_{\{STRONG\}}$
           $[_{VP} \text{ be someone}_{\{P:3; N:SG; CASE:?\}} \text{ here }]]$

(39)   a. $N_3 = \{John_0, T_1, v_0, expected_0, to_0, be_0, someone_0, here_0\}$

       b. $[_{vP} v_{\{P:?; N:?\}} [_{VP} \text{ expected } [_{TP} \text{ John}_{\{P:3; N:SG; CASE:?\}} \text{ to}_{\{STRONG\}} [_{VP} \text{ be}$
           $\text{someone}_{\{P:3; N:SG; CASE:?\}} \text{ here }]]]]$

(40)   a. $N_4 = \{John_0, T_1, v_0, expected_0, to_0, be_0, someone_0, here_0\}$

       b. $[_{vP} v_{\{P:3; N:SG\}} [_{VP} \text{ expected } [_{TP} \text{ John}_{\{P:3; N:SG; CASE:ACC\}} \text{ to}_{\{STRONG\}}$
           $[_{VP} \text{ be someone}_{\{P:3; N:SG; CASE:?\}} \text{ here }]]]]$

Given that *to* in (37) has an EPP-feature to be checked and *John* is still available for the computation, it merges with the structure in (37b) and

---

7 For arguments in favor of movement into theta positions, see among others Bošković (1994), Lasnik (1995b), Bošković and Takahashi (1998), Castillo, Drury, and Grohmann (1999), Hornstein (1999, 2001), Ferreira (2000), Grohmann, Drury, and Castillo (2000), Manzini and Roussou (2000), Pires (2001), Hornstein and Nunes (2002), Kiguchi (2002), Boeckx and Hornstein (2003, 2004), Grohmann (2003b), Hornstein and Kiguchi (2004), Nunes (2004), and Rodrigues (2004).

8 See Nunes (1995, 2004) and Hornstein (2001).

9 For purposes of presentation, the discussion will proceed under the Agree-based approach. But nothing would essentially change if we assumed covert movement of formal features, instead.

344   *Understanding Minimalism*

checks the EPP-feature, as shown in (38b). Further computations yield the structure in (39b), whose light verb must value its ϕ-features. It then enters into an agreeing relation with *John*, valuing its own ϕ-features and the Case-feature of *John*, as illustrated in (40b). Crucially, the light verb can't enter into an agreement relation with *someone* due to the intervention of *John*. From this point on, the derivation is doomed, regardless of whether or not *John* is allowed to move to [Spec,*v*P] in (40b) to be assigned to external θ-role. When T enters into the derivation, it won't be able to check its features: *John* is inactive because it has checked its Case-feature and *someone* is active but not close enough.

The derivation of (36a) therefore crashes and doesn't block the derivation of (29), which, after the step in (37), takes the derivational route in (41)–(45).

(41) a. $N_1 = \{John_1, T_1, v_1, expected_1, to_0, be_0, someone_0, here_0\}$
      b. $[_{TP}$ someone$_{\{P:3;\ N:SG;\ CASE:?\}_i}$ to$_{\{STRONG\}}$ $[_{VP}$ be t_i here $]\,]$

(42) a. $N_{2'} = \{John_1, T_1, v_0, expected_0, to_0, be_0, someone_0, here_0\}$
      b. $[_{vP}\ v_{\{P:?;\ N:?\}}\ [_{VP}$ expected $[_{TP}$ someone$_{\{P:3;\ N:SG;\ CASE:?\}}$ to$_{\{STRONG\}}$ $[_{VP}$ be t_i here $]\,]\,]\,]$

(43) a. $N_{2'} = \{John_1, T_1, v_0, expected_0, to_0, be_0, someone_0, here_0\}$
      b. $[_{vP}\ v_{\{P:3;\ N:SG\}}\ [_{VP}$ expected $[_{TP}$ someone$_{\{P:3;\ N:SG;\ CASE:ACC\}_i}$ to$_{\{STRONG\}}$ $[_{VP}$ be t_i here $]\,]\,]\,]$

(44) a. $N_{3'} = \{John_0, T_0, v_0, expected_0, to_0, be_0, someone_0, here_0\}$
      b. $[_{TP}$ T$_{\{P:?;\ N:?;\ STRONG\}}\ [_{vP}$ John$_{\{P:3;\ N:SG;\ CASE:?\}}$
      $[_{v'}\ v_{\{P:3;\ N:SG\}}\ [_{VP}$ expected $[_{TP}$ someone$_{\{P:3;\ N:SG;\ CASE:ACC\}_i}$ to$_{\{STRONG\}}$ $[_{VP}$ be t_i here $]\,]\,]\,]\,]$

(45) a. $N_{3'} = \{John_0, T_0, v_0, expected_0, to_0, be_0, someone_0, here_0\}$
      b. $[_{TP}$ John$_{\{P:3;\ N:SG;\ CASE:NOM\}_k}$ T$_{\{P:3;\ N:SG;\ STRONG\}}$
      $[_{vP}\ t_k\ [_{v'}\ v_{\{P:3;\ N:SG\}}\ [_{VP}$ expected $[_{TP}$ someone$_{\{P:3;\ N:SG;\ CASE:ACC\}_i}$ to$_{\{STRONG\}}$ $[_{VP}$ be t_i here $]\,]\,]\,]\,]\,]$

Someone checks the EPP-feature of *to* in (41b) and later enters into an agreement relation with the light verb (cf. (43b)). *John* is inserted in [Spec,*v*P], where it receives the external θ-role, and enters into an agreement relation with the finite T, checking the matrix EPP-features, as well (cf. (45b)). Once all [–interpretable] features are appropriately checked, the derivation converges, as desired.

To sum up, rather then presenting a problem, the contrast between (29) and (36a), repeated below in (46), actually provides support for the assumption that only convergent derivations are computed for economy purposes.

(46) a. John expected someone to be here.
      b. *John expected to be someone here.

The moral of the discussion thus far is that if we find a sentence resulting from a local violation of "Merge over Move," it must be the case that the competing derivation employing Merge doesn't converge.

Exercise 10.7

The data examined in this section seem to point to the conclusion that even if movement to θ-positions is allowed in the grammar, the resulting structures may run into Case problems. Discuss if this conclusion also holds with respect to the sentences in (i) under the derivations outlined in (ii) (see Lasnik 1992b, Hornstein 1999, 2001, and Grohmann 2000b, 2003b).

(i) a. John tried to solve the problem.
    b. John shaved

(ii) a. $[_{TP}$ John$_i$ $[_{vP}$ t$_i$ tried $[_{TP}$ t$_i$ to $[_{vP}$ t$_i$ solve the problem $]]]]$
    b. $[_{TP}$ John$_i$ $[_{vP}$ t$_i$ $[_{VP}$ shaved t$_i$ $]]]$

10.4 The derivation by phase

10.4.1 *More on economy and computational complexity*

Let's recap the general picture of economy computations discussed so far. First, the computational system doesn't compare any computation that can be made out of the whole lexicon but focuses on the computations that start from a given preselected array of lexical items, i.e. a numeration. Second, it'll only consider syntactic computations that are derivations; syntactic computations that don't exhaust the numeration or don't form a pair (π, λ), for instance, are discarded. The computational system further restricts the class of comparable derivations to the convergent ones. Finally, it only compares convergent derivations that share the same derivational history up to the point of comparison.

Assuming that computational complexity matters when economy issues are concerned, the restrictions reviewed above represent significant steps towards reducing the computational complexity involved in economy comparisons. However, there's still a very global feature in the way economy has been computed and this has to do with the well-grounded assumption that only convergent derivations can be computed for purposes of economy. Let's see how.

We've been assuming that convergence is a property of *derivations* and, furthermore, that a derivation must form a pair (π, λ). Thus, in order to decide whether or not to take an option at a given derivational step, the system must "look ahead" and see at the end of the day if the whole tree resulting from that specific option is convergent. Reconsider the derivational step in (37), repeated below in (47), for example.

(47)   a. $N_1 = \{John_1, T_1, v_1, expected_1, to_0, be_0, someone_0, here_0\}$
        b. $[_{TP} \text{ to}_{\{STRONG\}} [_{VP} \text{ be someone}_{\{P:3; \ N:SG; \ CASE:?\}} \text{ here }]]$

As discussed in section 10.3.3., the computational system has two options to check the EPP-feature of *to* in (47): merger of *John* or movement of *someone*. That is, both options are licit *at this derivational step*. The problem with the merger of *John* is, as we saw, that it'll prevent *someone* from checking its Case at some point further down the derivational road, causing the derivation to crash at the LF and PF levels. In other words, we'll have to build *the whole tree* in (48) below to learn that merger of *John* has bad derivational consequences and is not an option to be chosen at the derivational step in (47). This may seem a small burden in the case at hand, but given that sentences in natural languages can involve an unbounded number of recursions, (operational) computational complexity gets intractable very easily.

(48) $[_{TP} \text{ John}_k \text{ T } [_{vP} t_k [_{v'} v [_{VP} \text{ expected } [_{TP} t_k \text{ to be someone here }]]]]]$

Note that it's not obvious that the system doesn't have means to detect the Case problem resulting from the merger of *John* in (47) much earlier in the computation. Given that Case-checking relations are subject to minimality, as soon as the structure in (49) is formed, it's clear that the derivation won't converge: from this point on, *John* will block any potential Case-relation involving *someone*.

(49) $[_{TP} \text{ John}_{\{P:3; \ N:SG; \ CASE:?\}} \text{ to}_{\{STRONG\}}$
        $[_{VP} \text{ be someone}_{\{P:3; \ N:SG; \ CASE:?\}} \text{ here }]]$

Our task then is to search for a more local way to compute convergence in order to minimize the computational complexity involved in economy comparisons. We'll discuss one possible way to do it in the next section.

10.4.2   Phases

Take the two potential continuations of (47) sketched in (50), with merger of *John* represented in (50a) and movement of *someone* in (50b).

(50)   a. $[_{vP} v_{\{P:3; \ N:SG\}} [_{VP} \text{ expected } [_{TP} \text{ John}_{\{P:3; \ N:SG; \ CASE:ACC\}} \text{ to}_{\{STRONG\}}$
        $[_{VP} \text{ be someone}_{\{P:3; \ N:SG; \ CASE:?\}} \text{ here }]]]]$
        b. $[_{vP} v_{\{P:3; \ N:SG\}} [_{VP} \text{ expected } [_{TP} \text{ someone}_{\{P:3; \ N:SG; \ CASE:ACC\}_i}$
        $\text{to}_{\{STRONG\}} [_{VP} \text{ be } t_i \text{ here }]]]]$

As mentioned in section 10.4.1, no matter what happens after the structure in (50a) is assembled, the derivation won't converge because *someone* won't be able to check its Case due to the intervention of *John*. If the computational system could make use of this information, it wouldn't be required to proceed unnecessarily with the two computations in (50) in parallel until the derivations were fully completed. The question is how to do it in a general fashion.

Chomsky (2000) has observed that convergence is not a property inherent to the final syntactic object that reaches the interfaces; after all, any "partial" tree built along the computation may or may not be legible by the interfaces. Note, however, that if we allow the computational system to always check whether syntactic expressions are convergent, we would exclude not only unfixable structures such as one in (50a), but also structures that may become convergent at later steps of the derivation. The DP in (51a), for instance, only becomes a convergent expression after the *v*P in (51b) is built.

(51)   a. [$_{VP}$ love [$_{DP}$ the baby]$_{\{P:3; \ N:SG; \ CASE:?\}}$]
       b. [$_{vP}$ $v_{\{P:3; \ N:SG\}}$ [$_{VP}$ love [$_{DP}$ the baby]$_{\{P:3; \ N:SG; \ CASE:ACC\}}$]]

How can the system then be sure that some current lack of convergence can't be remedied later? Well, the specific contrast between (50a) and (51a) suggests that the issue may be settled once *v*P is formed. If the VPs of (50a) and (51a) are inspected for convergence after *v*P is formed, (50a) will be ruled out due to the unchecked Case-feature of *someone*, but (51a) will be ruled in, which is the desired result.

Chomsky (2000, 2001, 2004) has proposed that derivations indeed proceed in a piecemeal fashion along these lines, in the sense that convergence is inspected in installments as the computation unfolds. More concretely, Chomsky proposes that derivations proceed by *phases*, where a phase is a syntactic object whose parts (more specifically, the complement of its head) can be inspected for convergence.[10]

The *v*P headed by the Case-assigning light verb is a phase in these terms. Once a *v*P is assembled, Spell-Out applies to the complement of its head (i.e. VP), and the semantic and the phonological components inspect the shipped material. If it is legible by both interfaces (all of its features can receive an appropriate interpretation), as is the case of (50b) and (51b), the

---

10 As pointed out by Castillo, Drury, and Grohmann (1999) and Uriagereka (1999c), this
    proposal echoes the idea in Chomsky (1955, 1957) that *kernel sentences* – a term originally
    due to Harris (1951) – are the basic units of syntactic analysis and are subject to embedding
    rules.

derivation is allowed to proceed. If not, as is the case of (50a), the derivation is cancelled *at that derivational step*.

CP is also a phase in this approach. To see the motivation, let's examine the abstract structure in (52).

(52) $[_{vP} \, v \, [_{vP} \, V \, [_{CP} \, C \, [_{TP} \, DP_i \, T \, [_{vP} \, t_i \, [_{v'} \, v \, [\, V \, DP \,] \,] \,] \,] \,] \,] \,] \,]$

T heads may or may not be associated with a Case-feature. ECM and raising predicates select for a TP headed by a Caseless T, whereas C selects for a TP with a Case-marking T. In the latter circumstance, T will be associated with nominative Case if finite or null Case if non-finite (see section 4.3.4). If DP_i in (52) is PRO and T is non-finite or if DP_i is *John* and T is finite, the appropriate checking relations occur and the whole derivation may converge; whether it indeed converges or not will depend on the computations that follow. On the other hand, if the Case-properties of T and DP_i mismatch, the derivation won't converge regardless of the following computations even if the matrix light verb can check the Case of DP_i, T won't have its ϕ-features appropriately checked. In other words, the Case properties of TP in (52) are encapsulated in the sense that they are independent of a higher domain. Hence, CP may qualify as a phase in this regard. Once the computational system builds CP, it spells out the complement of C (i.e. TP), and if TP is not a convergent expression, the computation aborts *at this derivational point*.

Pushing the reduction of computational complexity further, Chomsky also assumes the *Phase Impenetrability Condition* (*PIC*) given in (53), where *edge* refers to specifiers and adjuncts to H or HP.[11]

(53)   *Phase Impenetrability Condition* (*PIC*)
        In a phase α with head H, the domain of H is not accessible to operations outside α, only H and its edge are accessible to such operations.

The intuition underlying the PIC is that once a given syntactic object has been judged convergent, it's taken to be "ready" and doesn't participate in any other syntactic computations. In other words, the computational system doesn't "backtrack" to reevaluate a previous convergent verdict under new scenarios. This makes a lot of sense, given our previous assumption that only active elements (i.e. elements with unvalued [–interpretable] features) may participate in a checking/agreeing relation (see section 9.4.3).

11 See Chomsky (2000, 2001, 2004) for different formulations and relevant discussion.

Hence, if a syntactic expression is judged convergent, all of its elements are by definition inactive for further computations.

For the sake of illustration, let's examine how the derivation of a sentence like (54) below is to proceed under this phase model of syntactic computations. After the computational builds the vP phase in (55d), the VP complement is shipped to the phonological and semantic interfaces by Spell-Out. Once all of its [–interpretable] features have been appropriately checked, the expression is judged to be convergent (annotated by "$\sqrt{}$") and the computation is allowed to proceed. Given the PIC in (53), the spelled-out material is, however, unavailable for further agreeing/checking relations.

(54)　　John thinks that Peter loves Mary

(55)　　*Phase 1*:

    a. [$_{VP}$ love Mary$_{\{P:3;\ N:SG;\ CASE:?\}}$]

    b. [$_{vP}$ $v_{\{P:?;\ N:?;\ STRONG\text{-}V\}}$ [$_{VP}$ love Mary$_{\{P:3;\ N:SG;\ CASE:?\}}$]]

    c. [$_{vP}$ love$_i$+$v_{\{P:3;\ N:SG;\ STRONG\text{-}V\}}$ [$_{VP}$ t_i Mary$_{\{P:3;\ N:SG;\ CASE:ACC\}}$]]

    d. [$_{vP}$ Peter$_{\{P:3;\ N:SG;\ CASE:?\}}$ [$_{v'}$ love$_i$+$v_{\{P:3;\ N:SG;\ STRONG\text{-}V\}}$ [$_{VP}$ t_i Mary$_{\{P:3;\ N:SG;\ CASE:ACC\}}$]]]

    e. *Spell-Out*:
       [$_{VP}$ t_i Mary$_{\{P:3;\ N:SG;\ CASE:ACC\}}$] $=\sqrt{}$

The computational system then builds the CP phase in (56c) below, where $VP^{\sqrt{}}$ annotates the fact that VP has already been judged a convergent expression and its contents are no longer available for syntactic computations. TP is spelled out (cf. (56d)) and since it has no unchecked [–interpretable] features, it converges. The computation then receives a green light, proceeding to the next phase, as shown in (57).

(56)　　*Phase 2*:

    a. [$_{TP}$ T$_{\{P:?;\ N:?;\ STRONG\}}$ [$_{vP}$ Peter$_{\{P:3;\ N:SG;\ CASE:?\}}$ [$_{v'}$ love$_i$ + $v_{\{P:3;\ N:SG;\ STRONG\text{-}V\}}$ VP$^{\sqrt{}}$]]]

    b. [$_{TP}$ Peter$_{\{P:3;\ N:SG;\ CASE:NOM\}_k}$ [$_{T'}$ T$_{\{P:3;\ N:SG;\ STRONG\}}$ [$_{vP}$ t_k [$_{v'}$ love$_i$ + $v_{\{P:3;\ N:SG;\ STRONG\text{-}V\}}$ VP$^{\sqrt{}}$]]]]

    c. [$_{CP}$ that [$_{TP}$ Peter$_{\{P:3;\ N:SG;\ CASE:NOM\}_k}$ [$_{T'}$ T$_{\{P:3;\ N:SG;\ STRONG\}}$ [$_{vP}$ t_k [$_{v'}$ love$_i$ + $v_{\{P:3;\ N:SG;\ STRONG\text{-}V\}}$ VP$^{\sqrt{}}$]]]]]

    d. *Spell-Out*: [$_{TP}$ Peter$_{\{P:3;\ N:SG;\ CASE:NOM\}_k}$ [$_{T'}$ T$_{\{P:3;\ N:SG;\ STRONG\}}$ [$_{vP}$ t_k [$_{v'}$ love$_i$ + $v_{\{P:3;\ N:SG;\ STRONG\text{-}V\}}$ VP$^{\sqrt{}}$]]]] $=\sqrt{}$

(57)　　*Phase 3*:

    a. [$_{vP}$$v_{\{P:?;\ N:?;\ STRONG\text{-}V\}}$ [$_{VP}$ think [$_{CP}$ that TP$^{\sqrt{}}$]]]

    b. [$_{vP}$ think$_m$ + $v_{\{P:3;\ N:SG;\ STRONG\text{-}V\}}$ [$_{VP}$ t_m [$_{CP}$ that TP$^{\sqrt{}}$]]]

    c. [$_{vP}$ John$_{\{P:3;\ N:SG;\ CASE:?\}}$ [$_{v'}$ think$_m$ + $v_{\{P:3;\ N:SG;\ STRONG\text{-}V\}}$ [$_{VP}$ t_m [$_{CP}$ that TP$^{\sqrt{}}$]]]]

    d. *Spell-Out*: [$_{VP}$ t_m [$_{CP}$ that TP$^{\sqrt{}}$]] $=\sqrt{}$

Assuming that CPs have {P:3; N:SG;} features, the light verb in (57a) is able to value its ϕ-features by agreeing with CP, and the vP phase in (57c) is assembled. Again, the spelled-out VP converges and the computation finally builds the CP phase in (58c) below. Spell-Out then applies to TP, which also converges. Finally, Spell-Out applies (by default) to the whole tree, and the derivation is judged to be convergent.

(58)   *Phase 4*:

    a. $[_{TP} T_{\{P:?;\ N:?;\ \textbf{STRONG}\}} [_{vP} John_{\{P:3;\ N:SG;\ CASE:?\}}$
       $[_{v'} think_m + v_{\{P:3;\ N:SG;\ STRONG\text{-}V\}} VP^{\surd}]]]$

    b. $[_{TP} John_{\{P:3;\ N:SG;\ CASE:NOM\}_w} [_{T'} T_{\{P:3;\ N:SG;\ STRONG\}}$
       $[_{vP} t_w [_{v'} think_m + v_{\{P:3;\ N:SG;\ STRONG\text{-}V\}} VP^{\surd}]]]]$

    c. $[_{CP} C [_{TP} John_{\{P:3;\ N:SG;\ CASE:NOM\}_w} [_{T'} T_{\{P:3;\ N:SG;\ STRONG\}}$
       $[_{vP} t_w [_{v'} think_m + v_{\{P:3;\ N:SG;\ STRONG\text{-}V\}} VP^{\surd}]]]]]$

    d. *Spell-Out*: $[_{TP} John_{\{P:3;\ N:SG;\ CASE:NOM\}_w} [_{T'}$
       $T_{\{P:3;\ N:SG;\ STRONG\}}$
       $[_{vP} t_w [_{v'} think_m + v_{\{P:3;\ N:SG;\ STRONG\text{-}V\}} VP^{\surd}]]]] = \surd$

    e. *Spell-Out*: $[_{CP} C\ TP^{\surd}] = \surd$

To summarize, by assuming that the computation of convergence proceeds phase by phase, we are able to both maintain the well-grounded assumption that only convergent derivations can be compared for economy purposes and reduce the computational complexity involved in such comparisons. Computational options (merger or movement, for instance) are compared within a single phase.

This approach raises several interesting conceptual questions. Note, for instance, the radical derivational nature of computations under this view. Not only are syntactic objects built in a step-by-step fashion, but the interfaces are fed with information as the derivation proceeds. This raises the possibility that as the derivation proceeds, the interfaces access syntactic computations directly, in a dynamic fashion, without the mediation of LF or PF.[12]

It should also be pointed out that the proposal that Spell-Out may apply multiple times is a welcome development from a conceptual point of view. One could have said that there's a vestige of S-Structure hidden under the assumption that Spell-Out applies only once, as in Chomsky's (1995) model (see discussion in section 2.3.1.6).[13] If the phase-based approach to syntactic computations is on the right track, on the other hand, there is no resemblance to an SS-like computational split, for the shipping of

---

12 See especially Epstein, Groat, Kawashima, and Kitahara (1998) for a worked out model.
13 See Uriagereka (1999c) for the original observation and further discussion.

relevant information to the interpretive components occurs several times, in a piecemeal fashion.

Another question that arises in this approach is why exactly *v*Ps and CPs should be phases and, more generally, how many kinds of phases there are.[14]

All of these questions are currently the subject of a very lively debate and we won't be able to explore them in depth here.[15] For the sake of presenting an overview of the whole approach, in the discussion that follows we'll focus on the role of CPs and *v*Ps as phases.

Exercise 10.8

Assuming the phase-based approach outlined in the text, present the complete derivation of the sentences in (i).

(i) a. There seems to be someone here.
     b. Someone seems to be here.
     c. John expected someone to be here.
     d. It seems that John was told that Mary won the competition.

Exercise 10.9

Chomsky (2000: 106) suggests that a phase should be "the closest syntactic counterpart to a proposition: either a verb phrase in which all θ-roles are assigned or a full clause including tense and force." If this reasoning is correct how many phases are there in the derivation of the sentences in (i)? Are there problems in conceiving a "closed" thematic unit a phase?

(i) a. John arrived.
     b. Bill was arrested.
     c. Mary's discussion of the paper was very illuminating.
     d. Joe considers Susan brilliant.

Exercise 10.10

In this section we've explored phases mainly from a Case perspective. More specifically, a phase was taken to be the projection of a head that defined its complement as an "encapsulated" Case domain. With this in mind, discuss whether PPs and DPs can in principle be analyzed as phases and if there are advantages in so doing.

14 See, e.g., Uriagereka (1999a, 2000b), Epstein and Seely (2002, 2005), Boeckx (2003a), and Grohmann (2003b), for critical discussion.
15 For relevant discussion, see among others Nissenbaum (2000), Bruening (2001), Bobaljik and Wurmbrand (2003), Hiraiwa (2003), Legate (2003), Matushansky (2003), Boeckx and Grohmann (2004), Müller (2004), Richards (2004), Chomsky (2005a, 2005b) and the references given in note 14.

10.4.3   Subarrays

In section 10.3.2. we discussed reasons for assuming that only derivations that start with the same numeration and share the same derivational history can be compared for economy purposes. With this in mind, consider the sentences in (59), whose derivations arguably start with the (simplified) numeration in (60).

(59)   a. Someone is wondering whether there is someone here.
        b. There is someone wondering whether someone is here.

(60)   a. $N_0 = \{C_1, someone_2, is_2, v_1, wondering_1, whether_1, there_1, here_1\}$

After some computations, we reach the derivational step in (61) below, where we have two options to check the EPP-feature of *is*: either merger of the expletive *there*, which is still available in the reduced numeration N_1, or movement of *someone*. Given the discussion in section 10.4.2, we need not wait until the completion of the whole derivation resulting from each of these options to compute convergence and decide which option to take. We should rather inspect convergence resulting from each option when the first phase following the step in (61) is completed. This is illustrated in (62), with merger of *there*, and (63), with movement of *someone*.

(61)   a. $N_1 = \{C_1, someone_1, is_1, v_1, wondering_1, whether_1, there_1, here_0\}$
        b. [$_{TP}$ is someone here]

(62)   a. $N_2 = \{C_1, someone_1, is_1, v_1, wondering_1, whether_0, there_0, here_0\}$
        b. [$_{CP}$ whether [$_{TP}$ there is someone here]]
        c. *Spell-Out*:
           [$_{TP}$ there is someone here] $= \checkmark$

(63)   a. $N_{2'} = \{C_1, someone_1, is_1, v_1, wondering_1, whether_0, there_1, here_0\}$
        b. [$_{CP}$ whether [$_{TP}$ someone$_i$ is t$_i$ here]]
        c. *Spell-Out*:
           [$_{TP}$ someone$_i$ is t$_i$ here] $= \checkmark$

Now here's the problem: as shown in (62c) and (63c), the two options lead to convergent results. Thus, these options are effectively eligible for economy comparison at the derivational step represented in (61), and the simpler option of merger should block the more complex option of movement (see section 10.3.2). In other words, we incorrectly predict that the derivation of (59a) should block the derivation of (59b).[16]

---

16 See Uriagereka (1997, 1999a), who attributes the observation of the problematic nature of pairs like the one in (59) to Juan Romero and Alec Marantz (but see Wilder and Gärtner 1997 for first discussion). For further discussion, see also Castillo, Drury, and Grohmann (1999) and Frampton and Gutmann (1999), among others.

Several reactions to these cases are reasonable. The economy account assumed above is tightly tied to the specific assumptions concerning the proper analysis of existential constructions. In particular, we've been assuming that the associate checks its Case against a finite T or a light verb and that *there* need not check Case at all. However, this analysis is not without its critics and slightly different assumptions may have important consequences in the current setting.

Suppose, for instance, that both the associate and the expletive need to check Case. If so, then it's reasonable to assume that it's *there* that checks its Case against a finite T or a matrix light verb. Whence the Case of the associate? A likely candidate would be the *be* that one finds in such constructions.[17] For the sake of the reasoning, let's then assume that there are two lexical entries for *be*: the "existential *be*," which is able to check Case, and the "copula *be*," which isn't. That this possibility is not unlikely is shown by the fact that many languages actually use different verbs for copula and existential constructions. In Brazilian Portuguese, for instance, the translation of the sentences in (59) would involve the existential *ter* 'have' and the copula *estar* 'be', as illustrated in (64).

(64)   *Brazilian Portuguese*
   a. Alguém está questionando se   tem alguém aqui.
      someone is   wondering   whether has someone here
      'Someone is wondering whether there is someone here.'
   b. Tem alguém questionando se   alguém está aqui.
      has someone wondering   whether somebody is   here.
      'There is someone wondering whether someone is here.'

If we do indeed have two different lexical entries for *be*, the acceptability of both sentences in (59) or (64) should pose no problems for economy computations. The sentences in (59), for example, should be built from the numeration in (65) below, rather than (60). Crucially, the distinct instances of *be* are appropriately encoded in (65). The derivations of (59a) and (59b) would then not be comparable because they wouldn't share the same derivational history. The derivation of (59a) would select the "existential *be*" first, as illustrated in (66), and the derivation of (59b) would select the "copula *be*" first, as shown in (67). Once the two derivations are not comparable, the fact that both lead to admissible results is not an issue.

17 See Belletti (1988) and Lasnik (1992a) for this proposal.

(65) $N_{0'} = \{C_1,$ someone$_2$, is$_{\{-\text{Case}\}_1}$, is$_{\{+\text{Case}\}_1}$, v_1, wondering$_1$, whether$_1$, there$_1$, here$_1\}$

(66)   a. $N_{1'} = \{C_1,$ someone$_1$, is$_{\{-\text{Case}\}_1}$, is$_{\{+\text{Case}\}_0}$, v_1, wondering$_1$, whether$_1$, there$_1$, here$_0\}$
         b. [$_{\text{TP}}$ is$_{\{+\text{Case}\}}$ someone here]

(67)   a. $N_{1''} = \{C_1,$ someone$_1$, is$_{\{-\text{Case}\}_0}$, is$_{\{+\text{Case}\}_1}$, v_1, wondering$_1$, whether$_1$, there$_1$, here$_0\}$
         b. [$_{\text{TP}}$ is$_{\{-\text{Case}\}}$ someone here]

Putting aside the motivations discussed in section 9.3.3 for assuming that *there* doesn't have a Case-feature, it should be pointed out that the analysis outlined above requires further duplication of lexical entries, for the potentially problematic cases are not restricted to *there*-constructions involving the verb *be*. The pairs of sentences in (68)–(70) present the same kind of violation of the preference for merger over movement.

(68)   a. There remains the fact that a problem developed.
         b. The fact remains that there developed a problem.

(69)   a. There arose the problem that a typo remained in the proofs.
         b. The problem arose that there remained a typo in the proofs.

(70)   a. There remains the suspicion that a problem exists.
         b. The suspicion remains that there exists a problem.

There's, however, an alternative account of the paradigm in (59) and (68)–(70) that doesn't force us to commit to *ad hoc* duplications of lexical entries. We've seen that resorting to a numeration as a starting point rather than allowing the computational system to have direct access to the lexicon is a way to reduce computational complexity. In section 10.4.2, we discussed a proposal to further reduce computational complexity by having the system compute convergence at phases, rather than at the end of the derivation only. Chomsky (2000, 2001, 2004) argues that these two proposals should be connected. More specifically, he proposes that a numeration is actually composed of subarrays, each of which containing one instance of a lexical item that can head a phase. If only CPs and vPs constitute phases, every numeration should then have the format illustrated in (71).

(71) $N = \{\{C_1, \ldots \}, \{v_1, \ldots \}, \ldots\}$

The intuition is that certain lexical items, the ones that can head a phase, introduce natural computational boundaries for inspecting convergence. Assuming that the system strives to reduce computational complexity, a numeration should then be structured around such items.

Taking this suggestion to be on the right track, a derivation proceeds in the following way. The computational system activates a subarray σ_1 from the numeration and builds a phase PH, using all the lexical items listed σ_1. It then spells out the complement of the head of PH. If the spelled-out expression is not convergent, the computation aborts and no further steps are taken. If it is convergent, the computation is allowed to proceed and the system activates a new subarray σ_2, repeating the previous procedures. A derivation is completed only after all subarrays have been exhausted.

With this picture in mind, let's return to the derivation of the sentences in (59), repeated here in (72), from the numeration in (60), repeated in (73).

(72)   a. Someone is wondering whether there is someone here.
        b. There is someone wondering whether someone is here.

(73) $N_0 = \{C_1,$ someone$_2,$ is$_2,$ $v_1,$ wondering$_1,$ whether$_1,$ there$_1,$ here$_1\}$

Under this new conception of how numerations should be internally organized, the lexical items of the numeration in (73) should be (arbitrarily) distributed among the subarrays containing the phase heads C, v, and *whether*. Two of the possible arrangements of the lexical items listed in (73) that may arise are given in (74) and (75).

(74) $N_1 = \{\{C_1,$ is$_1\},$ {someone$_1,$ $v_1,$ wondering$_1\},$ {whether$_1,$ there$_1,$ is$_1,$ someone$_1,$ here$_1\}\}$

(75) $N_2 = \{\{C_1,$ is$_1,$ there$_1\},$ {someone$_1,$ $v_1,$ wondering$_1\},$ {whether$_1,$ is$_1,$ someone$_1,$ here$_1\}\}$

N_1 and N_2 only differ in that *there* is part of the subarray defined by *whether* in (74), but part of the subarray defined by C in (75). However small, this distinction is sufficient to make them different. Hence, derivations starting from N_1 and N_2 can't be compared for the same reason the derivations of (76a) and (77a) can't be compared: they involve distinct arrays of lexical items!

(76)   a. There is someone here.
        b. $N = \{\{C_1,$ there$_1,$ is$_1,$ someone$_1,$ here$_1\}\}$

(77)   a. Someone is here.
        b. $N' = \{\{C_1,$ is$_1,$ someone$_1,$ here$_1\}\}$

We now have the key to account for the puzzle presented by the sentences in (72). Given the numeration N_1 in (74), if the system activates the array determined by *whether*, the computation may proceed until the derivational step in (78) below is reached. Given that *there* is available in the activated array, the preference for Merge over Move is ensured and the sentence in (72a) may be derived after further computations.

(78)   a. $N_{1'} = \{\{C_1, is_1\}, \{someone_1, v_1, wondering_1\}, \{whether_1, there_1, is_0, someone_0, here_0\}\}$
       b. [is someone here]

Given the numeration N_2 in (75), in turn, the system activates the subarray determined by *whether* and computes until it reaches the derivational step in (79) below. Here there's no choice with respect to the phase that is being computed; since there's no expletive in the activated subarray, *someone* must move to check the EPP-feature of *to* and further computations then derive the sentence in (72b).[18]

(79)   a. $N_{2'} = \{\{C_1, is_1, there_1\}, \{someone_1, v_1, wondering_1\}, \{whether_1, is_0, someone_0, here_0\}\}$
       b. [is someone here]

To summarize, in this section it was suggested that the computational system doesn't take into consideration all instances of the lexical items of a numeration at once; it instead operates with smaller subarrays that are defined in terms of lexical items that can head phases. This development substantially narrows the pool of potential options to be examined, thereby further reducing the computational complexity of syntactic derivations.

Exercise 10.11

Provide a detailed analysis of the derivations of the sentences in (70), repeated here in (i), paying special attention to the relevant phases and the subarrays that underlie them.

(i)   a. There remains the suspicion that a problem exists.
      b. The suspicion remains that there exists a problem.

Exercise 10.12

Which of the numerations in (ii) below should provide a convergent derivation for (i)? To put it in general terms, does it matter if the external argument belongs

---

18 For further discussion of the role of subarrays in the computation, see among others Nunes and Uriagereka (2000), Hornstein and Nunes (2002), and Nunes (2004).

to the subarray determined by the light verb or by the one determined by the complementizer?

(i)   John loves Mary.

(ii)   a. $N_1 = \{\{C_1, T_1\}, \{John_1, v_1, love_1, Mary_1\}\}$
      b. $N_2 = \{\{C_1, T_1, John_1\}, \{v_1, love_1, Mary_1\}\}$

Exercise 10.13

The numerations in (i) below involve the same lexical items. However, only one of them leads to convergent result. Which one is it? Why exactly do the computations starting with the other numerations fail?

(i)   a. $N_1 = \{\{C_1, T_1, the_2,\}, \{boy_1, v_1, saw_1, girl_1\}\}$
      b. $N_2 = \{\{C_1, T_1, the_1, boy_1\}, \{the_1, v_1, saw_1, girl_1\}\}$
      c. $N_3 = \{\{C_1, T_1, the_1, boy_1, saw_1\}, \{the_1, v_1, girl_1\}\}$

Exercise 10.14

In the text, we only examined derivations that start with the subarray that underlies the most embedded phase. Discuss whether this needs to be stipulated in the system.

Exercise 10.15

Suppose TPs should also count as phases. What should then be the relevant numerations underlying the derivation of the sentences in (i) below? Would we be able to account for the contrast between (ia) and (ib)? If so, how? If not, why not?

(i)   a.   There seems to be someone here.
      b.   *There seems someone to be here.

Exercise 10.16

In this section we assumed that a numeration determines which subarrays will feed the computation. Suppose, by contrast, that the computation works in a phase-by-phase fashion but doesn't resort to the notion of numeration. That is, the computational system dives into the lexical well, forms a subarray, builds a phase and spells out the complement of its head; if the spelled-out material is a convergent expression, the system then returns to the lexicon, forms a new subarray, and continues the computation. Compare this alternative to the one presented in the text and discuss if one is to be preferred over the other.

10.4.4   Working on the edge

So far we've focused our attention on A-relations (Case and ϕ-features checking). Let's now turn to A'-relations.

Let's start our discussion by considering the standard derivation of a *wh*-sentence such as (80a), for instance, as represented in (80b), where *wh*-movement proceeds in a successive-cyclic way, first targeting the embedded [Spec, CP] before reaching its final position.

(80)   a. What did you say that John ate?
        b. [$_{CP}$ what$_i$ did you say [$_{CP}$ t$_i$ [$_{IP}$ John ate t$_i$]]]

The evidence for successive-cyclic *wh*-movement is just overwhelming.[19] Over the years, it has received solid support from both the LF and the PF sides of the grammar. Support offered by the LF part is found, for instance, in the interpretive role played by traces in intermediate [Spec,CP] positions. The interpretation of the anaphor *himself* in (81a), for instance, receives a straightforward account if *wh*-movement leaves a copy of the *wh*-phrase in the embedded [Spec,CP], as shown in (81b), from where *himself* can be locally bound by *John* (see section 8.3.1).

(81)   a. Which picture of himself did John say that Mary liked?
        b. [$_{CP}$ [which picture of himself] did John say [$_{CP}$ [which picture of himself] that Mary liked [which picture of himself]]]

As for motivation coming from the PF side, it's not uncommon to find morphological reflexes of successive-cyclic *wh*-movement across languages. In Irish, for instance, the declarative complementizer is *go* 'that', as shown in (82a) below; however, it gets phonetically realized as the particle *aL* if a *wh*-phrase moves through its specifier, as illustrated in (82b).[20] As shown in (82c), *aL* also shows up in all C-positions along the way in a long-distance A'-dependency (here, multiple relativization).

---

19 The idea that long-distance dependencies are formed via more local steps goes back to Chomsky (1973). See, e.g., Chung (1998), McCloskey (2002), Boeckx (2003a), and Grohmann (2003c) for recent discussion.

20 *Gur* in (82a) is an inflected form of *go*; *L* in *aL* stands for (morpho-)phonological properties of the particle that induces lenition (*aL*). To complete the paradigm, the complementizer surfaces as *aN* (where *N* stands for properties of the particle that induce nasalization) when there is resumption within the clause, as in (i) below; notice that once long *wh*-movement is not involved, the lower complementizer of (ib) surfaces as *go*. See McCloskey (1990, 2002) for further data, extensive discussion, and additional references on complementizer properties in Irish.

(82) *Irish*
a. Creidim **gu-r** inis sé bréag.
   believe.1.SG GO-PAST tell he lie
   'I believe that he told a lie.'
b. Céacu ceann **a** dhíol tú?
   which one AL sold you
   'Which one did you sell?'
c. [[an t-ainm]ᵢ [**a** hinnseadh dúinn [**a** bhí tᵢ ar an áit]]]
   the name AL was.told to.us AL was on the place
   'the name that we were told was on the place'

In face of the robustness of the evidence for A′-movement through intermediate specifiers of CP, one can't help but wonder *why* there exists successive-cyclic movement in the grammar. Think of it. If a *wh*-element must move to enter into some relation with an interrogative complementizer, *why* must it also stop in the specifier of every non-interrogative complementizer on its way? Shouldn't there be some sort of feature mismatch in these intermediate movements? Within Chomsky's (1986a) *Barriers*-framework, this question was even more mysterious, for A′-moved elements were also required to adjoin to all intervening VPs. The derivation of the sentence in (80a), for instance, would proceed along the lines of (83), with *what* adjoining to both the matrix and the embedded VP on its way to the matrix [Spec,CP].

(83) [$_{CP}$ what$_i$ did$_k$ + Q [$_{IP}$ you t$_k$ [$_{VP}$ t$_i$ [$_{VP}$ say [$_{CP}$ t$_i$ [$_{IP}$ John [$_{VP}$ t$_i$ [$_{VP}$ ate t$_i$]]]]]]]]]

Although there are pressing questions of technical implementation without obvious answers, the phase-based approach developed in sections 10.4.2 and 10.4.3 provides an interesting rationale for successive-cyclic movement. To see this, take the derivation of (80a) under the phase-based approach. Given the numeration in (84), the computation proceeds until the derivational step in (85) is reached.

(i) *Irish*
a. Céacu ceann **a** bhuil dúil agat ann?
   which one AN is liking at.you in.it
   'Which one do you like?'
b. cúpla muirear **a** bhféadfá a rá **go** rabhadar bocht
   couple households AN could.2.SG say.NON-FIN GO were.3.PL poor
   'a few households that you could say were poor'

(84) $N_0 = \{\{Q_1, did_1\}, \{you_1, v_1, say_1\}, \{that_1, T_1\}, \{John_1, v_1, ate_1, what_1\}\}$

(85)   a. $N_1 = \{\{Q_1, did_1\}, \{you_1, v_1, say_1\}, \{that_1, T_1\}, \{John_0, v_0, ate_0, what_0\}\}$
        b. $[_{vP}$ John $[_{v'}$ v $[_{VP}$ eat what $]]]$

Now, if Spell-Out applies to VP in (85b), *what* will be unavailable for further computations, in compliance with the PIC, repeated below in (86). In particular, it won't be able to check the strong *wh*-feature of the interrogative complementizer, which will be later introduced in the derivation.

(86)   *Phase Impenetrability Condition (PIC)*
        In a phase α with head H, the domain of H is not accessible to operations outside α, only H and its edge are accessible to such operations.

Notice that, according to the PIC, the complement of the head of a phase is out of reach for further computations, but its edge is accessible. Now the role of successive cyclicity becomes clear. If *what* in (85) manages to move to the outer [Spec,vP], as shown in (87), *before* VP is spelled out, it'll be available for further computations.

(87)   a. $N_2 = \{\{Q_1, did_1\}, \{you_1, v_1, say_1\}, \{that_1, T_1\}, \{John_0, v_0, ate_0, what_0\}\}$
        b. $[_{vP}$ what$_i$ $[_{v'}$ John $[_{v'}$ v $[_{VP}$ eat t_i $]]]]$
        c. *Spell-Out*:
            $[_{VP}$ eat t_i $] = \checkmark$

The same considerations apply to the derivational step in (88) below, where the next phase is being built. If TP is spelled out, *what* will be trapped and won't be able to move. However, if it moves to the edge of the CP phase, as shown in (89), it'll still be in the game.

(88)   a. $N_3 = \{\{Q_1, did_1\}, \{you_1, v_1, say_1\}, \{that_0, T_0\}, \{John_0, v_0, ate_0, what_0\}\}$
        b. $[_{CP}$ that $[_{TP}$ John$_k$ T $[_{vP}$ what$_i$ $[_{v'}$ t_k $[_{v'}$ v VP$^{\checkmark}$ $]]]]]$

(89)   a. $N_3 = \{\{Q_1, did_1\}, \{you_1, v_1, say_1\}, \{that_0, T_0\}, \{John_0, v_0, ate_0, what_0\}\}$
        b. $[_{CP}$ what$_i$ $[_{C'}$ that $[_{TP}$ John$_k$ T $[_{vP}$ t_i $[_{v'}$ t_k $[_{v'}$ v VP$^{\checkmark}$ $]]]]]]$
        c. *Spell-Out*:
            $[_{TP}$ John$_k$ T $[_{vP}$ t_i $[_{v'}$ t_k $[_{v'}$ v VP$^{\checkmark}$ $]]]] = \checkmark$

Similar movement to the edge takes place in the next vP phase, as illustrated in (90), which finally allows *what* to reach the specifier of the interrogative complementizer, as shown in (91).

(90)   a. $N_4 = \{\{Q_1, did_1\}, \{you_0, v_0, say_0\}, \{that_0, T_0\}, \{John_0, v_0, ate_0, what_0\}\}$
        b. $[_{vP}$ what$_i$ $[_{v'}$ you $[_{v'}$ v $[_{VP}$ say $[_{CP}$ t_i $[_{C'}$ that TP$^{\checkmark}$ $]]]]]]$

c. *Spell-Out*:
   [$_{VP}$ say [$_{CP}$ t$_i$ [$_{C'}$ that TP$^\checkmark$]]] = $\checkmark$

(91)   a. N$_5$ = {{Q$_0$, did$_0$}, {you$_0$, v_0, say$_0$}, {that$_0$, T$_0$}, {John$_0$, v_0, ate$_0$, what$_0$}}
       b. [$_{CP}$ what$_i$ [$_{C'}$ did$_w$ + Q [$_{TP}$ you$_x$ [$_{vP}$ t$_i$ [$_{v'}$ t$_x$ [$_{v'}$ v VP$^\checkmark$]]]]]]
       c. *Spell-Out*:
          [$_{TP}$ you$_x$ [$_{vP}$ t$_i$ [$_{v'}$ t$_x$ [$_{v'}$ v VP$^\checkmark$]]]] = $\checkmark$
       d. *Spell-Out*:
          [$_{CP}$ what$_i$ [$_{C'}$ did$_w$ + Q TP$^\checkmark$]] = $\checkmark$

As mentioned above, although the phase model suggests a new way of looking at successive-cyclic A'-movement, at the moment it's not so clear how to technically implement it. Thus, we won't dwell on the issue of technical execution further here, not because it's unimportant, but because it's not even obvious that we have a good metric to choose among possibilities. The only thing that is clear is that by providing a completely fresh look at syntactic computations, the phase model resuscitates some aspects of the *Barriers*-framework with a cleaner apparatus. In particular, A'-movement must use the edge of vP as a escape hatch in a way similar to adjunction to VP in *Barriers*.

Interestingly, we also find evidence for these local movements to the edge both on the LF and PF sides. Consider the sentence in (92), for instance.

(92)   Which picture of himself does John expect Mary to buy?

Given that (92) is an ECM construction, the embedded clause arguably doesn't have a CP layer. That being so, we wouldn't be able to explain the licensing of *himself* if the *wh*-phrase moved directly to [Spec,CP], as illustrated in (93) below. By contrast, if syntactic computations must proceed by phases, the *wh*-phrase must pass through the outer [Spec,vP] both in the embedded and in the main clause, as illustrated in (94). Once there's a copy of the *wh*-phrase in the matrix vP, it may be used for interpretation and *himself* will be appropriately licensed by *John*.

(93)   [$_{CP}$ [which picture of himself]$_i$ does John expect [$_{IP}$ Mary to buy t$_i$]]

(94)   [$_{CP}$ [which picture of himself]$_i$ does John [$_{vP}$ t$_i$ [$_{v'}$ expect [$_{IP}$ Mary to [$_{vP}$ t$_i$ [$_{v'}$ buy t$_i$]]]]]]

Consider now the Bahasa Indonesia data in (95), which respectively illustrate *wh-in situ* and *wh*-movement constructions in this language.[21]

---

21 See Saddy (1991) for the data in (95) and relevant discussion of *wh*-relations in Bahasa Indonesia.

(95)   *Bahasa Indonesia*
    a. Bill men-gira Tom men-harap Fred men-cintai siapa?
        Bill TR-*thinks Tom* TR-*expects Fred* TR-*loves   who*
    b. Siapa yang Bill Ø-kira   Tom Ø-harap   Fred Ø-cintai?
        *who *FOC* Bill   think Tom   expect Fred   love*
        'Who did Bill think (that) Tom expects (that) Fred loves?'

Men- in (95a) is a prefix used with transitive verbs. The relevant point for us here is that this prefix is deleted if *wh*-movement takes place. Details aside, the dropping of the prefix may be interpreted as a morphological reflex of the movement of the *wh*-phrase to the edge of each *v*P phase.

To sum up. The phase model of syntactic computations was primarily motivated by A-type of relations. And this was due to the fact that certain syntactic objects constitute natural boundaries for Case and agreeing relations, which are considerably local. A′-relations, by contrast, are typically long-distance and this at first sight creates a potential problem for the phase model. We've shown, however, that despite the fact that there's much technical work yet to be done, the phase model may in fact establish a general framework in which it'll be possible to meaningfully address the tough question of *why* there's successive-cyclic movement in the grammar.

Exercise 10.17

Consider the following technical implementation for movement to the edge (see Chomsky 2000 for relevant discussion). Once a phase is finished and the computational system detects the presence of "A′-features" in the complement of the head of the phase, it assigns a kind of EPP-feature, call it an edge-feature, to the head of the phase, triggering successive-cyclic movement before Spell-Out. Discuss whether this suggestion is able to account for long-distance *wh*-movement sentences such as (ia) and exclude sentences such as (ib).

(i) a. What did you say John wrote?
     b. *Mary thinks what John ate.

Exercise 10.18

In this section it was suggested that successive-cyclic *wh*-movement is indirectly triggered by the PIC. Can this reasoning also be extended to instances of successive-cyclic A-movement such as (i)? If so, how? If not, why not?

(i) John is likely to be expected to be arrested.

Exercises 10.19

Can the phase analysis of *wh*-movement suggested in this section also be extended to *in situ wh*-phrases, as illustrated in (i)? If so, how? If not, why not?

   (i) Who gave what to whom?

Is your answer compatible with the Bahasa Indonesia data in (95)?

10.5   Economy of lexical resources

Another kind of economy thinking has been part of the descriptive armamentarium of generative grammar since its inception. Consider the classical paradigm of *do*-support in English illustrated in (96), for instance.

(96)   a. John loves bagels.
         b. *John does love bagels. [*do* unstressed]
         c. John does not love bagels.
         d. *John not loves bagels.

The contrast between (96c) and (96d) shows that *do* is required in negated sentences. The reason is that negation is thought to block affixation between the inflectional morphology and the verb (in effect, because of the negation, the verb and affix are too far apart to interact). *Do* is then inserted in this context to "support" the affixal material in T, thereby allowing the derivation to converge.[22] Of more interest for current purposes is the contrast between (96a) and (96b). In (96a) the tense material appears on the verb *loves*. What is curious is that we can't have (96b). The latter would be the result of inserting *do* and putting the material on it, much as we do in (96c). This, however, is forbidden. Why?

    The standard description is that *do*-support is only permitted where it is required. Restated in economy terms, this means that the acceptability of (96a) blocks the derivation of (96b). Chomsky (1991) provides the beginnings of a possible account of such a blocking in terms of least effort (see sections 1.3 and 5.2). Let's say that elements like *do* are expensive to use. There can be several reasons for this. Chomsky suggests that this might be because it is a language-particular "rescue" device. If so, then derivations that can converge without using *do* are more economical than those that

22 This sort of account has been a staple of generative analysis since Chomsky (1957) (see Lasnik with Depiante and Stepanov 2000). For more contemporary versions, see, e.g., Bobaljik (1995b) and Lasnik (1995a).

use it. Of course, if convergence is not possible without using *do*, as in (96c–d), then its use is permitted.

This is the standard description of *do*-support. What is interesting is that this description makes sense if grammars are indeed subject to economy considerations. We should now ask how this general idea is to be integrated with the technology we elaborated in the previous sections. Take the derivations of (96a) and (96b), for example. A good first guess would be that the numerations underlying these two derivations are the ones in (97) and (98), respectively.

(97) $N_1 = \{\{C_1, T_1\}, \{John_1, v_1, love_1, bagels_1\}\}$

(98) $N_2 = \{\{C_1, T_1, do_1\}, \{John_1, v_1, love_1, bagels_1\}\}$

But if this were correct, how could we compare the derivations of (96a) and (96b)? After all, the numerations in (97) and (98) are different and so the derivations built from them should not be comparable. In effect, both should converge, contrary to fact.[23]

The most straightforward way of capturing the intuition that the derivations of (96a) and (96b) do compete is to first examine if the numeration in (97) leads to a convergent result; *only if it doesn't* should the system then be allowed to add *do* to the computation. Given that (97) can yield a convergent derivation, namely, the one that generates (96a), the system doesn't trigger the alternative and (96b) isn't even taken into consideration.

The last resort nature of *do*-support thus suggests that *do* is a non-lexical grammatical formative whose use is costly. To put in general terms, it seems that the computational system is also subject to optimality considerations in the use of its lexical resources: it'll attempt to stick to the lexical items it has at its disposal and will consider other possibilities only if it is forced to.[24]

Exercise 10.20

The paradigm of negative concord in languages such as Italian, as illustrated in (i), resembles that of *do*-support in the sense that the negative element *non* is inserted only when a preverbal element is not negative (see Bošković 2001). Discuss if the paradigm in (i) can also be analyzed in terms of economy of lexical resources.

---

23 This problem was first pointed out by Mark Arnold (see Arnold 1995).

24 For relevant discussion, see also Bošković's (1997) proposal that economy may require that some clauses be realized as IPs (i.e. TPs) instead of CPs, and Hornstein's (2001) analysis of pronominalization as a costly lexical resource.

(i)   *Italian*
     a. *(Non)   ho   visto   nessuno.
        not   have.1.SG seen   nobody
        'I haven't seen anybody.'
     b. Nessuno (*non) ha   detto   niente.
        nobody   not   have.3.SG said   nothing
        'Nobody said anything.'

10.6   Conclusion

In this chapter, we've reviewed some motivations for introducing derivational comparisons into the grammar. The idea is that the computational system aims to accomplish its business optimally. It does this by using the "best" (in the sense of slightest) rules it can at any given point. We've discussed two general kinds of economy comparisons: economy of computations (Merge is preferred to Move as the latter is more complex than the former) and economy of lexical resources (non-lexical elements like *do* are inherently expensive). The general pursuit of computational simplicity also led us to the discussion of the notions of phases and subarrays, which lie at the heart of much contemporary research on syntactic theory within minimalism.

At this point, you are definitely prepared to dig into the original material and should get ready to take an active part in the minimalist enterprise. Good luck!

Glossary of minimalist definitions

(1) *Binding Theory*
    (i)   *Principle A*: If α is an anaphor, interpret it as coreferential with a c-commanding phrase in its domain.
    (ii)   *Principle B*: If α is a pronoun, interpret it as disjoint from every c-commanding phrase in its domain.
    (iii)   *Principle C*: If α is an R-expression, interpret it as disjoint from every c-commanding phrase.
    [see chap. 8 (61)]

(2) *C-Command*
    α c-commands β iff
    (i) α is a sister of β or
    (ii) α is a sister of γ and γ dominates β.
    [see chap. 7 (13)]

(3) *Equidistance*
    If two positions α and β are in the same MinD, they are equidistant from any other position.
    [see chap. 5 (57)/(73); for tentative formulations, see chap. 5 (22)/(51) and exercise 5.7]

(4) *Extension Condition*
    Applications of Merge can only target root syntactic objects.
    [see chap. 9 (55); for tentative formulations, see chap. 2 (90), chap. 4 (29), chap. 8 (73)/(74), and chap. 9 (7)/(25)/(54)]

(5) *Extended Minimal Domain*
    The MinD of a chain formed by adjoining the head Y^0 to the head X^0 is the union of $MinD(Y^0)$ and $MinD(X^0)$, excluding projections of Y^0.
    [see chap. 5 (21)/(42)]

(6)   *Inclusiveness Condition*
The LF object λ must be built only from the features of the lexical items of N.
[see chap. 2 (116)]

(7)   *Intermediate Projection: X'*
An intermediate projection is a syntactic object that is neither an X^0 nor an XP.
[see chap. 6 (61)]

(8)   *Last Resort*
A movement operation is licensed only if it allows the elimination of [–interpretable] formal features.
[see chap. 9 (11)]

(9)   *Linear Correspondence Axiom (LCA)*
A lexical item α precedes a lexical item β iff
(i) α asymmetrically c-commands β or
(ii)   an XP dominating α asymmetrically c-commands β.
[see chap. 7 (17); for a tentative formulation, see chap. 7 (14)]

(10)   *Maximal Projection: XP*
A maximal projection is a syntactic object that doesn't project.
[see chap. 6 (60)]

(11)   *Minimal Domain of α (MinD(α))*
The set of categories immediately contained or immediately dominated by projections of the head α, excluding projections of α.
[see chap. 5 (20)]

(12)   *Minimal Projection: X^0*
A minimal projection is a lexical item selected from the numeration.
[see chap. 6 (59)]

(13)   *Phase Impenetrability Condition (PIC)*
In a phase α with head H, the domain of H is not accessible to operations outside α, only H and its edge are accessible to such operations.
[see chap. 10 (53)/(101)]

(14)   *Predicate-Internal Subject Hypothesis (PISH)*
The thematic subject is base-generated inside the predicate.
[see chap. 3, section 3.2.2]

(15)   *Preference Principle*
Try to minimize the restriction in the operator position.
[see chap. 8 (47)]

(16)   *Theta-Role Assignment Principle (TRAP)*
θ-roles can only be assigned under a Merge operation.
[see chap. 2 (68)/(106)]

(17)   *Uniformity Condition*
The operations available in the covert component must be the same ones available in overt syntax.
[see chap. 2 (117)]

References

Abels, K. 2003. "Successive cyclicity, anti-locality, and adposition stranding," PhD thesis, University of Connecticut, Storrs.

Abney, S. R. 1987. "The noun phrase in its sentential aspect," PhD thesis, Massachusetts Institute of Technology, Cambridge.

Abraham, W. 1995. *Deutsche Syntax im Sprachenvergleich: Grundlegung einer typologischen Syntax des Deutschen*, Tübingen: Gunter Narr.

Ackerman, F. and J. Moore. 2001. *Proto-Properties and Grammatical Encoding: A Correspondence Theory of Argument Selection*, Stanford, CA: CSLI Publications.

Ackerman, F. and G. Webelhuth. 1998. *A Theory of Predicates*, Stanford, CA: CSLI Publications.

Adger, D. 1994. "Functional heads and interpretation," PhD thesis, University of Edinburgh.

Adger, D. 2003. *Core Syntax: A Minimalist Approach*, Oxford: Oxford University Press.

Adger, D. and G. Ramchand. 2005. "Merge and move: *Wh*-dependencies revisited," *Linguistic Inquiry* **36**, 161–93.

Agbayani, B. and E. Zoerner. 2004. "Gapping, pseudogapping and sideward movement," *Studia Linguistica* **58**, 185–211.

Albizu, P. 1997. "The syntax of person agreement," PhD thesis, University of Southern California, Los Angeles.

1998. "Generalized person-case constraint: A case for a syntax-driven inflectional morphology", in A. Mendikoetxea and M. Uribe-Etxebarria (eds.), *Theoretical Issues on the Morphology-Syntax Interface*, San Sebastian: Supplements of the *Anuario del Seminario Julio de Urquijo*, 1–34.

Alexiadou, A. 1997. *Adverb Placement: A Case Study in Antisymmetric Syntax*, Amsterdam: John Benjamins.

Alsina, A., J. Bresnan, and P. Sells. 1997. *Complex Predicates*, Stanford, CA: CSLI Publications.

Anagnostopoulou, E. 2003. *The Syntax of Ditransitives: Evidence from Clitics*, Berlin: Mouton de Gruyter.

Aoun, J. 1979. "On government, case marking, and clitic placement," ms., Massachusetts Institute of Technology, Cambridge.

1982. "On the logical nature of the binding principles: Quantifier lowering, double raising of *there* and the notion empty element," in J. Pustejovsky and

P. Sells (eds.), *Proceedings of NELS 12*, Amherst, MA: University of Massachusetts, GLSA Publications, 16–35.

Aoun, J., E. Benmamoun, and D. Sportiche. 1994. "Agreement, word order, and conjunction in some varieties of Arabic," *Linguistic Inquiry* **25**, 195–220.

Aoun, J. and R. Clark. 1985. "On non-overt operators," *Southern California Occasional Papers in Linguistics* **10**, 17–36.

Aoun, J., N. Hornstein, D. W. Lightfoot, and A. Weinberg. 1987. "Two types of locality," *Linguistic Inquiry* **18**, 537–77.

Aoun, J. and Y. -H. A. Li. 1993. *Syntax of Scope*, Cambridge, MA: MIT Press.

Aoun, J. and J. Nunes. 1997. "Vehicle change and Move-F," paper presented at the Colloque de syntaxe et sémantique à Paris, Université de Paris 7, October 16–18, 1997. [To appear as "Vehicle change phenomena as an argument for Move-F," *Linguistic Inquiry*.]

Aoun, J. and D. Sportiche. 1983. "On the formal theory of government," *The Linguistic Review* **2**, 211 36.

Archangeli, D. and T. Langendoen (eds.). 1997. *Optimality Theory: An Overview*, Oxford: Blackwell.

Arnold, M. D. 1995. "Case, periphrastic *do*, and the loss of verb movement in English," PhD thesis, University of Maryland, College Park.

Authier, J. -M. 1988. "The syntax of unselective binding," PhD thesis, University of Southern California, Los Angeles.

   1991. "V-governed expletives, case theory, and the projection principle," *Linguistic Inquiry* **22**, 721–42.

Bach, E. 1962. "The order of elements in a transformational grammar of German," *Language* **38**, 263–69.

Baker, C. L. 1978. *Introduction to Generative-Transformational Syntax*, Englewood Cliffs, NJ: Prentice-Hall.

Baker, M. C. 1988. *Incorporation: A Theory of Grammatical Function changing*, Chicago, IL: University of Chicago Press.

   1997. "Thematic roles and grammatical categories," in L. Haegeman (ed.), *Elements of Grammar: Handbook of Generative Syntax*, Dordrecht: Kluwer, 73–137.

   2001. *The Atoms of Language: The Mind's Hidden Rules of Grammar*, New York, NY: Basic Books.

   2003. *Lexical Categories: Verbs, Nouns, and Adjectives*, Cambridge: Cambridge University Press.

Baker, M. C., K. Johnson, and I. G. Roberts. 1989. "Passive arguments raised," *Linguistic Inquiry* **20**, 219–51.

Baltin, M. R. and C. Collins (eds.). 2001. *The Handbook of Contemporary Syntactic Theory*, Oxford: Blackwell.

Barss, A. 1986. "Chains and anaphoric dependencies," PhD thesis, Massachusetts Institute of Technology, Cambridge.

Barss, A. and H. Lasnik. 1986. "A note on anaphora and double objects," *Linguistic Inquiry* **17**, 347–54.

Bashir, E. 1987. "Agreement in Kashmiri infinitive complements," in E. Bashir, M. M. Deshpande, and P. E. Hook (eds.), *Select Papers from SALA-7*, Bloomington, IN: Indiana University Linguistics Club, 13–27.

Bastos, A. 2001. "*Fazer, eu faço!* Topicalização de constituintes verbais en português brasileiro," MA thesis, Universidade Estadual de Campinas.

Bayer, J. 1987. "The syntax of scalar predicates and so-called 'floating quantifiers'," ms., Max-Plank-Institut für Psycholinguistik, Nijmegen.

Beck, S. and K. Johnson. 2004. "Double objects again," *Linguistic Inquiry* **35**, 97–124.

Belletti, A. 1988. "The case of unaccusatives," *Linguistic Inquiry* **19**, 1–34.

1990. *Generalized Verb Movement: Aspects of Verb Syntax*, Turin: Rosenberg and Sellier.

(ed.). 2004. *Structures and Beyond: The Cartography of Syntactic Structures*, Vol. III, Oxford: Oxford University Press.

Belletti, A. and L. Rizzi. 1988. "Psych-verbs and θ-theory," *Natural Language & Linguistic Theory* **6**, 291–352.

Bergvall, V. L. 1987. "The position and properties of in situ and right-moved questions in Kikuyu," in D. Odden (ed.), *Current Approaches to African Linguistics*, Vol. IV, Dordrecht: Foris, 37–51.

Bernstein, J. 2001. "The DP hypothesis: Identifying clausal properties in the nominal domain," in Baltin and Collins (2001), 536–61.

Berwick, R. C. 1985. *The Acquisition of Syntactic Knowledge*, Cambridge, MA: MIT Press.

den Besten, H. 1977. "On the interaction of root transformations and lexical deletive verbs," ms., Massachusetts Institute of Technology, Cambridge and Universiteit van Amsterdam. [Appeared in den Besten (1989).]

1985. "The ergative hypothesis and free word order in Dutch and German," in J. Toman (ed.), *Studies in German Grammar*, Dordrecht: Foris, 23–64.

1989. "Studies in West Germanic syntax," PhD thesis, Katholieke Universiteit Brabant, Tilburg.

Bickerton, D. 1990. *Language and Species*, Chicago, IL: University of Chicago Press.

Bobaljik, J. D. 1995a. "In terms of merge: Copy and head movement," *MIT Working Papers in Linguistics* **27**, 41–64.

1995b. "Morphosyntax: The syntax of verbal inflection," PhD thesis, Massachusetts Institute of Technology, Cambridge.

2002. "A-chains at the PF-interface: Copies and 'covert' movement," *Natural Language & Linguistic Theory* **20**, 197–267.

2003. "Floating quantifiers: Handle with care," in L. L.-S. Cheng and R. Sybesma (eds.), *The Second Glot International State-of-the-Art Book*, Berlin: Mouton de Gruyter, 107–48.

Bobaljik, J. D. and S. Brown. 1997. "Inter-arboreal operations: Head-movement and the extension requirement," *Linguistic Inquiry* **28**, 345–56.

Bobaljik, J. D. and D. Jonas. 1996. "Subject positions and the roles of IP," *Linguistic Inquiry* **27**, 195–236.

Bobaljik, J. D. and H. Thráinsson. 1998. "Two heads aren't always better than one," *Syntax* **1**, 37–71.

Bobaljik, J. D. and S. Wurmbrand. 2003. "Relativizing phases," ms., McGill University, Montreal/University of Connecticut, Storrs. [To appear as "Domains of Agreement," *Natural Language & Linguistic Theory*.]

Boeckx, C. 2000. "EPP eliminated," ms., University of Connecticut, Storrs.
  2002. "On labels in syntax," ms., University of Illinois, Urbana-Champaign.
  2003a. *Islands and Chains*, Amsterdam: John Benjamins.
  2003b. "(In)direct binding," *Syntax* **6**, 213–36.
  2004. "Bare syntax," ms., Harvard University, Cambridge, MA.
Boeckx, C. and K. K. Grohmann. 2003. "Introduction," in C. Boeckx and
  K. K. Grohmann (eds.), *Multiple* Wh-*Fronting*, Amsterdam: John
  Benjamins, 1–15.
  2004. "Putting phases into perspective," ms., Harvard University, Cambridge,
  MA, and University of Cyprus, Nicosia. [To appear in *Syntax*.]
Boeckx, C. and N. Hornstein. 2003. "Reply to 'Control is not movement',"
  Linguistic Inquiry **34**, 269–80.
  2004. "Movement under control," *Linguistic Inquiry* **35**, 431–52.
Boeckx, C., N. Hornstein, and J. Nunes. 2004. "Overt copies in reflexive
  and control structures: A movement analysis," ms., Harvard University,
  Cambridge, MA, University of Maryland, College Park, and Universidade
  de São Paulo.
Bonet, E. 1991. "Morphology after syntax," PhD thesis, Massachusetts Institute of
  Technology, Cambridge.
Borer, H. 1984. *Parametric Syntax*, Dordrecht: Foris.
Bošković, Ž. 1994. "D-structure, theta criterion, and movement into theta posi-
  tions," *Linguistic Analysis* **24**, 247–86.
  1997. *The Syntax of Nonfinite Complementation: An Economy Approach*,
  Cambridge, MA: MIT Press.
  1998. "LF movement and the minimalist program", in P. N. Tamanji and
  K. Kusumoto (eds.), *Proceedings of NELS 28*, Amherst, MA: University of
  Massachusetts, GLSA Publications, 43–57.
  2001. *On the Nature of the Syntax-Phonology Interface: Cliticization and Related
  Phenomena*. Amsterdam: Elsevier Science.
  2002a. "On multiple *wh*-fronting," *Linguistic Inquiry* **33**, 351–83.
  2002b. "A-movement and the EPP," *Syntax* **5**, 167–218.
  2003. "On left branch extraction," in P. Kosta, J. Blaszczak, J. Frasek, L. Geist,
  and M. Żygis (eds.), *Investigations into Formal Slavic Linguistics:
  Contributions of the Fourth European Conference on Formal Description of
  Slavic Languages – FDSL IV*, Frankfurt am Main: Peter Lang, 543–77.
  2004. "Be careful where you float your quantifiers," *Natural Language &
  Linguistic Theory* **22**.
Bošković, Ž. and H. Lasnik. 2005. *The Minimalist Program: Essential Readings*,
  Oxford: Blackwell.
Bošković, Ž. and J. Nunes. 2004. "The copy theory of movement: A view
  from PF," ms., University of Connecticut, Storrs and Universidade de
  São Paulo.
Bošković, Ž. and D. Takahashi. 1998. "Scrambling and last resort," *Linguistic
  Inquiry* **29**, 347–66.
Bouchard, D. 1984. *On the Content of Empty Categories*, Dordrecht: Foris.
  1995. *The Semantics of Syntax*, Chicago, IL: University of Chicago Press.

Bowers, J. S. 1973. "Grammatical relations," PhD thesis, Massachusetts Institute of Technology, Cambridge. [Published 1981 as *The Theory of Grammatical Relations*, Ithaca, NY: Cornell University Press.]

Brame, M. 1982. "The head-selector theory of lexical specifications and the non-existence of coarse categories," *Linguistic Analysis* **10**, 321–25.

Bresnan, J. 1972. "On sentence stress and syntactic transformations," in M. Brame (ed.), *Contributions to Generative Phonology*, Austin, TX: University of Texas Press, 73–107.

   1982. *The Mental Representation of Grammatical Relations*, Cambridge, MA: MIT Press.

Brody, M. 1995. *Lexico-Logical Form*, Cambridge, MA: MIT Press.

Browning, M. A. 1987. "Null operator constructions," PhD thesis, Massachusetts Institute of Technology, Cambridge.

Bruening, B. 2001. Syntax at the edge: Cross-clausal phenomena and the Syntax of Passamaquoddy. PhD thesis, Massachusetts Institute of Technology, Cambridge.

Burton, S. and J. Grimshaw. 1992. "Coordination and VP-internal subjects," *Linguistic Inquiry* **23**, 305–13.

Burzio, L. 1986. *Italian Syntax*, Dordrecht: Reidel.

Butler, A. and E. Mathieu. 2004. *The Syntax and Semantics of Split Constructions: A Comparative Study*, Basingstoke: Palgrave-Macmillan.

Cann, R. 1999. "Specifiers as secondary heads," in D. Adger, S. Pintzuk, B. Plunkett, and G. Tsoulas (eds.), *Specifiers: Minimalist Approaches*, Oxford: Oxford University Press, 21–45.

Cardinaletti, A. and M.-T. Guasti (eds.). 1995. *Small Clauses*, San Diego, CA: Academic Press.

Cardinaletti, A. and M. Starke. 1999. "*The typology of structural deficiency: A case study of the three classes of pronouns*," in van Riemsdijk (1999), 145–233.

Carnie, A. 2001. *Syntax: A Generative Introduction*, Oxford: Blackwell.

Carston, R. 1996. "The architecture of the mind: Modularity and modularization," in D. W. Green (ed.), *Cognitive Science: An Introduction*, Oxford: Blackwell, 53–83.

Castillo, J. C., J. Drury, and K. K. Grohmann. 1999. "Merge over move and the extended projection principle," *University of Maryland Working Papers in Linguistics* **8**, 63–103.

Cattell, R. 1978. "On the source of interrogative adverbs," *Language* **54**, 61–77.

Chametzky, R. A. 2000. *Phrase Structure: From GB to Minimalism*, Oxford: Blackwell.

   2003. "Phrase structure," in R. Hendrick (ed.), *Minimalist Syntax*, Oxford: Blackwell, 192–225.

Chang, L. 1997. "*Wh-in situ* phenomena in French," MA thesis, University of British Columbia, Vancouver.

Cheng, L. L.-S. 1991. "On the typology of *wh*-questions," PhD thesis, Massachusetts Institute of Technology, Cambridge. [Published 1997, New York, NY: Garland.]

Cheng, L. L.-S. and J. Rooryck. 2000. "Licensing *wh-in situ*," *Syntax* **3**, 1–19.

Chomsky, N. 1955. "The logical structure of linguistic theory," ms., Harvard University and Massachusetts Institute of Technology, Cambridge. [Revised

1956 manuscript published in part as *The Logical Structure of Linguistic Theory* by New York, NY: Plenum, 1975; Chicago, IL: University of Chicago Press, 1985.]

1957. *Syntactic Structures*, The Hague: Mouton.

1964. *Current Issues in Linguistic Theory*, The Hague: Mouton.

1965. *Aspects of the Theory of Syntax*, Cambridge, MA: MIT Press.

1970. "Remarks on nominalizations," in R. A. Jacobs and P. S. Rosenbaum (eds.), *Readings in English Transformational Grammar*, Waltham, MA: Ginn and Company, 184–221.

1973. "Conditions on transformations," in S. R. Anderson and P. Kiparsky (eds.), *A Festschrift for Morris Halle*, New York, NY: Holt, Rinehart, and Winston, 232–86.

1977. "On *wh*-movement," in P. W. Culicover, T. Wasow, and A. Akmajian (eds.), *Formal Syntax*, New York, NY: Academic Press, 71–132.

1981. *Lectures on Government and Binding*, Dordrecht: Foris.

1982. *Some Concepts and Consequences of the Theory of Government and Binding*, Cambridge, MA: MIT Press.

1986a. *Barriers*, Cambridge, MA: MIT Press.

1986b. *Knowledge of Language: Its Nature, Origin and Use*, New York, NY: Praeger.

1991. "Some notes on economy of derivation and representation," in R. Freidin (ed), *Principles and Parameters in Generative Grammar*, Cambridge, MA: MIT Press, 417–54. [Reprinted in Chomsky (1995), 129–66.]

1993. "A minimalist program for linguistic theory," in K. Hale and S. J. Keyser (eds.), *The View from Building 20: Essays in Linguistics in Honor of Sylvain Bromberger*, Cambridge, MA: MIT Press, 1–52. [Reprinted in Chomsky (1995), 167–217.]

1995. *The Minimalist Program*, Cambridge, MA: MIT Press.

1999. "Derivation by phase," *MIT Occasional Papers in Linguistics* **18**. [Revised version appeared as Chomsky 2001.]

2000. "Minimalist inquiries: The framework," in R. Martin, D. Michaels, and J. Uriagereka (eds.), *Step by Step: Essays on Minimalist Syntax in Honor of Howard Lasnik*, Cambridge, MA: MIT Press, 89–155.

2001. "Derivation by phase," in M. Kenstowicz (ed.), *Ken Hale: A Life in Language*, Cambridge, MA: MIT Press, 1–52.

2004. "Beyond explanatory adequacy," in Belletti (2004), 104–31.

2005a. "Three factors in language design," *Linguistic Inquiry* **36**, 1–22.

2005b. "On phases," ms., Massachusetts Institute of Technology, Cambridge. [To appear in C. P. Otero et al. (eds.), *Foundational Issues in Linguistic Theory*, Cambridge, MA: MIT Press.]

Chomsky, N. and H. Lasnik. 1977. "Filters and control," *Linguistic Inquiry* **8**, 425–504.

1993. "The theory of principles and parameters," in J. Jacobs, A. von Stechow, W. Sternefeld, and T. Vennemann (eds.), *Syntax: An International Handbook of Contemporary Research*, Berlin: Walter de Gruyter, 506–69. [Reprinted in Chomsky (1995), 13–127.]

Chung, S. 1998. *The Design of Agreement: Evidence from Chamorro*, Chicago, IL: University of Chicago Press.

Cinque, G. 1984. "A′-bound *pro* vs. variable," ms., Università di Venezia.

1999. *Adverbs and Functional Heads: A Cross-Linguistic Perspective*, Oxford: Oxford University Press.

(ed.). 2002. *The Structure of IP and DP: The Cartography of Syntactic Structures*, Vol. I, Oxford: Oxford University Press.

Citko, B. 2005. "On the nature of merge: external merge, internal merge, and parallel merge," *Linguistic Inquiry* **36**.

Clark, R. and I. G. Roberts. 1993. "A computational model of language learnability and language change," *Linguistic Inquiry* **24**, 299–345.

Collins, C. 1996. *Local Economy*, Cambridge, MA: MIT Press.

2002. "Eliminating labels," in S. D. Epstein and T. D. Seely (eds.), *Derivation and Explanation in the Minimalist Program*, Oxford: Blackwell, 42–64.

Collins, C. and H. Thráinsson. 1996. "VP-internal structure and object shift in Icelandic," *Linguistic Inquiry* **27**, 391–444.

Contreras, H. 1987. "Small clauses in Spanish and English," *Natural Language & Linguistic Theory* **5**, 225–44.

1993. "On null operator structures," *Natural Language & Linguistic Theory* **11**, 1–30.

Cook, V. J. and M. Newson. 1996. *Chomsky's Universal Grammar: An Introduction*, Oxford: Blackwell, second edition.

Corver, N. 1990. "The syntax of left branch extractions," PhD thesis, Katholieke Universiteit Brabant, Tilburg.

Crain, S. and D. Lillo-Martin. 1999. *An Introduction to Linguistic Theory and Language Acquisition*, Oxford: Blackwell.

Crain, S. and P. Pietroski. 2001. "Nature, nurture and Universal Grammar," *Linguistics and Philosophy* **24**, 139–86.

Crain, S. and R. Thornton. 1998. *Investigations in Universal Grammar: A Guide to Experiments on the Acquisition of Syntax and Semantics*, Cambridge, MA: MIT Press.

Culicover, P. W. and P. M. Postal. 2001. *Parasitic Gaps*, Cambridge, MA: MIT Press.

Culicover, P. W. and W. K. Wilkins. 1984. *Locality in Linguistic Theory*, Orlando, FL: Academic Press.

Curtiss, S. 1977. *Genie: A Psycholinguistic Study of a Modern-Day "Wild Child"*, New York, NY: Academic Press.

Davis, H. 2001. "Is there a pronominal argument parameter?," paper presented at the Workshop on the Role of Agreement in Argument Structure, Utrecht Institute of Linguistics/OTS, Universiteit Utrecht, August 31–September 1, 2001.

deGraff, M. 1999a. "Creolization, language change, and language acquisition: A prolegomenon," in de Graff (1999b), 1–46.

(ed.). 1999b. *Language Creation and Language Change: Creolization, Diachrony, and Development*, Cambridge, MA: MIT Press.

DeLancey, S. 1997. "What an innatist argument should look like," in T. Haukioja, M. -L. Helasvuo, and M. Miestamo (eds.), *SKY 1997 (Yearbook of the*

Linguistic Association of Finland), Helsinki: Linguistic Association of Finland, 7–24.

den Dikken, M. 1995a. Particles: *On the Syntax of Verb-Particle, Triadic and Causative Constructions*, Oxford: Oxford University Press.

den Dikken, M. 1995b. "Binding, expletives and levels," *Linguistic Inquiry* **26**, 347–54.

den Dikken, M. and A. Giannakidou. 2002. "From *hell* to polarity: 'Aggressively non-D-linked' *wh*-phrases as polarity items," *Linguistic Inquiry* **33**, 31–61.

den Dikken, M. and R. Sybesma. 1998. "*Take* serials light up the middle," ms. CUNY Graduate Center, New York and Universiteit Leiden.

DiSciullo, A.-M. and E. Williams. 1987. *On the Definition of Word*, Cambridge, MA: MIT Press.

Dobrovie-Sorin, C. 1990. "Clitic-doubling, *wh*-movement and quantification," *Linguistic Inquiry* **22**, 1–27.

Dowty, D. 1991. "Thematic proto-roles, argument selection, and lexical semantic defaults," *Language* **67**, 547–619.

Dresher, B. E. 1998. "Charting the learning path: Cues to parameter setting," *Linguistic Inquiry* **29**, 27–67.

Eliseu, A. 1984. "Trabalho de síntese para provas de aptidão pedagógica e capacidade científica," ms., Universidade de Lisboa.

Emonds, J. E. 1976. *A Transformational Approach to English Syntax: Root, Structure-Preserving, and Local Transformations*, New York, NY: Academic Press.

1978. "The verbal complex V'-V in French," *Linguistic Inquiry* **9**, 151–75.

1985. *A Unified Theory of Syntactic Categories*, Dordrecht: Foris.

Emonds, J. E. and R. Ostler. 2005. "Double object constructions," in M. Everaert and H. van Riemsdijk (eds.), *The Blackwell Companion to Syntax*, Oxford: Blackwell.

Engdahl, E. 1983. "Parasitic gaps," *Linguistics and Philosophy* **6**, 5–34.

Epstein, S. D. 1999. "Un-principled syntax: The derivation of syntactic relations," in S. D. Epstein and N. Hornstein (eds.), *Working Minimalism*, Cambridge, MA: MIT Press, 317–45.

Epstein, S. D., E. M. Groat, R. Kawashima, and H. Kitahara. 1998. *A Derivational Approach to Syntactic Relations*, Oxford: Oxford University Press.

Epstein, S. D. and T. D. Seely. 2002. "Rule applications as cycles in a level-free syntax," in S. D. Epstein and T. D. Seely (eds.), *Derivation and Explanation in the Minimalist Program*, Oxford: Blackwell, 65–89.

2005. *Transformations and Derivations*, Cambridge: Cambridge University Press.

Ernst, T. 2001. *The Syntax of Adjuncts*, Cambridge: Cambridge University Press.

Fabb, N. 1984. "Syntactic affixation," PhD thesis, Massachusetts Institute of Technology, Cambridge.

Fanselow, G. 1992. "'Ergative' Verben und die Struktur des deutschen Mittelfelds," in L. Hoffmann (ed.), *Deutsche Syntax: Ansichten und Aussichten*, Berlin: de Gruyter, 276–303.

Fassi Fehri, A. 1980. "Some complement phenomena in Arabic, lexical grammar, the complementizer phrase hypothesis and the non-accessibility condition," ms., University of Rabat.

Felser, C. and L. M. Rupp. 2001. "Expletives as arguments: Germanic existential sentences revisited," *Linguistische Berichte* **187**, 289–324.

Ferreira, M. 2000. "Uma observação sobre a lugar da teoria da ligação e do critério temático dentro do programa minimalista," *DELTA* **16.1**, 139–48.

Fiengo, R. and R. May. 1994. *Indices and Identity*, Cambridge, MA: MIT Press.

Fodor, J. A. 1983. *The Modularity of Mind*, Cambridge, MA: MIT Press.

Fodor, J. D. 2001. "Setting syntactic parameters," in Baltin and Collins (2001), 730–67.

Fox, D. 1999. "Reconstruction, binding theory, and the interpretation of chains," *Linguistic Inquiry* **30**, 157–96.

Frampton, J. and S. Gutmann. 1999. "Cyclic computation, a computationally efficient minimalist syntax," *Syntax* **2**, 1–27.

Frank, R. 2002. *Phrase Structure Composition and Syntactic Dependencies*, Cambridge, MA: MIT Press.

Freidin, R. 1978. "Cyclicity and the theory of grammar," *Linguistic Inquiry* **9**, 519–49.

    1986. "Fundamental issues in the theory of binding," in B. Lust (ed.), *Studies in the Acquisition of Anaphora*, Dordrecht: Reidel, 151–81.

    (ed.). 1991. *Principles and Parameters in Comparative Grammar*, Cambridge, MA: MIT Press.

    1992. *Foundations of Generative Syntax*, Cambridge, MA: MIT Press.

    1999. "Cyclicity and minimalism," in S. D. Epstein and N. Hornstein (eds.), *Working Minimalism*, Cambridge, MA: MIT Press, 95–126.

Fukui, N. 1986. "A theory of category projection and its applications," PhD thesis, Massachusetts Institute of Technology, Cambridge.

    1988. "Deriving the differences between English and Japanese: A case study in parametric syntax," *English Linguistics* **5**, 249–70.

Gärtner, H. -M. 2002. *General Red Transformations and Beyond: Reflections on Minimalist Syntax*, Berlin: Akademie Verlag.

Gazdar, G. 1981. "Unbounded dependencies and coordinate structure," *Linguistic Inquiry* **12**, 155–84.

Gazdar, G., G. Pullum, I. A. Sag, and T. Wasow. 1982. "Coordination and transformational grammar," *Linguistic Inquiry* **13**, 663–77.

Georgopoulos, C. 1991. *Syntactic Variables: Resumptive Pronouns and A′-Binding in Palauan*, Dordrecht: Kluwer.

Gibson, E. and K. Wexler. 1994. "Triggers," *Linguistic Inquiry* **25**, 407–54.

Giusti, G. 1989. "Floating quantifiers, scrambling, and configurationality," *Linguistic Inquiry* **20**, 633–41.

Golston, C. 1995. "Syntax outranks phonology: Evidence from Ancient Greek," *Phonology* **12**, 343–68.

Goodall, G. 1987. *Parallel Structures in Syntax*, Cambridge: Cambridge University Press.

Green, L. J. 2002. *African American English: A Linguistic Introduction*, Cambridge: Cambridge University Press.

Grimshaw, J. and A. Mester. 1988. "Light verbs and theta-marking," *Linguistic Inquiry* **19**, 205–32.

Groat, E. M. 1995. "English expletives: A minimalist approach," *Linguistic Inquiry* **26**, 354–65.

Grohmann, K. K. 1998. "Syntactic inquiries into discourse restrictions on multiple interrogatives," *Groninger Arbeiten zur germanistischen Linguistik* **42**, 1–60.

  2000a. "Towards a syntactic understanding of prosodically reduced pronouns," *Theoretical Linguistics* **25**, 149–84.

  2000b. "Prolific peripheries: A radical view from the left," PhD thesis, University of Maryland, College Park.

  2003a. "German is a multiple *wh*-fronting language!" in C. Boeckx and K. K. Grohmann (eds.), *Multiple* Wh-*Fronting*, Amsterdam: John Benjamins, 99–130.

  2003b. *Prolific Domains: On the Anti-Locality of Movement Dependencies.* Amsterdam: John Benjamins.

  2003c. "Successive cyclicity under (anti-)local considerations," *Syntax* **6**, 260–312.

  2004. "Natural relations," ms., University of Cyprus, Nicosia.

Grohmann, K. K., J. Drury, and J. C. Castillo. 2000. "No more EPP," in R. Billerey and B. D. Lillehaugen (eds.), *WCCFL 19: Proceedings of the 19th West Coast Conference on Formal Linguistics*, Somerville, MA: Cascadilla Press, 153–66.

Grosu, A. 2003. "A unified theory of 'standard' and 'transparent' free relatives," *Natural Language & Linguistic Theory* **21**, 247–331.

Guasti, M.-T. 2002. *Language Acquisition: The Growth of Grammar*, Cambridge, MA: MIT Press.

Haegeman, L. 1994. *Introduction to Government & Binding Theory*, Oxford: Blackwell, second edition.

Haïk, I. 1985. "The syntax of operators," PhD thesis, Massachusetts Institute of Technology, Cambridge.

Hale, K. and S. J. Keyser. 1993. "On argument structure and the lexical expression of grammatical relations," in K. Hale and S. J. Keyser (eds.), *The View from Building 20: Essays in Linguistics in Honor of Sylvain Bromberger*, Cambridge, MA: MIT Press, 53–110.

  2002. *Prolegomenon to a Theory of Argument Structure*, Cambridge, MA: MIT Press.

Halle, M. and A. Marantz. 1993. "Distributed morphology and the pieces of inflection," in K. Hale and S. J. Keyser (eds.), *The View from Building 20: Essays in Linguistics in Honor of Sylvain Bromberger*, Cambridge, MA: MIT Press, 111–76.

Hamblin, C. L. 1973. "Questions in Montague English," *Foundations of Language* **10**, 41–53.

Harbert, W. 1995. "Binding theory, control, and *pro*," in Webelhuth (1995b), 177–240.

Harris, Z. 1951. *Methods in Structural Linguistics*, Chicago, IL: University of Chicago Press.

Henry, A. 1995. *Belfast English and Standard English: Dialect Variation and Parameter Setting*, Oxford: Oxford University Press.

Heycock, C. 1995. "Asymmetries in reconstruction," *Linguistic Inquiry* **26**, 547–70.

Hicks, G. 2003. " 'So easy to look at, so hard to define': *Tough* movement in the minimalist framework," MA thesis, University of York.

Higginbotham, J. 1983. "Logical form, binding, and nominals," *Linguistic Inquiry* **14**, 395–420.

  1985. "On semantics," *Linguistic Inquiry* **16**, 547–93.

Higginbotham, J. and R. May. 1981. "Questions, quantifiers, and crossing," *The Linguistic Review* **1**, 41–79.

Hiraiwa, K. 2003. "Cyclic locality", ms., Massachusetts Institute of Technology, Cambridge.

Hirose, T. 2003. "The syntax of D-linking," *Linguistic Inquiry* **34**, 499–506.

Holm, J. 1988. *Pidgins and Creoles, Vol. 1: Theory and Structure*, Cambridge: Cambridge University Press.

  2000. *An Introduction to Pidgins and Creoles*, Cambridge: Cambridge University Press.

Holmberg, A. 1986. "Word order and syntactic features in the Scandinavian languages and English," PhD thesis, Stockholms Universitet.

  1999. "Remarks on Holmberg's generalization," *Studia Linguistica* **53**, 1–39.

  2000. "Scandinavian stylistic fronting: how any category can become an expletive," *Linguistic Inquiry* **31**, 445–83.

  2005. "Stylistic Fronting," in M. Everaert and H. van Riemsdijk (eds.), *The Blackwell Companion to Syntax*, Oxford: Blackwell.

Holmberg, A. and C. Platzack. 1995. *The Role of Inflection in Scandinavian Syntax*, Oxford: Oxford University Press.

Holmer, A. 2002. "The Iberian-Caucasian connection in a typological perspective," ms., Lunds Universitet.

Hornstein, N. 1995. *Logical Form: From GB to Minimalism*, Oxford: Blackwell.

  1998. "Movement and chains," *Syntax* **1**, 99–127.

  1999. "Movement and control," *Linguistic Inquiry* **30**, 69–96.

  2000. "Existentials, A-chains, and reconstruction," in *DELTA* **16 special**, 45–79.

  2001. *Move! A Minimalist Theory of Construal*, Oxford: Blackwell.

  2003. "On control", in R. Hendrick (ed.), *Minimalist Syntax*, Oxford: Blackwell, 6–81.

Hornstein, N. and H. Kiguchi. 2004. "PRO gate and movement," *Proceedings of the 25th Annual Penn Linguistics Colloquium. University of Pennsylvania Working Papers in Linguistics* **8.1**, 33–46.

Hornstein, N. and D. W. Lightfoot. 1981. "Introduction," in N. Hornstein and D. W. Lightfoot (eds.), *Explanation in Linguistics: The Logical Problem of Language Acquisition*, London: Longman, 9–31.

Hornstein, N. and J. Nunes. 2002. "On asymmetries between parasitic gap and across-the-board constructions," *Syntax* **5**, 26–54.

Hornstein, N. and A. Weinberg. 1990. "On the necessity of LF," *The Linguistic Review* **7**, 129–67.

Huang, C.-T. J. 1982. "Logical relations in Chinese and the theory of grammar," PhD thesis, Massachusetts Institute of Technology, Cambridge.

1993. "Reconstruction and the structure of VP: Some theoretical consequences," *Linguistic Inquiry* **24**, 103–38.

Inkelas, S. and D. Zec (eds.). 1990. *The Phonology-Syntax Connection*, Chicago, IL: University of Chicago Press.

1995. "Syntax-phonology interface," in J. A. Goldsmith (ed.), *The Handbook of Phonological Theory*, Oxford: Blackwell, 535–49.

Jackendoff, R. 1972. *Semantic Interpretation in Generative Grammar*, Cambridge, MA: MIT Press.

1977. *X-Bar Syntax: A Study of Phrase Structure*, Cambridge, MA: MIT Press.

1990. "On Larson's account of the double object construction," *Linguistic Inquiry* **21**, 427–54.

Jacobs, R. and P. Rosenbaum. 1968. *English Transformational Grammar*, Waltham, MA: Blaisdell.

Jaeggli, O. 1982. *Topics in Romance Syntax*, Dordrecht: Foris.

1986. "Passive," *Linguistic Inquiry* **17**, 587–622.

Jaeggli, O. and K. Safir (eds.). 1989. *The Null Subject Parameter*, Dordrecht: Kluwer.

Janda, R. D. 1980. "On certain constructions of English's," in B. Caron, M. A. B. Hoffman, M. Silva, J. van Oosten, D. K. Alford, K. A. Hunold, M. Macauley, and J. Manley-Buser (eds.), *Proceedings of the Sixth Annual Meeting of the Berkeley Linguistics Society*, Berkeley, CA: BLS, 324–36.

Jenkins, L. 2000. *Biolinguistics: Exploring the Biology of Language*, Cambridge: Cambridge University Press.

Johnson, D. E. and S. Lappin. 1997. "A critique of the minimalist program," *Linguistics and Philosophy* **20**, 273–333.

1999. *Local Constraints vs. Economy*, Stanford, CA: CSLI Publications.

Jones, C. F. 1985. "Syntax and thematics of infinitival adjuncts," PhD thesis, University of Massachusetts, Amherst.

Jónsson, J. G. 1991. "Stylistic fronting in Icelandic," *Scandinavian Working Papers in Linguistics* **48**, 1–43.

Karttunen, L. 1977. "Presuppositions of compound sentences," *Linguistic Inquiry* **4**, 169–93.

Kato, M. 1999. "Strong pronouns, weak pronominals and the null subject parameter," *Probus* **11**, 1–37.

Kato, M. 2004. "Two types of *wh-in-situ* in Brazilian Portuguese," paper presented at the Georgetown University Round Table: Comparative and Cross-Linguistic Research in Syntax, Semantics, and Computational Linguistics (GURT 2004), March 26–29, 2004.

Kato, M. and J. Nunes. 1998. "Two sources for relative clause formation in Brazilian Portuguese," paper presented at the Eighth Colloquium on Generative Grammar, Universidade de Lisboa, April 19–22, 1998.

Kayne, R. S. 1975. *French Syntax: The Transformational Cycle*, Cambridge, MA: MIT Press.

1976. "French relative *que*," in F. Hensey and M. Luján (eds.), *Current Studies in Romance Linguistics*, Washington, DC: Georgetown University Press, 255–99.

1981. "ECP extensions," *Linguistic Inquiry* **12**, 93–133.

1984. *Connectedness and Binary Branching*, Dordrecht: Foris.

1985. "L'accord du participe passé en francais et en italien," *Modèles Linguistiques* 7, 73–89. [English version published as "Past participle agreement in French and Italian," in Kayne (2000), 10–24.]

1989. "Facets of Romance past participle agreement," in P. Benincà (ed.), *Dialect Variation and the Theory of Grammar*, Dordrecht: Foris, 85–104. [Reprinted in Kayne (2000), 25–39.]

1991. "Romance clitics, verb movement, and PRO," *Linguistic Inquiry* **22**, 647–86. [Reprinted in Kayne (2000), 60–97.]

1994. *The Antisymmetry of Syntax*, Cambridge, MA: MIT Press.

2000. *Parameters and Universals*, Oxford: Oxford University Press.

Kiguchi, H. 2002. "Syntax unchained," PhD thesis, University of Maryland, College Park.

É. Kiss, K. 2002. *The Syntax of Hungarian*, Cambridge: Cambridge University Press.

Kitagawa, Y. 1986. "Subjects in Japanese and English," PhD thesis, University of Massachusetts, Amherst.

Kitahara, H. 1997. *Elementary Operations and Optimal Derivations*, Cambridge, MA: MIT Press.

Koizumi, M. 1993. "Object agreement phrases and the split VP hypothesis," *MIT Working Papers in Linguistics* **18**, 99–148.

Koopman, H. 1984. *The Syntax of Verbs: From Verb Movement in the Kru Languages to Universal Grammar*, Dordrecht: Foris.

Koopman, H. and D. Sportiche. 1991. "The position of subjects," *Lingua* **85**, 211–58.

Koster, J. 1975. "Dutch as an SOV language," *Linguistic Analysis* **1**, 111–36.

1978. *Locality Principles in Syntax*, Dordrecht: Foris.

Kratzer, A. 1996. "Severing the external argument from its verb," in J. Rooryck and L. Zaring (eds.), *Phrase Structure and the Lexicon*, Dordrecht: Kluwer, 109–38.

Kural, M. and G. Tsoulas. 2005. "Indices and the theory of grammar," ms., University of California, Irvine and University of York.

Kuroda, S.-Y. 1988. "Whether we agree or not: A comparative syntax of English and Japanese," *Lingvisticae Investigationes* **12**, 1–47.

Labov, W., P. Cohen, C. Robins, and J. Lewis. 1968. "A study of the non-standard English of Negro and Puerto Rican Speakers in New York City," *Cooperative Research Report 3288*, Vols. I and II, Philadelphia, PA: US Regional Survey (Linguistics Laboratory, University of Pennsylvania).

Laenzlinger, C. 1998. *Comparative Studies in Word Order Variation: Adverbs, Pronouns and Clause Structure in Romance and Germanic*, Amsterdam: John Benjamins.

Laka, I. 1993. "Unergatives that assign ergative, unaccusatives that assign accusative," *MIT Working Papers in Linguistics* **18**, 149–72.

Landau, I. 1999. "Elements of control," PhD thesis, Massachusetts Institute of Technology, Cambridge. [Published 2001 as *Elements of Control: Structure and Meaning in Infinitival Constructions*, Dordrecht: Kluwer.]

Larson, R. K. 1988. "On the double object construction," *Linguistic Inquiry* **19**, 335–91.

1990. "Double objects revisited: Reply to Jackendoff," *Linguistic Inquiry* **21**, 589–632.

Lasnik, H. 1981. "Restricting the theory of transformations: A case study," in N. Hornstein and D. W. Lightfoot (eds.), *Explanations in Linguistics: The Logical Problem of Language Acquisition*, London: Longman, 152–73. [Reprinted in Lasnik, H. 1990. *Essays on Restrictiveness and Learnability*, Dordrecht: Kluwer, 125–45.]

1992a. "Case and expletives: Notes toward a parametric account," *Linguistic Inquiry* **23**, 381–405.

1992b. "Two notes on control and binding," in R. Larson, S. Iatridou, U. Lahiri, and J. Higginbotham (eds.), *Control and Grammar*, Dordrecht: Kluwer, 235–51.

1995a. "Verbal morphology: *Syntactic Structures* meets the minimalist program," in H. Campos and P. Kempchinsky (eds.), *Evolution and Revolution in Linguistic Theory: Essays in Honor of Carlos Otero*, Washington, DC: Georgetown University Press, 251–75. [Reprinted in Lasnik (1999), 97–119.]

1995b. "A note on pseudogapping," *MIT Working Papers in Linguistics* **27**, 143–63. [Reprinted in Lasnik (1999), 151–74.]

1995c. "Last resort and Attract F," in L. Gabriele, D. Hardison, and R. Westmoreland (eds.), *Proceedings of the Sixth Annual Meeting of the Formal Linguistics Society of Mid-America*, Bloomington, IN: Indiana University Linguistics Club, 62–81.

1995d. "Last resort," in S. Haraguchi and M. Funaki (eds.), *Minimalism and Linguistic Theory*, Tokyo: Hituzi Syobo Publishing, 1–32.

Lasnik, H. 1995e. "Case and expletives revisited," *Linguistic Inquiry* **26**, 615–33.

1998. "Some reconstruction riddles," *Proceedings of the 22nd Annual Penn Linguistics Colloquium. University of Pennsylvania Working Papers in Linguistics* **5.1**, 83–98.

1999. *Minimalist Analysis*, Oxford: Blackwell.

2001a. "Derivation vs. representation in modern transformational syntax," in Baltin and Collins (2001), 197–217.

2001b. "A note on the EPP," *Linguistic Inquiry* **32**, 356–62.

Lasnik, H. with M. Depiante and A. Stepanov. 2000. *Syntactic Structures Revisited: Contemporary Lectures on Classic Transformational Theory*, Cambridge, MA: MIT Press.

Lasnik, H. and R. Fiengo. 1974. "Complement object deletion," *Linguistic Inquiry* **5**, 535–71.

Lasnik, H. and M. Saito. 1984. "On the nature of proper government," *Linguistic Inquiry* **15**, 235–89.

1991. "On the subject of infinitives," in L. K. Dobrin, L. Nichols, and R. M. Rodriguez (eds.), *Papers from the 27th Regional Meeting of the Chicago Linguistic Society 1991. Part 1: The General Session*, Chicago, IL: Chicago Linguistics Society, 324–43.

1992. *Move α: Conditions on Its Applications and Outputs*, Cambridge, MA: MIT Press.

Lasnik, H. and T. Stowell 1991. "Weakest crossover," *Linguistic Inquiry* **22**, 687–720.

Lasnik, H. and J. Uriagereka. 1988. *A Course in GB Syntax: Lectures on Binding and Empty Categories*, Cambridge, MA: MIT Press.

Lasnik, H. and J. Uriagereka with Cedric Boeckx. 2005. *A Course in Minimalist Syntax: Foundations and Prospects*, Oxford: Blackwell.

Lebeaux, D. 1983. "A distributional difference between reciprocals and reflexives," *Linguistic Inquiry* **14**, 723–30.

  1988. "Language acquisition and the form of the grammar." PhD thesis, University of Massachusetts, Amherst. [Published 2000 as *Language Acquisition and the Form of the Grammar*, Amsterdam: John Benjamins.]

  1991. "Relative clauses, licensing, and the nature of the derivation," in S. D. Rothstein (ed.), *Perspective on Phrase Structure: Heads and Licensing*, San Diego, CA: Academic Press, 209–39.

  1995. "Where does the binding theory apply?," *University of Maryland Working Papers in Linguistics* **3**, 63–88.

Lefebvre, C. 1991. "*Take* serial verb constructions in Fon," in C. Lefebvre (ed.), *Serial Verbs: Grammatical, Comparative and Cognitive Approaches*, Amsterdam: John Benjamins, 37–78.

Legate, J. 2003. "Some interface properties of the phase," *Linguistic Inquiry* **34**, 506–16.

Legendre, G., J. Grimshaw, and S. Vikner (eds.). 2001. *Optimality-Theoretic Syntax*, Cambridge, MA: MIT Press.

Levin, B. and M. Rappaport-Hovav. 1995. *Unaccusativity: At the Syntax-Lexical Semantics Interface*, Cambridge, MA: MIT Press.

Levin, N. S. 1978. "Some identity-of-sense deletions puzzle me. Do they you?" in D. Farkas, W. M. Jacobsen, and K. W. Todrys (eds.), *Papers from the Fourteenth Regional Meeting of the Chicago Linguistic Society*, Chicago, IL: Chicago Linguistics Society, 229–40.

  1979. "Main verb ellipsis in spoken English," PhD thesis, Ohio State University, Columbus. [Published 1986 as *Main Verb Ellipsis in Spoken English*, New York, NY: Garland.]

Levine, R. 1984. "A note on right node raising, *tough* constructions and reanalysis rules," *Linguistic Analysis* **13**, 159–72.

Lidz, J. 2003. "Causation and reflexivity in Kannada," in V. Dayal and A. Mahajan (eds.), *Clause Structure in South Asian Languages*, Dordrecht: Kluwer, 93–130.

Lightfoot, D. W. 1991. *How to Set Parameters: Arguments from Language Change*, Cambridge, MA: MIT Press.

  1999. *The Development of Language: Acquisition, Change and Evolution*, Oxford: Blackwell.

Lin, T. -H. 2001. "Light verb syntax and the theory of phrase structure," PhD thesis, University of California, Irvine.

Lorimer, D. L. R. 1935. *The Burushaski Language, Vol. I: Introduction and Grammar*. Oslo: Instituttet for sammenlignende kulturforskning.

Lutz, U., G. Müller, and A. von Stechow (eds.). 2000. Wh-*Scope Marking*, Amsterdam: John Benjamins.

Lyon, J. 1968. *Introduction to Theoretical Linguistics*, Cambridge: Cambridge University Press.

Manzini, M. R. 1992. *Locality: A Theory and Some of Its Empirical Consequences*, Cambridge, MA: MIT Press.

Manzini, M. R. and A. Roussou. 2000. "A minimalist approach to A-movement and control," *Lingua* **110**, 409–47.

Manzini, M. R. and K. Wexler. 1987. "Parameters, binding theory, and learnability," *Linguistic Inquiry* **18**, 413–44.

Marácz, L. 1989. "Asymmetries in Hungarian," PhD thesis, Rijksuniversiteit Groningen.

Marantz, A. 1984. *On the Nature of Grammatical Relations*, Cambridge, MA: MIT Press.

   1997. "No escape from syntax: Don't try morphological analysis in the privacy of your own lexicon," *Proceedings of the 21st Annual Penn Linguistics Colloquium. University of Pennsylvania Working Papers in Linguistics* **4.2**, 201–25.

Martin, R. 1996. "A minimalist theory of PRO," PhD thesis, University of Connecticut, Storrs.

   2001. "Null case and the distribution of PRO," *Linguistic Inquiry* **32**, 141–66.

Martin, R. and J. Uriagereka. 1999. "Lectures on dynamic syntax," lecture series given at the LSA Summer Institute, University of Illinois, Urbana-Champaign, June 21–July 30, 1999.

Mathieu, E. 2002. "The syntax of non-canonical quantification: A comparative study," PhD thesis, University College London.

Matushansky, O. 2003. "Going through a phase," ms., CNRS/Université de Paris 8.

May, R. 1985. *Logical Form: Its Structure and Derivation*, Cambridge, MA: MIT Press.

McCawley, J. 1981. "An un-syntax," in E. A. Moravcsik and J. R. Wirth (eds.), *Current Approaches to Syntax*, New York, NY: Academic Press, 167–93.

McCloskey, J. 1990. "Resumptive pronouns, A-bar binding, and levels of representation in Irish," in R. Hendrick (ed.), *The Syntax of the Modern Celtic Languages*, San Diego, CA: Academic Press, 199–256.

   1997. "Subjecthood and subject positions," in L. Haegeman (ed.), *Elements of Grammar: Handbook of Generative Syntax*, Dordrecht: Kluwer, 197–235.

   2001. "On the distribution of subject properties in Irish," in W. D. Davies and S. Dubinsky (eds.), *Objects and Other Subjects: Grammatical Functions, Functional Categories and Configurationality*, Dordrecht: Kluwer, 157–92.

   2002. "Resumption, successive cyclicity, and the locality of operations," in S. D. Epstein and T. D. Seely (eds.), *Derivation and Explanation in the Minimalist Program*, Oxford: Blackwell, 184–226.

McDaniel, D. 1986. "Conditions on *wh*-chains," PhD thesis, CUNY Graduate Center, New York.

   1989. "Partial and multiple *wh*-movement," *Natural Language & Linguistic Theory* **7**, 565–604.

Meisel, J. 1995. "Parameters in acquisition," in P. Fletcher and B. MacWhinney (eds.), *The Handbook of Child Language*, Oxford: Blackwell, 10–35.

Merchant, J. 1996. "Object scrambling and quantifier float in German," in
   K. Kusumoto (eds.), *Proceedings of NELS 26*, Amherst, MA: University of
   Massachusetts, GLSA, 179–93.
Miller, G. A. and N. Chomsky. 1963. "Finitary models of language users," in
   R. D. Luce, R. R. Bush, and E. Galanter (eds.), *Handbook of Mathematical
   Psychology*, Vol. II, New York, NY: Wiley, 419–91.
Mioto, C. 1994. "A s interrogativas no português brasileiro e o critério-*wh*," *Letras
   de Hoje* **96**, 19–33.
Miyamoto, T. 2000. *The Light Verb Construction in Japanese: The Role of the
   Verbal Noun*, Amsterdam: John Benjamins.
Mohammad, M. 1990. "The sentence structure of Arabic," PhD thesis, University
   of Southern California, Los Angeles.
Moro, A. 1989. "*There/Ci* as raised predicates," ms., Massachusetts Institute of
   Technology, Cambridge.
Moro, A. 1997. *The Raising of Predicates*, Cambridge: Cambridge University
   Press.
   2000. *Dynamic Antisymmetry*. Cambridge, MA: MIT Press.
Müller, G. 2003. "Optionality in optimality-theoretic syntax," in L. L.-S. Cheng
   and R. Sybesma (eds.), *The Second Glot International State-of-the-Art Book*,
   Berlin: Mouton de Gruyter, 289–321.
   2004. "Verb second as *v*P-first," *The Journal of Comparative Germanic Syntax* **7**,
   179–234.
Munn, A. 1993. "Topics in the syntax and semantics of coordinate structures,"
   PhD thesis, University of Maryland, College Park.
Muysken, P. 1982. "Parametrizing the notion 'head'," *Journal of Linguistic
   Research* **2**, 57–75.
Nasu, N. 2002. "Aspects of the syntax of A-movement: A study of English infini-
   tival constructions and related phenomena," PhD thesis, University of Essex,
   Colchester.
Neeleman, A. 1994. "Complex predicates," PhD thesis, Universiteit Utrecht.
Neidle, C., J. Kegl, B. Bahan, D. Aarons, and D. MacLaughlin. 1997. "Rightward
   wh–movement in American Sign Language," in D. Beerman, D. LeBlanc, and
   H. van Riemsdijk (eds.), *Rightward Movement*, Amsterdam: John Benjamins,
   247–78.
Nissenbaum, J. 2000. "Investigations of covert phrase movement," PhD thesis,
   Massachusetts Institute of Technology, Cambridge.
Nunes, J. 1995. "The copy theory of movement and linearization of chains in the
   minimalist program," PhD thesis, University of Maryland, College Park.
   1998. "Bare X′-theory and structures formed by movement," *Linguistic Inquiry*
   29, 160–68.
   1999. "Linearization of chains and phonetic realization of chain links," in
   S. D. Epstein and N. Hornstein (eds.), *Working Minimalism*, Cambridge,
   MA: MIT Press, 217–49.
   2000. "Erasing erasure," *DELTA* **16.2**, 415–29.
   2001. "Sideward movement," *Linguistic Inquiry* **31**, 303–44.

2004. *Linearization of Chains and Sideward Movement*, Cambridge, MA: MIT Press.

Nunes, J. and E. Thompson. 1998. "Appendix," in Uriagereka (1998), 497–521.

Nunes, J. and J. Uriagereka. 2000. "Cyclicity and extraction domains," *Syntax* **3**, 20–43.

Nunes, J. and C. Zocca. 2005. "Morphological identity in ellipsis," *Leiden Papers in Linguistics* **2.2**, 29–42.

Obenauer, H.-G. 1976. *Etudes de syntaxe interrogative du Français*, Tübingen: Niemeyer.

1984. "On the identification of empty categories," *The Linguistic Review* **4**, 153–202.

1994. "Aspects de la syntaxe A-barre: Effets d'intervention et mouvement des quantifieurs," Thèse de doctorat d'Etat, Université de Paris VIII.

Oishi, M. 1990. "*Conceptual problems of upward X-bar theory*," ms., Tohoku Gakuin University.

Oishi, M. 1997. "Procrastinate to feature strength," *Interdisciplinary Information Sciences* **3**, 65–70.

Oishi, M. 2003. "When linearity meets bare phrase structure," *Current Issues in Linguistics: Special Publications of the English Linguistics Society of Japan*, **2**, 18–41.

Ormazabal, J. 1995. "The syntax of complementation: On the relation between syntactic structure and selection," PhD thesis, University of Connecticut, Storrs.

Ormazabal, J. and J. Romero. 1998. "On the syntactic nature of the *me-lui* and the person-case constraint," *Anuario del Seminario Julio de Urquijo* **XXXII–2**, 415–33.

Ormazabal, J., J. Uriagereka, and M. Uribe-Etxebarria. 1994. "Word order and *wh*-movement: Towards a parametric account," paper presented at the 17th GLOW Colloquium, Vienna, April 6–8, 1994.

Ouhalla, J. 1994. "Verb movement and word order in Arabic," in D. W. Lightfoot and N. Hornstein (eds.), *Verb Movement*, Cambridge: Cambridge University Press, 73–85.

Parsons, T. 1990. *Events in the Semantics of English*, Cambridge, MA: MIT Press.

Perlmutter, D. 1971. *Deep and Surface Constraints in Generative Grammar*, New York, NY: Holt, Rinehart, and Winston.

1978. "Impersonal passives and the unaccusative hypothesis," in J. Jaeger, A. C. Woodbury, and F. Ackerman (eds.), *Proceedings of the Fourth Annual Meeting of the Berkeley Linguistics Society*, Berkeley, CA: University of California, BLS, 157–89.

Perlmutter, D. and S. Soames. 1979. *Syntactic Argumentation and the Structure of English*, Berkeley, CA: University of California Press.

Pesetsky, D. 1987. "*Wh*-in situ: Movement and unselective binding," in A. G. B. ter Meulen and E. Reuland (eds.), *The Representation of (In)definiteness*, Cambridge, MA: MIT Press, 98–129.

1995. *Zero Syntax: Experiencers and Cascades*, Cambridge, MA: MIT Press.

2000. *Phrasal Movement and Its Kin*, Cambridge, MA: MIT Press.

Petronio, K. and D. Lillo-Martin. 1997. "*Wh*-movement and the position of Spec-CP: Evidence from American Sign Language," *Language* **73**, 18–57.

Pietroski, P. 2004. *Events and Semantic Architecture*, Oxford: Oxford University Press.

Pires, A. 2001. "The syntax of gerunds and infinitives: Subjects, case and control," PhD thesis, University of Maryland, College Park.

du Plessis, H. 1977. "*Wh*-movement in Afrikaans," *Linguistic Inquiry* **8**, 723–26.

Pollard, C. and I. A. Sag. 1994. *Head-Driven Phrase Structure Grammar*, Chicago, IL: University of Chicago Press.

Pollock, J.-Y. 1989. "Verb movement, UG and the structure of IP," *Linguistic Inquiry* **20**, 365–424.

Postal, P. M. 1966. "On the so-called 'pronouns' in English," *Monograph Series in Language and Linguistics* **19**, 177–206. [Reprinted in D. A. Reibel and S. A. Schane (eds.). 1969. *Modern Studies in English*, Englewood Cliffs, NJ: Prentice-Hall, 201–24 and in R. A. Jacobs and P. S. Rosenbaum (eds.). 1970. *Readings in Transformational Grammar*, Waltham, MA: Ginn and Company, 56–82.]

1974. *On Raising: One Rule of English Grammar and Its Theoretical Implications*, Cambridge, MA: MIT Press.

Postal, P. and J. R. Ross 1971. "Tough movement si, tough deletion no!" *Linguistic Inquiry* **2**, 544–46.

Radford, A. 1981. *Transformational Syntax: A Student's Guide to Chomsky's Extended Standard Theory*, Cambridge: Cambridge University Press.

1988. *Transformational Grammar: A First Course*, Cambridge: Cambridge University Press.

Raposo, E. 1973. "Sobre a forma *o* em Português," *Boletim de Filologia* **XXII**, 364–415.

Raposo, E. and J. Uriagereka. 1990. "Long distance case assignment," *Linguistic Inquiry* **21**, 505–37.

Reinhart, T. 1976. "The syntactic domain of anaphora," PhD thesis, Massachusetts Institute of Technology, Cambridge.

2004. *The Theta System*, Cambridge, MA: MIT Press.

Richards, M. D. 2004. "Object Shift and Scrambling in North and West Germanic: A case study in symmetrical Syntax," PhD thesis, University of Cambridge.

Richards, N. 2001. *Movement in Language: Interactions and Architectures*. Oxford: Oxford University Press.

2002. "A distinctness condition on linearization," ms., Massachusetts Institute of Technology, Cambridge.

van Riemsdijk, H. 1978. *A Case Study in Syntactic Markedness: The Binding Nature of Prepositional Phrases*, Dordrecht: Foris.

(ed.). 1999. *Clitics in the Languages of Europe*, Berlin: Mouton de Gruyter.

van Riemsdijk, H. and E. Williams. 1981. "NP-structure," *The Linguistic Review* **1**, 171–217.

1986. *Introduction to the Theory of Grammar*, Cambridge, MA: MIT Press.

Ritter, E. 1991. "Two functional categories in noun phrases: Evidence from Modern Hebrew," in S. D. Rothstein (ed.), *Perspectives on Phrase Structure*, San Diego, CA: Academic Press, 37–62.

Rizzi, L. 1980. "Negation, *wh*-movement and the *pro*-drop parameter," paper presented at the 3rd GLOW Colloquium, Max-Planck Institut für Psycholinguistik, Nijmegen, April 10–13, 1980. [Published as "Negation, *wh*-movement and the null-subject parameter" in Rizzi (1982), 117–84.]

1982. *Issues in Italian Syntax*, Dordrecht: Foris.

1986. "Null objects in Italian and the theory of *pro*," *Linguistic Inquiry* **17**, 501–57.

1990. *Relativized Minimality*, Cambridge, MA: MIT Press.

1997. "The fine structure of the left periphery," in L. Haegeman (ed.), *Elements of Grammar: Handbook of Generative Syntax*, Dordrecht: Kluwer, 281–337.

2001. 'Relativized minimality effects', in Baltin and Collins (2001), 89–110.

(ed.). 2004. *The Structure of CP and IP: The Cartography of Syntactic Structures*, Vol. II, Oxford: Oxford University Press.

Roberts, I. G. 1985. "Agreement parameters and the development of English modal auxiliaries," *Natural Language & Linguistic Theory* **3**, 21–58.

1993. *Verbs and Diachronic Syntax: A Comparative History of English and French*, Dordrecht: Kluwer.

1996. *Comparative Syntax*, London: Edward Arnold.

1998. "*Have/Be* raising, Move F, and procrastinate," *Linguistic Inquiry* **29**, 113–25.

2001. "Head movement," in Baltin and Collins (2001), 113–47.

Rodrigues, C. 2004. "Thematic chains," *DELTA* **20.1**, 123–47.

Rosenbaum, P. S. 1967. *The Grammar of English Predicate Complement Constructions*, Cambridge, MA: MIT Press.

1970. "A principle governing deletion in English sentential complementation," in R. A. Jacobs and P. S. Rosenbaum (eds.), *Readings in English Transformational Grammar*, Waltham, MA: Ginn and Company, 20–29.

Ross, J. R. 1967. "Constraints on variables in syntax," PhD thesis, Massachusetts Institute of Technology, Cambridge. [Published 1986 as *Infinite Syntax!*, Norwood, NJ: Ablex.]

Rothstein, S. D. 1995. "Small clauses and copular constructions," in A. Cardinaletti and M- T. Guasti (eds.), *Small Clauses*, San Diego, CA: Academic Press, 27–48.

Rouveret, A. 1991. "Functional categories and agreement," *The Linguistic Review* **8**, 353–87.

Rubin, E. 2002. "The structure of modifiers," ms., University of Utah, Salt Lake City. [To appear with Cambridge, MA: MIT Press.]

2003. "Determining pair-merge," *Linguistic Inquiry* **34**, 660–68.

Rudin, C. 1988a. "On multiple questions and multiple *wh*-fronting," *Natural Language & Linguistic Theory* **6**, 445–501.

1988b. "Finiteness and opacity: Evidence from the Balkans," in M. Hammond, E. A. Moravcsik, and J. R. Wirth (eds.), *Studies in Syntactic Typology*, Amsterdam: John Benjamins, 37–51.

Runner, J. 1995. "Noun phrase licensing and interpretation," PhD thesis, University of Massachusetts, Amherst. [Published 1998 as *Noun Phrase Licensing*, New York, NY: Garland.]

2005. "The accusative plus infinitive construction in English," in M. Everaert and H. van Riemsdijk (eds.), *The Blackwell Companion to Syntax*, Oxford: Blackwell.

Sabel, J. 1996. *Restrukturierung und Lokalität: Universelle Beschränkungen für Wortstellungsvarianten*, Berlin: Akademie Verlag.

1998. "Principles and parameters of *wh*-movement," Habilitationsschrift, Johann Wolfgang Goethe-Universität Frankfurt am Main.

2000. "Expletives as features," in R. Billerey and B. D. Lillehaugen (eds.), *WCCFL 19: Proceedings of the 19th West Coast Conference on Formal Linguistics*, Somerville, MA: Cascadilla Press, 411–24.

Saddy, D. 1991. "*Wh*-scope mechanisms in Bahasa Indonesia," *MIT Working Papers in Linguistics* **15**, 183–218.

Sag, I. A., G. Gazdar, T. Wasow, and S. Weisler. 1985. "Coordination and how to distinguish categories," *Natural Language & Linguistic Theory* **3**, 117–71.

Sag, I. A. and T. Wasow. 1999. *Syntactic Theory: A Formal Introduction*, Stanford, CA: CSLI Publications.

Salo, P. 2003. "Causatives and the empty lexicon: A minimalist perspective," PhD thesis, University of Helsinki.

Schachter, P. 1976. "The subject in Philippine languages: Topic, actor, actor-topic, or none of the above?," in C. N. Li (ed.), *Subject and Topic*, New York, NY: Academic Press, 493–518.

1977. "Reference-related and role-related properties of subjects," in P. Cole and J. M. Sadock (eds.), *Grammatical Relations*, New York, NY: Academic Press, 279–306.

Schein, B. 1993. *Plurals and Events*, Cambridge, MA: MIT Press.

Selkirk, L. 1984. *Phonology and Syntax: The Relation Between Sound and Structure*, Cambridge, MA: MIT Press.

1986. "On derived domains in sentence phonology," *Phonology Yearbook* **3**, 371–405.

Sells, P., J. Rickford, and T. Wasow. 1996. "An optimality-theoretic approach to variation in negative inversion in AAVE," *Natural Language & Linguistic Theory* **14**, 591–627.

Simpson, A. 2000. Wh-*Movement and the Theory of Feature-Checking*. Amsterdam: John Benjamins.

Smith, N. V. and I. -M. Tsimpli. 1995. *The Mind of a Savant: Language-Learning and Modularity*, Oxford: Blackwell.

Speas, M. 1986. "Adjunctions and projections in syntax," PhD thesis, Massachusetts Institute of Technology, Cambridge.

1990. *Phrase Structure in Natural Language*, Dordrecht: Kluwer.

1991. "Generalized transformations and the S-structure position of adjuncts," in S. D. Rothstein (ed.), *Perspective on Phrase Structure: Heads and Licensing*, San Diego, CA: Academic Press, 241–57.

Sportiche, D. 1988. "A theory of floating quantifiers and its corollaries for constituent structure," *Linguistic Inquiry* **19**, 425–49.

Starke, M. 2001. "Move dissolves into merge: A theory of locality," PhD thesis, Université de Genève.

Stowell, T. 1981. "Origins of phrase structure," PhD thesis, Massachusetts Institute of Technology, Cambridge.

1984. "Null operators and the theory of proper government," ms., University of California, Los Angeles.

Sultan, U. 2002. *"On a few case and agreement puzzles in Standard Arabic,"* ms., University of Maryland, College Park.

Svenonius, P. (ed.). 2000. *The Derivation of VO and OV*, Amsterdam: John Benjamins.

2001. "Locality, phases, and the cycle," ms., Universitetet i Tromsø.

2004. "On the edge", in D. Adger, C. de Cat, and G. Tsoulas (eds.), *Peripheries*, Dordrecht: Kluwer, 259–87.

Szabolcsi, A. 1983. "The possessor that ran away from home," *The Linguistic Review* **3**, 89–102.

Takahashi, D. 1994. "Minimality of movement," PhD thesis, University of Connccticut, Storrs.

Taraldsen, K. T. 1981. "On the theoretical interpretation of a class of 'marked' extractions," in A. Belletti, L. Brandi, and L. Rizzi (eds.), *The Theory of Markedness in Generative Grammar*, Pisa: Scuola Normale Superiore, 475–516.

Thiersch, C. 1978. "Topics in German syntax," PhD thesis, Massachusetts Institute of Technology, Cambridge.

Trask, R. L. 1993. *A Dictionary of Grammatical Terms in Linguistics*, London: Routledge.

Travis, L. deMena. 1984. "Parameters and effects of word order variation," PhD thesis, Massachusetts Institute of Technology, Cambridge.

Truckenbrodt, H. 1995. "Phonological phrases: Their relation to syntax, focus, and prominence," PhD thesis, Massachusetts Institute of Technology, Cambridge.

1999. "On the relation between syntactic phrases and phonological phrases," *Linguistic Inquiry* **30**, 219–55.

Tuller, L. A. 1992. "Postverbal focus constructions in Chadic," *Natural Language & Linguistic Theory* **10**, 303–34.

Ura, H. 1994. "Varieties of raising and the feature-based theory of movement," *MIT Occasional Papers in Linguistics* **7**.

Uriagereka, J. 1988. "On government," PhD thesis, University of Connecticut, Storrs.

1997. "Multiple spell-out," *Groninger Arbeiten zur germanistischen Linguistik* **40**, 109–35.

1998. *Rhyme and Reason: An Introduction to Minimalist Syntax*, Cambridge, MA: MIT Press.

1999a. "Comments on 'Minimalist inquiries: The framework'," ms., University of Maryland, College Park.

1999b. "Review of Chomsky (1995)," *Lingua* **107**, 267–73.

1999c. "Multiple spell-out," in S. D. Epstein and N. Hornstein (eds.), *Working Minimalism*, Cambridge, MA: MIT Press, 251–82.

1999d. "Minimal restrictions on Basque movement," *Natural Language & Linguistic Theory* **17**, 403–44.

2000a. "Warps: Some thoughts on categorization," *Theoretical Linguistics* **25**, 31–73.

2000b. "Comments on 'Derivation by Phase'," ms., University of Maryland, College Park.

2001. "Pure adjuncts," ms., University of Maryland, College Park.

2002. *Derivations*, London: Routledge.

Uribe-Etxebarria, M. 1989. "Some notes on the structure of IP in Basque," ms., University of Connecticut, Storrs.

van Valin, R. 1986. "An empty category as the subject of tensed S in English," *Linguistic Inquiry* **17**, 581–86.

Vergnaud, J.-R. 1982. "Dépendances et niveaux de représentations en syntaxe," Thèse de doctorat d'Etat, Université Paris VII.

Vikner, S. 1995. *Verb Movement and Expletive Subjects in the Germanic Languages*, Oxford: Oxford University Press.

Webelhuth, G. 1995a. "X-bar theory and case theory," in Webelhuth (1995b), 15–95.

(ed.). 1995b. *Government and Binding Theory and the Minimalist Program*, Oxford: Blackwell.

Wilder, C. and H.-M. Gärtner. 1997. Introduction. In Wilder, Gärtner, and Bierwisch (1997), 1–35.

Wilder, C., H.-M. Gärtner, and M. Bierwisch (eds.). 1997. *The Role of Economy Principles in Linguistic Theory*, Berlin: Akademie Verlag.

Williams, E. 1977. "Discourse and logical form," *Linguistic Inquiry* **8**, 101–39.

1978. "Across-the-board rule application," *Linguistic Inquiry* **9**, 31–43.

1981. "Argument structure and morphology," *The Linguistic Review* **1**, 81–114.

1983. "Syntactic vs. semantic categories," *Linguistics and Philosophy* **6**, 423–46.

1994. *Thematic Structure in Syntax*, Cambridge, MA: MIT Press.

1995. "Theta theory," in Webelhuth (1995b), 97–124.

2003. *Representation Theory*, Cambridge, MA: MIT Press.

vanden Wyngaerd, G. 1994. *PRO-Legomena: Distribution and Reference of Infinitival Subjects*, Berlin: Mouton de Gruyter.

Zagona, K. 1982. "Government and proper government of verbal projections," PhD thesis, University of Washington, Seattle.

Zocca, C. 2003. "O que não está lá? Um estudo sobre morfologia flexional em elipses," MA thesis, Universidade Estadual de Campinas.

Zwart, C.J.-W. 1992. "Dutch expletives and small clause predicate raising," in K. Broderick (eds.), *Proceedings of NELS 22*, Amherst, MA: University of Massachusetts, GLSA Publications, 477–91.

1993. "Dutch syntax: A minimalist approach," PhD thesis, Rijksuniversiteit Groningen.

1997. *Morphosyntax of Verb Movement: A Minimalist Approach to the Syntax of Dutch*, Dordrecht: Kluwer.

Index of languages

Index of names

Index of subjects